THE BEST WAY TO ROB A BANK IS TO OWN ONE

WILLIAM K. BLACK

THE BEST WAY TO ROB A BANK IS TO OWN ONE

HOW CORPORATE EXECUTIVES AND POLITICIANS LOOTED THE S&L INDUSTRY

University of Texas Press ⟨⟩ *Austin*

♾ The paper used in this book meets the minimum requirements of
ANSI/NISO Z39.48-1992 (R1997) (Permanence of Paper).

LIBRARY OF CONGRESS CATALOGING-IN-PUBLICATION DATA

Black, William K. (William Kurt), 1951–
    The best way to rob a bank is to own one : how corporate executives and politi-
cians looted the S&L industry / William K. Black.— 1st ed.
        p.   cm.
    Includes bibliographical references and index.
    ISBN: 0-292-72139-0
    1. Savings and loan associations—Corrupt practices—United States.   2. Savings
and loan association failures—United States.   3. Savings and loan bailout, 1989–
1995.   I. Title.
    HG2151.B52   2005
    332.3'2'0973—dc22
                                                              2004021232

To June: I'm glad Joy burned the soup.

CONTENTS

ABBREVIATIONS

AA	Arthur Andersen, a "Big 8" accounting firm
ACC	American Continental Corporation; Keating holding company used to buy Lincoln Savings
ACFE	Association for Certified Fraud Examiners
ADC	acquisition, development, and construction
AICPA	American Institute of Certified Public Accountants
ARM	adjustable-rate mortgage
AY	Arthur Young & Company, a "Big 8" accounting firm
C&D	cease and desist order
CDSL	California Department of Savings and Loans
CEBA	Competitive Equality in Banking Act (of 1987); authorized the FSLIC recapitalization
CEO	chief executive officer
CFO	chief financial officer
CPA	certified public accountant
CRA	Community Reinvestment Act
CRAP	creative regulatory accounting principles
DCCC	Democratic Congressional Campaign Committee
DNC	Democratic National Committee
DOJ	United States Department of Justice
ERC	Enforcement Review Committee
FAS	Financial Accounting Standards
FASB	Financial Accounting Standards Board; top accounting-profession standard-setting body
FBI	Federal Bureau of Investigation

FCPA	Foreign Corrupt Practices Act; forbids bribery of foreign officials
FDIC	Federal Deposit Insurance Corporation; federal banking insurance agency
FHLB	Federal Home Loan Bank; a regional bank that regulated and made loans to S&Ls
FHLBB	Federal Home Loan Bank Board; federal S&L regulator
FHLBSF	Federal Home Loan Bank of San Francisco; FHLB with jurisdiction over California, Arizona, and Nevada
FICO	Financial Corporation set up to "recapitalize" FSLIC
FSLIC	Federal Savings and Loan Insurance Corporation; federal deposit insurer for S&Ls
FY	fiscal year
GAAP	generally accepted accounting principles
GAO	General Accounting Office; federal auditors (recently renamed the Government Accountability Office)
GPRA	Government Performance Results Act of 1993
IRS	Internal Revenue Service; federal tax agency
KIO	Kuwaiti Investment Office; co-owner with Lincoln Savings of the Phoenician Hotel
LTOB	bank board regulation that restricted "loans-to-one-borrower"
MBS	mortgage backed securities
MCP	management consignment program
MOU	Memorandum of Understanding
NAHB	National Association of Home Builders
NAR	National Association of Realtors
NASSLS	National Association of State Savings and Loan Supervisors
NCFIRRE	National Commission on Financial Institution Reform, Recovery and Enforcement; appointed to study the causes of the S&L debacle
NRV	net realizable value
OCC	Office of the Comptroller of the Currency; federal regulator of national banks
OE	Office of Enforcement; enforcement office at the Bank Board
OES	Office of Examinations and Supervision; original name of the supervisory office at the Bank Board
OGC	Office of General Counsel

OMB	Office of Management and Budget; budgetary agency of the federal executive branch
OPER	Office of Policy and Economic Research; economic office of the Bank Board
OPM	Office of Personnel Management; federal personnel agency
ORPOS	Office of Regulatory Policy, Oversight, and Supervision; supervisory office of the Bank Board
OTS	Office of Thrift Supervision
PAC	political action committee
PR	public relations
PSA	Principal Supervisory Agent
RAP	regulatory accounting principles
RCA	risk-controlled arbitrage
REPO	Reverse Purchase Obligations
RTC	Resolution Trust Corporation
S&L	savings and loan
SEC	Securities and Exchange Commission; federal securities law regulator
TDR	troubled-debt restructuring
TFR	Thrift Financial Report
TRO	temporary restraining order

PREFACE

In 2003, the United States Department of Justice reported that property crimes had continued their trend and fallen to an all-time low. In fact, property crimes have surged to an all-time high since Enron collapsed in late 2001. The reason for the contradiction is that the Justice Department does not count serious property crimes because it excludes white-collar crimes from its data keeping. A wave of frauds led by the men who control large corporations, what I term "control fraud," caused the massive losses from property crimes.

In the 1980s, a wave of control frauds ravaged the savings and loan (S&L) industry. I was a regulator during the heart of that crisis. As the book shows, I had an uncanny ability to end up in the wrong place at the wrong time and a talent for getting powerful politicians furious at me.[1] After the crisis, I went back to school at the University of California at Irvine to learn to be a criminologist. I knew that the S&L crisis had grown out of systemic fraud. My dissertation studied California S&L control frauds.

This book arose from my concerns that we had failed to learn the lessons of the S&L debacle and that the failure meant that we walked blind into the ongoing wave of control frauds. The defrauders use companies as both sword and shield. They have shown themselves capable of fooling the most sophisticated market participants and academic experts. They are financial superpredators who use accounting fraud as a weapon and a shield against prosecution.

Several factors make control frauds uniquely dangerous. The person who controls a company (or country) can defeat all internal and external controls because he is ultimately in charge of those controls. Fraudulent CEOs do not simply defeat controls; they suborn them and turn them into allies. Top law firms, under the pretense of rendering zealous advocacy to the client, have helped fraudulent CEOs loot and destroy the client.

Top-tier audit firms are even more valuable allies (Black 1993e). Every S&L control fraud, and all of the major control frauds that have surfaced recently, were able to get clean opinions from them. Control frauds, using accounting fraud as their primary weapon and shield, typically report sensational profits, followed by catastrophic failure. These fictitious profits provide the means for sophisticated, fraudulent CEOs to use common corporate mechanisms such as stock bonuses to convert firm assets to their personal benefit. In short, they camouflage themselves as legitimate leaders and take advantage of the presumption of regularity (and psychic rewards) that CEOs receive.

Fraudulent CEOs can transform the firm and the regulatory environment to aid control fraud. They can use the full resources of the firm to bring about these changes. Control frauds frequently make (directly and indirectly) large political contributions. They may lobby in favor of deregulation or tort reform, or seek to remove the chief regulator. They can place the firm in the lines of businesses that offer the best opportunities for accounting fraud. This generally means investing in assets that have no readily ascertainable market value and arranging reciprocal "sales" of goods, which can transform real losses into fictional profits (Black 1993b). It can also mean, however, targeting poorly regulated industries. They can make the firm grow rapidly and become a Ponzi scheme.

The result is a dangerous package that appears healthy and legitimate but is not and that has extraordinary resources available for use by a fraudulent CEO. Control frauds have shown the ability to fool the most sophisticated market participants. They can be massively insolvent and still be touted by experts as among the very best firms in the world. The conventional economic wisdom about the S&L debacle assumed that "high flier" S&Ls existed solely because of deposit insurance. Scholars asserted that private market discipline would prevent any excessive risk taking in industries that had no government guarantee. This view was incorrect: S&L control frauds consistently showed the ability to deceive uninsured private creditors and shareholders. Elliot Levitas, one of the commissioners appointed to investigate the causes of the debacle as part of the National Commission on Financial Institution Reform, Recovery and Enforcement (NCFIRRE), emphasized this point in 1993, but no economist took him seriously. The current wave of control frauds has proved his point conclusively.

The scariest aspect of control frauds, however, is that they can occur in waves, causing systemic damage. The S&L debacle was contained before it damaged our overall economy, but this book explains how near a thing that was. Waves of control fraud have occurred in many nations, often with devastating consequences. Russia's privatization campaign was ruined by such a wave.

The current wave of control fraud has done great systemic damage. It need not have happened, had we learned the appropriate lessons from the S&L debacle. Unfortunately, the lessons we learned made us more vulnerable to control fraud, not less. This occurred because the conventional economic wisdom about the S&L debacle is fallacious.

According to the conventional wisdom:

1. The high fliers could not have occurred absent deposit insurance.
2. Fraud was trivial, and studying fraud distracts from proper public policy.
3. The high fliers were honest gamblers for resurrection.
4. Unfortunately, many gambles failed, which caused the debacle.
5. The industry "captured" the Federal Home Loan Bank Board (Bank Board).
6. Deregulation did not cause greater losses.
7. The 1986 tax act exacerbated total losses.
8. The 1989 reregulatory legislation caused the junk bond market to collapse.
9. The 1982 deregulation act was flawed because economists were excluded.

In fact, all of these statements are false, for the following reasons:

- I explained above that both waves of control fraud disproved the first claim.
- As to points 2 and 3, control frauds were leading contributors to the debacle. Over 1,000 S&L insiders were convicted of felonies. Studies of the worst failures almost invariably find control fraud. The pattern of failures is logically consistent with a wave of control fraud and inconsistent with honest gambling. Far from being a distraction, studying S&L control frauds more closely would have allowed us to avoid the present wave of control fraud.

- *Every S&L high flier failed.* They were all control frauds. Traditional S&Ls did "gamble for resurrection" by continuing to take material interest-rate risk in 1982–1985. These gambles were highly successful because interest rates fell sharply. The gambles greatly reduced the cost of bailing out the Federal Savings and Loan Insurance Corporation (FSLIC). Traditional S&Ls did not gamble in the way predicted by "moral hazard" theory, which predicted that they would maximize their exposure to risk.
- The S&L industry did not capture the Bank Board during the debacle. Indeed, each Bank Board chairman during the debacle was hostile to the trade group.
- Deregulation and "desupervision" added greatly to the debacle because they permitted S&Ls to invest in assets that were superb vehicles for control fraud.
- The 1986 tax act greatly reduced the cost of the debacle by bursting regional real estate bubbles. The 1981 tax act and the S&L control frauds in the Southwest contributed to the debacle by causing and inflating the bubble. Bubbles pop. Without the 1986 tax act, the Arizona, Texas, and Louisiana real estate bubbles would have continued to inflate. The resultant real estate crash would have been far worse.
- S&Ls were a small (overall) player in the junk bond markets. They were important because several of them, including Lincoln Savings, were "captives" of Michael Milken and Drexel Burnham Lambert (Black 1993c).
- Economists controlled the drafting of the 1982 St Germain Act.

The key lessons that proponents of the conventional wisdom drew were that "a rule against fraud is not an essential or even necessarily an important ingredient of securities markets" (Easterbrook and Fischel 1991, 285), that private market discipline turned presumed conflicts of interest into positive synergies, and that regulators like the Securities and Exchange Commission (SEC) were more harmful than helpful.

In sum, the lessons we learned from the debacle were false. The guidance that law and economics professors provided left us more susceptible to control fraud. This book is often critical of particular economists, but I am not dismissive of economics. Indeed, I write in large part to help build a new economic theory of fraud arising from George Akerlof's classic theory of lemons markets (1970) and Henry Pontell's work on "systems capacity" limitations in regulation that may increase the risk of waves of control fraud (Calavita, Pontell, and Tillman 1997, 136).

This book explains why private market discipline fails to prevent waves of control frauds. It also studies how S&L control frauds sought to manipulate public sector actors. Charles Keating and his Texas counterparts achieved staggering successes. Keating, perpetrator of the worst control fraud in the nation, caused the Reagan administration to attempt to give him majority control of the Bank Board. He enlisted Speaker Wright and the five U.S. senators who became known as the "Keating Five" as his allies. He was able to get a majority of the House of Representatives to cosponsor a resolution designed to block the reregulation proposed by Ed Gray, the Bank Board chairman.

Keating used this immense political power and the threat of lawsuits to intimidate the Bank Board under Danny Wall. The board issued the equivalent of a cease-and-desist order against itself.

Control frauds' key skill is manipulation. Fraudulent CEOs' ability to manipulate was limited primarily by their audacity and the leadership and moral strength of their opponents.

Ed Gray emerged as the most unlikely of heroes. President Reagan made him Bank Board chairman because he supported greater deregulation. Within four months, however, Gray began his transformation into the great reregulator and became the bane of the S&L control frauds and their allies. He immediately developed an impressive list of enemies. Joseph Stiglitz wrote in *The Roaring Nineties* that he believes in underlying forces, not heroes (2003, 272). I believe in both, and this book discusses both.

People matter in part because they vary in their concepts of duty, integrity, and courage. This book presents morally complex individuals, not stick figures. One aspect of that complexity is that individuals who were strongly criticized for moral lapses proved vital to preventing an S&L catastrophe. The other side of the coin is that officials who believed that they had superior morals allied themselves with the worst control frauds.

Morals matter, but people are capable of doing immoral acts while believing they are morally superior. I believe that part of the answer is that it is so hard to accept that a CEO can be a crook and that, because he owns substantial stock in the company, the risk *increases* that he will engage in control fraud if the firm is failing. This seems counterintuitive to most people. If officials understood control frauds, they would be more willing to see CEOs as potential criminals and to maintain the kind of healthy skepticism that could reduce future scandals.

Gray's reregulation set off two wars involving the S&L control frauds. The Bank Board rules limiting growth struck at the most vulnerable chink in control frauds' shields. Every control fraud collapsed within four years.

The control frauds, however, counterattacked using their political power, and blocked any chance that the president would renominate Gray for a second term. Gray's successor, Danny Wall, and his key lieutenants tried to appease Keating. This set off a civil war within the Bank Board. The appeasement produced the most expensive failure (over $3 billion) of a financial institution in U.S. history and ultimately forced Wall's resignation.

Unfortunately, neither regulators nor politicians have learned enough from the S&L debacle. They are repeating the many mistakes we made in fighting the S&L control frauds, but few of our successes. To date, the effort to "reinvent" government has failed to show any utility against waves of fraud. The Government Performance and Results Act (GPRA) was the central reinvention plank. It led to two practices that could have prevented a new wave of control fraud. GPRA required agencies to formally define their mission and to develop strategic plans to achieve those missions. The General Accounting Office (GAO) was assigned the task of identifying high-risk government activities.

The SEC, for example, properly defines itself in its recent strategic plans as "a civil law enforcement agency" (SEC Annual Report for 2002, 1). The SEC's annual reports during the 1990s, however, despite the record-setting, inflating stock market bubble, never defined a wave of control fraud as a central risk to the accomplishment of its mission. The SEC had grossly inadequate resources, did not see the wave of control frauds coming, and was overwhelmed. The GAO's definition of high-risk functions includes fraud risk as a key factor. The GAO, however, limited its concept of fraud risk to situations in which someone was stealing from a public agency. It did not consider a fraud risk that would impair the SEC's ability to meet its mission as a law enforcement agency and protect the pubic from trillions of dollars of losses. Indeed, the GAO still has not classified the SEC's antifraud function as high risk.

This book is the first true insider account of the S&L debacle from a regulator's perspective. (Three Bank Board economists have written books about the debacle, but each of them avoided that perspective.)

I bring many different "hats" to the task. My education and work experience include the following: economics major, lawyer, former regulator, and white-collar criminologist. I teach intermediate microeconomics, management, public financial management and regulation, and white-collar crime at the LBJ School of Public Affairs at the University of Texas at Austin. I also dabble in ethics.

My central message is that we can do things to detect and terminate individual control frauds and to prevent, or at least reduce substantially, future waves of control fraud. To do so, however, we have to take it seriously. One step is to no longer ignore serious frauds in our data collection. A second step is to realize that we need to train people to understand fraud mechanisms and how to spot and end fraud. The SEC's professional staff, for example, consists overwhelmingly of lawyers, accountants, and economists. Historically, none of these three disciplines taught their students anything about fraud. Even today, when securities-fraud scandals are legion and when Joe Well's Association of Certified Fraud Examiners (ACFE) has offered to provide free materials to schools that teach fraud examination, only a small percentage of new business school graduates are trained to fight fraud. The University of Texas has launched a new Institute for Fraud Studies to help bring about these reforms.

ACKNOWLEDGMENTS

This book springs from a career and a life. My first debt is to my mother, who taught me and helped set my moral compass. Bill Valentine and my teachers at the University of Michigan were treasures.

Jack Lansdale showed me that law could, and must be, practiced at the highest level of excellence and integrity. He exemplified the professional ethos at Squire, Sanders & Dempsey.

I owe too many people at the Bank Board and OTS too much to name them individually. Dorothy Nichols made the Litigation Division functional, humane, and fun; Ed Gray and Larry White, in their completely different manners, fought the good fight; and Mary Ellen Taylor did her best at the impossible task of keeping me out of trouble.

With regard to the Federal Home Loan Bank of San Francisco, I face the same quandary. I will mention only Jim Cirona, who could have made his job secure had he fired me; Mike Patriarca, who demonstrated every day the ultimate class and integrity as a leader; Chuck Deardorff, who kept supervision from disaster for decades; and my predecessor, Dirk Adams, who recruited the superb staff that made my work such a pleasure.

Thanks to Jim Leach, Buddy Roemer, Thomas Carper, and the late Henry Gonzalez. You saved the nation billions of dollars by opposing the efforts of the control frauds, but you also saved me from cynicism about elected officials when I had cause to be cynical.

James Pierce gave me the opportunity of a lifetime when he asked me to serve as his deputy and introduced me to George Akerlof. Both of you have been leading influences on my research, and your support has been critical.

Kitty Calavita, Gil Geis, Paul Jesilow, and Henry Pontell recruited me to come to UC-Irvine for my doctorate in criminology, taught me criminology, and have supported me throughout. I entered as a student and left as a colleague and friend.

Jamie Galbraith was instrumental in my coming to the LBJ School of Public Affairs at the University of Texas at Austin and has, with Bob Auerbach and Elspeth Rostow, been my greatest supporter. Jamie also got Jake Bernstein interested in doing a long interview with me for the *Texas Observer,* which led to Molly Ivins talking about control fraud in her column, which led Bill Bishel at UT Press to ask whether I was working on a book, which led to this book. Elspeth Rostow's grants for research made the book possible.

Writing a manuscript does not complete a book. I have been the immense beneficiary of the team assembled by UT Press to edit the book, Kip Keller and Lynne Chapman. Their care and professionalism is top drawer. Our eldest, Kenny, served as my research assistant. My spouse, June Carbone, author of a book on family law, was an inspiration and someone I could bounce ideas off. Travis Hale and Debra Moore gave me editing assistance. Henry Pontell and George Akerlof served as outside reviewers for the book, and their comments, along with those of Ed Kane, were of great use to me in improving the draft. Kirk Hanson helped me complete the book by allowing me to serve as a visiting scholar at the Markkula Center for Applied Ethics.

Thank you all. And, yes, the remaining errors are mine alone.

1. THEFT BY DECEPTION: CONTROL FRAUD IN THE S&L INDUSTRY

The best way to rob a bank is to own one.

WILLIAM CRAWFORD, COMMISSIONER OF THE CALIFORNIA
DEPARTMENT OF SAVINGS AND LOANS, INTRODUCING HIS
CONGRESSIONAL TESTIMONY BEFORE THE U.S. HOUSE
COMMITTEE ON GOVERNMENT OPERATIONS IN 1988

WHAT IS A CONTROL FRAUD?

A control fraud is a company run by a criminal who uses it as a weapon and shield to defraud others and makes it difficult to detect and punish the fraud (Wheeler and Rothman 1982). (I also use the phrase in some places to refer to the person who directs the fraud.) Fraud is theft by deception: one creates and exploits trust to cheat others. That is one of the reasons the ongoing wave of corporate fraud is so devastating: fraud erodes trust. Trust is vital to making markets, societies, polities, and relationships work, so fraud is particularly pernicious. In a financial context, less trust means more risk, and more risk causes lower asset values. As I write, stocks have lost trillions of dollars in market capitalization. To use a term from economics, fraud causes terrible "negative externalities" because it inflicts injury on those who were not parties to the fraudulent transaction.

Control frauds are financial superpredators that cause vastly larger losses than blue-collar thieves. They cause catastrophic business failures. Control frauds can occur in waves that imperil the general economy. The savings and loan (S&L) debacle was one such wave.

WHAT PERSONAL QUALITIES MAKE
A CONTROL FRAUD A SUCCESS?

Successful control frauds have one primary skill: identifying and exploiting human weakness. Audacity is the trait that sets control frauds apart. Charles Keating was the most notorious control fraud. His ability to manipulate politicians became legendary. Any control fraud could have done what Keating did in the political sphere, but only a few tried.

WHY DO CONTROL FRAUDS END IN CATASTROPHIC FAILURE?

Well-run companies have substantial internal and external controls designed to stop thieves. The chief executive officer (CEO), however, can defeat all of those controls because he is in charge of them.[1] Every S&L control fraud succeeded in getting at least one clean opinion from a top-tier audit firm (then called the "Big 8"). They generally were able to get them for years. The ongoing wave of control frauds shows that they are still routinely able to defeat external audit controls. The outside auditor is a control fraud's most valuable ally. Keating called his accountants a profit center. Control frauds shop for accommodating accountants, appraisers, and attorneys.

Control frauds create a "fraud friendly" corporate culture by hiring yes-men. They combine excessive pay, ego strokes (e.g., calling the employees "geniuses"), and terror to get employees who will not cross the CEO. Control frauds are control freaks (Black 2000).

The second reason control frauds are so destructive is that the CEO optimizes the firm as a fraud vehicle and can optimize the regulatory environment. The CEO causes the firm to engage in transactions that are ideal for fraud. Control frauds are accounting frauds. Investments that have no readily ascertainable market value are superior vehicles for accounting fraud because professionals, e.g., appraisers, value them. S&Ls shopped for outside professionals who would support fraudulent accounting and appraisals. Control frauds use an elegant fraud mechanism, the seemingly arm's-length (independent) transaction that accountants consider the best evidence of value. They transact with each other or with "straws" on what appears to be an arm's-length basis, but is really a fraud that massively overvalues assets in order to create fictitious income and hide real losses.

Control frauds grow rapidly (Black 1993d). The worst control frauds are Ponzi schemes, named after Carlo Ponzi, an early American fraud. A Ponzi must bring in new money continuously to pay off old investors, and the fraudster pockets a percentage of the take. The record "income" that the accounting fraud produces makes it possible for the Ponzi scheme to grow. S&Ls made superb control frauds because deposit insurance permitted even insolvent S&Ls to grow. The high-tech bubble of the 1990s allowed similarly massive growth.

Control frauds are predators. They spot and attack human and regulatory weaknesses. The CEO moves the company to the best spot for accounting fraud and weak regulation.

Audacious control frauds transform the environment to aid their frauds. The keys are to protect and even expand the range of accounting abuses and to weaken regulation. Only a control fraud can use the full resources of the company to change the environment. Political contributions and supportive economic studies secure deregulation. Control frauds use the company's resources to buy, bully, bamboozle, or bury the regulators. In my case, Keating used the S&L's resources to sue me for $400 million and to hire private detectives to investigate me (Tuohey 1987).

The third reason control frauds are so destructive is that they provide a "legitimate" way for the CEO to convert company assets to personal assets. All fraudsters have to balance the potential gains from fraud with the risks.[2] The most efficient fraud mechanism for the CEO is to steal cash from the company, e.g., by wiring it to his account at an offshore bank. No S&L control fraud, and none of the ongoing huge frauds, did so. Stealing from the till in large amounts from a large company guarantees detection and makes the prosecutor's task simple. The strategy could appeal only to those willing to live in hiding or in exile in a country without an extradition treaty. Marc Rich (pardoned by President Clinton) notwithstanding, few fraudulent CEOs follow this strategy.

Accounting frauds are ideal for control fraud. They inflate income and hide losses of even deeply insolvent companies. This allows the control fraud to convert company funds to his personal use through seemingly normal, legitimate means. American CEOs, especially those who run highly profitable companies, make staggering amounts of money. They receive top salaries, bonuses, stock options, and luxurious perks. Control frauds almost always report fabulous profits, and top-tier audit firms bless those financial statements. The S&L control frauds used a fraud mechanism that produced record profits and virtually no loan defaults, and had the ability to quickly transform any (real) loss found by an examiner into a (fictitious) gain that would be blessed by a Big 8 audit firm. It doesn't get any better than this in the world of fraud! Chapter 3 discusses this fraud mechanism.

Almost no one gives highly profitable firms a hard time: not (normal) regulators, not creditors or investors, and certainly not stock analysts. This is why our war on the control frauds was so audacious: at a time when hundreds of S&Ls were reporting that they were insolvent, we sought to close the S&Ls reporting that they were the most profitable and generally left the known insolvents open. Our political opponents thought us insane. There was only one way our war could be rational: there would have to be hundreds of control frauds; they would have to be massively overstating income and understating losses; and this had to be happening because the most prestigious accounting firms were giving clean opinions to fraudulent financials.

Control frauds are human; they enjoy the psychological rewards of running one of the most "profitable" firms. The press, local business elites, politicians, employees, and the charities that receive (typically large) contributions from the company invariably label the CEO a genius. In fact, they are pathetic businessmen. If they had been able to run a profitable, honest company in a tough business climate, they would have done so.

Control frauds who take money from the company through normal mechanisms (with the blessing of auditors) and receive the adulation of elite opinion makers are extremely difficult to prosecute. The control frauds we convicted became too greedy and began to take funds through "straw" borrowers.[3] A prosecutor who detects the straw can win a conviction.

The CEO who owns a controlling interest in the company maximizes the seeming legitimacy of his actions. Ordinary individuals, academic economists, even otherwise suspicious reporters simply cannot conceive of a CEO ever finding it rational to defraud "his" own company. Similarly, law-and-economics scholars argue that it would be irrational for any top-tier audit firm to put its reputation on the line by blessing a control fraud's financial statements (Prentice 2000, 136–137). It is easy to see why they reject control fraud theory: they think it requires them to believe that the CEO and auditor are acting irrationally. Rationality is the bedrock assumption of neoclassical economics, so these scholars must reject that paradigm in order to see control fraud as real. Control fraud theory does not require irrationality.

HOW DO WAVES OF CONTROL FRAUD ENDANGER
THE GENERAL OR REGIONAL ECONOMY?

Individual control frauds should be a central regulatory concern because they cause massive losses. The worst aspect of control frauds is that they can cluster. The two variants of corporate control fraud, "opportunistic" and "reactive," can occur in conjunction. Opportunists are looking for an opportunity to commit fraud. Reactive control frauds occur when a business is failing. A CEO who has been honest for decades may react to the fear of failure by engaging in fraud.

Economists distinguish between systemic risk that applies generally to an industry and risks that are unique to a particular company. Systemic risks can endanger a regional or even a national economy. Systemic risks pose a danger of creating many control frauds. In the S&L case, the systemic risk in 1979 was to interest rates. S&L assets were long-term (thirty-year), fixed-rate mortgages, but depositors could withdraw their money from the S&L at any time. If interest rates rose sharply, every S&L would be insolvent.

In 1979, the Federal Reserve became convinced that only it had the will to stop inflation. Chairman Paul Volcker doubled interest rates. By mid-1982, on a market-value basis, the S&L industry was insolvent by $150 billion. This maximized the incentive to engage in reactive control fraud and made it far cheaper for opportunists to purchase an S&L. These factors ensured that there would be an upsurge in control fraud, but the cover-up of the industry's mass insolvency (and with it, that of the federal insurance fund), deregulation, and desupervision combined to create the perfect environment for a wave of control frauds. Criminologists call an environment that produces crime "criminogenic."

Control frauds' investments are concentrated and driven by fraud, not markets. This causes systemic regional, or even national, economic problems. One of the remarkable things about the S&L debacle is how alike the control frauds were. Almost all of them concentrated in large, speculative real estate investments, typically the construction of commercial office buildings. (In this context, "speculative" means that there are no tenant commitments to rent the space.) Because the control frauds grew at astonishing rates, this quickly produced a glut of commercial real estate in markets where the control frauds were dominant (Texas and Arizona were the leading examples). Moreover, being Ponzi schemes, they increased their speculative real estate loans even as vacancy rates reached record levels and real estate values collapsed. Waves of control frauds produce bubbles that must collapse. They delay the collapse by continuing to lend, thus hyperinflating the bubble. The bigger the bubble and the longer it continues, the worse the problems it causes. The control frauds were major contributors to, not victims of, the real estate recessions in Texas and Arizona in the 1980s.[4]

What we have, then, is a triple concentration. Systemic risk causes control frauds to occur at the same time. They concentrate in the particular industries that foster the best criminogenic environments. They also concentrate in investments best suited for accounting fraud. That triple concentration means that waves of control fraud will create, inflate, and extend bubbles.

MORAL HAZARD

Moral hazard is the temptation to seek gain by engaging in abusive, destructive behavior, either fraud or excessive risk taking. Failing firms expose their owners to moral hazard. This is not unique to S&Ls; it is in the nature of corporations. Moral hazard arises when gains and losses are asymmetrical. A company with $100 million in assets and $101 million in liabilities is insolvent. If it is liquidated (sells its assets), the stockholders will get nothing because they are paid only after all the creditors are paid in full. In my example, the assets are not sufficient to repay the creditors' claims (liabilities), so liquidation would wipe out the shareholders' interest in the company. The CEO runs the company until it is forced into liquidation. There are two other keys. Limited liability limits a shareholder's loss to the value of his stock. He is not liable for the company's debts, no matter how insolvent it becomes. The creditors lose if the insolvency deepens.

The "upside" potential of a failing company is enjoyed by the shareholders. They win big if investments succeed. Assume that my hypothetical insolvent company makes a movie that produces a $70 million profit. That gain will go almost entirely to the shareholders.

Risk and reward are asymmetric when a corporation is insolvent but left under the control of the shareholders. If the corporation makes an extremely risky investment and it fails, the loss is borne entirely by the creditors. If the investment is a spectacular success, the gain goes overwhelmingly to the shareholders. The shareholders have a perverse incentive to take unduly large risks rather than to make the most productive investments.

The examples of moral hazard I have used involve unduly risky behavior. The theory, however, is not limited to honest risk taking. Moral hazard theory also explains why failing firms have an incentive to engage in reactive control fraud (White 1991, 41). Indeed, since S&L control fraud was a sure thing (it was certain to produce, for a time, record profits), reactive control fraud was a better option than an ultra-high-risk gamble.

WHY THE S&L INDUSTRY SUFFERED
A WAVE OF CONTROL FRAUD

Bad regulation exposed the S&L industry to systemic interest-rate risk and caused the first phase of the debacle. Bank Board rules prohibited adjustable-rate mortgages (ARMs). ARMs would have reduced interest-rate risk.[5] This prohibition caused a wave of reactive control fraud, though it is remarkable how small that wave was.

Opportunistic control fraud can also occur in waves. Opportunists seek out the best field for fraud. Four factors are critical: ease of obtaining control, weak regulation, ample accounting abuses, and the ability to grow rapidly.

These characteristics are often interrelated. An industry with weak rules against fraud is likely to invite abusive accounting. Industries with abusive accounting have superior opportunities for growth because they produce the kinds of (fictitious) profits and net worth that cause investors and creditors to provide ever-greater funds to the control fraud.

The interrelationship between the opportunities for reactive and opportunistic control fraud made the regulatory and business environments ideal for control fraud. Interest rate risk rendered every S&L insolvent (in market value) in 1979–1982, making it far cheaper and easier for opportunists to get control. Owners and regulators were desperate to sell S&Ls; opportunists were eager to buy. The Bank Board and accountants used absurd "goodwill" accounting to spur sales.

In another common dynamic, a financially troubled industry, particularly one with an implicit or explicit governmental guarantee (e.g., deposit insurance), is one most likely to abuse accounting practices and to restrain vigorous regulation. (Appendix B is a copy of a candid letter from Norman Strunk, the former head of the S&L trade association, to his successor, Bill O'Connell. It explains how the industry used its power over the administration and Congress to limit the Bank Board's supervisory powers.) Regulators, fearful of being blamed for the industry failing on their watch, experience their own version of moral hazard.

The temptation (shared with the industry) is to engage in a cover-up. The industry will lobby regulators, the administration, and Congress to aid the cover-up by endorsing accounting abuses and minimizing take-overs of insolvents.

Taken together, these factors mean that the incentives to engage in opportunistic and reactive control fraud will vary over time and by industry and that they can both peak at the same time and place (Tillman and Pontell 1995). This is not a random event, and it is not dependent on an industry having a heavy initial endowment of evil CEOs. Control fraud was a major contributor to the S&L debacle because the industry environment was the best in the country for both reactive and opportunistic fraud. The wonder is not that the control frauds caused so much damage, but that we stopped them before they hurt the overall economy. This is not a regulatory success story. The control frauds caused scores of billions of dollars of losses. However, a betting person in the mid-1980s would have judged the agency's chances of removing every control fraud from power within five years as none, not slim. The Bank Board did put the control frauds out of business and, remarkably, did so despite Danny Wall—a serial appeaser of control frauds—becoming chairman in mid-1987.

The fact that characteristic business and regulatory environments cause waves of control fraud is critical for public policy. It means that we can predict the fields that are most at risk and choose policies that will reduce, instead of encourage, waves of control fraud. Similarly, we can identify likely control frauds by knowing their characteristic practices. We can attack them because we can aim at growth, their Achilles' heel.

The reason the S&L control frauds died even when Bank Board chairman Wall reached a separate peace with them is that they were Ponzis. Former chairman Gray's restrictions on growth were fatal to them. The irony is that although Wall desperately wished to avoid closing S&Ls like Lincoln Savings, he never understood that he was dealing with Ponzi schemes. As a result, he never understood the need to change the rule limiting growth. The control frauds that Gray lacked the funds to close collapsed during Wall's term, to his horror and bafflement.

THE COVER-UP OF THE INSOLVENCY OF THE INDUSTRY AND THE FSLIC

The cover-up of the S&L debacle was the dominant dynamic during the Reagan administration. If the industry was insolvent by $150 billion, then the Federal Savings and Loan Insurance Corporation (FSLIC) fund (with $6 billion in the till) was insolvent by nearly $150 billion. The U.S. Treasury stands behind the federal insurance funds, so the FSLIC fund's insolvency meant that the U.S. Treasury should show a contingent liability of $150 billion. That translates as follows: the federal budget deficit was $150 billion worse than reported because the S&L industry's insolvency was not on the books.

No one wanted to recognize that contingent liability. The Reagan administration didn't want to because it was trying to get the 1981 tax cuts passed and was already facing criticism that it would not meet its campaign promise to balance the budget. The industry didn't want to admit that it was insolvent. The agency's nightmare, which I shared once I joined it on April 2, 1984, was a nationwide run sparked by depositors who might "do the math" and realize that $150 billion was considerably greater than the $6 billion in FSLIC.

Congress wanted a cover-up. Americans loved the S&L industry because S&Ls made loans to people, not corporations, and made possible the American dream (owning a home). The industry was superb at burnishing its reputation. (It also helped that the public thought of Jimmy Stewart and *It's a Wonderful Life* when they thought of S&Ls.) Politicians loved S&Ls because Americans did, because S&Ls were large contributors, and because they had the best grassroots lobbyists. Their trade association, the United States League of Savings Institutions (the League), was a force of nature, as were its allies the National Association of Homebuilders (NAHB) and the National Association of Realtors (NAR). (Their PACs traveled in packs.)

Moreover, cuts in government programs would deepen if the budget deficit were $150 billion worse. Members of Congress did not want to cut popular programs.

One testament to the times is that the Federal Deposit Insurance Corporation (FDIC) also engaged in a cover-up of the savings banks it regulated. The FDIC, which was much more staid than the Bank Board, used phony accounting to hide the insolvency of savings banks. Their industry was much smaller than the S&L industry, and the FDIC considered regulating savings banks a distraction from its "real" job of regulating commercial banks, so savings banks had little influence with the FDIC. The FDIC fund was far larger than the FSLIC fund, and the FDIC had no fear of a systemic run on savings banks even should the public learn of their insolvency. Despite all these differences, the FDIC adopted phony accounting for savings banks to hide their insolvency and stopped closing them, showing how strong the pressures were for cover-ups in the 1980s.

THE S&L COVER-UP OPTIMIZED
THE INDUSTRY FOR CONTROL FRAUD

No one intentionally designed the cover-up to optimize the industry for control fraud. Indeed, if someone had set out to optimize the problem, I am sure he would have failed. The interaction of a series of steps made the industry ideal for control fraud.

There are five central facts that explain why the Bank Board's implementation of the cover-up proved so harmful. First, it came from the top, and it came via consensus. Chairman Pratt endorsed and designed the cover-up. He did so with the aid of other leaders. The infamous Joint Task Force on Profitability combined the talents of senior Bank Board economists and regulators and the most prominent outside accountant specializing in the S&L industry. The task force endorsed accounting abuses, but it was the manner in which it did so that makes such depressing reading. It didn't hold its nose and say we need to do this as an unpleasant emergency measure. Instead, it endorsed absurd accounting abuses like "loan loss deferral" (which meant not recognizing losses currently) as purportedly superior accounting treatments under economic and accounting theory.[6] The task force also encouraged fast growth and interest-rate risk in a get-rich-quick scheme called "risk-controlled arbitrage" (RCA).[7]

Second, the design and implementation of the cover-up guaranteed a disaster. Moral hazard theory unambiguously predicts that if you greatly weaken restraints on abuse at a time of mass, intense moral hazard, you will suffer severe abuses. Had you asked Richard Pratt, when he was still a graduate student, to write a paper on the effect of removing restraints at a time of mass insolvency, I am confident that you would have received a sound analysis predicting disaster. Moreover, you didn't need a PhD in economics to figure any of this out. Common sense would have worked just fine. Daniel Fischel (1995, 211) says that the second stage of the debacle was "completely predictable." A cover-up works by grossly inflating net worth and net income, but to close an S&L the regulator often needs to show insolvency. This can make it very hard to close control frauds prior to their failing catastrophically (e.g., losses exceeding 30 percent of liabilities).

Third, no economist contemporaneously predicted that the administration's policies would produce a disaster.[8] Worse, they predicted the opposite, that Pratt's policies were the industry's best hope. As future Bank Board member and financial economist Larry White would famously write (1991, 90), there were "no Cassandras" among economists.

Fourth, although no economist spotted the problems, roughly two hundred opportunistic control frauds promptly spotted the opportunities and rushed to enter the industry. Larry White (1991, 92) makes this point at the close of his discussion of the lack of Cassandras:

> The *enhanced* opportunities-capabilities-incentives nexus was simply not seen—except by entrepreneurs who would take advantage of it. (emphasis in original)

Fifth, the Bank Board lost vital moral capital when it abused accounting practices to cover up the industry's and the FSLIC's insolvency. A regulator succeeds largely on the basis of moral suasion. When a regulator embraces fraudulent accounting, it loses legitimacy and will have great difficulty convincing, for example, courts that an S&L CEO should go to jail for using (different) fraudulent accounting methods to inflate net worth and income.

THE COVER-UP LED THE REAGAN ADMINISTRATION
TO OPPOSE GRAY'S WAR ON THE FRAUDS

No prior book has noted the centrality of the cover-up to the debacle, the control frauds, and the administration's war on Gray. Gray's war on the control frauds threatened the administration. First, closure of the frauds would reveal the industry's insolvency just when the Administration was pronouncing it cured. Reregulation was the second threat. Regulation was vital for defeating the frauds, but it was ideologically anathema and considered political suicide. The administration designed, implemented, and praised the deregulation that attracted the control frauds and made them superpredators. Reregulation would have been an admission of guilt.[9]

WHY DID ECONOMISTS AND THE ADMINISTRATION
GET THE DEBACLE SO WRONG?

White does not discuss why only the entrepreneurs saw this nexus and responded immediately by entering the S&L industry. (As will become clear, I disagree with White's view that the entrants were primarily honest entrepreneurs.) Surely this is an important question. One group, with extensive professional training, the aid of a theory that unambiguously predicts that the policy they designed will be disastrous, and a disciplinary emphasis on how individuals respond to incentives, got it entirely wrong. They designed the blunder, they opined that it was the solution, and they did not even warn of the inevitable problems it would produce. Fischel (1995) is right that the second stage of the debacle was "completely predictable" under standard economic theory, but like every other economist he failed to predict it, and does not discuss why he failed. Indeed, Fischel's villain is Gray, the "press flack" who did predict it (ibid.).

Economists refused to admit that the administration had created a disaster, and they stalled our efforts to end both individual control frauds and the wave of fraud. They are still in denial about the role of deregulation and fraud in the debacle.

Why is it that economists performed so badly and became, with the accountants and lawyers, leading allies of the control frauds? Why did the Reagan administration listen only to their perspective? I believe that the answer has four parts. Economists know almost nothing about fraud. The dominant law-and-economics theory is that there is no serious control fraud, so it is not worth studying. There is no coherent theory of fraud, though there is finally some interest in developing one.

Second, prominent U.S. economists generally believe that regulation is the problem and deregulation is the solution. The deregulators' ideology was the initial problem, but the fact that their policies led to disaster also brought on acute embarrassment. They had the normal human wish to avoid taking responsibility for their mistakes. Their embarrassment was particularly acute because they consider themselves the only true social scientists and believe that theory and facts, not ideology, drive their views. As I explained, their theory did not fail them. It predicted that the policies they recommended would cause a disaster. All of this strengthens the desire to avoid admitting error.

Third, economists (and the administration) were like generals preparing to fight the last war. In the S&L context, this meant concentrating on interest-rate risk. Thus, traditional S&Ls were the problem and high fliers the solution. The high fliers, unfortunately, were frauds.

Fourth, economists missed the problem because of social class and self-interest. Few economists are prepared to see business people, particularly patrons, as criminals. Many of the top financial economists worked for the control frauds, and the collapse created such embarrassment that they felt compelled to deny that their employers were frauds. (The most famous economic study of fraud was conducted by Bert Ely, a financial consultant who, as an expert witness, assisted in the defense of S&L managers and outside auditors. In fact, the study did not cover fraud [Black, Calavita, and Pontell 1995].) This self-interest was not unique to economists; it applied fully to accountants and lawyers. Economists are particularly vulnerable to this fault, however, when the CEO is the dominant shareholder. The leading law-and-economics text asserts that this is the ideal structure because it ensures managers' fidelity to shareholders' interests (Easterbrook and Fischel 1991, 106, 120). This is one of the areas where the field's lack of knowledge of fraud has embarrassed it, for William Crawford had it exactly right: the best way to rob a bank is to own it. The person with the greatest incentives to engage in fraud is the CEO owner of a failing firm.

Fifth, economists developed a conventional wisdom about the debacle and have not reexamined it. The conventional wisdom is that moral hazard explains the debacle, that control fraud was trivial, and that insolvent S&Ls honestly made ultrarisky investments (and became high fliers) that often failed. All aspects of the conventional wisdom proved false upon examination. Traditional S&Ls gambled for resurrection by continuing to expose themselves to interest-rate risk in 1982–1984. They won these gambles and greatly reduced the cost of the debacle (NCFIRRE 1993a, 1–2). Next, the high fliers were not honest gamblers, but control frauds. Studies of failed high fliers invariably found control frauds (ibid., 3–4). There were over 1,000 felony convictions of S&L insiders. The pattern of failures shows that the high fliers were control frauds. They invariably reported high initial profits, and they all failed. Honest gambling cannot explain any aspect of the pattern (Black, Calavita, and Pontell 1995). Finally, the high fliers invested in a manner (particularly by embracing adverse selection and consistently underwriting incompetently) that would have been irrational for honest gamblers (ibid.).

THE MANY FRONTS IN GRAY'S WAR
AGAINST THE CONTROL FRAUDS

The great controversies during the S&L debacle almost universally involved control frauds. There was no real controversy about how to deal with the 1979–1982 crisis in interest-rate risk. There was uniform belief that the twin answers were a cover-up and deregulation. It did not occur to anyone involved in making policy that combining the mass insolvency of an industry, deposit insurance, extraordinarily inadequate examination and supervision, a cover-up based on accounting abuses, and deregulation would create an ideal environment for control fraud. The idea of asking a white-collar criminologist whether the policy could spur crime never arose. We consider it normal that nearly every federal agency (and many of their subunits) has a chief economist and that no agency has a chief criminologist; indeed, the federal government has no job category for criminologist. As a result, we never ask vital regulatory questions.

The control frauds did not create this optimal environment for fraud. They exploited the criminogenic environment and led the campaign to maintain and even improve it.

The control frauds, of course, did not announce that they were entering the industry to loot it, and since the essence of control fraud is the vast inflating of income, they appeared to be the most profitable S&Ls in America. As a result, Pratt never identified and put out of business a control fraud and never identified the wave of control frauds entering the industry. He praised them as entrepreneurs. Pratt disdained traditional S&L CEOs and considered them the problem. The control frauds had dug in for two years before Gray began to fight back.

Gray had a huge problem that no book about the debacle has noted. The Bank Board staff often worked sixty-hour weeks with no overtime and at low rates of pay. In particular, the FSLIC staff did this for Pratt, a charismatic leader. They approved 500 goodwill mergers in two years. Pratt praised them for their efforts, which he said had saved the FSLIC fund from disaster. Senior supervisors praised the CEOs who bought failed S&Ls in the mergers, and lauded the high profits the entrepreneurs reported. No matter how we sugarcoated the message, the FSLIC staff knew what Gray's war meant. The incredible hours they had worked for years were worse than useless: they had made things worse. The goodwill mergers did not resolve failed S&Ls; they created fictitious income and hid real losses. The accounting was fraudulent, the goodwill was worthless, and the new managers weren't geniuses. Indeed, they were often criminals.

This was an inherently unattractive message for the staff to receive. But the comparison between Pratt and Gray was worse. Pratt was dynamic, quick, funny (he is brilliant at self-deprecation), ultracompetent, organized, efficient, and self-assured, and he looks like the former football player he is. Gray was not quick and not funny. He was disorganized and unfocused, and he radiated nervousness and indecision. Instead of self-deprecating humor, he compared himself to Winston Churchill. Pratt was an expert in the field, and Gray was a press flack who had worked for an S&L.

You can see why the Bank Board staff often did not adopt Gray's view that their labors had been harmful, particularly since he was contradicting everything Pratt had told them; in addition, the administration and the industry were shouting that Gray was wrong and Pratt was right. The staff knew that Pratt had tried to keep the administration from making Gray his successor. This could explain why Gray was trashing Pratt's policies. This dynamic got worse as Gray promoted those who shared his views about the control frauds. Each promotion can upset a dozen other staff members. The Bank Board leaked, and the leaks were aimed at Gray.

Gray had poor relationships with Don Hovde and Mary Grigsby, his colleagues on the Bank Board. Neither of them really supported reregulation. They felt oppressed by Gray's constant pressure to intensify the war against the control frauds. Hovde wanted to succeed Gray as chairman, and he became a source for Keating and reporters. He later tried to help Keating's "straw" make a phony purchase of Lincoln Savings.

Whereas the control frauds knew our strategy, we knew little about theirs. We could learn about them through whistle-blowers or effective examination. There were virtually no whistle-blowers at the control frauds. I cannot remember any. Control frauds are control freaks: they hire yes-men and yes-women and get rid of people who ask tough questions. Bank examiners are valuable as investigators, but even their bosses usually miss their other critical role as scouts. An effective force making frequent exams gives its leaders not only the facts about a particular field of battle, but information on overall intentions and common tactics that is critical to intelligence analysts.[10] When you don't have effective scouts, you walk into ambushes — and that produces massacres. The Bank Board did not have remotely enough scouts.[11] One of the reasons Gray was invaluable was that he spotted the control fraud pattern on the basis of skimpy initial information.

ECONOMIC HINDSIGHT PROVES 20:2000

Hindsight is not always 20:20. If it were, we would always learn the lessons of the past and not be condemned to repeat them. The ongoing financial crisis shows how poorly we learned the lessons that the S&L debacle should have taught. First, control frauds will cause the worst losses. The markets will not detect them timely. Outside professionals will aid, not restrain, control frauds. Directors provide camouflage for frauds. Stock options further misalign the interests of shareholders and control frauds because CEOs structure them to maximize their self-interest and use them as a means of converting firm assets to personal use.

Ed Kane developed a famous analogy to sum up his view of the S&L debacle. He said that the Bank Board's distorted accounting left the agency like the driver of a car with a muddy windshield (Kane 1989, 167–169). Control frauds, however, create something far worse than a muddy windshield. Mud is noticeable, an irritant. The driver knows the view is obstructed and has a strong incentive to get out and clean the windshield.

Control frauds use accounting fraud to deliberately make everything appear brilliantly transparent. They are like the side mirrors that seem to reflect so normally that the government requires a permanent warning to be affixed to them: "Objects in this mirror are closer than they appear."[12] Massive insolvency is far closer than it appears for control frauds.

THE CIVIL WAR AMONG THE REGULATORS

I will examine how the control frauds were able to manipulate politicians and regulators and even to spark a civil war among the regulators. Key administration officials, senior staff members, and presidential appointees at the Bank Board aided the control frauds. Only one of these individuals was corrupt, but Humbert Wolfe's poem captures the ambiguous import of this fact:

> You cannot hope
> to bribe or twist,
> thank God! the
> British journalist.
> But, seeing what
> the man will do
> unbribed, there's
> no occasion to.[13]

2. "COMPETITION IN LAXITY"

Economists describing how regulators competed for "customers" by promising to be laxer in supervision coined two of the most telling phrases to come out of the S&L debacle: "competition in laxity" and "race to the bottom." The novel aspect is that economists endorsed these pejorative terms because the race was toward greater deregulation. In the early 1980s, economists knew that regulation was the problem, so anything that reduced regulation was desirable. Richard Pratt shared this mindset when President Reagan appointed him Bank Board chairman in 1981.

FOR THE BANK BOARD, THE RACE TO THE BOTTOM WAS A SHORT ONE

The Bank Board was at the bottom of the federal financial regulatory heap before Pratt's deregulation and desupervision. Jim Ring Adams (1990, 40) aptly described it as "the doormat" of federal regulators. I describe the problems that the board had with examination, supervision, and enforcement briefly, but they were among the most important contributors to the debacle, and a similar problem with SEC resources is one of the most important causes of the ongoing financial scandals at the time I write. Criminologists call this a "system capacity" problem (Calavita, Pontell, and Tillman 1997, 136). The regulatory and criminal justice systems lacked the resources (and often the will) to stop the control frauds.

The first problem was institutional structure. Agencies need to integrate examination and supervision, and the banking agencies did so. The Bank Board separated them in the worst possible manner. Examiners and supervisors worked for different bosses and different employers! The examiners were federal employees; the supervisors were Federal Home Loan Bank (FHLB) employees. Member S&Ls owned the twelve FHLBs. This posed an obvious potential conflict of interest. The FHLBs were not subject to federal limits on staffing or salary. We paid supervisory agents far more than examiners. The life of an examiner was constant travel and frustration; the life of a supervisor was cushy. The examiners had little authority. Only supervisors could recommend actions or issue directives. Naturally, the two groups often disagreed and were antagonistic.

The first common boss for examiners and supervisors was the Bank Board chairman, so no one else could resolve disputes. The Bank Board called its top supervisor the director of the Office of Examinations and Supervision (OES), but supervisory agents reported to the "principal supervisory agent" (PSA)—the president of each FHLB—not to the OES. The PSAs reported to the chairman of the Bank Board, not to the OES director. Each FHLB was a separate duchy with substantial political power through its industry membership. The structure violated every rule of proper management and proved disastrous.

Second, examiners used state-of-the-art techniques—from the *1930s*. As late as 1986, examiners drafted each report in pencil. It took an average of two months to type a report.

Third, the industry hated the concept of examiners' and supervisors' exercising judgment, which is how banking regulators act (see Appendix B). S&L regulators could only enforce rules (Strunk and Case 1988). If an S&L was doing something unsafe, it could do so with impunity unless it violated a rule. If an S&L was acting sensibly but violating a rule, then supervisors would order it to stop. The enforcement branch reinforced this tendency. It would not take action absent a violation of an express rule (NCFIRRE 1993a, 50–51).

Fourth, the Bank Board virtually never made criminal referrals when it found fraud, and the Justice Department rarely prosecuted. The Bank Board had no formal criminal referral system. The attorney general, Edwin Meese, exacerbated the critical shortage of white-collar prosecutors by transferring many of them to prosecute pornography. (Meese acted to please the nation's leading antiporn activist—*Charles Keating*.)

Fifth, the Bank Board got all of its money from industry assessments, but was subject to federal restrictions on how many examiners it could hire and how much it could pay them. Worse, its banking regulator "competitors" were exempt from many of these limits. Good examiners could make a lot more money by joining the banking agencies — the starting difference in annual salary was about $3,000; it grew to over $10,000 for senior analysts (Strunk and Case 1988, 141). Bank examiners had greater authority and prestige (and computers instead of pencils). There were exceptions, but the system ensured that Bank Board examiners generally would be low in quality.

THE REAGAN ADMINISTRATION DECIDES TO COVER UP THE S&L CRISIS IN 1981

Pratt faced an impossible situation. Virtually every S&L was insolvent on a market-value basis by 1981.[1] By mid-1982, the industry was insolvent by roughly $150 billion (NCFIRRE 1993a, 1). The FSLIC fund had only $6 billion in reserves, so it was hopelessly insolvent. The Reagan administration refused to admit that the industry was insolvent, refused to give the FSLIC any additional money to close failed S&Ls, and ordered Pratt not to use the FSLIC's statutory right to borrow even the paltry sum of $750 million from the treasury. Pratt's orders were to cover up the S&L crisis.

The cover-up was particularly critical to the administration in 1981. Ronald Reagan's campaign promises were to cut taxes, increase defense spending, and balance the budget. Those three promises, of course, were inconsistent, as his budget director, David Stockman, would later admit.[2] The administration knew that if the public realized that the budget deficit was really $150 billion larger than reported, the resulting outcry could have prevented passage of the large tax cuts that the Economic Recovery Tax Act of 1981 (generally called the 1981 Tax Act) provided for.

The industry supported the cover-up because it didn't want to report that it was insolvent. Pratt supported the cover-up because Bank Board officials shared the same nightmare, a national run on S&Ls. Pratt did not cause the interest rate crisis, but many would blame him if the system failed on his watch. Pratt made sure this did not happen. Congress supported the cover-up because the alternative was to cut popular social programs.

THE COVER-UP SETS THE STAGE
FOR THE WAVE OF CONTROL FRAUDS

The cover-up optimized the industry for control fraud in several ways. The most direct contribution was abusive accounting. The Bank Board's regulatory accounting principles (RAP) trumped generally accepted accounting principles (GAAP) for regulatory reporting purposes. Pratt developed "creative regulatory accounting principles"—the acronym said it all! I discussed the worst of these, loan loss deferral, in the introduction. The creative RAP provisions were the cherry on the sundae of accounting insanity. Two GAAP provisions composed the sundae. The largest accounting abuse came from GAAP's failure to recognize market-value losses caused by interest rate changes. GAAP did not recognize the $150 billion loss in market value caused by interest rate increases.[3]

GOODWILL: PRATT'S PATENT
MEDICINE FOR A SICK INDUSTRY

The other huge GAAP abuse was "goodwill accounting." A word of encouragement: you will be able to understand it, you will be amazed at the scam, and you will know why policy makers must understand such scams. You will also be joining an elite group, for few understood it. In other books you can read that goodwill accounting was abusive, but not about how the scam worked. I describe in detail only the two accounting frauds central to the debacle; goodwill is the first.

It all starts with a simple, logical assumption drawn from economics: the best proof of market value is what an arm's-length buyer pays for an asset. An arm's-length buyer is an independent buyer acting in his own interests. (When economists assume "rationality," they err if they fail to take into account what's rational for a fraud.) Goodwill accounting among 1980s S&Ls was overwhelmingly fraudulent. Pratt's priorities, because the FSLIC had only trivial amounts of money relative to the scale of the industry's insolvency, were to avoid spending FSLIC funds to resolve failed S&Ls and to cover up the insolvency of the industry and the FSLIC. That meant that the FSLIC rarely used the normal means of resolving failures, i.e., paying a healthy firm to acquire the failed S&L. Instead, Pratt induced roughly 300 buyers to acquire failed S&Ls without any FSLIC assistance. Pratt called these "resolutions" and took credit for developing innovative techniques that reduced the average cost of resolving such failures by about 75 percent.

White-collar criminologists' mantra is "if it sounds too good to be true, it probably is." The obvious question is why entities knowingly took on net liabilities without FSLIC assistance. (A firm whose debts exceed its assets is insolvent; it is a net liability.) Accountants' answer was "goodwill." A firm can have greater value than the sum of its tangible assets less its debts. McDonalds is an example. It is worth far more than what it could sell its physical assets for, less its debts. It has a reputation for safety and cleanliness and is famous worldwide. This favorable reputation has great value, and we call that value "goodwill." Accounting literature, however, calls it a "general, unidentified intangible" (FASB Statement 72), and I will explain later why that phrase is important to the S&L scam. The "intangible" part just means it isn't a physical asset. The words "general" and "unidentified" indicate that the goodwill isn't attributable to any specific, identifiable physical asset, such as the golden arches.

The concept of goodwill and the assumption of rationality are both reasonable propositions. Together, however, in the context of the mass insolvency of the S&L industry, goodwill created insane financial results. It optimized the S&L environment for control fraud. It helped cover up the mass insolvency of the industry. It allowed Pratt to claim that he had resolved failures at minimal cost and had contained the crisis, which allowed him to resign in triumph and begin a lucrative career at Merrill Lynch, trading mortgage products with the industry.

Here's how the assumption of rationality and the concept of goodwill produced insanity. When you purchased an S&L through a merger, the assets and liabilities of the S&L you were buying were "marked-to-market."[4] As a practical matter, that meant that the S&L's mortgage assets would lose roughly 20 percent of their value.[5] Note that this result stems from the first GAAP accounting abuse that I discussed, the failure to recognize market-value losses caused by interest rate changes. Most S&Ls were insolvent on a market-value basis in 1981 by roughly 20 percent of their reported GAAP assets, so my example is realistic. This brings us to the fundamental balance sheet equation: assets − liabilities = capital. A typical acquired S&L might have reported under GAAP that it had $200 million in assets and $205 million in liabilities. Its GAAP insolvency was $5 million.

Here's how the mark-to-market valuation transforms the situation.

On a market-value basis, the S&L's assets are worth 20 percent less than on a GAAP basis: $160 million, not $200 million. The market value of the liabilities is the same as their GAAP value, $205 million. You might think that this demonstrates that the S&L being acquired was insolvent by $45 million on a market-value basis, but if you think so, you have forgotten rationality and goodwill. It would be irrational knowingly and voluntarily to buy an S&L that was insolvent by $45 million without getting at least $45 million in financial assistance from the FSLIC. But buyers got zero FSLIC assistance. The deals were done knowingly; the mark-to-market prior to completing the deal ensured that. The deals were voluntary. The FSLIC had no leverage with which to extort buyers. If the deal was done knowingly and voluntarily, then it was an arm's-length deal, and that made it the best possible evidence of the true market value of the S&L being purchased. The logic was inescapable: the S&L being acquired must not really be insolvent. It must have enormous goodwill value that accountants could not value directly in the mark-to-market. Indeed, in this example it had to have a minimum value of $45 million because if it had any lesser value, the S&L would be a net liability and it would be irrational to purchase it. Accountants recognized this value by creating a $45 million goodwill asset on the acquirer's books.

Note how circular and irrefutable this chain of logic is: there is no need (indeed, no way) for the auditor to check whether the S&L being acquired really has any goodwill at all, much less $45 million of it. There is no need because the arm's-length nature of the deal makes it the best evidence of market value; the auditor has no superior process. It is also impossible for the auditor to check because "general, unidentified intangible" is a fancy way to say "ghost." The accounting jargon means "we don't know where to look for it, and even if we did, it wouldn't matter because it can't be seen or measured."

Stepping back from the circular arguments, however, allows one to take the criminology perspective: this is too good to be true. Five hundred S&Ls that are deeply insolvent on a market-value basis aren't really insolvent on a market-value basis because they all turn out to have enormous amounts of goodwill? Then there is the odd way in which goodwill tracks insolvency. If one purchased the S&L a year later, when the mark-to-market showed it was insolvent by $60 million instead of $45 million, the accountants would put $60 million of goodwill on the books. The more insolvent the S&L being acquired, the greater its goodwill. That was, to say the least, illogical.

There was, in fact, no goodwill at the vast majority of failed S&Ls. Accountants did not consider what the source of the enormous goodwill could be. It couldn't be deposit insurance or even the broad asset powers granted by states with the greatest degree of deregulation. One could start a new S&L that would be solvent and would have deposit insurance and the same asset powers. Everyone doing the deals knew that the goodwill was fictitious, but it was in their interest to pretend it was real, so they did.

Why did buyers do these deals? Some of the deals were honest. For example, a large S&L would buy a much smaller S&L that was its major competitor for deposits in a metropolitan area. The large S&L would then have the market power to pay less for deposits and charge slightly more for home loans. Or, a very large S&L would buy a smaller S&L that had a good branch network in a part of a state where the large S&L had no presence and wanted to expand. In both cases, there would be real intangible value, but it would be identifiable; in the second example, it was attributable to the branch network.

The bulk of the goodwill mergers, however, were accounting scams. The buyers weren't irrational; they were taking advantage of an accounting abuse with the encouragement of the Bank Board and the blessing of a Big 8 audit firm. There are two keys to understanding why it was rational to merge despite fictitious goodwill. First the buyer was normally an insolvent S&L. Second, goodwill accounting was so perverse that the more insolvent the S&L acquired, the more "profit" reported.

The owner of an insolvent S&L and the owner of a healthy one had very different incentives when it came to making acquisitions. It was rational for an insolvent S&L to buy, without FSLIC assistance, another insolvent S&L. The insolvent buyer had no downside: limited liability meant that once the S&L was insolvent, the creditors bore any new losses. The owner of the insolvent S&L was no worse off if the merger made the S&L insolvent by an additional $45 million (as in my first example).

Goodwill mergers guaranteed that fraudulent, insolvent buyers won a trifecta even when the goodwill was bogus. First, buying an insolvent S&L was an elegant way for a control fraud to optimize the S&L as a fraud vehicle. Life is full of trade-offs, even for frauds. Control frauds normally have to trade off several factors. The ideal fraud vehicle would be a large company: there is more to steal and the prestige is greater. The larger an S&L's assets in the early 1980s, however, the greater its insolvency. Control frauds do not want to report that they are insolvent: a regulator can close them down or restrict their operations. A goodwill merger was perfect because it gave one control of a huge S&L and "eliminated" the insolvency of the purchased S&L. Under honest accounting methods, merging with a deeply insolvent S&L without FSLIC assistance should hurt profitability: the acquirer takes on more liabilities than assets, and so it should lose money.

That takes us to the second leg of the trifecta. I was serious about the claim that the more insolvent the S&L acquired, the higher the reported income. Goodwill mergers created fictitious profits in three ways. The principal means was "gains trading." Remember that the problem in the early 1980s was that S&Ls had lent most of their mortgage money in the 1970s at much lower interest rates and that the fixed-rate mortgages had thirty-year maturities. When interest rates go up, the value of long-term fixed-rate debt instruments (mortgages, bonds, treasury bills) goes down.

The S&L industry had roughly $750 billion in assets during the worst of the interest-rate crisis. Those assets were overwhelmingly long-term (typically thirty-year) fixed-rate mortgages. Fixed-rate assets do not earn higher rates of interest when market interest rates rise. As a result, they can lose a great deal of their market value when rates rise (no one wants to buy a mortgage if it is only earning 10 percent when he can buy a recently issued mortgage and earn 20 percent interest). By mid-1982, the S&L industry had lost about $150 billion in the market value of its mortgages. That works out to a 20 percent loss of total asset values. I will use that percentage loss in my hypothetical examples to provide a realistic explanation of why a "goodwill" merger could produce tremendous, albeit fictitious, profits.

For simplicity, assume the same insolvent S&L example I have been using. We buy an S&L that has $200 million (book value) in mortgages that the S&L lent in 1977 at an 8 percent interest rate. On a market-value basis, however, they are only worth $160 million because the market interest rate for a comparable mortgage is now 16 percent. The key is that we create a new book value when we acquire these mortgages through the merger. Their book value becomes $160 million. The $205 million in liabilities at the S&L we are buying are very short-term deposits. Short-term deposits do not change materially in value when interest rates change, so their book value is unchanged by the merger accounting.

Now assume that interest rates begin to fall after we buy the S&L. One year later the market interest rate for a comparable mortgage is 12 percent. Remember: interest rates and the market values of mortgages go in opposite directions. Interest rates have fallen by 25 percent since the merger, and the mortgages we acquired in the merger have increased in market value to $180 million. We sell the mortgages for $180 million and book a $20 million "gain on sale."

There were four remarkable things about this "gains trading" scam that made it one of the most perfect frauds of all time. First, one books an enormous profit through a deal that actually locks in an enormous loss. In my example, the acquirer assumes $205 million in liabilities to do this deal. The liabilities are real. The acquirer has just sold every asset acquired in the merger for $180 million. The sale locked in a $25 million loss. The merger has been disastrous, but one reports record profits! And these record profits are derived from GAAP, not creative regulatory accounting principles. Consider the policy implications of this. If one held the mortgages and if interest rates had continued to fall until the market value of the mortgages came back to $200 million, one might have survived. If one sold at $180 million, then it is irrelevant whether rates continue to fall. The other implication is that the acquirer knows that the profit is fictitious and that failure is certain, which maximizes the perverse incentives to engage in reactive control fraud.

Second, the Internal Revenue Service (IRS) treats this transaction for tax purposes as a loss. The IRS says that if one started with assets that had a book value of $200 million and sold them for $180 million, there is a $20 million loss for tax purposes that can be used to offset tax liability on GAAP profits. This is the second way in which goodwill mergers increased net income.[6]

Third, one could maximize this fictitious income only through a merger. Here's a simple way to understand the point. Assume the buyer was an S&L with assets and liabilities identical to those of the seller. (That is not a bizarre assumption. Most S&L acquirers were other S&Ls, and virtually every S&L was insolvent on a market-value basis during the peak merger years.) The important thing to understand is that only the seller's mortgages are marked-to-market by the merger. Again, we assume that market interest rates for comparable mortgages are 16 percent at the time of the merger and fall one year later to 12 percent. One could sell only the acquired mortgages for a gain because only they got a new (lower) book value through the mark-to-market. The buyer's mortgages have market, but not book, values identical to those of the mortgages acquired through the merger. The book value of the buyer's mortgages is still $200 million. If we sell them one year after the merger for their market price of $180 million, we have to book a $20 million loss under GAAP.

The S&L league seriously proposed that the entire industry mark its assets to market and create $150 billion in goodwill so that S&Ls could engage in gains trading without finding a merger partner. Even the administration thought this was beyond the pale. One can now see why S&Ls were desperate to acquire other S&Ls.

The fourth bit of elegance comes from an arcane point whose importance I promised to explain. Gains trading would not have been very attractive if one had had to reduce the goodwill asset figure when selling mortgages. A reduction in goodwill would have caused a dollar-for-dollar reduction in capital, and would soon have led to recognition of the GAAP insolvency of the S&L. It seems obvious that selling the assets obtained in the merger must also reduce any goodwill. But here is where the words "general" and "unidentified" proved so useful to the scams. Because the goodwill was not associated with any tangible acquired asset, it was not written off, even if every tangible asset acquired in the merger was sold.

In addition to gains trading and the IRS treatment of the gain as a loss for tax purposes, goodwill mergers created fictitious income through a device so arcane that perhaps one accountant in a thousand knew about it. Here's the quick and dirty version. Accountants actually created two new accounts when there was a goodwill merger. In addition to goodwill they created an account called "discount." Why they did this is not important to this discussion.[7] For S&Ls in the early 1980s, discount and goodwill were nearly identical in size. A percentage of goodwill had to be recognized every year as an expense. Pratt and the buyers, of course, wanted to minimize expense recognition in order to inflate net income. They found a blunt but effective way to do so. S&Ls had to recognize only 2.5 percent of goodwill a year as expense.[8] In my example of a $45 million goodwill figure, that would mean a bit over $1 million a year. S&Ls recognized a portion of discount as income every year. (Note that neither the expense nor the income represents cash flows.) The rate at which discount was recognized as income was significantly greater than the rate at which goodwill was recognized as expense.[9] Given my first point, the nearly identical size of goodwill and discount, this meant that the more insolvent the S&L acquired, the more "income" it produced.[10] The increased income from discount could be three times the increased expense from goodwill.[11]

Years later, brilliant lawyers produced an unexpected, fourth source of income from these goodwill scams. In 1989, Congress finally began cleaning up the S&L rot through the Financial Institution Reform, Recovery, and Enforcement Act (FIRREA). One of the abuses it ended was fictitious goodwill. The beneficiaries of that fictitious goodwill hired lawyers who managed to convince the Supreme Court that the Congress was taking something of value from these scam artists and that the Constitution requires the taxpayers to compensate them for the fictitious goodwill. We may have to pay $20 billion to the least deserving claimants in the history of takings litigation!

I have now explained two benefits of mergers to control frauds. Both the ability to control a large S&L without having to recognize its insolvency and the multiple sources of fictitious income are relevant to the third leg of the trifecta. The mergers protected the buyers from regulators and supercharged the S&Ls as control-fraud vehicles.

I explained that most acquirers were themselves insolvent S&Ls. Again, I want to emphasize that some of the goodwill mergers were legitimate acquisitions designed to strengthen branch networks. They should not be tarred with what I am about to explain. The goodwill mergers gave the acquirers de facto immunity from regulatory controls for several related reasons. The most obvious stems from my discussion of the fictitious income the mergers produced. Both the buyer and the S&L it was about to acquire would, in 1979–1982, have reported losing money. The merger would occur, and, miraculously, the combined entity would almost immediately be profitable—extremely profitable. It is very difficult to take supervisory action against a firm that is profitable.

The profit turnaround was "too good to be true," but Pratt hailed it as proof that his strategy for rescuing failed S&Ls was not only much cheaper than other solutions, but was also transforming the industry by attracting entrepreneurs whose superior management produced profits in awful economic times. Pratt knew better, as shown by his testimony before the National Commission on Financial Institution Reform, Recovery and Enforcement (NCFIRRE 1993c, 12).

> Under GAAP, as they were applied in the early 1980s, two institutions with massive negative earnings could merge, and the combined entity could show positive income without the operations of either institution changing (NCFIRRE 1993a, 38).

The acquiring CEOs responded with becoming modesty or bravado, depending on their personality, and raked in the rewards (raises, bonuses, and perks) that their superior skills and the responsibility of running a much larger S&L entitled them to. The values of stock S&Ls

(depositors owned many S&Ls in "mutual" form) surged after mergers in response to the "profits."

The remarkable profits of the goodwill mergers caused nearly everyone to view the CEOs as stars. From the Bank Board perspective, the acquirer was not simply a star manager—he was someone who deserved the agency's gratitude for resolving a failure at no cost to the FSLIC. The Bank Board wanted to believe that the profits were real. Pratt proclaimed that the profits proved his policies were correct. It would take a very brave or a very stupid examiner to say that the goodwill, income, and "successes" of the mergers were equally fictitious.[12]

The fact that senior field supervisors often recruited the acquirers in the goodwill mergers was a particular problem. The supervisor would recommend approval of the merger, vouching for the character of the principals. The merger produced the inevitable surge in "profits." The supervisor would write a glowing letter praising the new management, and, in turn, would receive a bonus and a letter in her file praising the merger. The supervisor would then ask the CEO to come to dog and pony shows where she would try to interest other acquirers. She would introduce the CEO as her prime example of how superior management produced great profits, and she would regale the group with odes to the CEO's brilliance. The CEO would tell his fellow real estate developers that we had met lots of jerky regulators, but his friend Mary was great.

Regulators are human. We are grateful to those who help us, particularly in times of greatest need. We are sensitive to the criticism that we are too negative; we like to say positive things. We deal constantly with the industry and make friends. We are reluctant to see our friends as crooks, and we know how embarrassing it would be if the CEO we recruited and praised turned out to be a fraud. We are subject to cognitive dissonance.

The combination of these factors meant that Bank Board supervisors were very unlikely to expose the goodwill accounting scams. Two other things compounded this problem. Very few people, even within the Bank Board, understood how the scam worked. I don't want to overstate this point—many people were skeptical that goodwill was real—but only a handful knew how goodwill and mark-to-market virtually guaranteed substantial fictitious profits if the insolvency of the acquired S&L was large relative to the size of the acquirer. This problem became even worse once Pratt and his senior staff left the agency, for the folks who remained were even less likely to understand.[13]

The acquirers, however, did not rely solely on these human weaknesses. They had lawyers, and they typically got forbearance provisions that said that the Bank Board could not take supervisory action against them even if they were in violation of the agency's pathetically weak net-worth requirements if the failure was due to acquiring the failed S&L. This meant that it was difficult to crack down on S&Ls involved in goodwill mergers even if they were highly unprofitable.

HOW THE GOODWILL MERGERS SERVED THE COVER-UP

The goodwill mergers were central to Pratt's cover-up. Every merger transmuted net liabilities into fictitious assets. This is accounting al-chemy. Every dollar of goodwill made a dollar of insolvency disappear. By the end of 1983, the industry had over $20 billion in goodwill. The goodwill mergers also produced, as I explained, large amounts of ficti-tious income. This effect was so large that the industry reported a net profit in 1993, but would have reported a net loss if not for the "income" produced by the mergers (NCFIRRE 1993a, 39). The goodwill mergers let Pratt declare victory and leave.

CREATIVE REGULATORY ACCOUNTING PRINCIPLES

Some books on the debacle have concentrated on lambasting Pratt for his creative RAP. That criticism is misdirected. GAAP created far more consequential accounting abuses than creative RAP. That fact, how-ever, is no defense of Pratt's creative RAP. The last thing that an indus-try engaged in rampant GAAP-sanctioned accounting abuses needed was additional abuse. The provisions were indefensible. Control frauds used several of Pratt's creative RAP provisions, but they were not criti-cal to the success of the frauds. I do not discuss them other than to recall that loan loss deferral damaged Pratt's purported strategy of waiting for a fall in interest rates.

DEREGULATION

I have explained that according to economic theory, deregulating an in-dustry that is massively and pervasively insolvent and has deposit insur-ance guarantees disaster. Pratt designed the Bank Board's deregulation, and the deregulatory Garn–St Germain Act of 1982. Pratt and Roger Mehle, an assistant secretary of the treasury, drafted the legislation.

Pratt's deregulation was doomed from the outset because he used the worst possible model of deregulation, Texas, to guide his efforts. He gave Texas an award in recognition of serving as his model. Texas-chartered S&Ls caused by far the worst losses during the debacle. Pratt chose Texas as his model for a logical reason. Texas S&Ls were more deregulated than those in any other state, and they reported smaller losses during 1979–1981 than almost any others. Again, stupid regulation was a major cause of the interest rate crisis, and almost everyone assumed that deregulation was the answer to the crisis. Pratt ignored the fact that dubious accounting drove the superior results in Texas.

Pratt's first major deregulation was a good one. The interest rate crisis had discredited the members of Congress who had prevented the Bank Board from approving adjustable-rate mortgages (ARMs), so Pratt was able to adopt a rule allowing ARMs.

The second major avenue of deregulation was the removal of controls on how much interest S&Ls and banks could pay depositors ("Reg Q"). This occurred in complex legislation and rulemaking, and the details are not important to this book. This deregulation was harmful—it was critical to making S&Ls the ideal Ponzi scheme—but it was also essential. Unless the nation was prepared to extend interest rate controls to money market funds (which was impossible politically and would have been very bad economics), S&Ls and banks had to be allowed to pay competitive rates of interest, or else depositors would have removed most of their deposits and transferred them to money market funds that were paying three times the interest rate permitted under Reg Q. The administration, not Pratt, led the charge to repeal Reg Q.

Another act that critics often blame incorrectly for the resulting S&L debacle was Congress's raising the deposit insurance limit from $40,000 to $100,000. In fact, this played no meaningful role in the debacle. The way that Congress increased the limit was wrong, and it showed the extreme clout of the S&L league, but the higher limit had no substantive effect. The thing to understand is that the limit was $40,000 at each S&L and that there were roughly 3,000 S&Ls. Under the lower limit, one could take $120 million to a deposit broker (Merrill Lynch was the largest) and have them deposit $40,000 into each of these 3,000 S&Ls, and every dollar deposited would be fully insured. There are only a handful of entities that might wish to deposit more than $120 million. And I haven't mentioned banks and credit unions, each with the same insurance limit. Altogether, that made about 20,000 insured depositories, which meant one could deposit about $800 million in insured funds under the old limit. In short, the old limit imposed no meaningful restraint, so the new limit's only impact was a tiny reduction in transaction costs, because Merrill Lynch's computers no longer had to divide a $80,000 deposit into two $40,000 deposits to attain full insurance coverage.

Other than approving ARMs, every act of deregulation that Pratt undertook contributed to the debacle. Pratt was a whirlwind who deregulated a broad range of activities. I discuss the seven areas most responsible for producing the wave of control frauds. The first two related directly to what CEOs could do. First, Pratt made it possible for one man to own an S&L. Pratt eliminated the Bank Board rules that prevented an individual from owning more than 15 percent of the stock and that required there be at least 400 shareholders. Second, Pratt relaxed conflict-of-interest rules that restricted officers and directors from using their positions for personal gain.

Pratt's deregulation spurred massive growth in several ways. The third key facet of deregulation was Pratt's further weakening of the net-worth requirement. He did so in two ways. The obvious change was reducing the net-worth requirement to 3 percent of total liabilities. That is a ludicrously low level of capital. A typical manufacturing company in the 1970s would have had fifteen times as much capital. An S&L with 3 percent capital is a few bad loans away from failure. The less obvious change came from all the income and assets attributable to abusive GAAP and creative RAP. An S&L that was deeply insolvent could report under both GAAP and RAP that it exceeded its required net worth. Pratt's fourth key measure spurred growth by ending restrictions on deposit brokers.

We need to view these deregulatory steps in conjunction with prior acts of deregulation that Pratt inherited but did not change. He inherited two insane rules that encouraged massive growth. One was five-year averaging. An S&L's capital requirement could be far less than the nominal requirement because it could, for example, meet the 3 percent requirement by showing that its capital represented 3 percent of its average liabilities over the last five years. The next footnote provides an example that illustrates the point; but the perverse bottom line was that *the faster you grew, the lower your effective percentage capital requirement.*[14] By lowering the nominal requirement to 3 percent and continuing five-year averaging, Pratt knew that he was essentially eliminating the capital requirement, and that came on top of the pervasive accounting abuses.

The combination of very low nominal capital requirements and five-year averaging meant that the fastest growing control frauds could grow by roughly $1 billion for every additional $1 million of "capital" they could report. This thousand-to-one leverage opportunity was one of keys to the astonishing growth that made the control frauds ideal vehicles for Ponzi schemes and imposed horrific damages on taxpayers. *Every $1 million in fraudulent accounting income could put the taxpayers at risk by an additional $1 billion.*

I will only mention the other similar act of capital depravity that Pratt inherited and then exploited instead of ending. "Twenty-year phase-in" provided that a newly created (de novo) S&L did not have to meet the nominal capital requirement. It only had to meet one-twentieth of the requirement by the end of year one, one-tenth of it by the end of year two, etc. De novos had no real capital requirement in their early years of operation. Five-year averaging and twenty-year phase-in were indefensible and disastrous. Pratt did not create them, but instead of ending them, he exploited them and made them worse by lowering the nominal capital requirement and encouraging fictitious accounting income.

The final three key acts of deregulation made construction lending the ideal Ponzi scheme. Pratt's fifth step was allowing federally chartered S&Ls to place a much higher portion of their assets (40 percent) in construction lending. Sixth, Pratt weakened the "loan-to-one-borrower" (LTOB) requirement to permit S&Ls to loan 100 percent of their RAP net worth to a single borrower. Pratt had inflated RAP, even beyond the enormous inflation provided by GAAP, so an S&L loaning at its LTOB limit was loaning far more than the total of its real capital to a single borrower. That meant that the S&L was one bad loan away from insolvency. (Of course, this discussion assumes the S&L had real, positive net worth to begin with, which it usually did not in 1982.) Seventh, Pratt ended the requirement for a down payment on secured real estate loans. S&Ls could loan 100 percent of the collateral's appraised value. If the loan defaulted (and default rates on speculative commercial real estate construction are high), the S&L was sure to suffer losses, even if the appraiser only slightly overvalued the project.

DESUPERVISION

Pratt's desupervision of the industry compounded the disaster his deregulation caused. Desupervision helped make the industry ideal for control fraud. First, and most disastrously, Pratt froze and then reduced the number of examiners. This was a terrible mistake, but Pratt was not alone in making it. President Reagan's first act was to freeze new hires.

The Office of Management and Budget (OMB) wanted the Bank Board to reduce its examiners and supervisors. President Reagan appointed Vice President Bush to head his financial deregulation task force. Bush recommended that financial regulators rely more on computer analyses of industry financial statements and cut both the frequency of examinations and the number of examiners. Martin Lowy (1991, 36) says that Pratt fought with the administration for new examiners and was denied them.

The OMB went so far as to threaten Pratt with criminal sanctions if he didn't obey its spending restrictions. On another occasion, the OMB cut off FSLIC funds for liquidations (ibid.).

Deregulation requires *increased* supervision in an industry with deposit insurance. An NCFIRRE consultant interviewed Paul Allen Schott, an assistant general counsel for the Treasury Department in 1981–1985. Treasury and the OMB worked together throughout that time to try to prevent the Bank Board from hiring additional examiners. Schott explained:

When OMB [blocked] efforts to hire more examiners, the thought was deregulation meant not supervising the institutions. There was a misguided perception that supervision wasn't needed. (NCFIRRE 1993b)

Examinations fell sharply from 1981 to 1983 as a result of the combination of deregulation, the cut in the number of examiners, the loss of experienced examiners, and the wave of control frauds. Deregulation meant examiners had to review much more complex assets, and control frauds meant that they could not rely on the S&L's records or personnel to be truthful. Both conditions vastly increased the required examination time and examiners' required expertise. Experienced examiners are far more efficient. The Bank Board conducted 3,171 exams in 1991, 2,800 in 1982, and 2,131 in 1983. At a time when greatly increasing the number of examinations was vital, desupervision led to one-third fewer exams.

Pratt inherited an undermanned staff paid so poorly relative to its counterparts in the banking agencies that examiner quality was poor. Pratt knew how desperately inadequate Bank Board examination, supervision, and enforcement were. He could have used the Garn–St Germain Act and his powers as chairman to fix these problems. Specifically, the Bank Board needed the statutory authority to pay competitive wages, and it needed a chairman who would dramatically improve Bank

Board examination and supervision. The Bank Board also needed to make the organization of its examiners and supervisors rational and to adopt modern examination techniques; as I've written, its examiners were still writing out reports in pencil in 1986. Pratt, however, produced no meaningful improvements. He missed his critical opportunity against the control frauds. The administration actively made things worse.

The administration took extraordinary steps to prevent Pratt from closing insolvent S&Ls. The first act was the congressional testimony of Roger Mehle, the assistant secretary that Treasury Secretary Donald Regan chose to take the lead in the S&L crisis. Mehle's testimony started with a fact: GAAP financial statements did not reflect the true market value of S&Ls. That was bad news, for their market values were deeply negative, but Mehle tried to make it good news by arguing that because GAAP was irrelevant, insolvency was irrelevant. He said the industry was "sound" (Black 1993a, 20). Market-value insolvency, however, is critical. If an S&L's liabilities exceed its assets, the insurance fund suffers a loss; and if the liabilities of the insurance fund exceed its assets, the taxpayers bear the loss.

Mehle had an answer to that: we bear the loss only if we close the S&L, so we should not close failed S&Ls. Mehle argued that an S&L needed to be closed only if it could not raise the cash to pay its current obligations. He noted that deposit insurance meant that this should never occur because the insolvent S&L could grow and use new deposits to pay interest on old deposits. *The administration encouraged insolvent S&Ls to engage in Ponzi schemes.* Mehle was not on a frolic of his own; he testified for the administration.

Mehle's second act was even more amazing. While still the senior Treasury Department official with responsibility for S&Ls, he testified on behalf of an S&L suing the Bank Board. Pratt's predecessor placed Telegraph Savings in receivership because it was insolvent. The owners filed suit challenging the receivership. Had the plaintiffs won, they doubtless would have sought damages for an unlawful takeover—from the Treasury Department! It was, therefore, bizarre that Treasury permitted Mehle to testify on the owners' behalf against the agency. Mehle was a dream witness for the plaintiffs, testifying that it was arbitrary for the agency to close an S&L because it was insolvent. He said that the S&L industry had to be healthy because it was growing rapidly. He even testified that it was irrelevant whether an S&L was already insolvent and had growing losses because "It can solve it by borrowing" or bringing in additional deposits (Black 1993a, 20). (Bankrupt companies solve their problems when they borrow more and go more heavily into debt?) After he left the administration, Mehle helped form a "shadow financial regulatory committee" that gave similarly expert advice on how to regulate.

The courts found Mehle unpersuasive, but the administration succeeded in its real goal: ensuring that Pratt would not close enough S&Ls to reveal the cover-up. The numbers tell the story: Pratt spent just enough FSLIC money in 1981 and 1982 to report that FSLIC reserves increased very slightly to $6.15 billion and then to $6.3 billion (Kane 1989, 9). The FSLIC fund, of course, was massively insolvent on a market-value basis because the industry was massively insolvent. Government accounting standards required the FSLIC to recognize that liability and to report that it was insolvent. Needless to say, Pratt (like his predecessors) did not do so. Pratt should have reduced the FSLIC fund by resolving failed S&Ls. Pratt, however, wanted the FSLIC fund to grow in order to aid the cover-up, to project an image of strength that would reduce the risk of a run, and to provide emergency liquidity if there were a run.

Third, I have explained how Pratt welcomed and praised the entrepreneurs and how this attitude plus the fictitious profits produced by the goodwill mergers made it very unlikely that the agency would take timely action against the control frauds. And, in fact, the agency did not take effective action against any control fraud during Pratt's tenure. Indeed, the agency took few enforcement actions. The goodwill mergers and the wave of new entrants that Pratt encouraged diverted critical supervisory resources into (non)resolutions at precisely the time they were desperately needed to counter the wave of control frauds.

TEXAS AND CALIFORNIA—THE STATES
THAT WON THE RACE TO THE BOTTOM

Another term for "competition in laxity" was "the race to the bottom." S&Ls could change freely from a federal to a state charter (the permission from the government to run an S&L) and still be insured by the FSLIC. The charter determined what the S&L could invest in. Texas led the race by deregulating in the 1970s, and California followed the lead. Many federally chartered S&Ls in those states converted to state charters. By granting federally chartered S&Ls greater investment powers, the Garn–St Germain Act and Pratt's deregulation led many

Texas and California charters to convert quickly to federal charters. Texas had the equivalent of a "most favored nation" clause in its charters that allowed Texas-chartered S&Ls to do whatever federally chartered ones could, so the rush to convert to federal charters was greatest in California. California responded to the Garn–St Germain Act with the Nolan Act (named after its sponsoring senator, the notably corrupt and soon-to-be-convicted Pat Nolan). The Nolan Act became effective on January 1, 1983. It won the race to the bottom by going directly to the bottom. A California-chartered S&L could invest 100 percent of its assets in *anything* (with the commissioner's approval).

Despite Nolan's corruption, this was not a conspiracy, but a bungled mess of epic proportions. No one was clever enough to design this disaster. The conversion of large numbers of California-chartered S&Ls into federal ones caused the state legislature and the industry to push for immediate adoption of the Nolan Act.[15]

A similar dynamic occurred in Texas. The result was that scores of federally chartered S&Ls converted to California and Texas charters. The second wave was the rush for de novo Texas and California charters—particularly California. The theory was that the state was supposed to be the primary regulator of state-chartered S&Ls. But neither Texas nor California had enough examiners and supervisors to handle their existing charters; the loss of assessment income gutted the ranks of both types of regulators. The surge of charter conversions overwhelmed them. It far outpaced the rate at which they could hire and train additional staff. In these circumstances, the last thing a rational state commissioner would have done is to encourage a wave of de novos: she would have had to turn her already hopelessly inadequate staff into application reviewers. The industry was suffering from mass insolvency and was undergoing unprecedented deregulation; it needed vastly more examination and supervisory resources to avoid catastrophe.

Naturally, Texas and California did the worst possible thing, at the worst possible time, in the worst possible manner. Their commissioners encouraged hundreds of de novo applicants for state charters, and they directed their overwhelmed staffs to expedite approval of the applications with little or no review for quality. They approved the applications of hundreds of real estate developers who were insolvent, had poor track records, and had severe conflicts of interest for de novo charters. Larry Taggart, commissioner of the California Department of Savings and Loans (CDSL), did not deny any de novo charters.

The second worst control fraud, Don Dixon's Vernon Savings &

Loan (aka "Vermin"), provided prostitutes to the Texas commissioner, Lin Bowman.[16] Taggart was worse. He went on to work for the three most notorious control frauds and tried to get the administration to fire Gray. His judgment was so poor that he put the following in writing in his August 4, 1986, letter to Donald Regan, now the president's chief of staff (and the man leading the administration's effort to force Gray to resign):

> [T]hese actions being done to the industry by the current chief regula-
> tor of the Federal Home Loan Bank Board are likely to have a very ad-
> verse impact on the ability of our Party to raise needed campaign funds
> in the upcoming elections. Many who have been very supportive of the
> Administration are involved with savings and loans associations which
> are either being closed by the FHLBB, or threatened with closure. (U.S.
> House Banking Committee, 1989, 3:630)

The wave of opportunistic control frauds entered the industry over-whelmingly through Texas and California charters in 1981–1984. The state commissioners were not simply ineffective; they were often the frauds' allies. In the states with the greatest deregulation and the great-est need for supervision, examinations became rare and supervision farcical.

THE 1981 TAX ACT: DROPPING NAPALM ON A FOREST FIRE

In addition to cutting the marginal rate of taxation, the 1981 Tax Act created abusive tax shelters and encouraged investments in real estate that were driven by tax, rather than normal economic, considerations. The inevitable result was a bubble in real estate values, particularly in commercial real estate. The bubble helped S&L control frauds claim record profits and increased the ultimate losses to the taxpayers once the bubble burst. A recurrent myth is that the 1986 Tax Reform Act, which removed most of the abusive provisions of the 1981 act, caused real estate recessions and greater losses to the FSLIC. As the investigat-ing commission explained in its report on the debacle:

> Many observers blamed the 1986 Tax Act for the woes that befell the
> S&L industry, but it was the 1981 Act that created an unsustainable
> boom, and encouraged "over-building." The 1986 law hastened the
> collapse in the Southwest, much of whose expansion had been based

on expectations of continued inflation in property values. But had the 1986 act not been passed, over-building would have been even greater, and the eventual collapse in real-estate values deeper. (NCFIRRE 1993a, 55)

SCAMS THAT OPPORTUNISTIC CONTROL FRAUDS USED TO ACQUIRE S&Ls FOR FREE (OR LESS!)

To an opportunistic control fraud, obtaining control more cheaply is the bronze standard, doing so for free wins a silver medal, and getting paid to take control takes the gold. Opportunistic control frauds lived up to the name I gave them: they were champions at getting something for nothing. I'll explain the most common scams. (The scams were not necessarily mutually exclusive; some opportunists combined them.) The most common fraud mechanism was to have Hermann K. Beebe fund the purchase of an S&L. Beebe was a control fraud, a convicted felon running a Louisiana insurance company. He was an associate of the New Orleans mob. Beebe helped scores of control frauds acquire S&Ls and banks in the Southwest (Mayer 1990, 226). Beebe would loan the money to buy the S&L. The buyer would, in turn, cause his S&L to make far larger loans to Beebe's straws. The straws, of course, would not repay the loans. Beebe won, the S&L owner won, and the taxpayers lost.

Similarly, Michael Milken, the "junk bond king" of Drexel Burnham Lambert, financed Charles Keating's purchase of Lincoln Savings and David Paul's purchase of CenTrust Savings (Black 1993c). Keating did not have to spend a penny of his own money to buy the S&L.

Another scam was to have the existing shareholders of the S&L direct it to fund the acquisition. I've explained that S&Ls were overwhelmingly insolvent in the early 1980s and that shareholders should receive nothing when the company is insolvent. They, however, do not want to receive nothing, and if they control the S&L (and have no ethical constraints), they may decide to have the S&L make a very large loan to a potential acquirer. The acquirer uses the loan proceeds to buy their stock (at a substantial premium above its true, i.e., nonexistent, market value). This gives the acquirer control of the S&L without having to use any of his own cash.

Pratt changed Bank Board rules to allow acquirers to contribute capital to the S&L in the form of real estate instead of cash. The acquirer had to present a real estate appraisal supporting the claimed value. I am confident that the reader can predict what happened, even though Pratt, the expert, did not: this change proved disastrous. In every case that I studied, the value assigned to the real estate was grossly inflated. David Paul, who, like Keating, was a Drexel "captive," used this scam. Contributed capital was overwhelmingly fictitious. Again, the key is that every $1 million of fictitious capital allowed the control fraud to grow by up to $1 billion and increased the risk to the taxpayers by the same amount. The acquirers who won gold medals for fraud used an elegant variant of this scam. They would say that they wished to contribute $5 million in capital to "their" S&L. Unfortunately, the only way they could do so was to contribute a large real estate parcel. The parcel had an appraised value of $20 million. They would contribute the parcel to their S&L, and *the S&L would pay them $15 million in cash.* The parcel might, in fact, be worth as little as $2 million.

HOW CONTROL FRAUDS SHOP FOR PROFESSIONALS

Outside professionals are like British journalists. There's no need to bribe them. More precisely, you bribe them in a way such that no one considers it a bribe.

Here's how it works with appraisers. The appraisal fee is larger for commercial real estate than for residential, and it is greater in absolute size for more expensive than for less expensive properties. As a result, both appraisers and S&L control frauds gained if the S&L did more commercial real estate lending on more expensive projects. The S&L loan officer calls the appraiser and asks him for a favor. The loan officer has to make a recommendation on a proposed $60 million loan in two weeks. Could the appraiser please give him a preliminary, oral estimate of value as soon as possible, before completing the written appraisal report? (Note that the loan officer has communicated the size of the loan to the appraiser.) The S&L can't make the loan without violating Bank Board rules if the appraiser does not come back with a value of at least $60 million. The appraiser calls with preliminary estimate of value. If it is at least $60 million, the loan officer tells him to finalize the written appraisal, pays his full fee, and uses him in the future. If he comes back under $60 million the loan officer thanks him effusively, says that there is no need to complete the written appraisal given the inadequate value of the property, pays a reduced fee, and the S&L never uses the appraiser again. Functionally paying an appraiser a fee to value property (that is, say, really worth $35 million) at over $60 million is equivalent to a bribe. But it is a "perfect crime," impossible to prosecute. Control frauds know that they only need a tiny group of appraisers to inflate property values; there is no need to suborn the entire profession. The thing that most people don't understand is that this whole process can (and typically was) done in a way that a transcript of the conversation could appear on the front page of the local newspaper without embarrassing the appraiser or the loan officer.

Shopping for an accommodating auditor involves a similar process. The dynamics differ because control frauds virtually always use top-tier audit firms, whereas appraisers are often sole proprietors. Institutions matter a great deal, and control frauds are adept at finding the weak link in any institutional chain.

The law-and-economics movement claims that top-tier audit firms will never aid a control fraud because the financial loss resulting from a diminished reputation is so much greater than any possible gain from assisting the fraud (Easterbrook and Fischel 1991, 282). Judge Easterbrook has gone to the extreme of preventing a plaintiff from presenting a case charging an auditor with aiding a fraud, stating that it would be irrational for an audit firm to act as alleged, given its reputational interest (Prentice 2000, 136). As I noted earlier, whenever economists assume rationality but ignore fraud, the predictions are likely to fail. Every S&L control fraud got a clean opinion from a top-tier audit firm—usually they got several years worth of clean opinions—even though they were deeply insolvent and engaged in pervasive accounting fraud. All of the current control frauds got clean opinions from top-tier audit firms, even when they were deeply insolvent and engaged in massive accounting fraud. Control frauds are routinely able to find auditors to assist their frauds. Indeed, a prestigious audit firm is a control fraud's most valuable ally.

The NCFIRRE report (1993a, 76) provides the bottom line:

> The result was a sort of "Gresham's law" in which the bad [accounting] professionals forced out the good.

3. THE MOST UNLIKELY OF HEROES

President Reagan appointed Edwin J. Gray to the Bank Board in early 1983 with the expectation that he would become chairman when Pratt resigned a few months later. Gray was a longtime friend of the president, and had served as his press secretary in California and then as a public-relations officer for a large San Diego S&L run by Gordon Luce, a member of the President's "kitchen cabinet." Gray served in the White House as a domestic policy advisor for President Reagan. He was valedictorian of his high school and received his BA in journalism. Like the president, he was a Democrat who became a conservative Republican. Gray led an antitax initiative in San Diego. He loved the president and his policies. Gray believed in deregulation. He freely told people that the president appointed him to make the league happy—it considered him a patsy.

Gray soon took positions that put him in opposition to the president he loved, his party, and his own philosophical views. He had nothing to gain from this transformation. He did not welcome it. He knew it would ruin his career and that he would lose what he most treasured, Ronald and Nancy Reagan's support and friendship. He knew that the counterattack would be savage, personal, and effective. He would make too many powerful enemies and he would have few effective allies.

Some people fight because they enjoy it, others because that is how they were trained; some because they are thin skinned, others because they are bullies; some because they are irrational, and others because they are cornered and have no other hope of survival. Soldiers fight mostly for their close comrades. Young males fight because they are desperately afraid of being afraid. Drug sellers fight because if they do not intimidate, they die. Most of the reasons people fight are bad ones. Gray did not fight for any of these reasons. Gray was not cornered: if he were unwilling to support S&L deregulation, he could have gone home to San Diego.

Gray was not naturally brave. His hands shook, he couldn't sleep, he chain-smoked, and his face became pallid. He shrank from confrontation. He was not calm under pressure. He was so nervous that he could not concentrate. He projected nervousness, making others uncomfortable. He did not have "the right stuff." John Glenn, the astronaut who exemplified the right stuff, disdained Gray. Glenn became one of the Keating Five (the five U.S. senators who tried, at Charles Keating's behest, to intimidate Gray), and Gray refused to back down to their pressure. Perhaps we should reexamine our definition of "the right stuff." It is how far Gray had to move philosophically, at what personal cost, and in a manner so at odds with his basic personality that makes him both the most unlikely of heroes and so heroic. But that is not how Gray's chairmanship began.

GRAY'S INITIAL PRATFALLS

Gray continued Pratt's policies during his first five months as chairman. He imposed a hiring freeze. He adopted a creative RAP rule. He approved disastrous acquisitions by men who would become infamous control frauds. He gave speeches lauding deregulation and urging S&Ls to make use of the new powers. He fought the last war, constantly reminding S&Ls of the need to reduce interest rate risk. He slowed the rate of S&L closures. Like Pratt, he capped FSLIC spending at a ridiculously inadequate level in order to show a small increase in the FSLIC fund at the end of 1983 ($6.4 billion). He approved goodwill mergers.

He made no improvement in the moribund enforcement efforts or in the dysfunctional examination and supervision systems. Indeed, he harmed supervision by agreeing to a proposal to move the headquarters of the 9th District from Little Rock, Arkansas, to Dallas, Texas. The new FHLB-Dallas decided to save money by being cheap when paying for relocation. The overwhelming majority of its supervisors resigned in late 1983.

Gray did not clean up the "change of control" system that allowed almost anyone to acquire an S&L. By continuing Pratt's policies, Gray increased the damage the control frauds later caused.

RIGHT WAR, WRONG TARGET

Donald Regan was the head of Merrill Lynch before he became treasury secretary during President Reagan's first term. He made Merrill Lynch the dominant deposit broker.[1]

Deposit brokers seek S&Ls and banks offering the highest interest rate on insured deposits. Deregulation allowed banks and S&Ls to compete on interest rates. Insured depositors had no risk of loss or even inconvenience. In order to maintain public confidence, if the FSLIC liquidated an S&L, it paid the depositors in full within days. An insolvent S&L that was closed on Friday afternoon would reopen on Monday morning. Deposit brokers fueled the growth that made control frauds ideal Ponzi schemes. An S&L could raise hundreds of millions of dollars in as little as three days through the brokers.

The Bank Board and the FDIC simultaneously adopted rules in March 1984 restricting insurance for accounts placed by brokers. The rules could not work. S&Ls could grow almost as rapidly by advertising a slightly higher interest rate and then "dialing for dollars." S&Ls created phone banks to call prospective depositors and solicit deposits. Any S&L could raise tens of millions of dollars in a week without using brokers.

The Bank Board's authority to restrict deposit insurance for brokered deposits was weak. My predecessor as Bank Board litigation director, Harvey Simon, advised Gray that the brokers would likely win their lawsuit if he adopted the rule. Simon proved correct.

Treasury Secretary Regan opposed the rule. He believed in deregulation, and he thought that brokers helped customers. Regan was Mehle's boss when he testified that insolvent S&Ls should grow rapidly and that the industry's fast growth showed that it was sound. Regan was convinced that President Reagan shared his views. Gray made a powerful enemy. Regan sought to drive him to resign.

The deposit broker rule was a mistake. It would not have worked even if we had won the case. We had more effective ways of limiting growth and the clear statutory authority to use them. The rule diverted resources we could have used more profitably against the control frauds.[2]

GRAY'S "ROAD TO DAMASCUS" EXPERIENCE

Empire Savings made famous the "land flip." The S&L paid the small fry (which it called "minnows" or "guppies") up to $50,000 to lend their name to this fraud. The guppies sat at a long table. A big fish started the land flip by selling a piece of undeveloped ("raw") land to Guppy One for $2,000 an acre. Guppy One sells it to Guppy Two for $4,000 an acre. This continued until another big fish agreed to pay $50,000 an acre. The S&L would then loan money to the big fish to purchase the raw land at this price. In five minutes, the "market" value of the land rose twenty-five-fold. The big fish was a residential real estate developer who was purportedly going to build thousands of townhouses.

It was impossible, of course, for such a developer to create a profitable project. The developer was part of a fraud, and he made money in several different ways. The S&L paid him an up-front "profit." The developer hired related entities at generous rates to do the construction. The developer gained directly by having a hidden interest in the construction group or through kickbacks for awarding contracts. The construction group charged high rates but provided inferior work and pocketed the difference. One of the scams that caused losses at Empire Savings occurred when contractors used one-fifth of the concrete needed to construct a road properly. The roads soon buckled. Empire Savings also funded the construction loans in full without tying disbursements to completion of construction.

The result was a disaster of epic proportions. Because other control frauds joined with Empire Savings to run the same scam and because they all (semi-) built their projects in the same area (along the "I-30 corridor" in Garland, Texas, near Dallas), the disaster was concentrated and stretched for miles.

The Bank Board examiners hired an old-time Texas real estate expert to help them figure out how bad the mess was. He decided that you had to see it to believe it. He videotaped a tour of the I-30 corridor. There were thousands of partially completed units left open to the elements and arsonists. Many units had no construction, just the concrete pad. We dubbed them "Martian landing pads." The images on the tape were so revolting that they created horror in everyone who saw them. He shot some of it from a small plane, which provided panoramic views of devastation. His narration increased the effect. It was so disturbing because it was artless. Imagine a strong Texas accent that remains calm and matter-of-fact while presenting a nightmare. Gray watched the film on March 14, 1984 (Day 1993, 156–157). He told me he wanted to throw up when he saw it.

He showed the tape to as many senior officials as possible, including Paul Volcker (Day 1993, 162). Kathleen Day interviewed one of the key people Gray showed the tape to, the House Banking Committee chief of staff, Paul Nelson. Whereas Volcker was horrified, Nelson responded, "Gray's the regulator, not us. . . . That's his job to stop this. Why am I watching this?" (ibid.) The smaller incidents are often the most revealing. Paul Nelson's reaction illustrates why congressional oversight failed throughout the critical years of the debacle. Gray was stunned, outraged, and determined to prevent any future Empire Savings from spawning similar horrors. Nelson and House Banking Committee chairman St Germain did not see that their deregulation had created the environment that produced the wave of control fraud. They were annoyed with the messenger.

Notably, he did not try to show the film to President Reagan. Gray and the president (who became famous as "the great communicator") neither met nor talked while he was chairman. Even when Regan was pushing for his resignation, Gray never tried to use his friendship with the president to have him call off the dogs. Many of us asked him why. His answer was always the same: "You don't know him. You can't do it; it's impossible." The president was an extraordinarily hands-off manager. He did not ask people like Gray for advice about how to deal with the debacle. Treasury and the OMB talked to him. They had two contradictory messages throughout his presidency—there is no crisis, and our top priority is making sure that the public does not learn of the crisis. President Reagan's autobiography ignored the debacle, at the time the largest financial scandal in U.S. history.

The mythic part of the story about the Empire Savings videotape is that it produced an instantaneous transformation in Gray: he rode in as a deregulator, the truths in the film knocked him off his horse, and he awoke as the Great Reregulator. Gray had begun transforming himself into a reregulator before he saw the film. Further, Gray did not complete his transformation until years after he saw the film. The film was, however, important in speeding Gray's transformation and the intensity of the war against the control frauds.

GRAY MAKES ENEMIES BY STOPPING TEXAS, CALIFORNIA, AND FLORIDA FROM CREATING NEW S&Ls

Gray's first effective counterattack against the control frauds assaulted the de novos. Taggart (the California Department of Savings & Loans commissioner) approved 200 new California charters by early 1984. Texas and Florida approved dozens of new charters. Gray adopted a rule in November 1983 requiring de novos to have 7 percent capital — over twice the requirement for other S&Ls — in order to receive FSLIC insurance.

Gray's second act was more decisive. He refused to approve FSLIC insurance for de novos from California, Texas, and Florida unless they improved their regulation. This was one of the most effective actions possible against control frauds. There would have been hundreds of additional control frauds but for Gray's moratorium. However, it enraged all three state commissioners and state and federal politicians representing California, Texas, and Florida, states with powerful congressional and state officials. The list of Gray's powerful opponents grew.

The related problem was that Gray had no clear legal basis for imposing a moratorium. His action was logical: none of the states had remotely adequate regulatory resources to deal with their existing charters. It was irresponsible of them to increase the number of charters. Gray tried to convince them to stop the approvals until they could build up their staffs. The three commissioners refused. Gray's action was desirable; but was it legal?[3]

UNRESTRICTED WARFARE: THE NET WORTH AND DIRECT INVESTMENT RULES

Gray proposed the net worth and direct investment rules in early 1984. He focused, however, on the deposit broker rule. He saw it as a direct way to limit growth, which he considered the central problem. When the courts struck down the deposit broker rule, these other two rules became his top priority. The Bank Board designed them to stop any future Empire Savings.

The de novo rule and Gray's moratorium on granting FSLIC insurance to new charters in California, Texas, and Florida had substantial support within the industry; they restricted future competitors. The deposit broker rule had some support within the traditional S&Ls. The proposed direct investment rule (which limited such investments to 10 percent of total assets) did not affect many S&Ls.[4] Gray did not expect the direct investment rule to spur major opposition. Gray designed the net worth rule to end extreme growth. He knew that the industry would oppose it because so many S&Ls were trying to "grow out of their problems."

GROWING PAINS

The idea of growing out of their problems was seductive to many S&Ls. The amount of growth required, however, was enormous. When interest rates are high, home sales slow and it is hard for a mortgage lender to grow, even slowly. The solution was to grow rapidly by investing in much higher-yield (and higher-risk) assets. The higher the yield of the new assets, the less growth an S&L needed in order to grow out of its problems. Deregulation made this solution possible.

FALLACY OF COMPOSITION

One of the standard logical fallacies is that of composition. Logicians warn that the fact that something is true in a particular case does not prove that it will hold true when applied simultaneously to many cases. An individual S&L might be able to grow out of its problems, but an industry cannot. Indeed, it is a prescription for disaster to try.

Some critics claim that Pratt expressly encouraged S&Ls to grow out of their problems. Pratt was generally careful to avoid going that far. Nevertheless, he gave the industry the ability to grow massively, and he took no action to stop the large number of S&Ls that began to grow rapidly. The results were, predictably, disastrous.

THE ADC PONZI SCHEME

The proposed net worth rule restricted growth by increasing capital requirements for faster growing S&Ls. Gray proposed to reverse the Bank Board's prior policy, five-year averaging, which reduced the capital requirement for fast growers. Gray acted because of the tendency of fast growers to become the worst failures. The agency did not understand the acquisition, development, and construction (ADC) Ponzi scheme fully when it drafted the rule. This was ironic because the rule struck the control frauds' Achilles' heel and proved the most critical act of reregulation. A Ponzi scheme operates by growing rapidly and using a portion of the new money brought in to pay off the old investors while the fraudster pockets the remainder. Pilots say, "Speed is life." For a Ponzi, growth is life.

S&L Ponzis invested in assets that had no readily ascertainable market value and that allowed S&Ls to treat (fictitious) noncash income as real for GAAP purposes. Professionals, like appraisers, determine value when there is no clear market value for an asset. Every S&L control fraud was able to get top professionals to overstate asset values massively and to get a clean opinion from a Big 8 auditor blessing its fake financial statements. The advantage of using noncash "income" as a fraud vehicle was that it guaranteed production of the income.

The "acquisition" in ADC refers to buying raw land. "Development" means adding improvements like sewers, utility lines, and roads. "Construction" meant creating a commercial building or a multifamily residential project. Control frauds called their ADC transactions loans and structured them as loans, but the typical ADC loan was really a direct investment. The law, the fields of economics and finance, and accounting all agree: if the economic reality is that the lender is taking an equity risk, then the transaction is a direct or equity investment, not a loan. If the success of the underlying project (such as the commercial office building being constructed) determines whether the borrower repays the S&L, then the lender is assuming an equity risk.

Big 8 auditors — despite three attempts by the profession to prevent the abuse — consistently blessed the accounting of ADC transactions as loans. Treating ADC deals as loans created extraordinary (fraudulent) income and hid enormous real losses. S&Ls combined accounting fraud with deregulation and massive growth to create the ideal Ponzi. If the auditors had required the control frauds to account for their ADCs as direct investments, they could not have recognized the fictitious income.

The typical control fraud made ADC loans with the following characteristics.

- There was no down payment.
- There were substantial up-front points and fees.
- All of those points and fees were self-funded: the S&L loaned the buyer the money to pay the S&L the points and fees.
- The term of the loan was two or three years.
- There was no repayment of principal on the loan prior to maturity. (The loan was interest-only, or nonamortizing.)

- The S&L self-funded all of the interest payments. The S&L paid itself the interest when it came due out of an interest reserve. The S&L increased the borrower's debt by an amount equal to the interest reserve.
- The interest rate on the loans was considerably above prime.
- The borrower had no personal liability on the debt (the loan was non-recourse). His construction company was indebted, but the developer was not. He did not provide any meaningful personal guarantee of his company's debt.
- The developer pledged the real estate project (the collateral) to secure the loan.
- The loan amount equaled the (purported) value of the collateral.
- It was common for the borrower to receive at closing a developer's profit that could represent up to 2 percent of the loan balance.
- It was common for borrowers to give S&Ls an equity kicker, an interest in the developer's net profits on the project. At first, these kickers often exceeded 50 percent. After the accounting profession issued a "notice to practitioners" that said a 50 percent equity kicker was evidence that the transaction was not a true loan, it became common to give a 49 percent interest. (For the characteristics in this list, see NCFIRRE 1993a; Black 1993b; Lowy 1991; O'Shea 1991; Strunk and Case 1988; Mayer 1990; Pizzo, Fricker, and Muolo 1989; Calavita, Pontell, and Tillman 1997.)

The implications of these characteristics are not obvious. One has to understand the fraud mechanism, Bank Board regulation, and a bit about accounting to see how elegant a Ponzi the control frauds created. The first implication is that one can see why the S&Ls were taking an equity risk, not making a loan. The real estate developers were not personally liable to repay the loan. Their companies were not really on the hook either: they used shell companies with no assets to sign the note. The developer would not repay the S&L unless the real estate project succeeded. Indeed, it had to succeed fully because the loan was 100 percent of the projected value; the S&L would lose money if the appraiser inflated that value even slightly. These were not close calls: the typical ADC Ponzi loan was clearly an equity investment. This makes their audit partners' consistent treatment of them as true loans all the more disturbing.

Cash moved in one direction in an ADC Ponzi scheme: out of the S&L to the developer. The developer typically did not provide an S&L control fraud with any cash—no down payment, no fees or points, and no interest payment. The developer was only required to pay cash when the loan matured, and as I'll explain, they rarely paid cash even then.

This may seem to be a foolish way to run a fraud, but it is actually clever. The first advantage is that an ADC loan can never default prior to maturity. The Bank Board based its supervisory system on rates of loan defaults and delinquencies. Those are very good leading indicators of failure in conventional home mortgage lending. Supervisors considered S&Ls with low delinquency rates to be safe and sound. ADC lending looked safe and highly profitable. That was, of course, too good to be true, but few supervisors thought like white-collar criminologists in the early years. Pratt praised the new entrepreneurs' managerial skills. Managerial expertise brings profits. A Big 8 audit firm blessed it. It must be true.

The second implication is that an S&L running an ADC Ponzi was certain to report extraordinarily high "income" as long as the auditor allowed it to classify the deals as loans instead of as investments. Every control fraud was able to get its auditor to misclassify its ADC deals as loans, so that caveat had no effect. It was simply a matter of math (and some additional abusive accounting). ADC Ponzis booked most of the points and fees that they self-funded, i.e., paid themselves as immediate income. Roughly 3 percent of the total loan amount instantly became income.[5]

ADC Ponzis recognized the self-funded interest as income every month or quarter when interest came due, crediting the borrower for paying interest to the S&L from the interest reserve. Because of the high fees and interest rates, all of it self-funded, a control fraud was certain to report high profits. The extremely rapid growth rate of the ADC Ponzis guaranteed that these profits would be extraordinary. Any S&L that grew rapidly and made primarily ADC loans was mathematically guaranteed to report extraordinary profits. This is why the worst control frauds invariably reported that they were among the most profitable S&Ls. Indeed, one of the best ways to spot control frauds was to concentrate examination efforts on the S&Ls reporting the highest profits. This also demonstrates how fully the frauds suborned their Big 8 audit partners. They were routinely able to get clean opinions attesting that they were among the most profitable S&Ls while in fact being massively insolvent.

The consistent patterns used to optimize a control fraud made it easier for the agency to spot them. The frauds' first requisite was to make their auditors their allies. After that, the three keys were growth rate, the dollar amount of ADC loans, and the magnitude of the interest rate, fees, and equity kicker. ADC Ponzis frequently grew more than 100 percent in a year; they typically grew by more than 50 percent; some grew by more than 1,000 percent. Deregulation was a major cause of the debacle not because it permitted far greater investment in risky assets, but because the permitted investment assets were optimal for creating fictitious income and hiding real losses. Deregulation combined with weak supervision and deposit insurance to create the ideal Ponzi. The worst control frauds were Texas- and California-chartered S&Ls because they could put 100 percent of their assets in investments that were the best vehicles for fraud—typically, ADC loans. (The auditors' failure to treat ADC loans as investments was harmful. Texas S&Ls could put only a small percentage of their assets in equity investments, but 100 percent of their assets into ADC loans.) Control frauds routinely made ADC loans that were substantially greater than the market value of even the completed project, because the total dollar amount of the ADC loans drove income. The rules prohibited this practice, so control frauds engaged in "appraiser shopping" to secure grossly inflated appraised values for the real estate.

Control frauds sought to make loans to uncreditworthy developers because they were willing to pay the highest interest rates and fees and to provide the largest equity kickers (Pierce 1993; Akerlof and Romer 1993; Calavita, Pontell, and Tillman 1997; O'Shea 1991; Lowy 1991; Pizzo, Fricker, and Muolo 1989; Mayer 1990). Deliberately seeking to make loans to the worst developers strikes most people as absurd. Surely, it is in the interest of control frauds to make profitable loans so they can stay in business and continue to loot the corporation? Most people (fortunately) do not think like white-collar criminals. Control frauds operate by different, perverse rules that harm society, but that does not mean they are irrational.

A Ponzi scheme invariably collapses, but that does not mean that the fraud fails: the corrupt CEO can make a great deal of money looting the company. The purported profitability of the Ponzi schemes, combined with deposit insurance, meant that S&Ls could grow rapidly for several years before they collapsed. Such CEOs did not have the option of making money honestly, as my discussion about the inability to grow out of your problem illustrated. ADC accounting frauds created fictitious income that allowed CEOs to convert firm assets to personal use through normal and seemingly legitimate corporate mechanisms: raises, bonuses, stock options, and perks.[6]

The worst real estate developers agreed to pay the highest interest rates because they had much to gain. The S&L often paid the developer an up-front developer's profit. The developer profited even more if the S&L arranged to have another entity purchase the project at a price that exceeded the loan amount. (I will explain why such purchases were both common and fraudulent.) The profit on such a sale was, because of the equity kicker, split between the developer and the S&L. Developers could also profit by engaging in types of fraud that are endemic in construction, such as receiving kickbacks from the construction contractors, embezzling funds intended to pay for construction, substituting cheaper, poor-quality materials during construction, and similar means.

Poor-quality real estate developers had no meaningful downside to agreeing to pay high fees, interest rates, and equity participations to the control fraud. They took no financial risk. They *did not actually pay* high interest rates and fees. The ADC loans did not require bad developers to pay a penny of their own money or to put a penny of their own money at risk. All their payments were actually made by the S&L; there was no down payment; and they did not have to guarantee the loan personally. When the loan defaulted, they could walk away from it.

A good developer could have also walked away from the default without any direct financial loss, but he would have suffered a loss of reputation. A reputation as a high-quality developer has substantial indirect financial value. A developer who had no favorable reputation, or even a poor reputation, however, would suffer little or no loss of reputation when the loan defaulted (as it was very likely to do given the typical inflated appraisal and the poor business acumen of the developer). Developers who had poor reputations could not get similar loans from a reputable lender. This maximized the fraudulent S&Ls' leverage over them.[7]

Everyone agrees that underwriting by the S&L high fliers was pervasively horrific (Patriarca 1987, 3–5; GAO Thrift Failures 1989, 31–38). They frequently made massive ADC loans to individuals without conducting credit checks or appraising the value of the real estate. This maximized adverse selection (and losses). It was a perversely rational practice for a control fraud precisely because it maximized adverse selection. Moreover, if the initial appraisal would have shown a large loss (or the credit check would have shown the developer to be uncreditworthy), it was better to make the loan without the damning appraisal or credit check in the file, where the Bank Board examiners could find it and use it to prove that the loans were unsafe and unsound.

This pattern would be illogical if the high fliers had been honest "gamblers for resurrection" (Black, Calavita, and Pontell 1995). Honest, rational gamblers would attempt to do high-quality underwriting before engaging in ultra-high-risk investments (which is what the conventional economic wisdom posits). Honest gamblers prosper only if the ultra-high-risk investments succeed. The odds of that occurring are inherently poor, but if one does not do superb underwriting, failure is certain.

The cover-up phase of the ADC Ponzis made bad developers (and informal alliances with other control frauds) critical. Adverse selection and the perverse incentive of control frauds to increase their ADC lending in the teeth of a glut of commercial real estate meant that the ADC projects were likely to fail and the loans would default at maturity. Control frauds hid these defaults and turned them into new sources of fraudulent income and new means of deceiving the regulators. In increasing order of elegance: S&Ls would refinance their ADC loans, engage in "cash for trash" deals with bad borrowers, trade "my dead horse for your dead cow" with other control frauds, and perform intricate transactions with "daisy chains" of control frauds. The fundamental gambit was to remove the real loss and create fictitious income through fraudulent loans and sales. Control frauds used equity kickers to create fictitious profits from sham sales.

The crudest way to prevent default was to refinance the ADC loan. The Ponzi would start the whole game again by self-funding the fees and interest. The problem was that this was easy for auditors and examiners to spot and should have raised warning flags. Remarkably, Arthur Young & Company gave clean opinions to two of the most notorious Texas control frauds, Vernon Savings and Western Savings, even though they routinely refinanced all their ADC loans.[8]

Cash-for-trash deals are harder to spot because they create seemingly arm's-length sales. The best evidence of market value is a recent arm's-length sale. A good rule, except when there is fraud. A cash-for-trash deal started with an uncreditworthy borrower asking the S&L for a $3 million ADC loan. The loan officer responds that the S&L will not loan him $3 million, but it will loan him $33 million. The catch is that the borrower has to use $30 million of the loan proceeds (the "cash") to buy a particular property (the "trash"). The property is a soon-to-fail real estate project that the S&L funded with an ADC loan.[9]

In this example, the initial ADC loan was valued on the S&L's books at $25 million. The Bank Board examiners found that the property is really worth only $12 million and ordered the S&L to recognize a $13 million loss, which would cause the S&L to fail its minimum capital requirement. The S&L fights the order and says that the project not only has no loss, but is profitable. By buying the property for $30 million, the new borrower proves there is no loss. The old borrower uses $25 million of the purchase price to repay the S&L in full. Assume that the original ADC loan had a 50 percent equity kicker. The old borrower made a $5 million profit on the sale of the project ($30 million–$25 million). He now pays the S&L its one-half interest in his net profits ($2.5 million). The S&L is able to remove the $13 million loss from its books that the Bank Board ordered and to book a $2.5 million gain from the equity kicker. It also books the self-funded points, fees, and interest it pays itself for the second ADC loan. It avoids the red flag of a major loan default and fires a shot across the regulator's bow to warn it not to question the control fraud's valuations in the future. After all, the markets have just proven the regulators wrong once again. The best part is that the second borrower appears fully independent of the S&L. How can the examiners prove it is a scam?

"I'll trade you my dead horse for your dead cow" works the same accounting alchemy. "Mustang" S&L buys a troubled project from one of "Longhorn" S&L's ADC borrowers that is about to default, and Longhorn S&L reciprocates. Both S&Ls pay well above book value, allowing both S&Ls to avoid default and loss recognition while booking a substantial gain. The examiners are very unlikely to spot this because the control frauds hide the linkage. However, it is possible that examiners will review both deals.

The most elegant scam was impossible to spot by examining an S&L. "Daisy chains" of control frauds operated in some parts of the country. This was not some vast, directed conspiracy, but a large mutual aid society. Daisy chains allowed S&L A to buy S&L C's problem asset, while S&L B bought A's and C bought B's. No examiner, no manner how suspicious, could find from the records of A, B, or C that the purchases were linked, because no single S&L's records could demonstrate the link.

WHY CONTROL FRAUD FAILURES
TYPICALLY CAUSED SUCH LARGE LOSSES

This discussion explains the first two reasons that ADC Ponzis produced such large losses. First, making bad loans to bad developers maximized control fraud profits.

Second, because control frauds used adverse selection to attract the worst borrowers, they increased the risk that junior officers and the borrower would engage in independent fraud schemes.[10] One reason control fraud through an ADC Ponzi was so elegant is that the CEO never had to openly direct an officer or employee to act fraudulently. All the CEO had to do was to emphasize that the business plan was to grow extremely rapidly and invest in ADC loans, that career advancement and bonuses were dependent on ADC volumes, and that he valued aggressive team players who were creative. It became immediately apparent, as the CEO approved one insane ADC loan after another, that credit quality was irrelevant.

ADC Ponzis were particularly susceptible to insider and borrower fraud because of the nature of construction. As I explained, fraud is always a major problem in that industry. Such fraud sometimes meant, as at Empire Savings, that it was cheaper to raze the construction than to repair it.[11]

Control frauds produced catastrophic real estate losses because they maximized their fraudulent take by making an enormous number of wildly inflated ADC loans to the worst borrowers for unneeded projects. Surging vacancy rates increased the need to make additional bad ADC loans and added to the record glut of commercial office space and multifamily housing. Those dynamics meant that an ADC Ponzi had to make progressively more and worse ADC loans to delay its collapse. (Remember, a Ponzi's mantra is "growth is life.")

Because the ADC Ponzi was the best available fraud mechanism, it made sense for other S&L (and bank) control frauds to follow the same strategy. The control frauds came in a wave: about 300 S&Ls (and scores of banks) were dumping ever greater amounts of unneeded projects into the same glutted markets. Worse, the fraudulent S&Ls were concentrated in the states with the greatest deregulation and the weakest state regulation, so they drove the Texas and Arizona real estate markets. This, together with the perverse incentive created by the 1981 Tax Act to build uneconomic real estate projects, produced first the bubble in Texas real estate values in the early 1980s and then the horrific crash (Akerlof and Romer 1993; NCFIRRE 1993a; Black 1993c). The fact that oil prices fell at the same time made the losses all the greater. Prominent Texas politicians intervened on behalf of the Texas control frauds to blunt Gray's war against them. They premised their efforts on the view that the high fliers were innocent victims of a regional recession. In fact, they were the villains of the piece. The politicians added to the ultimate cost to the taxpayers, as I will soon explain.

REREGULATION ON THE ROCKS

Gray had three good ideas in proposing to raise capital requirements and to restrict growth and direct investments. He also had three problems. The problems immediately blocked reregulation. The elegance of the ADC Ponzi made it very difficult for the Bank Board to prove a need for regulation; his opponents were numerous, politically powerful, and skilled; and he led a dysfunctional agency without allies. ADC Ponzis looked superb: they reported far higher income, higher capital levels, and low default rates. S&Ls that grew faster and made more direct investments reported record profits. Any reregulation would have enraged the administration, but Gray's proposals seemed irrational on their face.

This substantive problem made it easy for Gray's critics to attack his motives and competence; this was his second problem. Critics had a ready explanation for the irrationality. Gray had worked for a large California S&L. The large traditional S&Ls (with inept managers) were losing the competition with the innovative, entrepreneurial entrants. The economic literature is full of examples of politically powerful businesses running to the legislature or the regulators to hamstring their superior competitors. The literature also shows that old-line firms typically disparage the morals of the new competitors and call them names like high fliers (Fischel 1995). Gray was falling for this old *ad hominem* assault on the new because he was dumb and an industry tool.

Gray's opponents also made his substantive problems worse by hiring lawyers and economists, including Alan Greenspan, who explained why the agency had no statutory authority to adopt the rules and conducted studies proving that faster growth and greater direct investments produced higher profits and healthier S&Ls. Keating expanded the ranks and virulence of Gray's opponents through a wide-ranging effort to build allies in the administration, the press, and Congress and among the state S&L commissioners.

The first two problems were grave, but the third was disabling. The Bank Board was dysfunctional for many reasons, and Gray often contributed to that problem. He was a terrible manager. Meetings never ran on time, agendas were never real. He wandered in and out of meetings.

There was no strategic planning. The Office of Policy and Economic Research (OPER) was in charge of developing policy, but had neither the expertise nor the orientation to do so. OPER faced the common problem of how to attract good economists when government pay caps made their salaries uncompetitive. OPER met that problem by hiring some more-prestigious economists on short-term appointments, who were attracted by the prospect of using agency data to push their research agendas. That was sensible, but it meant that the economists often had little institutional orientation and were interested almost exclusively in their own research. There were two telling results. First, only a small percentage of OPER studies had any direct tie to the problems presented by the high fliers. There was no attempt by OPER to determine whether they were gamblers or control frauds. I know of only one OPER study of fraud. It was finished in 1989 after the Bank Board had removed the last high flier. There was no relevant OPER research when Gray proposed the rules on capital and on direct investments. OPER remained focused on interest-rate risk into 1984, then lost focus as its staff pursued individual research agendas.

OPER controlled what information the industry reported to the Bank Board in the "Thrift Financial Reports." Everyone agrees that ADC lending caused the worst losses, yet OPER never gathered data on ADC lending and never studied the ADC Ponzi schemes.[12]

OPER posed two other problems: its staff reflexively opposed reregulation, and they were not very good at translating economics into English. That was unfortunate, because the lawyers who drafted the rules and, more importantly, the rationale for the rules, which the courts would review for sufficiency, were economically illiterate and did not know anything about examination, supervision, or fraud. The "regulations and legislation" ("Regs and Legs") division could craft a convoluted rule, and had no problems with reregulating, but they could not communicate with the economists or the supervisors.

The supervisors were a mixed bag. They were generally former supervisory agents with one of the FHLBs. They meant well, and most of them came to favor reregulation, but they were rarely examiners, and they often had not been hands-on supervisors for many years. They often lagged in understanding fraud mechanisms and emerging patterns.

Altogether, reregulation was a very uneven contest. Gray had the best lawyers in the world against him; they had prestigious economists as experts who produced economic studies showing that the rules were harmful; the administration opposed the rules; the industry attacked him; and his staff was, by disposition or talent, poorly poised to support him. Eric Hemel, the OPER director, sent a copy of Lincoln Savings' comments on the proposed direct investment rule to Norm Raiden, Gray's general counsel, warning him that the Bank Board's "preamble" had not made a strong case for the rule. Lincoln Savings was promising to sue to strike down the rules. Norm asked me, his new litigation director, to look at the preamble.[13]

ENLISTING IN GRAY'S WAR AGAINST THE CONTROL FRAUDS

This request transformed my career. It led me to become Gray's principal aide for reregulation, and it changed the way the agency approached the war against the control frauds.[14] The Bank Board had done no economic studies supporting either rule. It had not explained why economic theory supported both proposals. The preamble cited only one example of a direct investment causing problems: ADC loans at Empire Savings. It did not explain why ADC loans were really direct investments.

RESURRECTING REREGULATION

I advised Gray that he needed to repropose both the capital and the direct investment rules because the preambles had so little support that we would likely lose both rules to court challenges. One of the impressive things about Gray is that he took that advice and reproposed the rules.[15] Gray tasked me with getting the rules in shape to survive the legal challenges. I asked the supervisory staff to write up case studies of our dismal experience with control frauds. They proved incapable of doing so. I had to assign the drafting to my litigation attorneys who were handling the lawsuits arising from the control frauds. They provided concrete examples of how excessive growth and direct investments led to serious losses. The supervisors reviewed the litigators' case studies and agreed they were accurate. They signed the final memoranda and were supportive.

I asked our economists to carry out studies to examine the need for the rules. They were largely at a loss as to how to do so. In their view, economic theory suggested that the direct investment rule was unnecessary and harmful. They believed that increased capital requirements were desirable, but had no idea how to show that empirically. I ended up designing several economic studies, an unusual job for a litigation director.[16]

The Bank Board was able to adopt the reproposed rules in late 1984. We know that Keating had planned to sue to strike them down. The quality of the support for the rules caused his lawyers to advise him not to sue. This was a remarkable turnaround, and it gave Gray the confidence to proceed with additional reregulation. Gray's reregulation did not prevent the debacle, but it saved the nation from disaster. Without the restriction on growth imposed by the rule on capital, the control frauds would have grown large enough to cause losses that would have threatened the general economy by the end of Gray's term. Without the growth rule, the control frauds would have grown massively during Wall's chairmanship, and their political power would have endangered the nation.

THE CATASTROPHE GRAY SO NARROWLY AVERTED

Because S&L control frauds were Ponzi schemes, the consequences of delay in stopping their growth were horrific. Without Gray's war on the control frauds, their growth would have increased throughout his term. His successor, Danny Wall, would not have taken on the control frauds for reasons made clear later in this book. Indeed, he helped the most notorious control fraud escape regulatory control. Eventually, the expanding wave of control fraud would have caused such a massive bubble in real estate values that it would have collapsed. Since Japan's real estate and stock market bubbles grew for a full decade during the 1980s without the growth advantages provided by deposit insurance, a U.S. bubble could have lasted for over a decade. Therefore, the wave of control fraud could have extended throughout the Reagan and Bush administrations had it not been for Gray's desperate war against the control frauds.

There were over 300 control frauds. My study found that the 11th District (California, Arizona, and Nevada) had 58 control frauds (Black 1998). Texas had over 100. Together, California and Texas had over half of the control frauds and produced over half the total losses. Prosecutors convicted over 1,000 S&L insiders of felonies. (That was an unprecedented level of success, particularly given the grossly inadequate resources provided by the Justice Department.) Every detailed study of the most expensive S&L failures found a common pattern that included control fraud (Black, Calavita, and Pontell 1995; Black 1998).

The typical large failure was a stockholder-owned, state-chartered institution in Texas or California where regulation and supervision were
most lax. . . . The failed institution typically had experienced a change
of control and was tightly held, dominated by an individual with substantial conflicts of interest — that is, one who used the institution's capital to support personal business ventures. The typical large failure had
grown at an extremely rapid rate, achieving high concentrations of assets in risky ventures such as . . . ADC loans and/or direct investments
of various kinds. . . . In the typical large failure, every accounting trick
available was used to make the institution look profitable, safe, and solvent. Evidence of fraud was invariably present as was the ability of the
operators to "milk" the organization through high dividends and salaries, bonuses, perks and other means. In short, the typical large failure
was one in which management exploited virtually all the perverse incentives created by government policy. (NCFIRRE 1993a, 3-4)

The S&L industry grew by 18.6 percent in 1983, and that staggering
rate of growth increased to 19.9 percent in 1984. The industry would
roughly double in size every four years at that rate (because growth
rates, like interest, compound). Nominal GNP grew at less than half that
rate, and commercial banks grew at only one-fourth the rate of the S&L
industry in 1984. The growth in the S&L industry was concentrated
disproportionately in the worst S&Ls. The soon-to-fail group grew at
101 percent, over twice the industry rate, between 1982 and 1985 (White
1991, 100-101). But the high fliers lived up to their name: 74 of them
grew by more than *400 percent* during those same years. In 1984, more
than 300 S&Ls grew by more than 50 percent (NCFIRRE 1993a, 52).
Half of those ultrafast growers were located in Texas, California, and
Florida (Strunk and Case 1988, 133). Over 700 S&Ls grew by more than
25 percent in the first half of 1984 (ibid., 132).

Growth was fastest in the states with the greatest deregulation and the
weakest state supervision (White 1991, 100). Forty Texas S&Ls grew by
more than 300 percent between 1982 and 1985. The percentage of assets
best suited to creating fictitious accounting income increased dramatically at the high fliers between 1982 and 1985 (ibid., 102-103). The fastest growing S&Ls reported a return on assets that was nine times larger
than the slowest (positive growth) S&Ls.

The number of high fliers also grew rapidly. Some of them were reactive control frauds; others acquired S&Ls that converted from mutual
to stock form; the most destructive group acquired failed S&Ls through

mergers; and over 100 entered as de novos. Without Gray's late 1984 moratorium on new California, Texas, and Florida charters' receiving FSLIC insurance, there would have been hundreds of new control frauds during his term.

The capital rule and other steps that Gray took to toughen supervision reduced growth dramatically. The industry rate of growth fell by more than half in 1985 to 9.5 percent (White 1991, 100). The cuts in growth were, of course, much greater for the control frauds that drove much of the ultrarapid growth in 1983 and 1984. Ponzis have to grow faster over time; Gray's rule required them to cut their growth rates dramatically. Gray had found their Achilles' heel, and his reregulation delivered a fatal blow. The Ponzis had only two options. They could drive Gray from office and get a replacement who would not enforce the rule, or they could violate the rule and use political interference to prevent the Bank Board from taking effective enforcement action. The growth rule did not simply impair the existing control frauds. It made the industry a far less attractive vehicle for control fraud and, in conjunction with Gray's moratorium on new charters, largely ended the entry of new opportunistic control frauds.

So what would have happened in the absence of Gray's war against the control frauds? There would have been no capital rule and no moratorium on de novos. The industry's rate of growth would have increased substantially as the control frauds' much higher growth rate and the entry of hundreds of additional control frauds increasingly drove overall industry growth. The major control frauds that Gray closed in 1986 and 1987 would have remained open and would have grown massively. Remember, without the capital rule's restriction on growth, Ponzis could have used deposit insurance to grow extremely rapidly and could have continued to report record profits for many years. The Bank Board would not have closed control frauds that reported record profits. By the end of Gray's term (June 30, 1987), the industry would have had total assets of well over $2 trillion. By the end of his next term (he would have been reappointed had he not reregulated) or Wall's term, the industry would have had over $6 trillion in total assets. Control frauds would have held a majority of those assets.

The ADC Ponzis would have hyperinflated real estate markets throughout the nation, resulting in a staggering glut of commercial office space. There is no way of knowing in what year the real estate bubble would have collapsed. The only sure things are that it had to collapse and that the more the bubble inflated, the greater the devastation of the general economy. Japan, as I write, has not recovered from the collapse of its twin bubbles in *1990*.

The best estimate of the cost of the S&L debacle (measured in 1993 dollars) is $150–175 billion (NCFIRRE 1993a, 4). (You may have read much larger estimates; they are misleading because they treat interest improperly.) An S&L industry with over $6 trillion in assets, and more than half those assets held by control frauds engaged in ADC Ponzi schemes, would have caused trillions of dollars in losses directly to the taxpayers and would have injured national real estate markets badly enough to gravely damage the national economy. If Ed Gray had not become our most unlikely of heroes, that would have been our fate.

4. KEATING'S UNHOLY WAR AGAINST THE BANK BOARD

Charles Keating had already put on a full-court press to prevent the Bank Board from adopting the rules on capital, growth, and direct investment. We were impressed by his expensive lawyers and economists. We were utterly amazed, however, by his political power. Within a few weeks, Keating was able to get a majority of House members to cosponsor a resolution designed to kill the rule. We had never seen such raw political power. Gray went forward with the rule even though the administration, the House, and the industry opposed it.

We discovered later that one of Keating's effective lobbying tactics was to have the state commissioners complain to their congressional delegations about any Bank Board rule that reduced state-granted investment powers. Keating made allies of the state commissioners by offering to sue to have the direct-investment rule declared invalid and by providing small gifts to what was then called the National Association of State Savings and Loan Commissioners (NASSLS). NASSLS was a very poor organization, so Keating's money allowed its members to stay in places that were not dumps and to have a hospitality suite with alcohol. They were very appreciative.

Keating continued to wine and dine the commissioners despite the failure in late 1984 of the House resolution to stop reregulation. His efforts were so successful that NASSLS was on the verge of voting in 1987, with only one dissent (Bill Crawford, Taggart's successor), to file a "friend of the court" brief supporting Keating's lawsuit against the direct-investment rule. Fortunately, just before NASSLS authorized filing the brief, Keating told the press, "There's no regulator alive who knows what he's doing" (Kammer 1987). Crawford told his counterparts about Keating's statements, which killed the brief.

Keating was new to the S&L industry, but he already had a bad track record. An SEC investigation found that he and his mentor, Carl Lindner, had engaged in fraud and insider abuse at Provident Bank. Keating and Lindner signed consent decrees in which they admitted no guilt, but also promised not to do it again (U.S. House Banking Committee 1989, 4:289). The taint led the Reagan administration not to go forward with its plan to make Keating (a major Republican contributor) U.S. ambassador to the Bahamas (U.S. Senate Committee 1990–1991a, 4:101). It obviously should have led to at least the presumption that Keating was unfit to run an S&L, but the agency's "change of control" tests were a farce in 1984.[1]

The second reason to fear Keating's entry into the industry was that he was paying a premium price to the existing shareholders to acquire an S&L that was insolvent by $100 million on a market-value basis. He knew that it was market-value insolvent because of the mark-to-market. A great deal of Lincoln Savings' reported income in the first two years arose from selling the mortgages he acquired from Lincoln Savings at a loss but accounting for them as a gain.

Nobody asked the question a white-collar criminologist would have asked: Why would any honest buyer agree to pay a substantial amount of money (over $50 million) to the shareholders of an S&L that was insolvent on a market-value basis by over $100 million, when the acquirer was not an S&L and would experience no possible (honest) synergies by acquiring Lincoln Savings' branch structure? Overpaying makes no sense for an honest buyer. It makes sense for control frauds because they manufacture fictitious profits, and the key determinant of their profits is how quickly they get control of the S&L and cause it to grow massively.

Norm Raiden, before becoming Gray's general counsel, represented Lincoln Savings in its sale to Keating. He was amazed when Keating wanted the complex deal done so quickly that he was willing to accept contract terms that Norm drafted to be totally one-sided in favor of the seller. Norm anticipated that this would lead to negotiations and compromise language, but Keating simply signed.

In 1993, when I served as the NCFIRRE's deputy staff director, one of the members of the commission told me that Keating called him immediately after buying Lincoln Savings to offer him the job of CEO. Keating told him having a California charter was "a license to steal" and guaranteed his salary would exceed $1 million. He declined Keating's offer.

The third reason to fear Keating was that not a penny of his purchase of Lincoln Savings came from his pocket. Michael Milken and the junk bond operations he controlled at Drexel Burnham Lambert provided all the cash for the deal. Milken had a standard operating procedure in such cases. Drexel greatly overfunded the buyer. Keating needed $51 million to purchase Lincoln Savings, but Drexel issued over $125 million in junk bonds out of American Continental Corp. (ACC), the holding company that Keating used to acquire Lincoln Savings. ACC was a failing real estate development company even before it had this crushing debt dumped on it (Binstein and Bowden 1993, 164; U.S. House Banking Committee 1989, 2:370; Black 1985). Milken wanted companies like ACC to be in desperate circumstances; that maximized his leverage over Keating.[2]

The fourth warning that Keating would be trouble was that he was a major contributor to the Republican Party and was "known for buying politicians."[3]

The agency was eventually mesmerized by Keating's political power, but we did not have the luxury of concentrating on him. He was one of hundreds of high fliers. The agency felt overwhelmed by what had become a deluge of increasingly shrill warnings from the field that things were wholly out of control, particularly in Texas.

PREPARE TO REPEL BOARDERS— KEATING'S PLAN TO TAKE OVER THE BANK BOARD

In the case of Charles Keating, we have the unusual advantage of having found a planning document. (The full document is reproduced as Appendix A.) It is an August 28, 1985, letter from Michael R. ("Mickey") Gardner to Charles Keating. The context of the letter is important. Gardner was a lawyer in the Washington, D.C., office of Akin, Gump, Strauss, Hauer & Feld. Akin, Gump (as the firm is called) began in Texas and is one of the premiere lobbying firms in the United States. The firm was predominately Democratic, but Mickey was a senior Republican lobbyist. Robert (Bob) Strauss was the most famous partner, the grand old man of the Democratic Party and its former national chairman. Gardner's expertise was communications law (which largely means knowing your way around the Federal Communications Commission, the FCC).

One of the great advantages that white-collar criminals have over blue-collar criminals is the ability to use top lawyers, not only at trial but also before criminal investigations even begin. Control frauds maximize this advantage by paying for the lawyers who help the controlling insider loot the firm. Then, as evidence of their legitimacy, control frauds trumpet that they sought legal counsel and that the counsel advised them that their activities were lawful.

One of Keating's first big plays after acquiring Lincoln Savings was to "greenmail" Gulf Broadcasting.[4]

Gardner had at least one, and reportedly two, roles in all this. He contended that Lincoln Savings put him on retainer to run Gulf Broadcasting if Lincoln Savings were to buy a controlling interest in it. Lincoln Savings paid $900,000 to Gardner in connection with Gulf Broadcasting. Lincoln Savings did not pay this fee to Akin, Gump, but to Gardner directly at his home address. Since the fee was so substantial and since members of a firm are required to send all fees for legal services to the firm for distribution, Akin, Gump induced Gardner to resign from the firm when the government discovered the payments years later.

Gardner's claim that this large fee was a retainer to secure his services as CEO is improbable. He had no expertise as a CEO. He did not have to give up any opportunity to make money to be available to act as CEO should Keating gain control of Gulf Broadcasting. The other potential role Gardner had was as a source of inside information, since Akin, Gump represented Gulf Broadcasting. Such inside information would be worth millions to a greenmailer.

By August 1985, Keating knew that he had to neutralize Gray or risk having Lincoln Savings taken over by the Bank Board. Gray had just pushed through the first three of what would become the four pillars of reregulation. Gray restricted direct investments, limited growth, and increased real capital requirements. Gray was pushing the fourth pillar, the power to "classify" assets. Gray was also implementing his two great efforts to improve supervision. He was transferring the examination function to the FHLBs, which were not subject to OMB and Office of Personnel Management (OPM) limits on staff and pay, and recruiting tougher supervisors for key positions.

GARDNER'S PROPOSED PLAN

Gardner was one of several outside professionals whom Keating used to help plan his war against Gray and the Bank Board. Other professionals were usually clever enough to give their advice orally, but Gardner was more brazen. His August 28, 1985, letter to Keating begins by recounting the original strategy that Gardner and Keating developed: have the Reagan administration "dismiss" Gray and replace Hovde with someone selected by Keating. Gardner checked with his "good friends in the Administration" about whether it was doable. He reports: "Regrettably, the consensus is a bit gloomier . . . than our earlier prognosis." Gardner was frustrated that "the President's illness" means he is concentrating on only a few major priorities, namely, "the budget and tax bills, and the Gorbach[e]v meeting" rather than "our goal of getting some near-term relief for Lincoln."[5]

Gardner is a highly partisan Republican writing to another highly partisan Republican, so his negative views about President Reagan are revealing. His greatest frustration is that Gray is a longtime associate of the president. Gray "is unquestionably a disaster but still 'a nice guy' to the Reagan inner circle." The administration cares far more for its cronies than it cares whether they are causing a "disaster." Gardner writes that Gray, "like so many before him in this Administration, would have to be criminally liable or worse before they [*sic*] would be removed." The irony is exquisite. Gardner is complaining to Keating that the principal weakness in their plan to pervert public policy is that the Reagan administration is too tolerant of sleaze and incompetence.

Because they cannot convince Reagan to dismiss Gray, Gardner suggests a revised, two-track strategy. One track is "to make life unbearable for Gray." The goal is to push Gray to resign. The second track is to destroy the effectiveness of the Bank Board until Gray can be removed. Gardner advises that essential action for both tracks will be to induce the Reagan administration to appoint "your new [Bank] Board Member." Note the possessive: "your" Bank Board member. Gardner explains the advantages that Keating will derive from having his own Bank Board member.

It would . . . serve notice on Gray and his staff . . . that he is out of favor with the White House. This is key since most Reagan-appointed Chairmen of regulatory commissions enjoy great influence over the selection of their fellow commissioners. By robbing Gray of this important perogative [*sic*], you could hurt him both psychologically and practically, thereby making his early resignation more likely.

Gardner was correct. Note that he understands that the effect will be felt not just by Gray but also by his staff.

Gardner's next point showed how well he understood agency dynamics.

> Chairmen who lose their influence over Board appointments often find that the loyalties of their own staffs become shallow at best. This could temper the action of key FHLBB staff, both in Washington and in . . . San Francisco.

There are two reasons for this loss of staff loyalty. The chairman is "damaged goods": he is on the wrong side of the White House because he is following policies they oppose. The chairman may not be able to help loyal staff advance to high-level positions that require White House approval. The new appointee represents the true views of the White House. The staff, seeing which way the wind is blowing, will not want to antagonize the appointee, who may soon be chairman.

Gardner suggested that Keating direct his new appointee to take an active role on Keating's behalf.

> Once confirmed, the Hovde replacement immediately could start to issue strong dissents that could provide your litigators with some good material for appeals to the Federal Courts.

As a litigator who has both defended and brought lawsuits asking the courts to strike down agency regulations, I can confirm that it would be of immense value to control a presidential appointee who would "issue strong dissents" calculated to aid one's legal case.

Gardner then turned to another key player: the third Bank Board member, Mary Grigsby, a Texan. If Keating's Bank Board member could get her to vote with him, Keating would have effective control of the board.

> With an enlightened Hovde replacement on the horizon, the now-cowed female Member of the Board may take a more independent approach, including occasionally dissenting from the Chairman. The obvious displeasure of Texans, including the Vice President, with the Gray Chairmanship could further enhance this Member's independence from Gray if she sensed she wasn't alone.

Other than the sexism, Gardner was again perceptive. George Bush was a major proponent of S&L deregulation, so Gray's reregulation was anathema to him, and Bush shared the "obvious displeasure" so many Texans had for Gray.

Gardner also understood the importance of other actors, including Congress.

> Congressional leaders would have a greatly improved opportunity to show in public hearings the folly of the Gray approach since all three Board Members would be testifying with the replacement presenting an opposing viewpoint to Gray's. Nothing could better educate Members of Congress and the Administration as to the FHLBB problems and opportunities than an enlightened Board Member who could publicly disagree with Gray.

I testified frequently on behalf of the Bank Board before Congress, and I agree that had Gardner's plan been implemented successfully our congressional appearances would have been a disaster. Keating's board member would have attacked our positions and our motives, claiming that we were biased and were suppressing information adverse to our arguments. He would have stressed, accurately, that we were acting contrary to the policies and beliefs of the administration. A public civil war among board members at a congressional hearing would have guaranteed wide, intense media coverage by the major networks and C-SPAN. The chairman always loses in these circumstances: it looks like he is incapable of exercising effective leadership.

Gardner then turned to the other major actor that would be decisive against us, the media.

> [T]he PR value of the Hovde replacement would be unlimited. . . . [Y]our new Board Member could articulate an intelligent approach, and do so with the mantel [*sic*] of authority that goes along with membership . . . on the FHLBB.

The press would have had a field day with publicly feuding Bank Board members. Keating's member would have had *instant* credibility because of his position. Again, the chairman has to lose in such a war.

Gardner stressed the need "to pursue a number of actions in tandem" in order to "successfully replace Hovde and to simultaneously make life unbearable for Gray." The actions were mutually reinforcing, designed to force Gray out and to make it impossible for the Bank Board to act against Lincoln Savings in the interim. Appointing Keating's board

member would serve both purposes. The difficulty was that President
Reagan was focused on only a few critical items, and Keating's desires
were "barely a bleep [*sic*] on the far right-hand corner of the White
House's radar screen." Gardner had a plan to make Keating's desires a
White House priority.

Part of his plan was conventional: intense lobbying of "important
members of the Executive branch." Part of the plan reveals Gardner's
view of George Benston.

> Surrogates like Professor Benston should be used to call on key mem-
> bers and staff, and to testify in open Congressional hearings about the
> counter-productive, re-regulatory approach the Gray Board is pursuing.
> If we don't provide articulate surrogates for Lincoln, the robust point of
> view that you need to have expressed simply won't occur.

Gardner also suggested that "Gershon Kekst and Company [Keat-
ing's PR firm] mount a major public relations program in responsible
print media" against Gray. The idea was to plant stories in the media
that could then be "offered as 'objective' information pieces for officials
of the Executive Branch, Congressional members and even important
Kitchen Cabinet members."

Gardner proposed that Keating use his congressional allies to
pressure the administration to appoint Keating's choice as Hovde's
replacement.

> Congressional pressure also should be kept on Don Regan [the presi-
> dent's chief of staff] and Bob Tuttle [the president's director of person-
> nel] to insure that the White House feels the *real* anxiety of key members
> of the Senate and House about the Hovde replacement. This pressure
> should start immediately after the Labor Day Recess and continue
> throughout September and October when the White House will prob-
> ably be very much in need of Congressional votes on the budget and tax
> bills. Achieving significant changes in the make-up of the FHLBB by the
> Christmas recess must become the quid pro quo for some key Members
> whose votes on these crucial bills will be vital to the White House. (em-
> phasis in original)

Gardner's plan is to extort the president by holding his top priorities
(the tax and budget bills) hostage. Keating must convince key members
of the Senate and House to tell the president that they will kill the budget

bill or the tax bill unless he appoints Keating's choice to the Bank Board. Think about that. A senator is supposed to tell President Reagan that he will kill the tax bill, legislation of critical national importance, unless Keating's demand that he select his own regulator is granted. Gardner understands that it would be difficult for a senator to make this threat credible, which is why he emphasizes the word "real."

This portion of the letter reveals a great deal about Gardner and Keating and about their views of Gray, Congress, and the Reagan administration. First, Gardner knew that Keating believed he could get senators to condition key votes on whether the administration appointed Keating's choice to the Bank Board. Gardner had already received enormous sums from Keating and plainly wanted to stay in his employ. He would not have recommended a strategy that Keating would view as absurd. This demonstrates that Gardner and Keating believed that they had enormous influence over the senators. Second, Gardner thought it was realistic that the White House would give in to such extortion (particularly if the publicity campaign to tarnish Gray's reputation were successful). Third, it is clear that neutralizing and then removing Gray was Keating's sole priority. Think of the political capital that Keating was willing to expend in this effort. Keating had senators who would kill critical national legislation on his behalf, and he was prepared to use up all those chits to get rid of Gray faster. These two partisan Republicans, purported Reaganites, were willing to prevent implementation of Reagan's top priorities if they felt it would help Keating remain in charge of Lincoln Savings.

Gardner's plan to ruin Gray's reputation was cleverly designed to intimidate the Bank Board and throw sand into its gears without revealing Lincoln Savings' hand.

> We should use every possible hearing (oversight or routine) as a means of assaulting Gray through planted, informed questions. The recent Dingell Oversight Hearing illustrated the aggressive approach that we should be taking behind the scenes to make Gray, his staff, and other Board Members feel extremely uncomfortable about current FHLBB operations. If done properly, the Board Members should not necessarily know what segment of the industry is generating the heat, only that the heat is there and will be increasing. Following each of these hearings, letters asking for additional information should inundate Gray's office from appropriate Congressional sources. Together, these efforts should make Gray feel very much under attack by responsible members of Congress.

KEATING IMPROVED ON GARDNER'S PLAN

It is remarkable how well Gardner's revised plan anticipated the future and how much fidelity Keating showed to the revised plan. Keating improvised, always in the direction of making the plan more audacious, but the key elements of the plan were implemented as Gardner had proposed.

Gardner's letter shows that parts of the original plan were implemented before it was written. Keating and Gardner had developed the overall plan in earlier conversations. The 1985 Dingell hearing is cited as an example of how to hit the Bank Board and Gray secretly. John Dingell regularly won polls in this era as the "most feared member of Congress" (Barry 1989).[6] He is very bright and often nasty. When the Democrats controlled the House and he was chairman of the Energy and Commerce Committee, he took an imperial view of his jurisdiction, and was noted for his extraordinarily adversarial investigative hearings. Dingell had just held hearings on the Bank Board's poor performance concerning Beverly Hills Savings. Dingell had flayed the Bank Board quite effectively. Gardner's letter (and the reports of Jim Grogan, Keating's top lobbyist) show that Lincoln Savings' lawyers helped prime him for assaulting Gray through "planted, informed questions . . . behind the scene." The Bank Board's general counsel was humiliated. Dingell proceeded to conduct a series of equally aggressive hearings on failed S&Ls, including one in which he threatened to jail me. After each hearing, Dingell followed up with an enormous demand for confidential documents to be produced under impossible deadlines. Keating followed Gardner's game plan, and it seemed to be working even better than they could have hoped.

Gray was attacked at a series of hostile congressional hearings. Dingell chaired some, but not all, of these. They were followed up with demands for masses of agency documents on very short notice. What of the other elements of the plan? They were followed rather faithfully. News stories attacking Gray were regularly planted, particularly with Kathleen Day, a business reporter with the *Washington Post,* It is likely that they were then presented to key leaders in the executive branch, Congress, and the kitchen cabinet. Gardner had proposed hitting Gray with a *coup de main* (a hard, unexpected strike) by placing Keating's member on the Bank Board. Keating decided to stage a *coup d'état:* he would take control of the Bank Board and topple Gray by convincing

President Reagan to appoint two Bank Board members selected by Keating. That would give him majority control over the Bank Board.

HOW SUCCESSFUL WERE THE HOSTILE
HEARINGS AND PUBLICITY TACTICS?

Keating's attacks on Gray and the Bank Board had important consequences, but not the ones he intended. The goal was to intimidate Gray into failing to act against Lincoln Savings or to discredit any action he proposed. The lesser goal was to tie up the agency by having it meet congressional demands for documents. Keating attained his lesser goal, but that just meant that Bank Board staff worked even harder to meet the congressional deadlines. His tactics failed to achieve his primary goal because he did not understand that hard-hitting attacks on the agency in 1985 would have to be premised on its regulatory laxity, not oppressiveness.

Indeed, Gardner's strategy had already backfired by the time he wrote the letter. Dingell's criticism of the agency was embarrassing, but it led to greater regulatory toughness. Gardner's tactics assumed that he could intimidate Gray through a drumbeat of criticism and that the nature of the attacks was not critical. Gardner was happy because Dingell's attack was intense and embarrassing to the Bank Board. As a result of Dingell's attack, Gray required supervisory agents to refer all unresolved, substantial violations of rules or materially unsafe or unsound practices to Washington, D.C., and then either to request enforcement or to explain why enforcement was inappropriate. This part of Gardner's plan proved the old adage: be careful in what you ask for, for you may receive it.

The series of congressional hearings that Keating helped spur had several important chance effects that affected Keating in ways no one could have anticipated. The most improbable result was that Dingell eventually came to view Gray and the agency favorably, and he helped Gray in the struggle with Speaker Wright (who became an ally of Keating's).

The hearings also changed my role in Washington. After the first Dingell hearing, which so embarrassed the agency and our general counsel, I was tasked with representing our witnesses as counsel at the next hearing. I thought the questioning was abusive and misleading at many points, and spoke up to object to such questions. Dingell had a standard way of trying to intimidate lawyers at such moments: he swore them in as witnesses. The Democratic members of the committee would then pound the lawyer with a barrage of hostile questions. (One of the key reasons Dingell was so effective in using his investigative committee was that the Republicans on the Committee were intimidated by him and did not protect administration witnesses.) Dingell even threatened to put me in the congressional lockup until the end of the session!

The premise of Dingell's attack, however, was wrong. He assumed that we were pushing the cover-up and would testify that the industry and the FSLIC were in fine shape. I was able to turn the tables on him by stressing that our testimony was exactly the opposite. I took him through all the reregulatory steps Gray had taken and all the steps to toughen supervision that he had implemented before Dingell had announced the first hearing. I explained how Gray's actions had caused him and the agency to be viewed as the enemy and attacked by the industry, particularly the high fliers. Without saying it explicitly, I got the idea across that Gray had taken on the Reagan administration by backing reregulation. Dingell favored Gray's approach. It made no sense for him (a Democrat) to attack Gray.[7]

The second Dingell hearing caused me to become involved in a whole series of issues involving Keating and Speaker Wright. Keating and Wright developed a common antipathy to Gray and me that helped make them allies. No one could have predicted such an improbable chain of events.

Keating's strategy of using the Dingell hearings to attack Gray had another unintended effect that helped Keating. In response to Dingell's criticisms of the lack of timely, vigorous regulatory action against Beverly Hills Savings, Gray looked around for acts he could take quickly to emphasize his commitment to toughness. He decided to make the enforcement attorneys (who, like the litigators, were a sub-subunit in the Office of General Counsel) into a separate office reporting directly to the chairman. Responding to the pressure from Dingell, Gray immediately promoted the associate general counsel in charge of the enforcement staff to the rank of office director (the equivalent of a two-level promotion). That attorney was Rosemary Stewart, and within the Bank Board she became Keating's most aggressive defender and the primary opponent of the FHLB in San Francisco (FHLBSF) in general and me in particular. The irony, therefore, is that Keating's strategy thrust fairly junior staffers — one who would become his leading agency opponent and one his principal proponent — into senior roles.

REGULATORY CAPTURE AS REALITY, NOT METAPHOR

By early 1986, Keating realized that he had a chance to take majority control of the Bank Board. No S&L would be closed, no enforcement action taken, and no regulation adopted without the approval of Keating's members. They would also be able to repeal any existing rule. It would not matter whether Gray stayed, for he would be powerless. Moreover, Keating's capture of the Bank Board would be so humiliating that Gray would almost certainly resign. Keating could defraud Lincoln Savings with complete impunity.

Keating chose two replacements for Hovde and Grigsby. The first was George Benston, Lincoln Savings' "surrogate." Benston was also attractive to Keating because the law forbade all three Bank Board members to come from the same party. Benston was a Democrat, albeit a Reagan Democrat.

Keating's other choice was Lee Henkel. Henkel was a Republican from Georgia who had worked for Keating when he ran former Texas governor John Connally's campaign to be nominated as the Republican Party's candidate for president. He was a tax lawyer who had held a senior position with the IRS. Henkel and his law firm did legal work for Lincoln Savings. Henkel was a joint-venture partner with Lincoln Savings in real estate deals. (Importantly, a joint venture was a direct investment under the Bank Board rule that Keating was determined to destroy.) Henkel was also a large, uncreditworthy borrower from Lincoln Savings.

One of the least-understood facts about the S&L debacle is how close the nation came to a Japanese-style banking industry disaster. The S&L debacle was one of the greatest financial scandals in U.S. history, and the $150 billion loss was enormous, but it was still quite small compared with the size of our economy, which is measured in the trillions of dollars. The S&L debacle had only a small effect on our overall economy, but only because, as I explained in Chapter 3, Gray reregulated.

Consider what the result would have been if Keating had gained control of the Bank Board. Gray's rules would have been promptly rescinded. Keating was a bitter opponent of the FHLBs. Gray's major supervisory reforms were the transfer of the Bank Board's examination function to the FHLBs (with the accompanying requirement to double the number of examiners and supervisors and to increase examiners' pay) and the hiring of individuals known for their supervisory rigor for key positions at the FHLBs. Keating would have killed all of those steps. Gray was also pushing for much tougher enforcement and vigorous litigation against those who had caused S&L failures through abusive or criminal acts. Keating's position was that enforcement and litigation were already too severe and abusive. Gray had tightened the rules to prevent the entry of real estate developers with conflicts of interests into the S&L industry and to eliminate new Texas- and California-chartered S&Ls. Keating called traditional S&L CEOs "morons" and said that the answer to the problems of the industry was to encourage more real estate developers to emulate his purchase of Lincoln Savings.

LEE HENKEL: KEATING'S BANK BOARD MEMBER

Gardner reported that Keating's war against Gray had substantial support within the Reagan administration. The three strongest areas of that support were Donald Regan, the OMB, and the office of the vice president (George Bush). Don Regan was Keating's "go-to guy" in the administration. Don Regan overruled Tuttle's recommendation that Henkel not be appointed, saying that the administration owed Senator DeConcini a reward for his support (U.S. Senate Committee 1990– 1991a, 3:705–707).[8] The reward was for DeConcini's absenting himself from the 1986 vote on Judge Manion's nomination. The nomination was approved by one vote.

Manion was an odd person to be the fulcrum that gave Keating the leverage to move the administration into giving him de facto control over the Bank Board. The Republicans controlled the Senate Judiciary Committee in 1986, but Manion could not get a committee vote recommending his nomination. He was an inexperienced lawyer who would normally not have been considered ready for an appointment to a federal appeals court. If the nomination failed, the president could have chosen among dozens of experienced, conservative Republican jurists who would have easily won Senate confirmation. There was no policy reason for the administration to make his nomination a major issue.

Keating and Gardner played their cards well: they found a vote that the administration felt it needed to win and a situation where one or two votes (and Keating represented that he could deliver five senate votes) would prove decisive. Keating and DeConcini even found a way in which DeConcini could provide the winning margin without having to vote for the administration. From their perspective, this was an elegant solution.

It should have been a troubling solution from the administration's perspective. Gardner had assumed that Keating would have to demonstrate the willingness, ability, and intent to kill the administration's two top priorities (the budget and taxes) to induce President Reagan to appoint a single Bank Board member of Keating's choice. Instead, the administration was willing to give Keating majority control of the Bank Board (by appointing two members selected by Keating), and all Keating had had to do was hold hostage Manion's appointment to the U.S. Court of Appeals for the Seventh Circuit. The administration sold its soul to Charles Keating (a fair approximation of the devil) for *Manion*.[9]

The administration was about to appoint both Benston and Henkel to the agency on a recess basis. Benston got all the way to the official "intent to nominate" stage when random political opposition killed his nomination. The administration was still desperate to get another nominee on the Bank Board to outvote Gray, so they asked Benston to recommend a deregulatory Democrat who could be appointed quickly. He suggested Larry White, who had undergone the security checks and was about to be appointed to another agency. The administration appointed Henkel and White at the same time in late 1986. Grigsby and Hovde both resigned before these appointments, so without a quorum Gray was left helpless to take vital actions for a time. The timing seemed perfect for the administration and Keating. The direct investment rule had a "sunset" provision, and it would expire if not renewed by the Bank Board by the close of 1986. That was the rule Keating most hated (because he violated it so egregiously), and the administration opposed it as well. With two new deregulatory votes, the rule looked doomed.

BLOWING THE WHISTLE ON KEATING'S MOLE, LEE HENKEL

We knew Keating had gotten Henkel appointed to the agency and that Henkel had enormous conflicts of interest, but there seemed to be nothing we could do about it, and there was no chance of getting his vote. Henkel's first major act was to propose an amendment to the direct investment rule. The amendment, which had been secretly drafted by Lincoln Savings' lawyers, would have surreptitiously immunized Lincoln Savings from sanctions for its massive—$600 million—violation of the rule. I was the only one at the Bank Board to identify what Henkel was up to. I blew the whistle on Henkel, which led to his resignation in disgrace and eventually to an order by the Bank Board's successor agency removing him from the industry. Remarkably, the administration officially nominated him for a full four-year term after I blew the whistle, after they knew of his conflicts of interest and misdeeds, and after they knew that Lincoln Savings was in massive violation of the direct-investment rule.

Keating had invested enormous political capital in getting the administration to appoint Henkel, and he would have been immensely valuable as Keating's mole. All of this was lost when we exposed Henkel's misconduct. Keating now viewed me as his greatest problem.

Keating's real problem was that Bob Sahadi (the Bank Board's chief economist) and I won White's support for reregulation.[10] White has a keen mind and was open to ideas that challenged his initial positions. Our efforts to improve the Bank Board's research on direct investments, including designing and saving the key studies, were critical to this process. White was a deregulatory economist. He was initially suspicious of Gray and reregulation. The administration and Benston had reason to be confident that he would vote against Gray. At the Justice Department he had supported efforts to reduce substantially the circumstances under which it would bring antitrust actions. We had to have Larry White's vote to achieve further reregulation, because Henkel was a lost cause.

On Keating's behalf, Benston continued to file comments opposing the proposed equity-risk rule. His first study (in 1984) praised a group of S&Ls that had made material direct investments. They reported high profits. By 1987, however, when Gray and White passed a rule further restricting equity-risk investments, most of those S&Ls had failed. Many were control frauds. Indeed, all thirty-three of the S&Ls that Benston labeled safe and profitable failed (Mayer 1990, 139–140).[11]

THE CIVIL WAR WITHIN THE AGENCY BEGINS

In addition to the rule raising capital requirements and restricting growth, Gray's invigoration of supervision and examination was his critical contribution to the war against the control frauds. This inevitably led the political allies of the control frauds to launch a counterattack. That had terrible consequences for individual supervisors and for the taxpayers, but we knew it was a battle we would have to fight. The intra-agency civil war was unexpected and much more painful. The irony is that our enforcement director's ethical views caused her to view the people fighting the control frauds as the villains and the frauds as the victims. Stewart was convinced that Bank Board supervisors were too ready to abuse individuals' rights and that her ethical duty as head of enforcement was to exercise independent judgment to prevent this ever-present danger.

Regulators can be unprincipled and abusive, and ethical heads of enforcement and prosecutorial bodies should be an important check on such tyranny. But Stewart's view was idiosyncratic. Every independent scholar says that prior to Gray's bringing in tough new supervisors from the Office of the Comptroller of the Currency (OCC), Bank Board supervision was shockingly weak (NCFIRRE 1993a). Stewart's contrary views were first driven home to me in connection with Consolidated Savings Bank, a California control fraud. Consolidated was unusual in that the FBI warned us that "mob associates" ran the S&L. The number two officer, Mr. Angotti, told an FHLBSF examiner that he hoped the agency wasn't going to take over the S&L because if it did, someone was going to get hurt, and he hoped it wasn't the examiner! This sent shock waves though the examination team and the FHLBSF. They pulled the examiners out of the S&L and requested emergency action by the Office of Enforcement (OE). Stewart declined, and told the FHLBSF to go to the top officer at Consolidated, Mr. Ferrante, and complain about Angotti. Ferrante was famous for having survived a semiprofessional "hit" at close range from the front. He screamed, while bleeding profusely, at the police that he wouldn't help any (obscenity deleted) cops. The FHLBSF was amazed and appalled at Stewart's lack of support on such a critical matter. They called me and asked whether the litigation department could help. We pulled out all the stops and soon got a temporary restraining order against the threats.

The new supervisors were generally dismayed at the approach that the OE took. It was extraordinarily risk averse about losing a case, so it rarely brought any that might be contested (NCFIRRE 1993a, 51). That meant that its attorneys never developed much trial experience. The office generally did not seek to hire experienced trial attorneys for inhouse positions, and it refused to use experienced outside counsel.

And it drove the former OCC supervisors berserk when Stewart flatly told them that they were not clients. She said that "the agency" was the client, which meant that she was free to substitute her supervisory judgment for that of the senior field supervisors. The only way they could stop this was to have the chairman personally overrule her supervisory judgment. You cannot take dozens of enforcement disputes to the chairman for resolution without ruining the agency, so as a practical matter she was saying she could not be reversed. She had no training or experience as a supervisor, and her supervisory judgment was consistently in favor of weaker sanctions. She interpreted senior supervisors' protests at this laxity as proof that her ethical restraints were, in fact, needed to protect against frequent abuses.

Although Stewart had no supervisory experience, Mike Patriarca, who Gray had hired to run the FHLBSF's supervision department, was a former OCC enforcement attorney. He was in a very good position to evaluate her work and to compare it to that of OCC enforcement attorneys. His view of her was scathing.

Gray had bypassed any competitive selection process to elevate Stewart to office head in order to protect his rear politically after being savaged by Dingell. I considered her work and attitude disastrous for the agency. Julie Williams, the senior Bank Board attorney responsible for securities law compliance, shared that view. One of the telling things for me was that attorneys representing S&Ls that our supervisors had identified as control frauds tried to get the OE involved. At most agencies, regulatory lawyers fight desperately to resolve disputes without coming to the attention of the enforcement attorneys. An enforcement staff is supposed to be like the pit bull that you keep on a chain: there is an implicit threat that you will let it loose if the violators don't clean up their act voluntarily. When they succeeded in bringing the OE into the case, the control frauds' attorneys would go on at length about how delighted they were to have Stewart involved because they knew how fair she was. She believed them. Either she was blind to how that would make the supervisors seethe, or she interpreted their displeasure as more proof of their ethical flaws.

A clash was coming, and Lincoln Savings sparked it. There were three *causes célèbres* involving Lincoln Savings and Stewart during Gray's term. First, she was enraged when I blew the whistle on Henkel. Her rage was directed entirely at Gray and me; she never indicated any distress with Henkel or Keating. To her, Henkel and Keating were the victims.

Second, when the FHLBSF examiners began disclosing Keating's frauds in 1986, he responded with an unprecedented tactic. His litigation attorneys announced that the examiners could no longer examine the S&L's books and records or question its personnel. The examiners could request materials, and if Keating's litigator decided that the Bank Board needed to see the files, they might be provided. The statute, as one would expect, gives the Bank Board an absolute right to examine all aspects of any S&L. Keating's unlawful actions, if not ended promptly, would have created a terrible precedent, one that would have destroyed examination effectiveness. Any normal regulator would have realized that if an examination discovered one fraud, there was certain to be far worse information that the S&L was desperate to avoid being uncovered, and the scope of the examination should be expanded.

Stewart, however, would not take any enforcement action. Substituting her supervisory judgment for the examiners' once more, she decided that if the litigation attorney was based at Lincoln Savings in California, instead of in New York, the FHLBSF had to comply with the attorney's demands. This can have come only from her view that Keating was the victim and Patriarca the villain. The meeting that led to this settlement distressed me because Stewart allowed Lincoln's top outside litigator, Peter Fishbein, to, in essence, depose the unprepared and unsupported FHLBSF head of examination. I concluded that Stewart had no litigation sense.

A third incident enraged Stewart. Recall that Lincoln Savings was a captive of Drexel and had no involvement in decisions about its massive junk-bond portfolio. That was a major problem because, as Milken himself emphasized, a junk bond is really a commercial loan. Bank Board rules required an S&L to perform careful underwriting prior to making a commercial loan. Lincoln Savings had done no underwriting, which the FHLBSF examiners were sure to spot. Lincoln Savings decided, as always, that more deceit was the solution. Arthur Andersen was Lincoln Savings' auditor. The S&L now hired a large group of Andersen consultants to create what would appear to be contemporary underwriting documents.[12]

The amazing fact about this elegant fraud is that the FHLBSF discovered it. Specifically, Bart Dzivi noticed that the documents were not in a logical numerical sequence and spotted one place (in thousands of pages) where Andersen had mistakenly shown a date subsequent to the junk bond purchase.[13] Bart spotted it and understood the significance.

The FHLBSF alerted the OE to the fraud and the possible backdating and forging of documents. The OE received formal examination authority from the Bank Board and then did nothing. It did not take testimony from a single witness. The FHLBSF general counsel was about to leave in early 1987; the office offered me the position and flew me out to try to convince me to take it. I met with Mike Patriarca. He asked me to talk to Gray about two things: he wanted Gray to end the insane interest-rate gamble that American Savings was taking, and he wanted enforcement action taken against Lincoln Savings.

I talked with Gray; he was ready to end the gamble and sell American

Savings quickly. But he wanted nothing to do with directing Stewart to take action against Lincoln Savings. He told me to talk with my superiors in the Office of General Counsel. They arranged a meeting with Stewart's deputy, Steve Hershkowitz, who was handling the Lincoln Savings case. It was enlightening. I said that Mike Patriarca wanted to know when the OE was going to begin deposing witnesses. Steve said he might not take any depositions and that, in any event, it was not a priority matter. I was staggered; I told Steve that it was one of the highest priorities of the S&L's top supervisor. He responded that Lincoln Savings wasn't a priority matter because it wasn't insolvent. I replied, "Actually, Steve we like to keep it that way." He also said that the allegations didn't indicate any problems with management's integrity. I said that the allegations of file stuffing and document backdating certainly reflected on integrity. He told me that "those allegations haven't been proven." I replied, "That's *why* we do investigations."

Eventually, I had to assign one of my experienced litigators, Anne Sobol, to conduct the investigation (under Stewart's control). Sobol used outside counsel to assist with the investigation. The depositions revealed extensive forgeries and backdated documents, and documented the junk bond "file stuffing." This led to criminal referrals and eventually to felony pleas. The effect on Stewart, however, was to convince her that I was the prime villain and that Keating was somehow not very culpable.

I became convinced that Stewart was the greatest internal impediment to the accomplishment of the agency's mission. I considered the OE to be the land of the invertebrates. Patriarca and I pushed for Gray to move her to the side and bring in a vigorous enforcement director. Gray's term, however, was about to end, and Larry White did not want any major personnel changes before Danny Wall arrived as the new chairman. Gray elected not to proceed. It probably wouldn't have done any good if he had. Wall saw Gray's and my criticism of Stewart as the greatest possible endorsement of her. The stage was set for a broadscale civil war.

5. THE TEXAS
CONTROL FRAUDS
ENLIST JIM WRIGHT

INTRODUCTION

James (Jim) Wright, Jr., became Speaker of the House of Representatives in 1987. I will examine the following puzzles: How did the two worst control frauds recruit him as an ally? Why did he remain loyal to them even after it became clear that doing so would have disastrous consequences for his constituents, the nation, and his party? Why did he, after striving for decades to become Speaker, continue to support the control frauds, even though doing so cost him his life's ambition and his reputation? How did three control frauds and a real estate developer, each of whom voted for Ronald Reagan in 1980, get Wright, a populist Democrat, to champion wealthy GOP frauds despite the warnings of fellow Democrats?

Wright's actions on behalf of the control frauds had enormous direct consequences: they were decisive in forcing him to resign in disgrace from the House, and because they delayed the closure of dozens of (mostly Texas) control frauds, they led to billions of dollars in additional costs to the taxpayers.

The indirect consequences were even greater. The Speaker's support for the control frauds helped elect George Bush to the presidency in 1988. The clumsy interventions of members of Congress on behalf of the frauds obscured the Reagan-Bush administration's contributions to the control frauds' success and the creation of the debacle. Wright's actions proved critical in causing Gray's successor to appease Charles Keating. That, in turn, led to the worst failure of a financial institution in U.S. history, to the S&L debacle becoming a political scandal, to the resignation in disgrace of Gray's successor, to the termination of the Bank Board, and to an ethics investigation of the Keating Five by a reluctant Senate. The Speaker's intervention was a "hinge event" that changed a wide range of policies.

Wright's actions fit the classic definition of tragedy. He was not an intrinsically evil man or a fool. He did not know initially that the people he was aiding were control frauds. His tragic flaws were ambition and hubris. His driving ambition was to become Speaker of the House, and he had to be a champion fund-raiser in order to achieve it. Wright's pride and domineering personality led to him to surround himself with yes-men and to disdain warnings.

Studying how the frauds enlisted him to their cause is vital. First, they did it relatively easily. The political system remains vulnerable to similar enlistments, and elected officials should study the case of Jim Wright to learn how to avoid subornation by future control frauds. Second, Wright's actions—and the responses by his colleagues, the Reagan administration, and the regulators—are important to the development of a coherent theory of how elected officials and regulators behave. Scholars use public-choice theory to devise a "just so" story that purports to explain government officials' actions after the fact, but public-choice theory could not have predicted the behavior described here. A theory that relies on ad hoc and contradictory assumptions about behavior is not useful. Studying how government officials act during hinge events is important if scholars are to develop tenable theories.

Since John Barry had the immense good fortune to accompany Wright for months and to all manner of meetings for a behind-the-scenes book on the Speaker, our ability to understand Wright's actions is made much easier. Barry wrote a lengthy book, *The Ambition and the Power* (1989), filled with anecdotes. We are even more fortunate because Barry became a partisan defender of the Speaker. As Barry emphasizes, the Speaker was comfortable only with yes-men. If Barry had not come to identify so completely with him, the Speaker never would have been so open. Barry's book provides the Speaker's contemporaneous defense of his actions on behalf of the control frauds.[1]

The House ethics investigation of the Speaker and the Senate ethics investigation of the Keating Five also permit a rich study of the Speaker's actions on behalf of the Texas control frauds and his later aid to Keating. The Senate investigation immunized Keating's chief political fixer, Jim Grogan, who set up Keating's 1988 meeting with Senator

Glenn and Speaker Wright and attended the decisive meeting later that day with Bank Board chairman Wall at which Keating, by playing the Speaker card, induced Wall to appease him. Grogan's testimony about the Speaker is unusually credible because he was, clearly, wholly sympathetic to the Speaker and Keating, yet his testimony damned both.

I participated in the critical 1987 meeting with Speaker Wright and attempted to cope with his interventions on behalf of the Texas control frauds in 1986 and 1987. This meant that I dealt directly with all of the executive-branch and legislative officials involved. I led the Bank Board's eventual criticism of the Speaker. This adds to the richness of the case study but adds a risk of bias.

A FRIEND IN NEED IS A FRIEND INDEED

The first irony is that it was a very clever Republican political ploy that made it easy for the Texas control frauds to enlist Jim Wright in their cause. The second irony is that the issues involved had nothing to do with S&Ls. In 1984 the Republicans gained control of the Senate. President Reagan was enormously popular. The Republicans had been in the minority in the House for the bulk of the last fifty years. Being the minority power in the House is inherently unsatisfying, but the Republicans felt that the Democrats had gone out of their way to make their lives unpleasant. The Republicans began to believe that a historic realignment was taking shape, one that could restore them to majority control of the House. They were eager to hasten the process.

In 1985 Jim Wright was House majority leader and Thomas "Tip" O'Neill was Speaker. O'Neill was in ill health, and it was clear that he would soon retire. The Speaker can be the second-most powerful elected official in the United States because House rules place far more power in the Speaker's hands than the Senate rules vest in the Senate majority leader. Jim Wright would soon be Speaker, and his ambition to be a powerful Speaker was widely known.

The president appointed Representative Sam Hall, who represented a district around 100 miles east of Wright's, to the federal judiciary. The congressman was a Democrat, so appointing him to the judiciary removed the advantage of incumbency that the Democrats would have otherwise had in that district. When a vacancy occurs in the House, there is a special election to choose a successor. Republicans planned to humiliate Majority Leader Wright in this special election. If he could not get a Democrat elected in his own backyard, he would not be a credible Speaker. The Republicans hoped to deny him the speakership and publicize the realignment of the country along Republican lines (Jackson 1988, 265; O'Shea 1991, 167–169).

Texas was fertile political ground for the Republicans. Former governor John Connally had switched parties to become a Republican, and the state was becoming more conservative while the Democratic Party was becoming more liberal. The Republican Party and its supporters had far richer coffers than the Democrats, and poured large sums into the special election. In a special election, candidates have less time to develop name recognition with the voters, which maximizes the importance of existing name recognition and expensive political advertising on television (as Governor Schwarzenegger's huge victory proves). The Republican candidate was a well-known former collegiate football hero.

The Democrats sought with equal fervor to elect their candidate, Jim Chapman (Jackson 1988, 264–267). Representative Tony Coelho, chairman of the Democratic Congressional Campaign Committee (DCCC), urgently raised funds for Chapman. As Jim O'Shea, the journalist who wrote a book about Vernon Savings, explained, the Chapman election created the "ideal opportunity to curry favor" (1991, 167–169). Thomas Gaubert seized the opportunity even though he had voted for Reagan in 1980 (Jackson 1988, 263). He was the principal owner of a Texas S&L named Independent American. He had looted the S&L so badly that it was deeply insolvent, and the Bank Board had removed him from control through a consent agreement. The law permitted the DCCC to make only a small contribution to Chapman. Gaubert created a single-candidate political action committee (PAC) to fund Chapman's campaign.

> I decided to make a difference. I formed the PAC, I raised the money. I raised every dime that went into the PAC. I called everybody I knew. (*Washington Post*, May 5, 1988)

Within three months, Gaubert's PAC raised $100,920. He explained the pitch he used to raise funds:

> I don't know why you're not involved in their [politician's] business; they're involved in our [expletive] business every day. . . . The donations give you access. . . . They give you a chance to have a forum when you have a problem. (ibid.)

The S&L insiders who made these PAC contributions were an infamous collection of the worst Texas S&L control frauds, including Don Dixon of Vernon Savings (a Republican), John Harrell of Commodore Savings, and Ed McBirney of Sunbelt Savings (ibid.; O'Shea 1991, 167–169). In his even more graphic pitch to these criminal S&L owners, Gaubert cited his experiences with Bank Board supervision:

> Look what the SOB is doing to me and you're going to be next. If we don't get the Nazi [expletive] bastards out of here they're going to destroy the whole industry. (*Washington Post*, May 5, 1988)

The "SOB," of course, was Gray. Worse, these S&Ls frequently made illegal campaign contributions by directing their employees to make contributions and then reimbursing them the funds (Jackson 1988, 274–275; O'Shea 1991, 203–207). The same S&Ls gave about $200,000 to the DCCC from early 1985 to mid-1986 (*Washington Post,* May 5, 1988). Don Dixon explained, "It was the responsibility of Vernon Savings to grease the wheels of political America" (O'Shea 1991, 206). In fact, Gaubert's entire PAC was probably illegal because it gave far more money to Chapman than permitted, unless it was wholly independent of the DCCC, which it was not (Jackson 1988, 266). Gaubert's ability to convince so many S&Ls to contribute to his PAC is particularly impressive given that S&L regulation was not at issue in the special election.

Chapman very narrowly won the election. Wright became the Speaker, and Coelho became the House Democratic Whip thanks to his fund-raising successes. Gaubert, now a hero, became close to both Wright and Coelho. Gaubert and the control frauds had shown great sophistication in their strategy and tactics. He had found a situation that was absolutely critical to the party and to Coelho and Wright personally. He came in at their hour of greatest need and he delivered.

The scariest part of this recruitment was that the control frauds did it for about $100,000, a pittance. The insolvency of Independent American under Gaubert grew at the rate of about $1 million every working day, so it took Gaubert only a few minutes to lose a sum equivalent to the $5,000 that Independent American provided to that $100,000 contribution. My standard joke was that the frauds' highest return on investment always came from their political contributions.

In addition to helping two prominent and rising politicians at the time of their greatest need, Gaubert's contributions had four other important effects. The first one is so basic that we tend to forget it. To Jim Wright, these were not control frauds, but legitimate businessmen. The S&Ls and their owners had apparent legitimacy: control fraud is so effective because it hides behind a false front. The contributions aided the Democratic Party, not just individual officials, so the party was now indebted to the Texas control frauds.

The frauds asked nothing in return for their contributions; this is why it was useful that S&L regulation was not at issue in the election. This made it appear that the contributors belonged to that ideal group, those who support politicians financially because they believe in their policies.

The fourth characteristic was that there were no rival contributions to offset the political debt owed to Gaubert and the control frauds. Political scientists have theorized that political contributions are less influential than the public suspects because they often offset one another. If both the trade association representing the big banks and the rival association representing the small banks contribute to a politician, neither has decisive leverage on issues in which the two groups have opposing interests. The Bank Board, of course, could not make political contributions. The control frauds maximized their political leverage, therefore, on issues in which they opposed the Bank Board, and they opposed the Gray Bank Board on everything.

Gaubert's clever (albeit illegal) tactics defeated the clever Republican ploy designed to prevent Jim Wright from becoming Speaker. Wright and Coelho came out of the special election with increased power and reputations, poised to become the top leaders of the House. Gaubert's confederation of control frauds made it possible. What elected official would not be intensely grateful in such circumstances?

THOMAS GAUBERT

Wright and the Democratic Party rewarded Gaubert by appointing him finance chairman of the DCCC; his ambition was to become chairman of the Democratic National Committee (Jackson 1988, 263). Successful presidential candidates traditionally appoint the party chair to the cabinet or a plum ambassadorial post.

The Bank Board had forced Gaubert out of day-to-day control of Independent American in late 1984. By mid-1985, it was seeking a "removal and prohibition" order to keep him from ever reentering the industry. He knew that the Dallas fraud task force was planning to indict him. The S&L he owned was deeply insolvent; its new management, appointed by the FHLB-Dallas, was preparing a huge lawsuit against him. He realized that his wealth and his ambitions for higher political office were doomed unless the Bank Board released him from the removal-and-prohibition order and he regained control of Independent American. Gaubert had ample incentive to cultivate political support during the 1985 special election (U.S. House Conduct Committee 1989, 241).

Gaubert was cultivating fertile ground that had already been furrowed. Gray's proposed rules on growth and direct investments in 1984 had galvanized the control frauds in Texas and California. In 1984 Durward Curlee, a former senior Texas League official, formed a group, comprising the worst Texas S&Ls, to oppose reregulation (O'Shea 1991, 102, 165–167). The group met monthly to plot its strategy. Its primary focus was on lobbying the Texas congressional delegation. The Texas delegation was numerous and disproportionately powerful. Senators Phil Gramm (Republican) and Lloyd Bensten and Representative Jim Wright (Democrats) were its leaders. In 1986 Senator Gramm recommended that Curlee be named to the Bank Board (*National Thrift News,* May 26, 1986). He would have been as disastrous an appointment as Lee Henkel. The fact that the administration appointed Keating's choice instead of a prominent Republican senator's candidate indicates how extraordinary Keating's influence was with the White House.

1986: A YEAR OF CRISIS FOR THE CONTROL FRAUDS AND THE BANK BOARD

By 1986 the control frauds were desperate to remove Gray and reverse his initiatives. Texas and California control frauds were the most desperate. A series of hammer blows fell on them. The growth rule was beginning to bite. Deprived of growth, the Ponzis would die.

The Bank Board dramatically increased its human resources, particularly in Texas. The FHLB-Dallas hired more than 100 new examiners, and the Bank Board temporarily reassigned 250 examiners from other districts to Texas.

The Bank Board's leadership was greatly improved. Adding Joe Selby in Dallas and Mike Patriarca in San Francisco immediately injected vigor into the agency. The FHLBSF had already been a leader in closing problem S&Ls under the leadership of its president James

Cirona and its vigorous supervisor, Charles Deardorff; now it targeted the control frauds and took over record numbers of them. Selby faced a far greater crisis than Patriarca, so it took the FHLB-Dallas much longer to begin removing its control frauds.

Taking over the control frauds, however, required the FSLIC to spend its critically limited funds. By late 1986, the FSLIC had very little money left.

In 1986 the Bank Board and the administration proposed to recapitalize the FSLIC (i.e., give it a loan so it would have more cash to close the control frauds). The control frauds understood that the FSLIC "recap" would provide the funds to close them down. As Taggart, the former CDSL commissioner, explained in his August 4, 1986, letter urging Donald Regan to fire Gray:

> [Gray's actions] are likely to have a very adverse impact on the ability of our Party to raise needed campaign funds in the upcoming elections. Many who have been very supportive of the Administration are involved with savings and loan associations which are being closed by the FHLBB. . . .
>
> It is felt by many in the industry that the 250 extra federal examiners on temporary duty in Texas are poised awaiting passage of the Recapitalization Bill. . . . If approved, sufficient funds will then be available to the FSLIC to . . . close down associations. . . . It is then anticipated that a substantial number of these "loaned" examiners will be transferred to California. . . . [T]hose who are typically targeted for removal or takeover are sole shareholder associations . . . [which] are highly profitable and which have experienced substantial growth over the past three to five years. (U.S. House Banking Committee 1989, 3:630, 634)

The Bank Board was getting far more stringent, i.e., by eliminating most of the creative regulatory accounting principles. The regulators were also receiving additional powers. The classification-of-assets rule became effective January 1, 1986. Upon Selby's arrival in May 1986 through the remainder of that year, the FHLB-Dallas issued over 100 supervisory actions (U.S. House Conduct Committee 1989, 256). Enforcement actions, liability suits against directors and officers, and criminal investigations were all expanding rapidly.

Texas commercial real estate was in massive oversupply due to several things: the 1981 Tax Act, perverse (e.g., fraudulent) incentives for continuing to make ADC loans in the face of a glut, and the crash of oil prices. Passage of the 1986 Tax Reform Act and the crack down on the Texas S&L control frauds punctured the Texas real estate bubble.

The final straw came when the FHLB-Dallas put the first massive Texas control fraud, Western Savings in Gatesville, into the Management Consignment Program (MCP). It was a $2 billion S&L riddled with fraud, and it eventually cost the taxpayers over $1 billion. It was clear that the new Texas MCP managers, as their counterparts had done with failed California S&Ls, would expose massive losses and pervasive fraud once they took control and removed the insiders. It was equally certain that a wave of criminal referrals and lawsuits would follow. The Texas control frauds had reason to be worried: Dallas, uniquely, had a special financial-fraud task force of 100 professionals created to respond to the wave of frauds.

Texas had more control frauds than any other state. If the FSLIC recap passed, Gray and Selby would destroy the livelihoods and reputations of hundreds of control fraud insiders and defaulting borrowers. Thousands of noncriminal S&L executives also hated Gray. The S&L League reflected its membership's overwhelming enmity for him. The industry hated reregulation. It was in a panic about stringent supervision by regulators recruited from the Office of the Comptroller of the Currency because of their demonstrated toughness. The industry had fought for over fifty years to prevent the grant of any meaningful discretion to examiners. The classification-of-assets rule now gave examiners substantial discretion. This is the context in which the administration introduced the FSLIC recap bill.

1986: FSLIC RECAP

A BASTARDIZED PLAN EXPOSES THE BANK BOARD TO EXTORTION

The mechanics of the proposed recapitalization of the FSLIC are complex, and unnecessary for understanding the struggle over the bill. It is enough to know that the administration placed two absolute constraints on the plan and that those constraints were sure to cause severe problems. First, the Treasury Department would not kick in a penny to help the FSLIC. That was a bedrock administration demand — end of story. All the money had to come from the industry. Second, not a penny of the money spent could be "scored" for budgetary purposes as a federal expenditure; in other words, the whole plan had to be "off budget."

The goals were, first, to prevent the S&L crisis from becoming an issue the Democrats could use in the 1988 presidential election, and, second, to give the FSLIC a modest increase in funds for closing more of the worst control frauds. The FSLIC recap brilliantly accomplished the first goal, but for wholly unforeseen reasons. The idea was to stave off the FSLIC's collapse. Government accountants were in the process of (properly) declaring the FSLIC insolvent. A nationwide run was still a possibility if the public panicked, and that could have doomed George Bush's electoral chances. No one foresaw that the control frauds would hand George Bush a priceless political gift by enlisting Speaker Wright to help kill the FSLIC recap.

The recap failed to achieve the second goal for equally unforeseen reasons. The control frauds and the league combined to prevent passage of the FSLIC recap bill during Gray's tenure. Gray, therefore, never received any additional funds to close more control frauds. Gray's successor, Danny Wall, chose not to use the modest amount of funds that the FSLIC eventually received under the plan to close the worst control frauds. In Chapter 8 I explore why Wall made this decision.

The plan was to take a few billion dollars from the industry (out of FHLB capital—the S&Ls owned the FHLBs) and leverage those funds through additional borrowings. The bill would create a new entity to borrow $15 billion by selling bonds. The total additional revenue would be $15 billion over the next five years. That would be on top of the FSLIC's annual premium income of roughly $2.3 billion. The plan would repay the $15 billion debt over decades through investment earnings on the capital taken from the FHLBs (to help "defease" the debt) and from FSLIC insurance premiums that would go to the newly created bond authority instead of the FSLIC fund.

The plan had five obvious flaws. It did not provide remotely enough money for the FSLIC to close failed S&Ls. Second, it required the agency and the administration to cover up the true scope of the crisis: if the public knew how insolvent the industry and the FSLIC fund were, it would not buy the FSLIC recap bonds and the plan would collapse. The long-running cover-up of the crisis led the administration to design a plan that depended on deceiving investors. This was unprincipled and certain to fail unless the markets were badly inefficient. The administration officials designing the plan, however, were true believers in the efficient-markets hypothesis.

The third flaw was that this was a very expensive way for the federal government to borrow money. The treasury could have raised the funds at a much cheaper rate of interest, but that would have put the program on the budget. The plan, therefore, was a pure income transfer from taxpayers to the securities industry. The administration officials who designed the plan came from the securities industry.

The plan required the industry to pay an additional $15 billion over roughly twenty years. That figure, however, understated the effect of the recap on the healthy part of the industry. Over 600 S&Ls were insolvent on a market-value basis in 1986. The FSLIC did not receive any net increase in funds when an insolvent S&L paid it an insurance premium. It was a wash. Each dollar an insolvent S&L paid to the FSLIC increased FSLIC assets by a dollar and its (contingent) liabilities by a dollar. That meant that all the additional revenue provided to the FSLIC by the plan had to come from solvent S&Ls. Roughly 1,000 S&Ls were solvent but seriously undercapitalized. Increasing their insurance premiums was worse than a wash from the FSLIC's perspective because it could cause them to fail and impose serious costs on the FSLIC. Typically, the remaining 1,000 S&Ls had barely adequate capital. The aspect of the plan that took capital from the FHLBs to help repay the bonds threatened to make their capital inadequate. The third flaw fed back into this flaw. Anything that raised the cost of borrowing the funds would be borne by the healthy members of the industry.

The administration knew that the plan had these four flaws. It did not spot the last, and largest, flaw. The plan maximized the odds that the high fliers and the traditional S&Ls would ally themselves to defeat the plan. The high fliers were sure to oppose the plan. The traditional S&Ls and the high fliers generally held one another in mutual contempt. This had undercut their ability to work together to defeat Gray's reregulation. Traditional S&Ls knew that they would have to bear the cost of the plan, and the most capable CEOs knew the plan would not begin to cover the FSLIC's insolvency. An enormous federal bailout of the FSLIC was inevitable, and whoever won the 1988 presidential election would probably have to propose it as one of his first initiatives. If the league could defeat, delay, or reduce the FSLIC recap, the taxpayers would bear the expense of bailing out the high fliers.

There is very little good one can say about such a plan except that it was absolutely the best (or the least bad) plan that Gray could get the administration to support, and without administration support the cause was hopeless. I was not involved in structuring the plan, but I could not have done any better given the administration's constraints. Good public policy would have required an immediate infusion of tens of billions of dollars from the treasury.

What none of us at the Bank Board understood was how much the agency was exposing itself to extortion by seeking the FSLIC recap. One cannot blame this exposure entirely on the administration's insistence on keeping the debacle off budget. Even if the administration had proposed to provide treasury funds to the FSLIC, Congress would have had to pass legislation authorizing the bailout, and the control frauds and their political patrons could have tried to hold that legislation hostage in order to extort the Bank Board to go easy on the frauds. However, we would have been better able to defeat such extortion had the administration supported an on-budget plan.

The strongest arguments in favor of recapitalizing the FSLIC were that the industry was in crisis, that the FSLIC fund was deeply insolvent, and that the longer the control frauds remained open, the larger the losses would be to the taxpayers. We could not make those arguments as long as the administration insisted on covering up the deep insolvency of the industry and the FSLIC fund.

It would have been far more politically dangerous for a legislator to hold FSLIC recapitalization hostage if the administration and the Bank Board had made plain that the crisis was overwhelming. If the administration had made public the depth of the crisis and the major contribution of the control frauds to it, perhaps no member of Congress would have allied himself with any possibly fraudulent S&L to block the FSLIC recapitalization. I do not believe that either the Speaker or the Keating Five would have acted as they did had the administration made public the true scope and causes of the crisis. Unfortunately, the administration was absolutely opposed to such an approach.

The FSLIC recap made sense only if the FSLIC was in desperate shape. It seems impossible now that anyone thought there was no real problem then. But that gives too much weight to hindsight. Congress deals every day with agency heads who exaggerate their problems to get bigger budgets approved. The league was claiming at every opportunity that there was no real problem that necessitated the FSLIC recap. Congress looks on agency claims of crisis with well-earned skepticism. The only way we could convince Congress that we were in a true crisis was to make it clear that the situation was absolutely desperate. That maximized the leverage of any powerful member of Congress who wished to exploit the leverage our desperation inevitably produced.

FROZEN IN THE SENATE

The FSLIC recap initially fared quite well in both houses. It was not initially considered a controversial bill; it had administration support; and it was not a partisan issue. The GAO, the auditing and consulting arm of Congress, strongly supported the bill.[2] The bill received prompt consideration, favorable preliminary votes, and almost no opposition. The league was uncharacteristically slow to formulate a position on the FSLIC recap and mobilize its potent legion of lobbyists and contributors.

The chairman of the Senate Banking Committee, William Proxmire, wanted to make explicit the Bank Board's statutory authority to restrict state-chartered S&Ls' direct-investment powers. This would have removed Keating's best argument against the direct-investment rule. Senator Alan Cranston, at Keating's behest, put a freeze on the FSLIC recap to block Proxmire's effort.[3]

WRIGHT PUTS A HOLD IN THE HOUSE

The House Banking Committee voted 47–1 in favor of the FSLIC recap. Its chairman, Fernand St Germain, placed the bill on the "suspension calendar" in response to Gray's letter noting the need for the bill's urgent passage. This procedure suspends the normal House rules to allow prompt consideration of noncontroversial measures. There was a public announcement that the full House would vote on the bill on September 29, 1986. Instead, Wright's hold prevented the vote (U.S. House Conduct Committee 1989, 208).

The particular matter that decided the timing of Wright's hold was an arcane dispute involving a large insolvent Texas real estate developer, Craig Hall. However, Hall's particular dispute was only a small part of a much larger effort by the Texas control frauds to get Wright to use the FSLIC recap bill to extort concessions from Gray.

To get to Wright, the control frauds and their allies used two methods that were mutually reinforcing and added credibility to the claim, otherwise absurd on its face, that unduly tough regulation had caused the Texas S&L crisis. It would have been a snap to make the opposite case: the Bank Board's laxity under Pratt was notorious. But a big lie can lead to big success.

The DCCC, which was run by Coelho and had Gaubert as finance chairman, was the first entry point for the control frauds to get to the Speaker. Coelho, who was clever, never called the regulators himself.

He used Wright to do that dirty work. The control frauds would go to Coelho and get appointments with Wright. They could always get access to Coelho through Gaubert.

CRAIG HALL

Craig Hall was the wild card in Wright's S&L intervention. He was atypical both in how he got to Wright and in who he was. He was a Reagan supporter, but had made a large contribution to the DCCC shortly before meeting with Wright (O'Shea 1991, 227). Barry emphasizes early in his book that a principal source of Wright's power in the House came from his ability to help elect other Democrats. Fundraising, through Coelho and the DCCC, became the centerpiece of Wright's ability to elect other Democrats. Barry (1989, 217) says that although Hall had hired Akin, Gump, the premier Democratic lobbying firm in the nation, he was unable to meet Wright until a nephew of an old friend of Wright's arranged a meeting.

Hall was the only S&L borrower on whose behalf Wright personally intervened with the Bank Board. Hall was a very large S&L borrower—his loans from S&L's such as Westwood Savings in California totaled roughly $1 billion—and a well-regarded developer of large residential projects. By early 1986 he was deeply insolvent and did not have the cash to make the interest payments on his loans. When he defaulted, he attempted to arrange a "loan workout."[4] Hall's loans and similar ADC loans caused Westwood Savings, a fraudulent S&L, to fail. The Bank Board placed it in the MCP program. Westwood's new management, after much review and spirited debate, ultimately decided that restructuring Hall's debt would make Westwood worse off. Its "special representative," Scott Schultz, was an FHLBSF employee who communicated the decision to Hall.

Westwood rejected Hall's proposal and sued him to collect the debt. Hall went to Wright. Wright and other members of Congress objected to Gray. (Ominously, Danny Wall, who would be Gray's successor, wrote one of the hostile letters on behalf of his boss, Senator Jake Garn). Wright's efforts on behalf of Hall, however, were unique. He made repeated efforts to have Gray force Westwood to restructure the debt. The FHLBSF and I fought a tenacious rearguard action against this. Shannon Fairbanks, Gray's chief of staff, pushed for the agency to cave in to Wright. She argued that the FSLIC recap was the agency's highest priority and that Wright could kill its passage. I countered that if we gave in, we would only encourage further extortion. Gray wavered; he plainly hoped that someone would find an arguably principled basis for giving Wright what he wanted. Wright made the point moot by putting a hold on the FSLIC recap bill. Gray felt he had no choice. He gave in and Wright removed his hold.[5]

GEORGE MALLICK

The second access route the control frauds had to Wright was through George Mallick. Almost no one has heard about him, but he had a dramatic effect on the outcome of the 1988 presidential election and the downfall of Speaker Wright.

Mallick's importance grew from a paradox about Jim Wright. As Barry (1989, 234) reports: "'Jim's the hardest man to help I know of.' Bob Strauss sighed." Strauss was a fellow Texan, a former head of the Democratic National Committee, and an old colleague on friendly terms with Wright. He sighed because he had tried again, unsuccessfully, to warn Wright that Mallick was involving him in scandal. Jim Wright did not accept help when it came in the form of good, but critical, advice. He did not accept it even when it came from individuals who were not seeking any personal gain.

However, for those who were trying to help themselves, Wright was one of the easiest men to harm precisely because he accepted certain kinds of help so indiscriminately. Barry (1989, 93) reveals that Wright enjoyed even the most unctuous flattery. He also appreciated tangible help in the form of money and votes, and he did not investigate why his patrons were providing him tangible aid, even when a patron was obviously seeking personal gain from his ties to Wright. George Mallick wanted to help George Mallick, and he realized that the best way to do so was to help Jim Wright.

Barry explains that when Wright divorced his first wife, who was much loved in Fort Worth, and married a secretary, he was ostracized by the elites in that conservative, religious town. Wright still had to support his former wife and children, and his new wife had expensive tastes, so Wright's financial problems grew.

George Mallick seemed the answer to Wright's woes. He provided income by hiring Wright's new wife; he reduced their expenses by providing them with free housing and cars; and he welcomed the new Mrs. Wright as a friend in the midst of her social isolation (Barry 1989, 224–230). He flattered Jim Wright shamelessly. Like Gaubert, Mallick had found a way to help Wright in one of his hours of greatest need. Wright understandably displayed great loyalty to both men.

Mallick, who is of Lebanese descent, faced serious prejudice in Fort Worth. He was a perpetual outsider. The ostracism of Jim Wright and his new wife by the upper crust of Fort Worth, and the intense resentment with which the Wrights (and Mallick) responded to that ostracism, helped make their bond with George Mallick so strong.

Wright's association with George Mallick eventually forced him to resign in disgrace. Most of the problems related to Mallick's role as business partner and employer of the Speaker's wife, but one of Mallick's critical problems involved S&Ls.

OCTOBER 21, 1986: THE RIDGLEA MEETING AND ITS FALLOUT

After Wright successfully extorted Gray on behalf of Craig Hall, he asked Mallick to set up a meeting with Texas critics of the Bank Board. Barry (1989, 219) describes the result.

> They expected a lunch with ten or fifteen people. [On October 21, 1986,] one hundred and fifty thrift executives and builders showed up at the Ridgelea [*sic*] Country Club in Fort Worth.
>
> After the meeting, Herman Smith, former president of the National Association of Homebuilders, warned Wright's [best] friend Craig Raupe, "I looked around and saw some good, reliable businessmen. I also saw some crooks." But Raupe did not give Wright that message.[6]

One can understand why such a meeting would have convinced Wright of Gray and Selby's perfidy. First, since so many people attended a meeting that he had expected to be small, they must have felt that the Bank Board's actions were an important matter. They reinforced this point by saying that Selby and Gray would put most of them out of business if Congress passed the FSLIC recap. They all said the same thing: everyone who spoke told a horror story about the regulators, and most of them used the "nazi" comparison. Surely they couldn't all be lying. In addition, many of those who spoke up were substantial contributors to the Democratic Party and claimed that the Bank Board was targeting them because they were contributors.

Wright had no reason to believe the Bank Board. His intervention on behalf of Hall had convinced him that fools ran the Bank Board and that by getting involved he had prevented harm not simply to his constituents but to the FSLIC as well. Soon after Ridglea, Wright received information that led him to have a far more negative view of the Bank Board. The information seemed to confirm charges that the Bank Board was a bunch of nazis who were out to get Democrats.

> Federal investigators were offering to go easy on criminals if they could supply damaging information about anyone on a list with the names of four hundred Texas businessmen. Most were involved in the thrift industry, and many were Democratic contributors. . . . That could not be a legitimate criminal investigation; it had to be a fishing expedition. In fact, it had to be a witch hunt. Legitimate investigations first found a crime; then they looked for criminals. This investigation seemed to be starting with a list of people, trying to attach a crime to them. It was an outrageous abuse of power. (Barry 1989, 220)

Barry became so close to Wright that it is often not clear from the text which of these conclusions, e.g., "It was an outrageous abuse of power," are Wright's and which are Barry's. In late 1986 Wright could have understandably believed the claims of prosecutorial abuse because he received all of his information from the control frauds and their allies. Such beliefs were nonsensical in 1989, when Barry completed his book.

Note the first sentence: "[prosecutors] were offering to *go easy* on *criminals* if they could supply damaging information about . . . Texas *businessmen*" (emphasis added). No, the prosecutors were offering *criminal Texas businessmen* reduced sentences if they had information that would help convict *other criminal Texas businessmen*. That's how prosecutions of big cases work. The prosecutors were investigating dozens of criminal referrals prepared by the FHLB-Dallas identifying S&L control frauds. Those referrals identified the key participants in the daisy chain (as well as other frauds), and there were well over 400 participants. It was the frauds that were outrageous; the effort to stop their crimes and convict the guilty was praiseworthy. The Dallas Fraud Task Force produced well over 400 criminal convictions arising from the Texas control frauds. It remains the most successful white-collar prosecution effort in world history.

If you start with Wright's proposition that the regulators were acting like nazis, it is no stretch to assume that they were targeting Democratic contributors. In fact, it makes the nazi story less looney. Still, there were five obvious problems with the nazi theory even in 1986. First, remember that Taggart made precisely the opposite claim in 1986. Taggart told Don Regan that Gray was targeting Republican contributors. Don Regan was trying to drive Gray from office because he felt that Gray was not acting like a good Reagan Republican. Gray was the least likely person in the Reagan administration to be leading a partisan attack on Democrats.

Second, the staffer taking the lead in reregulation, pushing the decision that the FSLIC receivers should sell their Texas properties and supporting the change to far more vigorous supervision, was a Democrat who had never voted for a Republican. It was unlikely that I would lead a partisan attack on Democratic contributors.

Third, why would the Bank Board want to act like nazis? Closing S&Ls, particularly control frauds, is unpleasant work for regulators. They sue you for scores of millions of dollars in your individual capacity; they hire private investigators to try to find dirt on you; and they threaten you. Regulators are not famously masochistic; what was in it for us to act like nazis?

Fourth, for much of its history the Bank Board was notorious for being a shill for the industry. What elixir had transformed us from shills into nazis? The S&L industry was famous for its support for the Democratic Party and the strength of its trade association. Any Bank Board chairman who attempted to use the agency to punish Democrats would be walking into a buzz saw of his own creation.

Fifth, in 1986 the Bank Board was notable for how few Texas S&Ls it had closed. It was no fluke that Westwood Savings, a California S&L, was the only one of the thirty S&Ls that had made substantial loans to Craig Hall that had been taken over by the Bank Board in 1986. A disproportionate number of California S&Ls had been closed; and Gray was a Californian. Further, as Taggart stressed, the Bank Board closed many California control frauds run by Republicans. Barry (1989, 217) asserts that California S&Ls "pummeled" federal legislators for forbearance in 1986 because of sharp falls in California property values. In fact, California real estate values surged in 1986 and for several years afterwards.[7]

Representative Charles Pashayan (Republican) was the only legislator from California whom I recall "pummel[ing]" the Bank Board in 1986. He complained bitterly about the closure of North America Savings, a California control fraud. Pashayan was also a close ally of Keating. On July 31, 1986, Keating sent a letter to then-congressman John McCain calling Gray a "Mad Dog" and warning that the Republicans would lose control of the Senate because of his regulatory and enforcement actions (U.S. Senate Committee 1990–1991a, 1:593). The enclosure that was supposed to prove Gray's madness was a stringent cease and desist order preventing further fraud at North America Savings. The control frauds supported one another. Keating's letter was a follow-up to a July 1, 1986, letter to McCain in which he described the Bank Board as "Nazi" and made the same prediction that Gray's reregulation would cost Republicans control of the Senate.

Pashayan was part of a group of sixteen Republican congressmen (including Dick Cheney, Newt Gingrich, and Robert Dornan) who pressured the Bank Board to give Keating privileged Bank Board information in order to help him block the direct-investment rule (Mayer 1990, 238–239; Williamson 1990). The FHLBSF ignored his complaints and led the way in closing the control frauds. Pashayan was a member of the House Ethics Committee that investigated Speaker Wright. He detested Gray. (He even took me aside privately after I testified in the House ethics investigation of Wright to tell me how "vindictive" Gray was. He could not, however, provide any examples.) Barry (1989, 702) quotes with approval Pashayan's personal distaste for Gray. Barry does not explain why Gray's decision to close a notorious California control fraud in the face of threatened political retaliation by a fellow Republican should be viewed as anything other than praiseworthy.

But, if one simply accepted the premise that Gray was a raging Republican out to destroy Democratic contributors, it could explain why the agency staffers acted like nazis. Nixon had an "enemies list" and used government agencies like the IRS to attack Democrats (he justified this criminal conduct by claiming that Democratic predecessors had engaged in similar abuses.) If the regulators were abusive enough to act like nazis (which Wright assumed to be true), then it was a small step to assume that they would be selective in that abuse and target their political opponents.

Wright did not have to ignore the Republicans' hatred of the heretic Gray and their claims that he was shutting down Republican contributors, because he never learned of those facts. No one was there to point out inconvenient facts to him. Wright's (and Barry's) reaction to the 400 names on the subpoena shows how easily he assumed that damning "evidence" was true. "Many" of them were Democrats. And many were Republicans. And some were independents.

Most revealingly, many of the people on the list contributed to both parties. Indeed, real estate developers are infamous as political contributors. Many of them strike it big by getting a zoning change from the local commission or obtaining a license to develop a facility from a state agency. Real estate developers commonly donate to both parties.

In early 1987, Texas S&L insiders held a Republican fund-raiser at which Treasury Secretary Baker was the featured speaker. Baker sat next to Don Dixon of Vernon Savings. Dixon had also contributed to the DCCC. In 1987 he was the worst known control fraud in the nation; he was on the prosecutors' list of 400 names. When Wright saw his name on that list he thought "Democratic contributor." Similarly, Craig Hall contributed to the Republicans and the DCCC (O'Shea 1991, 227). Wright never considered that control frauds have compelling incentives to make contributions to powerful politicians of either party who might intervene on their behalf.

Barry told me about Wright's reaction to the subpoena with the 400 names. Wright promptly called a meeting of top House supporters. They were tasked with immediately making a series of phone calls and reporting back to the Speaker. Representative Robert Eckhardt (Texas), for example, phoned FBI director William H. "Judge" Webster to find out who had authorized the subpoena and to convey Wright's severe displeasure with the investigation. Representative Douglas Barnard (Georgia) was assigned to call the Bank Board. Dick Peterson, his top aide, called. Dick was extremely nervous about making the call. He was supposed to find out whether we had any role in creating the list of names. Curtis Prins, aide to Representative Frank Annunzio (Illinois), also called us, and threatened that if the Speaker discovered that the Bank Board had had anything to do with generating the list, there would be retribution. Even Barry was alarmed. He told me that his immediate thought was that "Somebody better protect the Speaker of the House on this *because I like the guy*" (emphasis added). I was so startled by Barry's tale that I grabbed a pad of paper and wrote that sentence down. Barry's concern was that the Speaker needed to be protected against obstruction-of-justice charges. Prins's attempt to intimidate the Bank Board from assisting the Justice Department's investigation of the Texas control frauds could have been construed as obstruction of justice.

Barry concluded that the Ridglea meeting had convinced Wright that the Bank Board, particularly Gray and Selby, were out-of-control nazis who were prevented from arbitrarily shutting down scores of Texas S&Ls solely by the FSLIC's lack of cash. Two things, therefore, became essential. The FSLIC recap had to be blocked, and forbearance provisions had to be added to the bill to curtail drastically the Bank Board's power to supervise and close S&Ls (Barry 1989, 219–220).

WRIGHT APPOINTS MALLICK HIS PRIVATE INSPECTOR GENERAL

Wright then involved Mallick in an even more formal manner by appointing him his agent to investigate the Texas S&L situation.

> Wright had asked Mallick to look into the savings and loan thing for him, had given him that letter of introduction in effect identifying Mallick as his agent. Mallick's extensive real estate holdings gave him at least the appearance of a conflict of interest, but that appearance did not deter Wright.
>
> "That letter was a sop to Mallick's ego," another man close to Wright said. "He waved that letter all over the Southwest and in New York. It caused some problems with Bob Strauss." (Barry 1989, 233)

The Mallick family had a real conflict of interest, not simply an apparent one. At the time of George Mallick's investigation on behalf of the Speaker, they were not-very-creditworthy borrowers from Texas S&Ls and banks. Mallick's son Michael was soon to default on a $1 million loan (cosigned, i.e., guaranteed, by George), and the S&L involved, Interwest Savings, was about to fail (U.S. House Conduct Committee 1989, 183). One of the things George Mallick proposed in his written report to Wright was a moratorium on foreclosures by S&Ls (ibid., 184). This would have been of immense direct personal benefit to the Mallicks.

The fact that Wright's letter upset Bob Strauss was important. It set in motion two unsuccessful efforts to convince the Speaker that the control frauds were using him and that his actions would harm him, the Democratic Party, and the nation. The fact that Wright took his guidance from Mallick rather than Bob Strauss, the grand old man of the Democratic Party, demonstrates how closely he bonded with Mallick.

It was of enormous value to the control frauds that Mallick served as their conduit to Wright. Mallick was many things to Jim and Betty Wright: their best friend, the financial partner who had saved them from humiliating ruin and returned them to security, her employer, and the provider of their dwelling and car. He was an expert on financial and real estate matters, the man the Wrights' trusted to handle their own investments (U.S. House Conduct Committee, 1989).

Mallick was the control frauds' ace in the hole. It was easy to recruit him. If the FSLIC recap bill became law, the Bank Board would appoint a receiver for the insolvent S&L that had made the large loan to his son. His son could not repay the loan, so the receiver would sue George, who had guaranteed it. He was facing imminent financial ruin. The Fort Worth elites who had always despised him would humiliate him if that happened. He would no longer be able to subsidize the Wrights, and they might find it politically embarrassing to associate with him if he were bankrupt. Mallick saw himself as an innocent victim. He and the control frauds had common interests. Wright got his advice on S&Ls exclusively from the control frauds and Mallick. It is no surprise that he believed that they were the victims, and Gray and Selby the villains.

THE FSLIC RECAP BILL FAILS IN 1986

The FSLIC recap was dead in 1986 after the Ridglea meeting. There was no way Wright would allow its passage. Things broke well for him. Unrelated technical matters also held up the recap: the partisan squabble over nonbank banks, the Congressional Budget Office's scoring of the Financing Corporation (FICO) bonds (the bonds to finance the FSLIC recap) for budgetary purposes under the Gramm-Rudman Act, and "exit" fees. (None of the arcane details behind this jargon are necessary to my tale.) The delays by Cranston, Pryor, and Wright meant there was no time to sort things out, particularly given the rush to recess during an election year. (The House began to sprout "Free the 99th Congress!" buttons as the session dragged.) The House and Senate could not go to a conference committee, reconcile the House and Senate bills, and vote out a final bill in the brief time remaining after Wright removed his hold on the bill. The FSLIC recap died with the end of the 1986 term; Wright did not need to block it again. Indeed, once it was clear that the bill would not even make it to a conference committee, he was clever enough to vote for it in the House. The Bank Board's highest priority in 1987 would be passage of the reintroduced bill.

WRIGHT'S SERIES OF INTERVENTIONS
IN LATE 1986 AND EARLY 1987

Predictably, after Wright's willingness to extort Gray, and his success in doing so, "S&L executives all over Texas flooded his office with complaints" (Barry 1989, 219). This helped lead to the Ridglea meeting and, equally predictably, that meeting led to still more complaints. Wright believed that the frequency, vigor, and uniformity of the new complaints demonstrated the validity of the charges. He also believed that the case of Craig Hall proved that the complaints were well founded and that his intervention had helped everyone concerned. This emboldened Wright to intervene repeatedly on behalf of some of the worst control frauds in the nation in late 1986 and early 1987.

There were a series of meetings and phone calls between Wright and Gray involving several different control frauds. I will limit my discussion to the three efforts that proved decisive for the FSLIC recap and Wright's career. The other matters fit the same pattern: Wright pushed and Gray caved.

THOMAS GAUBERT OF INDEPENDENT AMERICAN SAVINGS

I have explained how Gaubert became a close ally of Wright and Coelho. Gaubert was active behind the scenes in the Hall matter. Congressional contacts told Gray that the one thing he had to do before meeting with Wright about Hall was to find out everything he could about Gaubert (U.S. House Conduct Committee, 1989).

The Speaker pressured Gray to release Gaubert from the removal-and-prohibition agreement he had consented to, which would allow him to resume control of Independent Savings. The goal was to put one of the worst control frauds in the nation back in charge of an S&L that he had looted and made massively insolvent. Gray knew he couldn't agree to that. He sought an opportunity to explain to Wright why this was a terrible idea. Wright refused to be briefed (U.S. House Conduct Committee 1989, 245). Gray decided instead to arrange an independent review that would convince Wright that the Bank Board had acted properly. This occurred over Rosemary Stewart's and my vigorous objections. She objected to any investigation of her office, and I continued to argue that giving in to Wright's extortion would encourage greater extortion. Gray held off appointing a receiver for Independent American because of Wright's intervention (ibid., 248–249).

From a list of lawyers proposed by Gaubert's lawyers, we chose Aubrey Harwell to conduct the independent investigation. Harwell concluded that Gaubert was a criminal who had defrauded and looted the S&Ls he controlled. (He told me this in person.) His secondary conclusion was that our Office of Enforcement (OE) had not acted vigorously enough in its investigation of Gaubert and had missed areas of culpability (U.S. House Conduct Committee 1989, 250). He was critical of the Bank Board for two reasons. He thought it had been insane of the Bank Board to approve Gaubert's earlier acquisition of troubled S&Ls. Amen to that! He also thought that the OE should have told Gaubert that it was contemplating making criminal referrals about him. Harwell was wrong about that. Criminal referrals are highly confidential, and the Justice Department advises agencies not to reveal such matters to suspects. Otherwise, incriminating documents disappear.

Harwell's report is a detailed indictment of Gaubert's looting and a rejection of his claims of Bank Board perfidy (U.S. House Conduct Committee 1989, 250; Mayer 1990, 237; Jackson 1988, 279). Wright, however, continued to intervene on Gaubert's behalf even after the Bank Board gave him Harwell's report.

Martin Mayer (1990, 236) was livid about Barry's mischaracterization of the Harwell report:

> One notes that in his astonishing whitewash of Jim Wright, John M. Barry deals with the Gaubert matter in half a paragraph.

Mayer is slightly off on quantity, but Barry does not provide the reader with any of the uncontested facts about what Gaubert did wrong at an Iowa S&L.

Brooks Jackson's *Honest Graft* summarizes the findings of the Harwell report (1988, 267–269). I can provide the essence of the story in a paragraph. Gaubert purchased some real estate. Three months later he provided an appraisal report claiming that the property was worth eighteen times what he had paid for it. He approached Capitol Savings, an insolvent Iowa S&L. He had the S&L lend money to entities he controlled in order to have them to buy the real estate from him at this absurdly inflated value. He did not inform the S&L's board of directors that he controlled the entities. The entities he controlled defaulted on their enormous debts. Roughly ten days after the loans closed, Gaubert "loaned" the Capitol Savings officer who approved the deal $150,000. But the "borrower" did not sign a note ("IOU") and, as far as anyone could tell, never repaid any part of the loan.

A jury acquitted Gaubert even though the trial established these facts. That is a testament to the difficulty of securing a white-collar conviction for a complicated financial fraud. The obvious question, which Barry never asks, is why Wright continued to intervene on Gaubert's behalf after learning these facts. Whether or not a jury considered them criminal, they were certainly dishonest and dishonorable. Why would Wright continue to consort with Gaubert after he knew the man's character? Why would he intervene to try to return him to control of an S&L with billions of dollars of assets insured by the FSLIC?

The Justice Department eventually convicted Gaubert of other felonies. Despite these convictions, Wright defended him in his 1993 presentation to the National Commission on Financial Institution Reform, Recovery and Enforcement. He claimed that the government had a vendetta against Gaubert (NCFIRRE 1993d, 16–19).

DON DIXON OF "VERMIN" SAVINGS

At the time Wright intervened on behalf of Don Dixon, the Bank Board believed that he ran the worst control fraud in the nation, Vernon Savings, known to its regulators as "Vermin." This was the S&L, described in Chapter 2, that provided prostitutes to Texas S&L commissioner Bowman. Eventually, Charles Keating of Lincoln Savings managed to nip him at the wire for the not-so-coveted title of worst of the control frauds.

Dixon personified greed, immorality, incompetence, and audacity. Vernon is also the S&L, as I discussed in my explanation of ADC Ponzis, that made ADC loans with a six-month maturity so that it could maximize income from refinancing. This goosed Vernon's income stream so mightily that it reported itself to be the most profitable S&L in America. Its (fictitious) earnings were twice the (fictitious) earnings of the second-most profitable S&L (O'Shea 1991, 124). I noted that 96 percent of its ADC loans defaulted. Lest you think it was a victim of the Texas real estate recession, more than 90 percent of the ADC loans it made outside Texas also defaulted. Vernon was an important contributor to the Texas real-estate glut.

Recall that Dixon got control of Vernon Savings without putting up a penny of his own money. The felon Herman K. Beebe and the prior owner of Vernon Savings, who was conned by Dixon, funded the entire purchase.

Dixon did not limit his pimping to Bowman. He inherited a conservative board of elderly directors, many of them leaders in their very strict Baptist church. Not a problem! One of his first acts after the acquisition was to invite the board of directors along on an overnight trip. He tactfully told the female member of the board she wouldn't be comfortable on the boys' night out. Dixon flew the board members to California on a private jet with an open bar, took them and eight prostitutes on a romantic cruise in a very spiffy sailboat to an equally romantic island restaurant off San Diego, and brought them back to a fabulous beach house (O'Shea 1991, 68–70). He never had to worry about the board exercising any independent judgment after this soiree.

Vernon is a very small town (population 12,500) in northwest Texas, near the Oklahoma border. God did not bless Vernon with either great natural beauty or a temperate clime. Dixon had grown up in Vernon, but had then moved and seen other parts of the United States. He liked the beach, so he had Vernon Savings buy spectacular, multimillion-dollar homes on the beach in Southern California, and then spend tens of thousands of dollars keeping the homes in fresh flowers. One does not live a full life by beach alone, so Dixon also had Vernon buy a chalet, near former President Ford, at one of the nation's top ski resorts in Colorado. Naturally, one wishes to be able to enjoy such amenities without plebeian concerns such as baggage screening, restrictive flight schedules, or possibly having to sit next to a screaming child. Thus was born Vernon's air force. Once one has a fleet of private jets, one discovers that they have little to do most of the time. The answer is to provide them, often (illegally) without charge, to politicians. Wright was one of those who flew Air Vermin.

But what's an air force without a navy? Vernon is very far from any real body of water. Dixon made up for this drawback by having Vernon buy the sister ship of the presidential yacht, *The Sequoia.* (Dixon named the yacht, aptly, the *High Spirits.*) It couldn't be berthed anywhere near Vernon, Texas, so it was docked in the Potomac River near Washington, D.C. It served as a floating lobbying platform. Yes, the prostitutes showed up here as well. The DCCC held many fundraisers on the yacht without paying any of the costs. This was illegal, and the DCCC, to its humiliation, later had to pay tens of thousands of dollars to Vernon's receiver. Wright met Dixon at one of these shipboard parties (U.S. House Conduct Committee 1989, 264). The Republicans had their own parties on the yacht.

Once Dixon had sampled that which was sweetest in America, he began to dream of Europe. He made two grand forays. He wasn't Catholic, but he wanted to be part of high society, so he arranged a private audience with the pope. He befriended Bishop Maher of San Diego by becoming the largest donor to the (Catholic) University of San Diego (U.S. House Conduct Committee 1989, 150). The school put him on its board. Unfortunately, the donation was in the form of stock in Vernon's holding company, which was soon to become worthless (but which provided Dixon with a valuable tax deduction). Dixon also provided Maher and an aide with a fantastic all-expense-paid trip to Europe. They flew over on Vernon's air force. The bishop arranged the private audience with the pope. Vernon Savings donated an expensive painting to the pope, an Olaf Wieghorst original (ibid., 157). Vernon paid for everything.

Dixon arranged an even grander tour of Europe. He had Philippe Junot, Princess Caroline's former husband, on Vernon's payroll at huge expense for no real work. Philippe arranged a two-week tour of multiple-star restaurants in France. Dixon took friends along; one of them kept a diary of the tour, which she entitled *Gastronomique Fantastique!* (U.S. House Conduct Committee 1989, 63–66). Vernon, which is to say the taxpayers, paid for everything.

Vernon was in deep trouble with both the Bank Board and state regulators well before Wright began to intervene on Dixon's behalf. By September 1986, Texas had placed Vernon under state supervisory control (U.S. House Conduct Committee 1989, 261). Vernon consented to the appointment of the state supervisor. Note that Bowman was still commissioner and that he approved this action despite the obvious risk that Dixon would reveal that he had provided Bowman with prostitutes. Bowman was a complicated individual who often tried to do the right thing.

In December 1986, Dixon contacted Coelho, who referred the request to Wright. Dixon told Wright that the Bank Board was about to take over "his" S&L. He said that he needed only one additional day to complete a sale of the S&L that would allow him to save "his" investment. Wright called Gray to get his assurance that the Bank Board would not close Vernon Savings that week. Gray knew that there was no takeover planned because only the Bank Board members could approve a takeover, and they had not even scheduled one for Vernon. He explained this to Wright and said he would call the president of the FHLB-Dallas, Roy Green, and see if some other action was about to be taken. Gray called Green and found out that the FHLB-Dallas was about to present a "consent to merger" resolution to Vernon Savings' board of directors.

Gray and Green then tried to call Wright back to explain what the Bank Board planned. Wright had left the office, so Gray and Green asked to talk to his staff. Wright's staff, however, was moving from the Majority Leader's offices to the Speaker's offices that day, which caused a great deal of disruption. Gray and Green waited on hold for two hours to explain the matter. Wright's principal aide, John Mack, was then able to take their call. They explained, and thought all was well. Soon, however, Mack called Gray back. He was very angry and said that someone he did not identify (doubtless Dixon) informed him that a "consent to merger" resolution was equivalent to a takeover. Gray explained why this was not so, but Mack did not seem mollified (U.S. House Conduct Committee 1989, 264–267).

WRIGHT'S EFFORT TO GET JOE SELBY FIRED

The single most disgusting action Wright took was to try to force Gray to fire Joe Selby as the lead supervisor for the Dallas district. Wright denied that he did so. I will explain why I do not believe his denial is credible. Wright was not the only politician to try to get Selby fired. Danny Wall, then Senator Garn's top aide and soon to be Gray's successor, told Gray he should get rid of Selby. Wall found a way to force Selby out once he became Bank Board chairman.

According to Gray's testimony, Wright told him that

> Selby had established a ring of homosexual lawyers in Texas . . . and in order for people to deal with Federal Home Loan Bank [of Dallas] supervision people, they would have to deal with this ring of homosexual lawyers. . . .
>   [H]e said to me, "Isn't there anything you can do to get rid of Selby or ask him to leave or something." (U.S. House Conduct Committee 1989, 256–257)

Wright denied that he had ever mentioned his belief that Selby was a homosexual or that he had asked Gray to get rid of him. But the Speaker did just what Gray testified he did. Gray was apoplectic about it and told at least three of his senior aides immediately, including me. The story is so insane that no one could have made it up. (Moreover, Gray is a fundamentally honest person.) Barry (1989, 220) confirms Gray's testimony by providing the details of the rumors the Speaker heard and believed. In conversation with me, Barry tried to justify the Speaker's effort to get Selby fired. He premised his (rather inept and offensive) defense on the Speaker's belief that the rumors were true.

> Wright heard other, even more outrageous rumors. Texas S&L executives were saying that Selby, the regulator, was at the center of a ring of

sadistic homosexuals who liked to see men squirm. Thrift executives spoke of him with real hatred. After he forced owners of one thrift to sign over control, he reportedly laughed in their faces and said, "Now you can call Jim Wright." A seventy-year-old director, who had founded the thrift originally, replied, "Fuck you, you goddamn queer".

John Neibel, dean of the University of Houston Law Center, supposedly suggested firing him. There were even rumors that Selby was refusing to deal with thrift executives unless they hired homosexual lawyers, who were giving themselves immediate six-figure bonuses. They were bizarre, outrageous charges. They couldn't be true. Could they?

Wright called Gray and relayed some complaints about Selby. (Barry 1989, 220)

Barry confirmed to me that Wright did believe these rumors. The last bizarre, outrageous charge is the one Gray told us about immediately after talking to Wright. None of us, including Gray, had ever heard this smear before. Gray heard it from Wright. That means the Speaker's denial that he mentioned to Gray his belief that Selby was a homosexual was false. The rumors are in fact bizarre and outrageous. Nevertheless, Wright believed them. Barry's account cleared up a minor mystery. I could never figure out why Wright used the word "sadistic" to describe FHLB-Dallas supervision. That word seemed over the top even for Wright. Plainly, he believed the homophobic smear that gays are literally sadistic and get aroused by making straight men squirm. Only severe antipathy can explain this willingness to believe absurd smears: we believe the worst about those we hate. There are two evident sources of that personal malice. The most obvious source is virulent homophobia. Wright also believed that Selby was a nazi. These factors were mutually reinforcing.

There is every reason to believe that Gray was also telling the truth when he testified that Wright went on to request that he fire Selby. Wright was not shy about using his clout to try to get officials fired. He and his aides asked Danny Wall and his aides several times to fire me.

Gray refused to fire Selby. This was the first time he said no to Wright. Gray had personally recruited Selby. Selby was the top financial regulator in America. The control frauds were determined to get Selby fired because he was so competent. Selby and Gray were the two people doing the most to protect Texans from injury. The control frauds were steadily deepening the glut of Texas residential and commercial real estate and forcing Texas into an ever-deeper real estate recession. Scores of thousands of Texans were losing their houses as home prices plummeted. It was essential that the Bank Board bring the control frauds under control as soon as possible and replace their managers with honest people. Wright was again trying to force Gray to take actions that would harm Wright's constituents in order to aid DCCC contributors. Sadly, Wall did deliver Selby's head on a pike to Wright, which seriously increased losses in Texas.

Barry's effort to defend Wright's effort to get Selby fired and Barry's uncritical dissemination of rumors are illustrative of his book about Wright. I particularly like the innuendo that gays are naturally sadistic and like to make (straight) men squirm. Barry could, and should, have answered his own question:

> They were bizarre, outrageous charges. They couldn't be true. Could they?

All it would have taken was one word: "no." None of it was true (U.S. House Conduct Committee 1989, 257). But because the Speaker believed vicious, baseless smears spread by the control frauds, the nation lost its most valuable field supervisor at precisely the moment he was most vital. Texans, and all U.S. taxpayers, suffered billions of dollars of losses because Wright and Wall forced Selby from office.

6. "THE FAUSTIAN BARGAIN" 1987: FSLIC RECAP AND THE BEGINNING OF THE END FOR SPEAKER WRIGHT

RENEWING THE HOLD ON THE FSLIC RECAP

> The House Banking Committee leadership . . . promised the Administration and the Bank Board that FSLIC recapitalization would receive top priority in the new [100th] Congress. On January 6, 1987 [chairman St Germain and ranking minority member Wylie] reintroduced the recapitalizaton bill in substantially the form proposed by the Administration in the previous Congress. The goal was to bring the bill to the floor by March. (U.S. House Conduct Committee 1989, 209)

When a bill has bipartisan support and the industry affected by the bill is in crisis and the committee chair, ranking minority member, and administration all support the bill, it usually moves fast. The FSLIC recap, however, was DOA (dead on arrival) in January 1987. First, the newly elected Speaker of the House, Jim Wright, was determined to hold the bill hostage until he received Gray's unconditional surrender. Second, the S&L League had now decided that blocking the bill and then perverting it into a measure that would gut the Bank Board's supervisory powers was its sole priority.

THE LEAGUE'S FAUSTIAN BARGAIN

I have represented trade associations. All trade associations face the question of how to maintain solidarity. Although the league's solidarity made it a far more effective lobbying force than the fractious and divided banking industry, its solidarity came at a severe cost in 1987. The league faced its worst dilemma: appease the control frauds and alienate the honest owners, or vice versa. Roughly 5 percent of the industry was still in the hands of control frauds; roughly 30 percent of the industry was insolvent. Texas, Arkansas, Arizona, and Louisiana were suffering from severe real estate recessions that were being aggravated by the control frauds' lending in the teeth of the glut. It was greatly in the interests of the honest S&Ls that the Bank Board close the control frauds as quickly as possible.

A split potentially so divisive can fracture a trade association; a trade association that seeks to optimize solidarity has to adopt positions acceptable to the lowest common denominator among its membership. (This was ironic; the league constantly, albeit inaccurately, criticized Gray for regulating to the lowest common denominator.) When your membership includes scores of control frauds, that denominator is set at an unseemly level.

One of the things that made it easier for the league to achieve consensus was that the blocs within the industry had different priorities. This meant that one bloc could help the other get what it primarily wanted in return for support in obtaining its own priority. The league had a creative insight. The recap bill as proposed by the Bank Board and the administration had only one dimension: how much money the FSLIC would raise. The league recast the bill and added a second dimension: how much money and what kind of forbearance. The healthier S&Ls' priority was to reduce the amount of money they would have to pay. Forbearance was the highest priority of all insolvent or nearly insolvent S&Ls. Forbearance had a second advantage. The league claimed that it was the silver bullet that could painlessly restore solvency to the S&Ls and the FSLIC. Time heals all wounds.

Indeed, the only rift that opened among the league's members is that Texas S&Ls sometimes told us at the Bank Board (in private) that they would be happy to support a $15 billion FSLIC recap as long as the money was used to subsidize Texas S&Ls and the existing managers were left in place. Texas S&Ls wanted to have the rest of the nation subsidize them. Speaker Wright and Treasury Secretary Baker, two prominent Texans, supported this grand design.

The league was willing to hold its nose and ally itself with the control frauds because the full $15 billion FSLIC recap bill had come so close to passing in 1986. The bill would have become law but for Charles Keating, Craig Hall, Thomas Gaubert, Don Dixon, and their political allies (Senator Alan Cranston and Jim Wright). The league and the control frauds could rout the opposition if they combined their political power. The CEO of one of the best S&Ls in the country described the deal to me as "a Faustian bargain" (i.e., a deal with the devil).

SLAMMING ON THE BRAKES TO BLOCK THE FSLIC RECAP

On January 21 and 22, 1987, a House banking subcommittee held hearings on the FSLIC recap. The industry announced its opposition to any material recapitalization of the FSLIC and its support for forbearance. The other shoe soon dropped. Speaker Wright signaled his support for the leader of the Texas control frauds, Tom Gaubert, and the most notorious control fraud in the nation, Don Dixon. Wright used Representative Douglas Barnard as his surrogate.

After their testimony, league officials met the Speaker for lunch. Walter W. "Bo" McAllister III, director of the Texas Savings and Loan League, asked the Speaker to put a hold on the FSLIC recap until the administration added forbearance provisions acceptable to the Texas League to the bill. O'Shea (1991, 236) reports:

> McAllister later wrote in the Texas League's magazine, "We encouraged him to take this action and that is exactly what happened."

That same group of league officials met with Gray at the Bank Board to promote both forbearance and greatly reduced funding for the FSLIC. I was there. Gray had appointed me point man for the FSLIC recap about a week before this meeting. (Gray had appointed me deputy director of the FSLIC because the Hill responds well to titles and poorly to lawyers.) I've never forgotten two comments that league representatives made. The executive director, Bill O'Connell, responded to my statements about the depth of the crisis the FSLIC faced and the additional losses that the requested forbearance would cause with the kindly look one gives to an overenthusiastic youth. He assured me that he had heard the same warnings many times during his career, and it had always turned out that the agency grossly exaggerated the crisis. I asked Bo which Texas S&Ls the Bank Board had closed improperly. He said there weren't any—so much for the "nazi" theory. In one of those small-world events, Bo's San Antonio Savings Association (SASA) ended up managing Vernon after the Bank Board finally took it over. The SASA officials involved were appalled at the extent of the control fraud and could not understand how the regulators had failed to shut it down far earlier.

DUAL DUETS: GAUBERT AND DIXON, WRIGHT AND BARNARD

On the second day of the hearings, January 22, 1987, a very unusual act occurred at an open hearing of the House Banking Committee. Representative Barnard asked Gray about the Bank Board's treatment of two still-open Texas S&Ls—Tom Gaubert's Independent American and Don Dixon's Vernon Savings (U.S. House Conduct Committee 1989, 251). This had never happened in my experience. Publicly releasing confidential information about insolvent and fraudulent S&Ls could spark a run. Members of Congress feared that the media would blame them were a run to occur after they forced public disclosures; as a result, they do not ask such questions. Barnard asked the questions because Wright's staff requested it (U.S. House Conduct Committee 1989, 251–252). (Barry emphasizes throughout his book that Wright's staff never freelanced.) Tom Gaubert had drafted the question.

The reason Wright and Gaubert directed Barnard to ask Gray about both S&Ls was to add to the pressure on Gray and to signal the Speaker's continuing unhappiness with Gray's failure to do more for Gaubert and Dixon.

Gaubert later sued Gray and me for hundreds of millions of dollars in our individual capacities on the grounds that we had answered the questions that *Gaubert* had caused Barnard to ask us. Remember the old joke about the definition of "chutzpah"? A son kills his mom and dad and begs mercy from the judge because he's an orphan. Gaubert's actions provided an equally illustrative definition of the word.

Barnard's doing the bidding of Gaubert mystified us. He was from the banking industry and had been a banking regulator. He was the last person in the world you would expect to ask such a question in open session. It was obvious that he was asking the question at the behest of one or both of the control frauds that Speaker Wright had gone to bat for. Gray immediately arranged a luncheon meeting with Barnard and his principal aide, Dick Peterson, for the next day. Gray, Mary Ellen Taylor (his top legislative aide, who was a former colleague of Peterson's and friend of both Peterson's and Barnard's), and I attended. My staff prepared short memoranda on Vernon Savings and Independent American.

I first became aware of the existence and role of the George Mallick at this meeting. Barnard was so worried that he spoke openly of his fears. This was quite unusual because he was speaking largely of his fears for his party (the Democrats), and Gray and Taylor were both Republicans. He told us that he had asked the questions at the request of Wright's staff. He explained how concerned he was that unscrupulous people were using Wright in ways that would destroy his reputation and harm the party. He told us that Bob Strauss shared his concern.

Barnard was also concerned for the House. Barnard had a great deal of seniority and chaired important committees; he knew how to run congressional investigations. He thought it was terrible for Congress that Wright had given Mallick a letter on the Speaker's stationery saying that Mallick was acting on the Speaker's behalf in investigating the S&L crisis. Barnard was hearing that Mallick was running all over the place flaunting the letter as a demonstration of his importance, power, and close ties to the Speaker. Barnard believed that Mallick was one of the people using the Speaker and perhaps involving him in scandal.

As a Democrat, I saw the same danger that Barnard did. The Democratic Party's best issue in the upcoming election was "the sleaze factor." A number of President Reagan's top aides had gotten into hot water for alleged ethics violations. The obvious way for the Republican Party to neutralize the issue was to publicize Wright's extortion of Gray on behalf of Texas control frauds. Gray explained in some detail each of Wright's acts on behalf of the control frauds. Barnard and his aide grew morose.

That's when I began my discussion of the facts about Vernon Savings and Independent American. As I got going, Barnard and his aide blanched. They had feared that the two S&Ls would prove unsavory, but I was explaining that they were outright criminal and that Vernon was the worst S&L in the country. They had come to the meeting with ample fears; they left it realizing that the true horror exceeded their ability to imagine.

I briefed them from two- and three-page memoranda on Independent American and Vernon. My staff, Ruth Amberg and Mike Solomon, had scrambled to prepare them overnight immediately after we returned from the hearing. Barnard requested copies of the memoranda before our restaurant meeting broke up, saying he wanted to warn the Speaker immediately. I gave them the copies I used in briefing them. Barnard said he would use them to warn the Speaker of the need to cut all ties with Thomas Gaubert and Don Dixon and to point out how Mallick was involving him in a potential scandal. We sent much more extensive memoranda to Barnard on February 27 detailing the nature of both control frauds. Those memoranda were the formal answer to Barnard's request for a response at the open hearing.

INVESTIGATING THE BANK BOARD
INSTEAD OF THE CONTROL FRAUDS

Wright relentlessly kept up the pressure on the House Banking Committee in favor of the control frauds. He would not simply hold the FSLIC recap hostage; he would try to embarrass the Bank Board.

On January 29, Wright held a luncheon with Fernand St Germain and several other congressmen to discuss complaints about the Bank Board. According to St Germain, the Texas delegation complained of the Bank Board's "high-handedness." As a result of the luncheon, St Germain agreed to hold subcommittee hearings regarding the allegations (U.S. House Conduct Committee 1989, 210).

The control frauds were well on their way to perverting the FSLIC recap bill, transmogrifying it from a means to help the FSLIC close more control frauds into a means of gutting the FSLIC's power to stop them. Congress would now investigate the regulators, not the control frauds, and it would do so at the behest of the control frauds.

THE REMORAS JOIN THE TEXAS FEEDING FRENZY

Remoras use suckers to attach themselves to large rays and sharks. When the big fish feed, the remoras feast, too. Senior Texas state officials, primarily Democrats, smelled blood in the water and joined the feeding frenzy. The party's successful candidate for governor, Mark White, and the attorney general, Jim Mattox, had long received large political contributions from the Texas control frauds. A ten-gallon hat was often passed around the room and came back stuffed with large bills (O'Shea 1991, 32–33). Mattox received a $200,000 gift that resulted from a fraudulent "land flip" by the man who led the pathbreaking Texas control fraud, Empire Savings in Mesquite, Texas (Mayer 1990, 239). Mattox announced in March 1987 that he was beginning a criminal investigation of the Bank Board. He also threatened to bring suit "to stop use of federal regulatory procedures that discriminated against the State's savings and loan associations" (ibid.; Day 1993, 245). Roughly a week after announcing that he would begin such an investigation, and

without the aid of any investigation, he announced that the Bank Board
was guilty.

THE SETTING OF THE FEBRUARY 10, 1987, PEACE MEETING

Though I did not realize it at the time, Bob Strauss set up the February 10, 1987, meeting at which the Bank Board sought to make peace
with the Speaker. Strauss feared that George Mallick and unscrupulous
S&L leaders were leading the Speaker into scandal and ruining one of
the party's best issues for the 1988 presidential elections.

We sent a fairly large delegation to try to make peace with the Speaker.
The president of the FHLB-Dallas, Roy Green, along with Joe Selby and
Walter Faulk, came up from Texas. Faulk was a well-respected supervisor
who looked and sounded like a "down home" Texan: weather-beaten,
tall, and laconic. As the point man on the FSLIC recap, I attended along
with Bill Robertson, the top headquarters supervisor. The purpose of
the meeting was to convince the Speaker to stop blocking passage of the
FSLIC recap and to support a $15 billion plan without the forbearance
provisions designed to gut the Bank Board's supervisory powers.

We prepared carefully for the meeting. Faulk would take the lead and
our emphasis would be on the role of the high fliers in exacerbating the
Texas real-estate recession. He would show how Gaubert and Dixon
had looted Independent American and Vernon Savings. Selby would
take a backseat role; his presence was necessary to show that Gray and
Green backed him despite Wright's antipathy and that he was a top professional, not a nazi. Once Faulk had prepared the way, I would pitch
the need for the recap to help the honest Texas S&Ls whose deposit
costs were forced upwards by the control frauds. I would explain how
the control frauds exacerbated the real-estate glut and deepened the
real-estate recession. Bill Robertson would provide a national context,
explaining how control frauds in other states caused the same kind of
problems and how the Bank Board under Gray had shut down far more
S&Ls in California than in Texas.

Unfortunately, as the military saying goes, no plan ever survives contact with the enemy. The Speaker was not there to make peace. Despite our efforts to "backdoor" a warning to him—through Barnard
and Strauss—to stop aiding the Mallicks, Gauberts, and Dixons of the
world, Wright thought of us as the enemy. We were carrying our truce
flag and walking dumb and blind into what the military calls a kill sack.

We knew we were in trouble as soon as we entered the Speaker's outer offices, for George and Michael Mallick were there, obviously to attend the meeting. This destroyed our plans. We could not discuss confidential information about particular S&Ls with private individuals in the room. There was no way we could convince the Speaker to kick George Mallick—his best friend, business partner, and employer of his wife—out of the meeting. Barry also attended the meeting, making our inability to discuss confidential information total.

The Speaker also had a large group of people at the meeting. In addition to the Mallicks, his top aide, John Mack, was there. Barry has rightly emphasized how Wright was the most intimidating politician in America. Mack added greatly to that terror. He was the Speaker's hard man. Mack was brutal even by the standards of someone who is supposed to play the heavy. He once tried to rape a woman, a stranger to him. She resisted, and he smashed repeatedly at her with a hammer, then "slashed her throat with a knife" (Barry 1989, 734).[1] Mack stuffed her in the trunk of a car, drove it around a while, and eventually fled on foot. Miraculously, she was able to get the attention of a passerby, and emergency care saved her life. Mack went to prison, and Wright helped get him released early by offering him a job. Wright did this because a daughter of his was then married to Mack's brother. Mack worked his way up Wright's staff to become his most powerful aide. The Godfather had Luca Brasi, Wright had Mack. No one wanted to cross Mack.

I made the mistake of being the last of our group to enter the Speaker's inner office for the meeting. The open seat that remained was, just as in elementary school, directly in front of the teacher's, er, Speaker's desk. Seated next to me was Bill Robertson. Roy Green, Joe Selby, and Walter Faulk sat to the Speaker's far right.

The fact that the Mallicks were there meant that our effort to convince the Speaker by backdooring information to him about Don Dixon and Tom Gaubert had failed. It also meant that Barnard and Strauss had failed, even with the benefit of our briefings, to convince the Speaker that George Mallick was leading him and the Democratic Party into scandal. If Strauss couldn't convince him to stop aiding the worst S&L, Vernon Savings, then there was no chance that we would succeed. Indeed, Wright was signaling the closeness of his ties to Mallick and that Strauss's concerns about Mallick would avail us not a bit. We knew our mission to make peace with the Speaker would probably fail.

What we did not know is that we would not simply fail to make peace, but that Wright had agreed to the meeting in order to attack Gray personally and to put more pressure on the Bank Board to aid the Texas control frauds. Our ignorance was understandable. From our perspective, we had already made outrageous concessions to Wright. We could not know that from his perspective only our unconditional surrender was acceptable. Moreover, we had no way of knowing that Wright was acting under a glaring factual error deliberately sown by Don Dixon and that he believed Gray had lied to him in a prior conversation.

BLESSED ARE THE PEACEMAKERS

Roy Green began the meeting for us, talking about the depths of the Texas S&L crisis. Wright moved this theme quite skillfully into a suggestion that forbearance was the only possible answer. Wright expressed the view that the Bank Board was closing Texas S&Ls "willy-nilly" (Barry 1989, 235).

Selby made an attempt to clear the air. Wright had stated that Texas S&L owners feared Selby. Selby told the Speaker, "We just want to show you we don't have horns." It was a friendly, joking remark by one Texan to another. Barry (1989, 235) gives the Speaker's reaction:

> Wright eyed him, wondering whether Selby's comment was unintended irony or a deliberate provocation.

Wright's reaction to Selby's comment was visibly hostile. Given that Selby had done nothing in the meeting to prompt any hostility, it was clear that Wright was hostile to Selby before he ever met him. We expected that hostility, given Wright's efforts to get him fired, but it was still disheartening that Wright wouldn't even give Joe a chance to make peace. It was obvious that Selby was engaging in intended irony. The control frauds were telling the Speaker that Selby was the devil incarnate; Selby came to speak directly to the Speaker and show that he was neither a demon nor a nazi.

The idea that we were meeting with the Speaker to provoke him was so bizarre that we did not understand until months later that the Speaker and his staff were laboring under this misconception. We were there to make peace, not war. We had no clue to the extent of Wright's paranoia. Why anyone would think that we would want to provoke the most powerful and vindictive member of Congress—who would surely respond by blocking our desperately needed legislation and destroying our careers and reputations—was and is beyond me.

Wright then moved the discussion from the general topic of Texas S&Ls to the specific S&Ls he was intervening on behalf of. He wanted to make clear that Gray's concessions were "extremely unsatisfactory." (I am quoting here from my testimony to the House ethics committee.)

> I have gotten involved in three things, and the first one [i.e., Craig Hall] was handled very satisfactorily, worked out very well. . . . That worked out real good. I talked to the Chairman and we were able to work all that out. . . . *But the other two have been extremely unsatisfactory.* (U.S. House Conduct Committee 1989, 253; emphasis in original)

Wright made the same point in his testimony before the House Ethics Committee.

> So . . . with regard to Tom Gaubert [,] I asked an audience. *That didn't turn out as well as the first one* [i.e., the Craig Hall intervention]. (U.S. House Conduct Committee 1989, 252; emphasis and bracketed materials in original)

All of us from the regulatory ranks knew exactly what Wright meant when he referred to the "three things," and his use of the phrase indicated that he was confident we would understand exactly what he was saying. The first one, which worked so well, was Craig Hall. Note that Gray capitulated unconditionally on the Hall matter, removing Scott Schultz's authority over the troubled-debt restructuring (TDR) and causing his replacement to agree to Hall's proposed terms.

The second and third things Wright was seeking to get favorable action from Gray about were Don Dixon and Tom Gaubert. Remember, Gaubert, acting through Wright, had caused Representative Barnard to fire a shot across our bow over the treatment of Vernon and Independent American about two weeks before the meeting with the Speaker. Consider also that Gaubert chose to have Wright ask not simply about "his" S&L, Independent American, but also about Vernon. Plainly, Gaubert felt that combining the political weight of the two control frauds was useful to their common cause of intimidating Gray.

As I will explain, the discussion about Don Dixon led to Wright becoming enraged and effectively ending the meeting before any further discussion of Gaubert. Wright, however, had conveyed his central message in the paragraph quoted above: Gray had not done nearly enough for Gaubert and Dixon, and Wright would maintain the hold on the

FSLIC recap until he got the same kind of concessions "that worked out real well" in the case of Craig Hall. Peace could only come through unconditional surrender to the control frauds. Barry told me years later that he had not understood either the substance of this meeting or its importance.

After the comment about the three things he had become involved in, Wright turned to complaining about how unfairly the Bank Board had treated Don Dixon. This was pretty amazing stuff; Wright was still going to bat for the most notorious control fraud. It grew more surreal when Wright said that all Dixon wanted from the Bank Board was one week to try to protect "his investment" in Vernon Savings from loss by arranging for a buyer that would recapitalize Vernon Savings at no cost to the FSLIC. With the Mallicks and Barry in the room, we could not reiterate what we had already explained to Barnard and what we had put in the memoranda we had given him for backdoor delivery to Wright. Dixon did not have a penny of his own money invested in Vernon Savings.

Wright's entire focus was on Dixon, not the taxpayers who eventually paid about $1 billion to cover the expense of Dixon's control fraud. At no time during the meeting did Wright express any concern for possible losses to the FSLIC or the taxpayers. There was no way that any legitimate buyer was going to purchase a massively insolvent S&L without FSLIC assistance. The proposed purchase arranged by Dixon was a complete scam involving accounting fraud and worthless notes. In any event, the Bank Board had already given Dixon years, not days, to arrange a true sale.

We explained that Dixon had been given ample time to arrange a sale and that no sale would occur because Vernon Savings was publicly reporting that it was insolvent by over $500 million. This only upset Wright more. It served as the catalyst (or pretext) for his personal attack on Gray. Barry (1989, 221–222) describes the key conversation (which took place around Christmas 1986, as I described in the last chapter) between Gray and Wright, the one that led Wright to believe that Gray had lied to him, this way:

> Gray told him that closing an S&L required his approval, and he knew nothing about it. So whatever was happening, regulators couldn't be closing the S&L. Dixon would have his week. . . .
>
> Soon after the call to Gray, Wright learned that the regulators had in fact put Dixon out of business that day. Not technically—Vernon S&L

stayed open for another four months before regulators closed it. But Dixon had signed away all say in the business, had lost all ownership rights, and a regulator was physically at Vernon all day every day, making all decisions. Dixon was out.

At best, Wright thought, Gray was incompetent and did not know what was happening in his own agency. At worst, Gray had lied to him. *The only thing you have in politics is your word. Without that you have nothing.* Wright was absolutely furious.

He did not even know he had stepped into quicksand. (emphasis in original)

This is essentially the same story that Wright now told at the February 10 hearing. It is hard to know how much of this story Wright believed. Mack's testimony before the House Ethics Committee on this matter was important because Gray and Green talked with him about the matter. His testimony was clearly erroneous. He claimed that Gray told him the Bank Board was about to close Vernon Savings, but stopped in response to Wright's call (U.S. House Conduct Committee 1989, 266–267). Mack was, next to Barry and George Mair (who had not yet entered the picture), Wright's most intense defender, and Mack's testimony was very bad for the Speaker's ethics defense. This suggests to me that Mack was genuinely befuddled on this point, not intentionally lying. S&Ls can be closed only with an enormous amount of preparation; it is an objective fact that Vernon Savings was not about to be closed by the Bank Board in December 1986, and it is equally certain that Gray and Green knew this and would not have told Mack that Vernon was about to be closed. The Bank Board had not even scheduled Vernon for some future closure.

Wright's staff was extraordinarily weak, as Barry admits. Worse, before they testified before the House Ethics Committee, they made no effort to investigate Dixon's or Gaubert's claims (U.S. House Conduct Committee 1989, 264). Dixon apparently took advantage of their ineptitude, laziness, and ignorance of finance and regulation to convince Wright and his aides that Gray was lying to him when he said Vernon Savings was not about to be closed in December 1986. Gray's veracity on this point was clear by February 10: six weeks had gone by since the Christmas phone calls, and the Bank Board had not closed Vernon Savings. (And, no surprise, no remotely legitimate buyer had shown up.) Dixon now twisted the story to claim that Gray's statement was only "technically" true.

One can figure out from reading Barry's defense of Wright what Dixon's tale must have been. What was imminent by Christmas 1986 was a routine action by the field when an S&L is hopelessly insolvent. The field seeks a "consent to merger" resolution. Hundreds of S&Ls had adopted such resolutions. Here is the key passage again from Barry (1989, 221–222):

> Wright learned that the regulators had in fact put Dixon out of business that day. Not technically—Vernon S&L stayed open for another four months before regulators closed it. But Dixon had signed away all say in the business, had lost all ownership rights, and a regulator was physically at Vernon all day every day, making all decisions. Dixon was out.

This mishmash of lies and half-truths had to come from Dixon; Wright's staff wouldn't have understood enough to cook up such a stew on their own. Dixon had not "lost all ownership rights." He still was the dominant shareholder. If he or the FSLIC could sell the S&L at a profit (as he claimed), he would reap that profit. A regulator had long been in charge and physically at Vernon Savings: a Texas state regulator appointed in September 1986 (U.S. House Conduct Committee 1989, 261). The consent-to-merger resolution did not change that. Similarly, the state of Texas had previously obtained its own consent-to-merger resolution from Vernon Savings. The Bank Board did not "in fact" put Dixon "out of business that day."

The Phelan report (U.S. House Conduct Committee 1989, 268) has the facts.

> It is clear that Wright was willing to intervene on Dixon's behalf without performing even a rudimentary investigation of Dixon's dispute with the Bank Board or the legitimacy of his request. . . . Wright thereafter became wed to a mistaken version of the facts. He believed that Gray had promised that the Bank Board was not going to "close down" Vernon, but that it did so anyway. He further believed that the Bank Board had taken away Dixon's ability to arrange for a purchaser of Vernon when such was not the case. Gray was correct when he told Wright and Mack that the consent-to-merger agreement neither closed Vernon nor affected its ability to be sold.

Wright lashed out at Gray at the February 10 meeting. The Phelan report (U.S. House Conduct Committee 1989, 271) quotes my testimony about what Wright said:

When I talk to the head of a federal agency and he tells me something, you know, I believe him. And I asked Gray when they were going to shut down Vernon Savings & Loan and he personally assured me that they were not going to do that, and then I discover that you did just exactly that, and the very [same] day.

He called Gray's "misrepresentation" "outrageous."

At this point the full extent of the institutional disaster became clear to me. Our original hope for the meeting had been to bring the Speaker a peace treaty and begin converting him into a supporter of the FSLIC recap. Scratch that plan. As a fallback, we would follow up on Barnard and Strauss's backdoor approach and convince Wright to have nothing more to do with Dixon and Gaubert. The meeting was producing a failure beyond our worst fears. Wright was becoming more vigorous in his defense of Dixon and Gaubert.

But Wright's vitriolic attack on Gray was the worst news of all, and completely unanticipated. If Wright really believed that Gray had lied to him we were dead—period. No one listens to someone he thinks is a liar. We could not leave Wright's office without trying to make him understand that Gray had told him the truth and not misled him through subterfuge.

But now I began to realize that I faced a personal disaster. As I watched the Speaker rant about Gray's perfidy, I noticed that Roy Green was reverting to an elementary school trick. When your fifth grade teacher is furious with the class, you try very hard to avoid eye contact, sit back in your chair, and do not move. You pray fervently that the teacher will call on someone else. Roy had to speak up. He had been in on the conference call with Mack and Gray that the Speaker claimed was the key act of misrepresentation. Roy was also the leader of our delegation. But Roy was clearly not going to defend Gray. I was going to have to speak up, and that risked redirecting Wright's wrath my way.

I was not pleased. This was my first experience with a feeling I would later have many times. I knew that I was Wright's best friend in the world at that moment. I wanted the Democratic Party to win in 1988. I knew that Wright was about to throw away the party's best issue (the sleaze factor) and hand the Republicans a superb issue with which to bash the Speaker and the Democrats. I knew that I would advise and implore Gray to make public that the Speaker was holding the FSLIC recap hostage to extort favors for control frauds. I knew that if Gray agreed, I would likely lead the criticism of Wright's actions. I had no desire to hurt Wright and every desire to help him.

I was also the perfect person to help the Speaker. I knew the issues and had no personal axe to grind. If he would only permit a confidential briefing without the Mallicks and Barry, we felt that we might succeed. Faulk and I could warn him off helping the control frauds and explain why honest Texas S&Ls would be the first victims of forbearance. It was obvious that his aides had neither the ability nor the guts to warn him that he was acting improperly. It was clear that the Mallicks were leading him into scandal. It was also clear that Wright was acting under a completely erroneous view of the facts because the frauds were lying to him.

But I also knew before I started that I had only a faint chance of success. I was Wright's best friend precisely because I was the only one willing to tell him the truth and disagree with him when he was wrong. The facts were entirely on our side; the other side (Dixon) was the most notorious control fraud in the nation. But Wright could not see that. He looked at us and saw nazis. When he looked at me he also saw a kid. I am short and I was only thirty-five years old. If I was disagreeing with him and explaining that he had the facts reversed, I must be an impertinent liar. The impertinent part was a particular danger. I felt Wright was acting shamefully, and though I tried to hide that feeling, it may well have shown.

Wright was almost certain to look at me and see an enemy, not his best friend in the room. He saw Gray as an enemy and liar. Wright had staked out his position so stridently that it would be highly embarrassing for him to admit that he was wrong about the facts and had abused Gray without cause. I would be asking him to side with the Bank Board against his staff (Mack), his best friend and business partner (Mallick), and a DCCC contributor (Dixon). I knew enough about Wright to realize there was little chance he would admit to such an error, particularly in that setting.

I began my defense of Gray by encouraging Green to get involved. I said that unlike Green I had not been in on the phone call to Mack, but I had heard directly from Gray about the call and believed that Roy would confirm Gray's recollection. I said that there must have been a misunderstanding because Gray had taken fairly extraordinary actions to communicate accurately and promptly about Vernon Savings. I explained how Gray not only had assured him that Vernon Savings was not about to be closed, but had also called Green promptly to find out whether any other actions were imminent. Green informed him that the

FHLB-Dallas was about to request the consent-to-merger resolution. Green and Gray then stayed on hold for two hours trying to contact Wright to inform him about the resolution and its import. Wright had left the office and the support staff could not reach him; Green and Gray eventually reached Mack.

This is where things began to get very bad for me personally. Wright viewed this as an attack on him or his staff for leaving Gray and Green on hold for so long. I emphasized that I had been trying to explain how Gray took great efforts to communicate accurately and promptly with him because Gray perceived how important it was to maintain a good relationship with him. I told Wright that we understood the disruption caused by moving and were in no way criticizing him or his staff. Wright let me go on, but his body language signaled his barely contained rage.

I then explained why a consent-to-merger resolution was not a closure and left Dixon free to find a buyer. Indeed, the purpose of the resolution is to facilitate sales. At this point, Wright gave me one of those creepy smiles that Barry found so horrible. It was everything Barry said, and more: you had the feeling that a butcher was sizing you up to figure out which limb to hack off first.

Wright, still "smiling," said that I was "prevaricating" and that my explanation that a consent-to-merger resolution was not a closure was "just words" and "a distinction without a difference" (U.S. House Conduct Committee 1989, 272). So far at the meeting, everything possible had gone wrong. In trying to convince the Speaker that Gray had not lied to him, I had succeeded only in convincing him that I, too, was a liar. My next attempt, admittedly a weak one, was at humor. As the Bible counsels, I was hoping that a gentle answer might turneth away wrath. I joked that I was a Midwesterner and that Midwesterners did not prevaricate.

Barry is again remarkably useful for giving an insight into the idiosyncratic way that Wright (and Barry) viewed us. Barry (1989, 235) missed the attempted joke entirely and manufactured a "snort," but the key is the interpretation that he and Wright put on my response.

> Suddenly, virtually calling Wright a liar, [Black] snorted, "I'm not from Washington. I'm not talking words."

This sentence reveals a great deal about Barry and the Speaker. The Speaker had just called Gray a liar. Then he called me a liar. Both claims were clearly erroneous; both of us had told Wright the truth. But Barry doesn't think it is worth mentioning that Wright called people liars ("prevaricating" and making "outrageous" "misrepresentations"). The big deal to him and the Speaker was that I had supposedly "virtually call[ed] Wright a liar." How had I done this? By explaining to the Speaker that I hadn't been lying to him in my prior answer! As Barry presents the scene, this is a Catch-22. I could either confess (falsely) that I had lied to Wright, or I could accuse him of lying by denying that I was lying.

But it is a false Catch-22. I did not accuse the Speaker, "virtually" or actually, of lying. I did not then, and do not now, think the Speaker was lying about the consent-to-merger resolution. I knew that the Speaker was getting his "facts" from Dixon, and I knew that Dixon was a liar. I was trying to explain that the Speaker's view of the facts was erroneous and that Gray and I were telling the Speaker the truth about the consent-to-merger resolution.

I explained to the Speaker that the difference between a takeover and a consent-to-merger resolution was real, not just words. I tried again to explain why. Wright, having decided I was a liar, wasn't listening, and he lost all control of his temper. He would interject; I would stop. He paused; I tried again; he erupted! "Goddamn it! Goddamn it! I listened to you; now you Goddamn listen to me, Goddamn it!" His screwed up his face with pure malice and leaned across the table at me. Barry (1989, 236) got the words and the interruptions wrong, but he got Wright's voice right: "his words spat out in a tight, hissing, controlled rage." In this context, "controlled rage" meant directed rage. Wright lost control and spewed out his rage. I was the target. The room went absolutely silent. No one spoke or moved for a full twenty seconds. That may not seem like much, but it was an excruciatingly long, uncomfortable time in this setting.

A desultory discussion resumed, but the meeting was over. Wright shook my hand on the way out and said, "Don't worry," but he fooled no one. Wright was firmly in Dixon and Gaubert's camp and would continue to hold the FSLIC recap hostage unless we surrendered unconditionally.

Many politicians are famous for their swearing, but Wright was a lay preacher and, Barry (1989, 649) claims, "[Wright] used a four-letter word once every six months." This suggests that Dixon's and Gaubert's causes were of great importance to him and that he was extraordinarily upset with Gray for not caving in sufficiently on their behalf and for "prevaricating."

Although you will not find it in his book, Barry told me that our effort to explain to Wright that Gray had told him the truth was one of only two occasions during the many months he spent with Wright that anyone dared disagree with or try to correct the Speaker when he erred. (Barry told me that Wright also raged and screamed at the other poor fool.) Barry's book shows that Wright's staff, after the departure of Raupe, was composed entirely of yes-men. His inability to admit error, and the exclusion of anyone who dared point out his errors, caused his mistakes to persist and grow.

Gray's decision to oppose the Speaker

It was insane, of course, for Gray to take on Wright. He was already anathema to the industry. League officials were warning him that he would never be able to work in the industry again. The powers within the administration hated him. One of the reasons that Congress did not pass the FSLIC recap in 1986 was that the White House took no action to get the bill passed. George Gould, the treasury undersecretary who was the lead executive-branch official on the FSLIC recap, was solid and professional, but he had no power. The White House can reward and threaten the interests of members of Congress by promising or withholding support on other bills dear to the legislators' hearts, but an undersecretary can only ask for a legislator's support. The press was frequently bitterly derisive about Gray. The last thing Gray needed was another enemy, much less the most powerful and vindictive enemy one could make on Capitol Hill.

"Do not go gentle into that good night. Rage, rage against the dying of the light."

I explained to Gray how disastrous the meeting had been: the Speaker, who now viewed us as liars, believed we had not done enough for Dixon and Gaubert. I noted that giving in to Wright's extortion previously had made Wright only increase his demands; if we did anything further along these lines, Gray would not be able to look himself in a mirror. Wright had all the power as long as he could extort without paying any consequences. I proposed that we go public with what he was doing.

It was unconscionable to leave Vernon Savings open. The Bank Board should close it and signal that the Speaker could no longer intimidate the agency.

To the surprise of most Bank Board staff, but not me, Gray agreed. Frankly, he didn't take much convincing; I believe he had already reached the same conclusion when he heard our report on the February 10 meeting. Neither of us thought we could win, but we thought we should go out trying to do the right thing. The truly astonishing thing is that it worked as well as it did. It was an important reason why Wright eventually resigned to avoid censure.

WRIGHT KEEPS THE HOLD ON THE FSLIC RECAP AND MOVES TO ATTACK

Wright's pressure on the House Banking Committee to gut the FSLIC recap seemed successful in February 1987. The committee sent investigators out to hear charges that supervisors at the FHLB-Dallas were acting like nazis. The effort, however, backfired because the committee sent two honest, competent inspectors. They were former GAO auditors, Jim Deveney and Gary Bowser. They found that the Dallas district was awash with control frauds, had been ineptly run before Selby's arrival, and had properly taken action against fraudulent owners (U.S. House Conduct Committee 1989, 211–212).

On March 3 and 4, 1987, the key House banking subcommittee held hearings that focused on Texas, the FHLB-Dallas, reregulation, and forbearance.

> Deveney stated that the hearings supported his findings from his investigation of the FHLB-Dallas: The regulators made a good case and the savings and loan operators did not. Deveney was surprised when St Germain thereafter offered a $5 billion recapitalization plan. He recalled commenting to Bowser that he "was amazed at how things are accomplished up here on the Hill." (U.S. House Conduct Committee 1989, 212)

THE BANK BOARD'S EFFORTS TO SUPPORT THE FSLIC RECAP

We briefed the House Banking Committee staffers throughout this period, explaining about the control frauds and why they were not innocent victims of a bad economy, but lead perpetrators in the collapse of Texas real-estate values. I designed studies for our economists that elucidated these points, and we prepared simple charts and handouts that made the results clear. We received canny assistance from Mary Ellen Taylor and my aides Mike and Ruth, all of whom understood how the House Banking Committee worked. I made a series of presentations to the staff on what was really happening in Texas. Joe Selby and I made a joint presentation to another group of staffers. We explained how an ADC Ponzi scheme works. We knew the presentations were effective because of the staffers' reactions. The folks who were not active proponents of forbearance were very impressed, but the reaction of opposing staffers provided an even more sincere compliment. They were enraged, but had no ability to respond.

We spent most of our efforts trying to defeat the forbearance provisions designed to emasculate the Bank Board. We had to explain three major points: how the provisions would end our ability to deal with the control frauds; how regulatory weakness, not vigor, had caused the crisis; and how our opponents' argument, a variation of "It's the economy, stupid!" was wrong.

We emphasized that the California control frauds had failed, amidst a robust real estate market, to counter this last argument. We prepared simple graphics showing trend lines for the tangible capital of the control frauds in Texas and California; they were so similar that they made our point instantly understandable even to staffers who disliked math and economics. We showed that all parts of the Texas S&L industry did not look the same; the high fliers' (which we called the "Texas 40" on our charts) trend line looked very different from that of the rest of the industry. The Texas control frauds had been insolvent before oil prices crashed. We spent a great deal of our time explaining why leaving control frauds open was disastrous for the honest bulk of the industry and for Texas homeowners and why it could cost the taxpayers many billions of dollars.

Wright had prevented the House Ethics Committee from roasting St Germain, so he owed Wright.[2] Our sense, however, was that St Germain knew Wright was wrong and resented what he was being forced to do. No committee chairman likes to see the Speaker take over his or her committee. Behind the scenes, St Germain's staff was frequently helpful by providing us an opportunity to make our case. By March 1987, we had solid support among House Banking Committee staff and growing support among the members.

THE PRESS BEGINS TO TURN AGAINST
WRIGHT AND THE CONTROL FRAUDS

The first step was to get immediate public attention about the Speaker holding the FSLIC recap hostage in 1986 and 1987. Barry (1989, 237) provides the Speaker's reaction to our initial effort:

> Gray talked with an underling of Jack Anderson, and Anderson wrote a column—as many as eight hundred publications ran some of his columns—in mid-March accusing Wright of pressuring regulators to go easy on a sleazy operator. *Yes, I called Ed Gray,* Wright said with cold anger when he read it. *I would have done it for anyone in the same situation. I never met Dixon in my life.* The story bothered him mostly because it impugned his reputation.[3] (emphasis in original)

But Wright did not intervene with Gray on "anyone['s]" behalf. He intervened only on behalf of contributors to the Democratic Party, like Dixon. Worse, he intervened on behalf of DCCC contributors without investigating their complaints. As a result, outright criminals like Dixon and Gaubert used him. Wright clearly never thought about the negative consequences of intervention. Helping Dixon and Gaubert helped DCCC contributors by harming Wright's constituents—and all American taxpayers. There is no evidence that Wright ever recognized this—even when he knew they were convicted felons.

I began to visit the editorial boards of Texas papers and national papers like the *Wall Street Journal,* A series of stories and editorials criticizing Wright for holding the FSLIC recap bill hostage began to appear nationally and at the state level. Wright began to feel under siege from the press and would periodically lash out ineffectively in frustration.

THE FRUSTRATIONS OF THE
LEAGUE'S PROFESSIONAL LOBBYISTS

The league's professional lobbyists were all over the Hill, pushing forbearance and opposing any meaningful money for the FSLIC, but their arguments were internally inconsistent, and they were not winning the undecided. They had their usual stable of politicians who always sided with the league, and the intense support of politicians whom the control frauds influenced, but there was no member of Congress who was an effective advocate of their positions. The league's professional lobbyists did not strike out; they were too good and the league was too powerful for them to fail entirely. We were amateurs, and not simply in comparison with them. But we had by far the best case substantively, and we hammered away on the facts (our strength) instead of on schmoozing. We could tell that we were being effective because the league cranked up the volume of its complaints against the Bank Board until their rhetoric was indistinguishable from the control frauds'. The league was worried it might lose; we began to dare to hope.

Some of the major problems the league had in lobbying against the FSLIC recap were with the Texas League. The Texas League knew all about the control frauds that were destroying Texas. At the same time that it was lobbying against the FSLIC recap, it was working on a "Report on the Texas Thrift and Real Estate Crises" (released October 30, 1987). The report explained that "entrepreneurs with backgrounds in real estate development either own or owned 20 of the 24 most deeply insolvent thrifts in Texas (with the remaining four copying the tactics of the real estate entrepreneurs)" (18). The report emphasizes that ADC loans "turned out to be veritable ticking time bombs whose subsequent explosions devastated substantial numbers of Texas thrifts" (10). Concluding that "while there was not anything necessarily wrong with this 'grow out of it' strategy," it led to "frenzied growth" which "became an increasingly vicious cycle" (14, 15).

Many of the newcomers, as well as some of the existing owners, also began to engage in fraudulent and otherwise illegal schemes. (18)

The report repeatedly complains of appraiser fraud and inadequate supervisory vigilance (20, 32–33). Nevertheless, the report calls for greater forbearance, including elimination of any regulatory or supervisory agreements entered into as a result of prior failures to comply with regulatory capital requirements (44).

The report then goes on to call for the creation of additional creative RAP provisions and a prohibition against classifying assets if doing so would "cause" a Texas S&L to fail to meet its capital requirement (50–53, 56–57, 60). The report calls for a slowdown on the issuance of Bank Board rules and an end to "'regulation to the lowest common denominator' as was done by the FHLBB under Chairman Gray" (62).

This was obviously and logically incoherent. It confirmed that the worst Texas S&Ls were control frauds running ADC Ponzis; that there were large numbers of such frauds; that supervision in Texas was horribly weak; that the Bank Board under Gray had moved to get the control frauds under control; and that the key reform needed was to weaken supervision!

We had a field day responding to this kind of logic. The Texas League proposed a "get out of jail free" card (release insolvent S&Ls from supervisory agreements) plus an "immunity from arrest" card (the Bank Board cannot show that an S&L is insolvent by classifying its problem assets).

But illogic was not the only reason that the league discovered it could not rely on Texas League officials to establish the case for forbearance. They also had to deal with the problem that Bo McAllister (head of the Texas League) answered direct questions truthfully, e.g., his admission to me that the Bank Board had not closed any Texas S&L that should not have been closed. The honest members of the Texas S&L industry generally despised the control frauds. They were willing to enter into this Faustian bargain because the control frauds had such political clout with Speaker Wright and because their honest S&Ls were also insolvent. They were not willing to defend Gaubert, Dixon, and their ilk.

The national office of the league also had to deal with the Texas wild card factor. Texans are (proudly) quirky. Tom King, the Texas League's executive director, said that Texas needed "rinky-dink" accounting. The first rule, of course, in asking for rinky-dink accounting is to never call it by its true name.

In the absence of credible spokespersons in Congress or the Texas industry, the league had to rely on rhetoric. As I explained, when the league became more desperate, it ratcheted up its diatribes against Gray. The league had started out its 1987 attack on the FSLIC recap bill by saying that the industry had turned itself around and was profitable and overwhelmingly healthy. The league soon realized that this argument undercut its rationale for forbearance and promptly adopted a very different claim. As the league stressed in a letter to its members (*American Banker*, February 10, 1987, 1):

> *It should be emphasized that there is an essential linkage between the two elements of our program.* Frankly, if we do not get the necessary regulatory reforms and "stretch out" the resolution of problems in depressed areas, the amounts required by FSLIC will run easily into the tens of billions of dollars. But a series of time buying initiatives by the regulators will greatly reduce the demands on FSLIC. (emphasis in original)

The new league line was that there was a severe problem, confined to distressed areas, and that if the Bank Board dealt with it now it would cost "tens of billions of dollars," but forbearance would eliminate the vast bulk of that cost, leaving the $5 billion league plan adequate to fund all needs. The league was relying on a classic "silver bullet" solution, painless and surefire.

If forbearance was painless and surefire, it followed that Gray's reregulation and vigorous supervision policies must be irrational and disastrous. As the league argued on February 9 in a letter to Senator Boren:

> Arbitrary and excessive writedowns [are] dictated by current FHLBB rules and procedures. Those writedowns and reclassifications are unnecessarily forcing soundly-managed companies into insolvency and magnifying the FSLIC's caseload of troubled institutions. (U.S. League of Savings Institutions, Book 1, Tab C-16 at 1)

On March 6, 1987, the league wrote the comptroller general that there was no S&L crisis; that Gray's supervisory policies were causing the industry problems; and that no funds should be provided to the FSLIC until it stopped requiring insolvent S&Ls to admit their insolvency.

> The Board's failure to moderate its appraisal and classification rules for depressed areas is responsible in substantial part for the problems of FSLIC. . . .
> [B]ecause, among other things, of the regulatory appraisal and asset classification rules used by the Board, we are seriously troubled about the FSLIC's ability to use wisely monies provided to it. (U.S. League of Savings Institutions, Book 6, Tab C-4 at 1–2)

As it became clear that the league was in grave danger of losing in the House Banking Committee, its rhetoric reached a peak. On March 13 the league wrote to its members, urging them once more to lobby Congress in favor of forbearance and the league's $5 billion FSLIC recap plan. The Senate Banking Committee had just approved a $7.5 billion FSLIC recap plan.

> We do not want to provide so much money that the FSLIC will be able to indiscriminately close down well-managed institutions that are the victims of local economic conditions. . . .
> Frankly, with a [league] forbearance program in place, we don't

believe an extension of the FSLIC funding program [beyond $5 billion] will be necessary. (U.S. League of Savings Institutions, Book 5, Tab A-19 at 1)

No one could point to any well-managed S&L closed by the Bank Board. The league did not attempt to explain why the Bank Board would want to close down well-managed S&Ls indiscriminately, but some league lobbyists presented the nazi theory (though not in writing). The league was claiming that a one-shot $5 billion in extra FSLIC funding would be enough for all time. Indeed, a subsequent letter said that $5 billion would be more than was needed (Black 1993a).

WRIGHT AND THE LEAGUE: A VERY LIMITED ALLIANCE

Wright and the league allied themselves against the FSLIC recap in 1987. Indeed, Wright's defenders later emphasized this link because it bolstered the theory of his ethics defense that he was acting in the interest of the public, not individual contributors. As I quoted, the Texas League took credit for helping convince Wright to put a hold on the bill in 1987.

What is difficult to understand is how limited and uncoordinated this alliance was despite the strong common interests and expertise of both allies.

On February 10 the league wrote its members to explain that "key members of Congress are insisting that the Board take [forbearance steps] before any recapitalization program is adopted" (Black 1993a; U.S. League of Savings Institutions, Book 5, Tab A-16 at 2). The letter attached a news article noting that Wright and Congressman Steve Bartlett from Texas were working with the league and that Wright had gotten St Germain to cancel a planned vote on the FSLIC recap. The article quoted Wright as saying

We don't want to give them $15 billion to . . . close down an enormous lot of institutions. . . .
They need a little bit tighter tether.

"Tighter tether" was a variant of the phrase used by both the league and the control frauds. The idea was that by drastically reducing the amount of money provided to the FSLIC, Congress could ensure that it kept the Bank Board on a "short leash" and could make the agency responsive to political intervention designed to prevent the closure of insolvent S&Ls. The Bank Board, in this metaphor, was the dog that had not yet learned obedience. The Speaker of the House was the perfect man to ensure that the agency was "House" broken.

One of the few meetings between the league's leader and the Speaker occurred by chance.

> Wright ran into the [league] lobbyist and [Mr. O'Connell]. They thanked him for his help, then said, "We've got to do something about that reevaluation of property values. Let me give you those figures."
>
> "I can't talk about it now," Wright said.
>
> They insisted. Suddenly Wright exploded. "*Listen! My back got tired of carrying all you people.* When those bastards were writing all those stories about me, I was alone. Where were you then? This is a two-way street. That's the way things work up here. You come and tell me your problems but you don't tell the press. You don't do a damn thing to support yourselves or me. You left it to me to do it all." (Barry 1989, 240; emphasis in original)

Mr. O'Connell responded to the Speaker's criticisms by writing *Newsweek* and the *New York Times* to protest articles critical of the Speaker and to blame the Bank Board for industry problems.

It is clear from Wright's comments to O'Connell that there was little or no coordination even behind the scenes between Wright and either the national or Texas League. Overwhelmingly, Wright got S&L input not from the league, but the control frauds.

Wright was hopelessly unable to comprehend the substance of the S&L crisis. His staff never understood the S&L debacle; they did not try to counter us as we played the role of the tortoise and briefed House Banking Committee staffers (and members, where we could) about the merits. Bartlett, the Republican congressman who later became mayor of Dallas, led the push for forbearance in the committee. His party affiliation was a godsend to the committee Democrats who supported forbearance. It made it a bipartisan effort, so they were delighted to let him get out front on the issue. Bartlett, however, was not effective at arguing his case and his staff was even weaker. They came to our briefings of House Banking Committee staffers and glared, but they never attempted to counter our findings and charts.

One of the best testaments to Wright's tactical weaknesses in attempting to keep the House Banking Committee's increasingly restive members in line was that he came to rely a great deal on Curt Prins. Prins was Frank Annunzio's chief staffer. Annunzio, a senior Democrat on the committee, was from Chicago, the home of the league's national headquarters, and he was a strong supporter of the league. Indeed, his sons-in-law worked for the league and for relatives of the league's leader, Bill O'Connell (Day 1993, 211). Annunzio was also a close ally of Keating. Remember that Annunzio led the effort in the House to block the direct-investment rule. Annunzio passionately disliked Gray. Annunzio had always had a very poor reputation as a legislator, and by 1986 he was also in such bad health that he was reduced to reading questions prepared by his staff; often, he could not even manage that.

Prins tried to fill the role of representative (which Annunzio had essentially left vacant). Top aides, e.g., John Mack, often have formidable power, but members of Congress never consider them equals. Prins's efforts led other members of the committee to refer to him as "Representative Prins" (Day 1993, 213). That is a very unfriendly remark in the House. Prins was even deeper in Keating's pocket than Annunzio, and both remained deep in his pockets even in 1989, when Keating's frauds became obvious to everyone.

Prins told us that he "was carrying the Speaker's water to House Banking" on the FSLIC recap.

That use of Prins reflected how weak Wright's influence was with the rank and file on the committee. Wright could not rely on any Democratic committee member to carry water on behalf of Dixon and Gaubert. Even the ablest and best-regarded staffer is a lesser creature on Capitol Hill; only members count. Prins was neither able nor well respected. The members of the Committee, their staffs, and the media all despised Prins (Day 1993, 213). He was a vicious, unprincipled bigot (ibid.). Only desperation could have made Wright turn to Prins. Wright's other alternatives on the committee must have been even worse. St Germain, for example, had one of the poorest reputations of any member of Congress and was not popular among Democrats on the committee. Moreover, St Germain probably secretly opposed Wright's actions of the FSLIC recap bill.

FRIENDLY FIRE: TREASURY'S BLUNDER

The Treasury Department did a generally low-key, competent job of lobbying for the FSLIC recap in 1987. However, Treasury made a serious mistake that provided the league with its best substantive argument.

The blunder was trying to add another argument to an already winning argument: the supplementary argument ended up undercutting the winning argument. The issue was how much money the FSLIC recap should provide. Treasury always cared primarily about the money in the bill; by mid-1987 the Bank Board cared primarily about the forbearance measures. The industry wanted to minimize the amount of money they would have to pay to deal with the costs of the debacle. They said that the FSLIC would close too many S&Ls too quickly if Congress passed the $15 billion FSLIC recap bill, even though the premise of the FSLIC recap was that closing down the control frauds quickly would reduce the cost of the S&L cleanup.

Treasury, however, decided to argue that the FSLIC would not close many S&Ls if Congress approved the recap, because the FSLIC lacked the capability to spend more than $5 billion in a year effectively.[4] Treasury was wrong. Resolving the three worst S&Ls would have cost well over $5 billion. The FSLIC could have effectively closed at least fifty S&Ls annually. The standard industry joke was that if you landed at Dallas–Fort Worth Airport and resolved the insolvent S&Ls you drove past while taking a cab to Dallas, you would spend $15 billion before you arrived downtown. Treasury's argument also vitiated the rationale for a $15 billion recapitalization. The league's very competent lobbyists instantly recognized the immense value of the Treasury gaffe and used it to great advantage (NCFIRRE 1993c; Day 1993, 253–254).

7. THE MIRACLES, THE MASSACRE, AND THE SPEAKER'S FALL

It is not necessary to hope in order to attempt,
or to succeed in order to persevere.

ATTRIBUTED TO WILLIAM THE SILENT,
PRINCE OF ORANGE (1533-1584)

THE TWIN MARCH MIRACLES

The first March miracle was that the key House subcommittee voted in favor of a $15 billion FSLIC recap bill. The second was that the press began to come around, recognizing that Gray was following good policies in the face of intense political intervention by the Speaker on behalf of Texas control frauds. The second miracle helped explain the success of the FSLIC recap in the subcommittee, so I will discuss it first.

POSITIVE PRESS ABOUT GRAY

Gray's reregulatory efforts began to receive positive coverage in the mainstream and trade press. That was remarkable. Gray had received extraordinarily bad press coverage for his entire term, and it had been getting worse. Senior administration officials attacked him regularly, as did powerful members of Congress, most of the industry, and a fair number of his own staff. He was presented as venal (all the expensive trips), malicious, and dumb as a doornail.

Gray was an extremely poor spokesman for his own cause. He

typically wrote and typed his own speeches until four in the morning, showed up the next morning at a microphone looking like death warmed over, read a long speech that everyone had heard many times before, and praised himself as a latter-day Churchill. The speeches went over like a depleted-uranium balloon. To top it off, Gray could not understand why people did not react well to his speeches. He thought they were great. He sent them to every S&L in the country. (Their substance comes across very well when they are read now: he is constantly warning, accurately, that certain practices will lead to disaster.)

By March 1987, however, Gray was often dealing with a different part of the press. The S&L story had been a business story; it now became a political story. (It had always been both; the jurisdictional gulf between the business and political reporters was one of the reasons the press performed so miserably in dealing with the S&L debacle.) Better yet, it was a political scandal, which meant that a reporter could hope for more column inches to explain the story and a much more prominent placement in the paper. This new group of reporters investigated the issues from different perspectives and with different sources. Financial reporters spent their time talking to S&L leaders. They were close to unanimous in their contempt for Gray. Financial reporters had to be present for Gray's numerous speeches. They groaned and made fun of him (to one another) when he gave a speech.

Political reporters did not come to the story with that preconception. They knew that the story would work better if it had a protagonist. The idea of Gray as a protagonist was inconceivable to most financial reporters, but for someone writing about the politics of the debacle, Gray looked like a very attractive one. He had started as an impassioned deregulator; he was a friend and strong supporter of the president; he had become the great reregulator out of conviction (not ideology); and he had persisted despite the efforts of senior administration officials to drive him from office and the efforts of the control frauds to bribe him away. Now he was taking on the most feared person on the Hill, Speaker Wright, and Speaker Wright was trying to aid the control frauds.

Although the industry hated Gray, his peers praised him. William Seidman, the FDIC chairman, and Paul Volcker, the former chairman of the Federal Reserve, were strong supporters of Gray, and they had excellent relations with the press. Gray's conversion and his dogged willingness to take on the powerful made for one hell of a story. Political reporters also knew that when the powerful are criticized, they always respond by trying to smear their accusers. The efforts by Don Regan,

Charles Keating, and Speaker Wright to blacken Gray's name might have been proof of his courage, not his mendacity.

Jack Anderson criticized the Speaker in a syndicated column for putting a hold on the FSLIC recap in order to coerce favors for DCCC contributors. That, along with our efforts to explain what the Speaker was doing to block the recap, began to bear fruit in the form of very bad press for the Speaker. Barry (1989, 390) provides Wright's reaction:

> *Every time Wright thought he was shut of that damned issue, it came back to haunt him.* The savings and loan thing would not go away. *Newsweek* had done that story. *The New York Times* had done it. *Business Week* was doing it. The Texas papers, the *Houston Chronicle, Dallas Morning News, Austin American-Statesman, Dallas Times-Herald* had all done it over and over. In late September [1987], a writer asked him what disappointments he had suffered. Wright did not mention any policy. Instead he talked of the press coverage of his involvement in the S&L issue. (emphasis in original)

These articles greatly restricted the Speaker's ability to openly hold the FSLIC recap hostage and put him on the defensive. They also made it far more likely that members of the House Banking Committee would oppose the forbearance provisions drafted by the control frauds and support a $15 billion recap.

A March vote in favor of the $15 billion FSLIC recap bill

The other miracle was even more improbable: standing up to Wright and criticizing his actions almost led to passage of the FSLIC recap in a desirable form. The second (near) miracle was a testament to three things. First, Gray was on the right side of an important issue, and Wright and the league were on the wrong side. Second, our opposition's weaknesses kept Wright from responding effectively to our arguments in the House Banking Committee. Third, there were some truly good public servants on the House Banking Committee and its staff who were willing to buck the will of an exceptionally powerful and nasty Speaker and a powerful trade association. I have already addressed the first two points, so I will turn to the third.

My discussion up to this point has emphasized the efforts of the Bank Board and our opponents. This has the danger of implying that our efforts were decisive in producing the near miracle in the House Banking Committee. In fact, the most important factor was the strength of a bipartisan group of committee members who became convinced that the FSLIC recap was vital. The leaders of that group were (in alphabetical order) Tom Carper (Democrat from Delaware), Henry B. Gonzalez (Democrat from Texas), Jim Leach (Republican from Iowa), and Buddy Roemer (Democrat from Louisiana).[1]

That mere listing presents two very unlikely facts. First, although the group was bipartisan (and, indeed, nonpartisan), most were Democrats. That may not seem strange. Democrats were generally less enamored with deregulation than were Republicans, particularly by 1987. It always mystified Gray why so few Democrats supported his efforts at reregulation that so distressed the administration. But the FSLIC recap was an administration bill, so the first question was why there were so few strong supporters for the bill from the Republican side of the aisle. Jim Leach was one of the vanishing breed of Republican moderates who was famous for his willingness to buck the administration. None of the partisan Republicans on House Banking took a leadership role in support of the FSLIC recap.

The fact that most in the group were Democrats was important for another reason. It indicated that the Speaker had failed to sway them to his cause even though he had made clear his intense personal interest in their support, framed the issue as a partisan issue, and personally asked for their support. That third element is particularly important. As Barry (1989) repeatedly emphasizes:

> The most pressure a Speaker can apply is to ask. It is a lot. (102)

> Although he said he was not dictating anything—"Please let me know how you feel," he wrote [in his notes to the Democrats on Ways and Means]—between the lines came a stronger message: *There will be taxes. Are you with me or not? Are you friend or foe?* (147, emphasis in original)

> *Pressure? What's pressure? There's nothing higher than the Speaker asking for your help. There's nothing higher than that, . . .* (446, emphasis in original)

Wright's holding the FSLIC recap hostage at the behest of the control frauds was one of the key acts that began to erode the hill of sand on which he had built such apparent power. Barry (1989, 238) provides part of the tale.

> Inside the House Wright was having problems on the issue too. He wanted a $5-billion package. Strong sentiment existed on the Banking Committee for the $15-billion package. The industry was in shambles and the sooner it was cleaned up, the less expensive it would be in the long run. . . .
>
> Wright and his Texas colleague Mike Andrews testified before a closed caucus of Banking Committee Democrats [on March 19, 1987] about their concerns about the regulators, and their fears of giving them too much power.

The context of Wright's personal appeal to the Democrats on the House Banking Committee is revealing. As Barry's book makes clear, Wright was experiencing unbroken success in the House on his priorities during 1987 and gaining largely positive reviews in the press. Barry (1989, 387) describes the extent of his power:

> Wright seemed in absolute control of the House [by September 1987], about to challenge the President for supremacy.

He was in danger of losing only on this priority issue. He was losing despite having an enormous number of advantages. The FSLIC recap was, at best, a fourth- or fifth-tier administration "priority." His primary opponent, Gray, was weak as well as actively hated by the powers that be in the administration. The league was immensely powerful politically; its membership was united; the FSLIC recap was its sole priority; and it supported Wright fully. (We were able to garner support from the realtors and the National Association of Home Builders. This was quite a coup. Understandably, however, the FSLIC recap was never a priority for them, so their support was heartening but not active.) Wright had bipartisan support in the form of Representative Bartlett. The Texas delegation was famous for its strength and solidarity. Texas state officials, particularly Attorney General Mattox, lent their weight. Wright had the chairman of the committee, St Germain, in his palm because of his exposure on the ethics charges. Wright should have been crushing the opposition.

Instead, Wright knew from the intelligence provided by his whip organization (which Coelho chaired) that he was in grave danger of losing the vote in the House Banking Committee. Nothing had gone right for the Speaker on this issue. Yes, by meeting personally with St Germain and other senior Democrats in January he had been able to halt progress on the bill, but the cost in political capital and vulnerability to press criticism had exceeded the gain. The attempt to intimidate Gray by having Barnard ask him about Vernon Savings and Independent American had blown up in the Speaker's (and Gaubert's) face. The February 10 meeting had been a fiasco for the Speaker. The once-compliant Gray now refused to do any more regulatory favors. Coercing the House Banking Committee to investigate the Bank Board's supervision of Texas S&Ls had made matters far worse because it exposed the supposed victims as frauds and the supposed nazis as conscientious workers trying to do the job their predecessors had shirked. The hearing that was supposed to showcase the nazi reign of terror had embarrassed the proponents of forbearance. Mattox's threats against Gray and Selby had been so crude that they hurt his reputation, not theirs. The press had turned against Wright on this issue and, most galling of all, in favor of Gray. There was no one on the committee whom Wright could rely on to lead the effort against the FSLIC recap.

It was bad enough to lose, but to lose to Gray, a man he personally hated, was unthinkable. Wright decided to intervene personally.

This was the context when Wright and Andrews addressed the Democratic members of the House Banking Committee on March 19, 1987. A meeting like this—the Speaker addressing a closed session of a committee's Democratic caucus to plead for its members' support— was rare. It indicates that several things were going on. First, Wright knew that he was about to lose the House Banking Committee vote. Second, Wright cared enormously about the vote. He was expending tremendous political capital to try to win it. Worse, he was identifying his prestige as their leader with his success on the vote. If he lost the vote, he would damage the perception of power that he had so carefully cultivated. Indeed, the erosion had already begun: Democrats on the committee knew that Wright wanted very much to defeat the FSLIC recap, yet several were prepared to join Republicans to defeat Wright's position.

Third, he was asking colleagues, as Democrats, to support him. He was making a partisan issue out of defeating a bill that was not a partisan dispute and that had previously enjoyed bipartisan support. Mayer (1990, 238) reports what Wright told the caucus.

The [Texas] economy was passing through a hard time, but there wasn't, at bottom, anything wrong with the S&Ls. The problem was Gray and Roy Green of the Federal Home Loan Bank of Dallas, a nest of Republican regulators who were trying to kill off good Democrats, big contributors to the Democratic party [*sic*]. It was the duty of the Democrats on the committee to exert themselves and put a stop to that, first of all by holding down the FSLIC recap bill to $5 billion at the very most.

Henry Gonzalez recalled that Wright claimed the Bank Board was "saving the Republicans and damning the Democrats. . . . My request was, give me the documentation. And when the documentation was not forthcoming, I did not act" (Mayer 1990, 238). Barry doesn't discuss this failure. If Wright had been able to document his charges, he would have done so. Day (1993, 253) says that the Speaker told "horror stories" about the regulators.

After Wright made these repeated, highly unusual efforts to induce committee Democrats to support him on a matter they knew was dear to his heart and the interests of his constituents, it was particularly impressive when three Democrats became leaders in the struggle for the FSLIC recap. It was even more impressive considering that a vote to gut the bill did not seem likely to cause any political embarrassment and that their efforts on behalf of a good bill were almost certain to fail.

Two of the leaders supporting the FSLIC recap came from states where they were likely to suffer for their support: Gonzalez was from Texas (San Antonio) and Roemer was from Louisiana. Every S&L in Texas and Louisiana opposed the $15 billion FSLIC recap bill and supported ruinous forbearance. Although many of them privately blamed the control frauds, publicly they all blamed the sharp fall in oil prices for causing a regional recession. Gonzalez and Roemer were taking a real risk that their constituents would consider them traitors. Voting in favor of a $15 billion FSLIC recap bill could not win them a single vote or a dollar in campaign contributions.

All of this, of course, made them invaluable as supporters of the Bank Board. The fact that "oil patch" Democrats supported the Bank Board made the complaints that we were nazis seem even more ridiculous. If they were willing to anger powerful constituents for whom the bill was the first priority, surely other committee members from states with strong economies would not shrink from paying the small political price for supporting the FSLIC recap.[2] No one could claim that Gonzalez or Roemer was ignorant of, or unsympathetic to, the problems of Texas and Louisiana. And they were both Democrats willing to oppose the Speaker.

THE FOUR STALWARTS

The four members of the House Banking Committee who took the lead in supporting the FSLIC recap were Gonzalez, Leach, Carper, and Roemer, and they all shared several traits. Their colleagues knew they were independents and considered them reformers. They all had advanced degrees. Three of the four were moderates who were highly respected by their peers (the exception was Gonzalez).[3] These four were so effective that we actually had the potential to win in the House Banking Committee.

THE MARCH MIRACLE IN THE SUBCOMMITTEE

The Japanese love cherry blossoms. They bloom all in a rush, and a single day of wind or rain can sweep them away. Their attraction lies in the ephemeral nature of the bloom as much as in the pale beauty of the blossoms. Japan gave cherry trees to the United States for our nation's centennial. They ring the Tidal Basin in Washington, D.C. Our first two children were born while the trees were in bloom; we marveled at them on our drive home from the hospital. Blooming in late March or early April, they are the capital's quintessential symbol of spring, rebirth, and hope.

March 31, 1987, was cherry blossom day as far as the Bank Board was concerned. Wright's fears about the House Banking Committee vote were accurate. The Phelan report explains:

> On March 31, the Subcommittee on Financial Institutions considered the recapitalization bill. St Germain offered a $5 billion, two-year plan with forbearance provisions as a substitute for the $15 billion, five-year plan without forbearance provisions which he had introduced at the beginning of the session. Congressman Carper moved to amend St Germain's substitute bill by raising the recapitalization amount to $15 billion. The Carper amendment passed the Subcommittee by a vote of 23–20. (U.S. House Conduct Committee 1989, 212)

A bizarre incident immediately after the vote revealed to me how intense the pressure was on Gray. Carper had taken the lead in delivering a subcommittee vote in favor of the $15 billion FSLIC recap. Gray approached him as soon as Carper went back to his office. Carper probably expected Gray to congratulate him. Instead, Gray blazed away about how the bill they had just passed had exit fees that were too low. Gray feared that healthy S&Ls would convert to bank charters to avoid the costs imposed by the FSLIC recap. Gray had "lost it": the tension had overwhelmed him. Mary Ellen Taylor and I rushed to undo the damage. If I had been in Carper's shoes, I would have told Gray off. Carper was clearly startled, but he said nothing. He calmed himself and quietly explained to Gray that no one wins all the battles at the same time and that he would try to help improve the exit-fee provisions. Mary Ellen and I gave Carper the Bank Board's fulsome thanks for his efforts. Then we took Gray aside and calmed him down before he lit into another ally.

Gray aged noticeably during 1987; his hands now shook. He knew how faint were the chances of success on the FSLIC recap; he worried about how deeply he was in debt and how poor were his job prospects, given the powerful enemies he had made and the damage his reputation had suffered from attacks in the press. He had to force himself to continue, and he did.

APRIL FOOLS

The subcommittee included virtually all the members of the full House Banking Committee. The full committee would vote on the FSLIC recap the next day, April Fools' Day. Unless something drastic changed overnight, Wright was about to suffer his first major defeat as Speaker. But that night brought a chill deluge that swept all the blossoms off the cherry trees. Barry (1989, 238–239) explains:

> The vote stung Wright. That night Wright gave Jack Brooks a ride to a dinner. They talked about it. *Wasn't it a shame,* Wright said, *that Ed Gray would go to the newspapers and lie about him and then win?* Brooks had heard all the complaints from thrift executives too. The next day the full committee was going to vote on the bill. At breakfast, one Wright aide said, "I think I can turn the vote around. Should I?"
>
> "No!" Wright said firmly. This had already become stickier than he wanted. "Stay out of it. The forbearance language is all I care about and it's in there."
>
> Wright and his staff did nothing. But Brooks worked the committee hard. So did Andrews: "I talked to everybody I could get my hands on.

Probably fifteen. I went to younger members I knew well. I think I did some good." The full committee voted 25-24 to reverse the subcommittee. That only sparked more bad newspaper stories about Wright's involvement. (emphasis in original)

Wright gives Jack Brooks, a fellow Texan and staunch ally, a ride to dinner and says it's a shame that Gray could lie about him and win. Brooks knows that our disclosures to the press have made it impossible for Wright to repeat his open effort to gut the recap. Wright used Brooks and Andrews to do the dirty work and provide him with deniability. But Wright was too clever by half. The April 6 *Banking Report* from the Bureau of National Affairs reveals that "Carper said he had reconfirmed with Wright early April 1 that Wright was committed to Carper's $15 billion compromise recapitalization plan." Wright deceived Carper.

Barry does not even note the glaring contradiction in the passage just quoted. Why, if forbearance, which is in the Carper bill, is all that he cares about, is Wright "stung" by the Carper bill and furious that it has been passed? Why did the Speaker confirm to Carper on April 1 that he supported his bill when he was, in fact, furious that it had passed? Carper, disgusted with the Speaker's high-pressure tactics and dishonesty, said on the floor on April 1, 1987, that "I'll let today's vote and the broken arms speak for themselves" (Day 1993, 253).

Wright won by the narrowest of margins, 25-24. Congresswoman Kaptur switched her vote from Carper's $15 billion bill to Congressman Neal's $5 billion bill. Doug Barnard, Hamlet to the end, decided "not to be": he passed when the time came to vote. A tie vote would have meant the adoption of Carper's bill. St. Germain broke the tie by using the proxy of Walter Fauntroy (a delegate representing the District of Columbia) to kill the $15 billion FSLIC recap bill (Rom 1996, 181, 302n89); Fauntroy had promised Carper that he would vote for the $15 billion bill.

After losing the crucial vote on the $15 billion FSLIC recap bill in the full committee, Carper proceeded, undaunted, to try for a lesser amount. In the effort to rally support he was slightly late (*seconds* late) in raising the right procedural motion for offering his proposed amendment. St Germain ruled it out of order. St Germain had the power to do this, but it is the kind of thing you do not do in the modern world. St Germain's action caused an involuntary gasp from several spectators. Carper was clearly upset. I watched him struggle with his emotions for about five seconds. He then straightened his shoulders and in a mild, calm voice asked for unanimous consent to be able to raise his amendment. He did not protest, complain, or scowl. St Germain realized that he had made a mistake in barring Carper from offering his amendment. The room began to relax. Suddenly, Prins was whispering in Annunzio's ear. Annunzio objected; there was no unanimous consent.

Now St Germain was in even deeper trouble. He was aware that the press was going to criticize him for killing the $15 billion bill. Using a never-enforced technicality to prevent the committee from considering a $12.5 billion bill would look terrible not only to the press but also to the rest of his committee. Annunzio's action made it look even worse: the committee members believed that no two members of Congress were deeper in the league's pocket than St Germain and Annunzio. St Germain, especially, was notorious for his unethical ties to the league.

There was shock and then a tumult of noise after Annunzio raised his objection. Through it all, Carper sat ramrod straight with a look of great dignity. His presence demanded reasonable action, though he said nothing. Other senior members of the committee began hammering Annunzio. Prins's having caused him to raise the objection made it far worse. It took several minutes, but Annunzio backed down. The end was anticlimactic: the House voted down all of Carper's proposed amendments and approved the $5 billion bill the Speaker wanted. But Carper is the kind of guy I would want on my side.

Using Brooks and Andrews, neither of them a member of the House Banking Committee, to "break arms" reinforced the Speaker's weakness in dealing with the committee. Brooks was chairman of Government Operations, an extremely powerful committee. Between his direct leverage and the Speaker's power, it is remarkable that Wright still won by only one vote.

THE KEATING FIVE

Lee Henkel, Keating's Bank Board member, resigned March 31 (the second miracle that day), and it became public, appropriately enough, on April Fools' Day. Keating had told Gould, the Treasury undersecretary, that he could influence the votes of five senators on the FSLIC recap (Williamson 1991). The president often has difficulty delivering the votes of five U.S. senators. Keating was claiming unprecedented power for a private individual in the modern era. Even in the "robber baron" era, owning one senator was a coup. Gould was so offended that he ended the meeting and ordered the guards to bar Keating from entering the Treasury building.

On April 2, 1987, four U.S. senators made it clear that Keating was not bragging. They called Gray in to meet with them and told him not to bring any staff; they also excluded their own staff. The four senators who showed up were miffed that Senator Riegle had not joined them, despite indicating that he would be there. Seven days later, Riegle joined them in a meeting that would make them infamous as the Keating Five.[4] They wanted Gray not to take enforcement action against Lincoln Savings for its $600 million violation of the direct-investment rule. The defeat of the FSLIC recap in the House Banking Committee meant that the Bank Board's only hope lay in the Senate. The clout of five senators, added to the Speaker's power and the league's power, should have been an irresistible force. They would surely succeed for Keating where Henkel had failed. The story of the Keating Five is continued in later chapters.

WRIGHT WINS THE BATTLE AND LOSES THE WAR

In the end, Wright had not simply squandered his political capital in this barely successful effort on Dixon and Gaubert's behalf. He had done permanent damage to his reputation, helped elect George H. W. Bush president of the United States, caused large losses to the taxpayers, and made enemies of a substantial number of Democrats on the House Banking Committee.

Mayer (1990, 238) explains the import of the Speaker's asking them to support control frauds.

> Another congressman who was at the meeting told me in early 1989, when commentators still believed the ethics investigation of Wright would fail to produce any action, that if the Speaker got into any real danger, and it began to seem unlikely that he could retaliate, the Democrats on the Banking Committee would abandon him. There are, after all, very few ways a man can lose his seat in the House, and one of them is going to bat for the likes of Don Dixon and Tom Gaubert. Wright had asked members to do that, and they would not forgive him for it.

Wright caused problems that went beyond angering the Democratic members of the House Banking Committee. He nullified the Democrats' best issue, the "sleaze factor," against the Republican candidate in the rapidly approaching 1988 presidential election. He did it despite strong efforts by fellow Texan and party elder Bob Strauss to get him to stop. If the Democratic candidate lost the 1988 presidential election, there would be many Democrats furious with Wright and scared of what he might do next. House Democrats knew it would be unpleasant to be in the minority, which was where Wright's lack of judgment seemed to be taking them.

The real irony, however, is that none of it was necessary. Had the Speaker not felt personally stung by the vote and determined to reverse it, the league would have done his dirty work for him. The league, almost as terrified by a $15 billion FSLIC recap bill as were Dixon and Gaubert, was gearing up to kill the bill and chew up anyone who got in the way. The league and Wright, acting separately, each had enough muscle to pervert the FSLIC recap into a device for gutting the Bank Board's regulatory powers. But they were not acting separately; they were allies. Together they ensured that the FSLIC recap would face the May massacre.

THE ADMINISTRATION MAKES A SEPARATE, SECRET PEACE WITH THE SPEAKER

Barry makes clear that Wright had utter disdain for President Reagan; it is also clear that the contempt was mutual. The irony is that the administration almost saved the Speaker from himself. Having already unintentionally damaged chances for a $15 billion FSLIC recap bill with their "friendly fire" assertion of the FSLIC's purported inability to spend more than $5 billion in any year, the administration now engaged in intentional fire at Gray. With "allies" like this, who needed the league and the Speaker as opponents?

The Reagan administration decided to make a separate peace with Wright. In late April 1987, Treasury Secretary Baker asked Wright for a meeting on the FSLIC recap. Baker kept the meeting secret from Gray. The administration offered not to reappoint Gray as Bank Board chairman. His term expired June 30, 1987, so he would never control a penny of the FSLIC recap money. Danny Wall would be the new chairman, and he was a big believer in two things sure to please Wright: forbearance and trying very hard never to upset powerful politicians. Wall supported Craig Hall and suggested to Gray that he fire Selby, so he was on the "Wright" side of the issues.

Wright knew, of course, that because key administration officials loathed Gray, there was no chance that Reagan would reappoint him.

Wall's appointment was essentially a done deal. Thus, the administration wasn't really offering Wright anything in return for his support of a $15 billion FSLIC recap bill.

Wright had no real objection to a $15 billion recap if it subsidized Texas S&Ls and their borrowers. He said he would support the $15 billion recap if the administration agreed to support the forbearance language. The administration had always supported covering up the scope of the FSLIC crisis, so it was happy to agree to forbearance provisions.

This was, finally, a smart political and PR move on Wright's part. He would neutralize press criticism by publicly supporting a $15 billion FSLIC recap bill. Like Baker, he wasn't really offering anything. He could, behind the scenes, help kill the $15 billion recap. The $5 billion recap, with crippling forbearance language, was certain of passage given the unified front of the league, the control frauds, and the Speaker. He could have the best of both worlds. It was also, of course, a deeply cynical move that would hurt the public interest and future relations with the administration.

All really great disasters involve bad luck, and Wright experienced his share during the media focus on his blocking the FSLIC recap. A few days after he met with Secretary Baker, and before Wright announced his support of the recap, the Bank Board put Vernon Savings in receivership and immediately brought a civil suit alleging that Dixon had looted Vernon Savings and seeking to freeze Dixon's assets. We had put Vernon Savings on the front burner for a takeover as soon as Gray decided to take on the Speaker. The publicity was horrific for the Speaker. It was bad enough that Vernon had a private air force and navy; it was far worse that the Speaker had used both. The average person was stupefied that any S&L could have over 90 percent of its non-Texas loans in default. We kept the pressure on Wright with a series of news items on the *MacNeil/Lehrer NewsHour* featuring Vernon Savings.

Wright went ahead and announced the day after we filed suit against Dixon that he was supporting the $15 billion FSLIC recap. He said that his change of position had nothing to do with Vernon's closure. The world concluded that Wright had changed his position because his support for Dixon had become politically untenable, given the receivership. The irony is that Wright's supporters promptly sealed this conclusion by openly threatening Gray. Prins allowed the *Washington Post* to quote him by name, saying:

> If this is an attempt to embarrass Wright, then Mr. Gray is lucky that the Speaker is an advocate of the homeless, because after June, when

Mr. Gray is out of a job, he may be sleeping on a grate. (Day 1993, 245; Mayer 1990, 159; Binstein and Bowden 1993, 262–263)

Wright's hopes for good publicity over his purported decision to support the $15 billion recap turned sour.

THE MAY MASSACRE

We could compete with the league's professional lobbyists when the setting was the House Banking Committee. The members knew something about S&L issues; their staffs were often knowledgeable; and the number of members was large but not enormous. We could not possibly, however, compete with the league's grassroots lobbyists, i.e., the local S&L executives who were on a first name basis with the senator or representative, contributed to their campaigns, and ran their election committees. More particularly, we could not compete with 500 such grassroots lobbyists descending en masse on the Capitol and fanning out to meet every member of Congress in two days.

The league now called hundreds of S&L executives to Congress to lobby personally virtually every member of the House. As Mr. O'Connell testified in 1993 before the National Commission on Financial Institution Reform, Recovery and Enforcement:

> I was the guy who organized the grass roots political organization for the savings and loan business. I think I did a good job, and I think it was successful when we had to go to the Hill. We spent a fair amount of money from the trade association. . . .
>
> I tried to have political contact people from the business in each congressional district. [W]hen I wanted to get three, four, five hundred people in there, I got three, four, five hundred people there [on the Hill] and usually had all the congressional districts covered. (NCFIRRE 1993b, 181)

On April 30 the league faxed its members and said that Wright's and St Germain's "turnaround" created the "need to flood these Members' offices with phone calls" before the full House voted on the FSLIC recap on May 5 (Black 1993a, 47). The requested deluge occurred.

It was clear that we were going to suffer a defeat of epic proportions in the House. The league might have only trounced us if we had won the vote in the House Banking Committee, but because we had lost, other members had political cover for voting against the Bank Board.

Wright could have actually supported the $15 billion recap plan, and it still would have lost. This would have been of great benefit to him in fending off bad publicity and ethics charges. Instead, he tried to be too clever by half. This simply led to more bad press and the accurate perception on the part of the administration that Wright had deceived them.

Wright should have reconsidered his strategy of publicly supporting, while privately killing, the $15 billion recap once the storm of bad publicity about Vernon Savings broke. He did not. Undersecretary of the Treasury George Gould explained:

> We saw the Speaker go to the well and deliver an impassioned speech. But our people on the Hill told us it was hopeless: While Wright was speaking his whip Coelho had people all over the floor telling congressmen not to pay attention, the Speaker didn't mean it. And sure enough, the House repudiated its Speaker by a record margin. The hypocrisy was incredible. (Mayer 1990, 241)

The league's success seemed total. Martin Lowy (1991, 193–194) described the May 5 vote as

> the high-water mark of the League's political power. And certainly it was the night that everyone in Congress resented most when it turned out that the League had hornswoggled them.

According to Jim O'Shea (1991, 257),

> It was an incredible display of the U.S. League's legislative clout. . . .
> Virtually every congressman who received money from high-flying and traditional thrifts voted the way the industry wanted on at least two of the three votes [on May 5]. And when one or two lawmakers strayed from the League's path, it was usually a face-saving move like Wright's.

The league shared this view of its power. On May 8 it wrote each of its members:

> Thank you for your part in achieving one of the greatest grass roots legislative victories in our history. Your calls, letters and visits to your Members of Congress made the difference. . . .
> The *New York Times* called the vote "a major lobbying victory for the thrift industry's largest trade group, the . . . League . . . , and a dra-

matic display of the influence of local thrift institutions on their elected representatives. . . .

The lesson of this week's events is that it pays to be actively involved in politics in your local Congressional district and in legislative efforts affecting your business. Your voice and your vote count and nothing demonstrated this so dramatically as the House vote Tuesday on the FSLIC recap bill. As a Congressman who fought unsuccessfully for the $15 billion amendment said afterward, the vote for $5 billion "proves (former House Speaker) Tip O'Neill's axiom that 'all politics is local.' It is very hard for a Congressman to say no when his local S&L executive calls him about a vote." (U.S. League of Savings Institutions, Book 5, Tab A-22)

A majority of Republicans (98–72) voted against the administration bill. The Republicans voting to gut the FSLIC recap included Trent Lott, Newt Gingrich (the hysterical and hypocritical critic of Speaker Wright on S&L matters), and other luminaries. Overall, the vote for the $5 billion FSLIC recap bill with the ruinous forbearance provisions was 258–153. Democrats voted against the bill by more than a two-to-one margin. Gray had tried to stand in the way of the biggest sixteen-wheeler anyone had ever seen. The league ran us over, and so little was left that we did not even constitute road kill; we were just a smear on the pavement.

FORBEARANCE EQUALS A FIELD DAY FOR CONTROL FRAUDS

Representative Bartlett introduced the forbearance provisions. The Texas control frauds drafted the language. Their drafting combined sophistication and crudeness to dramatically reduce the Bank Board's ability to take action against them. The cleverest provision required the Bank Board to calculate real-estate losses no more stringently than under GAAP. That sounded reasonable. The view was that the Bank Board had many creative regulatory accounting principles (creative RAP) designed to hide real losses. GAAP was the normal standard. Adopting GAAP sounded like a reform.

The control frauds knew that Gray had gotten rid of virtually all the creative RAP and was about to sweep away the last vestiges. They also knew that the Bank Board RAP for loss recognition was more stringent than GAAP because GAAP understated real (market-value) losses on bad real-estate loans and investments.[5] Mandating the use of GAAP would lead to inflated values of real estate, which was very bad for taxpayers. By the time the Bank Board could establish that an S&L was insolvent according to GAAP, it would be severely insolvent on a market-value basis. When the FSLIC sold assets, no buyer would pay the inflated GAAP value. Buyers care about market values.

The even more severe problem, however, was that by making asset values a question of GAAP interpretation, the forbearance provisions could devastate supervision. The best possible tactical position for an insolvent control fraud would be to have the Bank Board forbidden to require the recognition of any losses greater than those required under GAAP. That meant that the controlling expertise was in GAAP, not in the actual (i.e., market) value of the asset. The experts in GAAP, of course, were the Big 8 audit firms. As previously explained, the control frauds routinely hired Big 8 firms and received clean opinions signed by an auditor who had a resume that made him or her look like God's accounting representative on earth. In a hearing or trial related to the S&L, the auditor would attest to the "fact" (i.e., fiction) that the S&L's financial statements were reported in accordance with GAAP. The Bank Board would then put its examiner, who might have taken two courses in accounting, on the stand. We had little doubt about whose view a judge was likely to credit. By the same token, the Bank Board was the expert under the classification-of-assets rule that the Bank Board and every other federal banking regulator used. On the issue of supervisory judgment as to the credit quality and risks of an asset, no Big 8 auditor could claim comparable expertise.

The Bank Board had to be able to demonstrate that an S&L had incurred great losses before it could take over an S&L or even take enforcement action. This forbearance provision would severely reduce the Bank Board's ability to act to protect the taxpayers.

A related forbearance provision called on the Bank Board to welcome abusive TDR accounting. The league's January 22, 1987, letter to its members favorably cited the GAAP provision that prevented current loss recognition for TDRs (FAS 15); the letter also supported allowing inflated asset values even for troubled assets that did not qualify for FAS 15 treatment (Black 1993a, 38). Though the league admitted that FAS 15 represented a "loophole in commercial bank regulatory discipline" (ibid., 30), it claimed that allowing such inflated values "represents a far more accurate accounting for the asset" (ibid., 33). This was patent nonsense.

The control frauds tried to gut the Bank Board's ability to require recognition of their losses by two other major means. One provision allowed S&Ls to defer recognizing loan losses due to poor credit quality over a ten-year period. Another mandated an appeals procedure that would allow the S&L or borrower to appeal any loss that the Bank Board required an S&L to recognize. The idea was to delay the recognition of losses for many months and to tie up agency personnel with hundreds of appeals.

Another proposal forced the agency to terminate its highly praised "R41c" appraisal standard. The control frauds targeted the appraisal standard because it required real estate to be valued at market value.

Collectively, the impact of these provisions would have been devastating on the agency. That was exactly what the control frauds intended.

FIGHTING AGAINST FORBEARANCE

We picked ourselves up after the May 5 massacre and continued the battle against forbearance. Indeed, we left the effort to get more money for the FSLIC almost entirely to Treasury and focused on the forbearance clauses: they represented a far greater danger than the slashing of funds to the FSLIC. Our battle against forbearance had four major components. First, we worked to dispel the "nazi" premise underlying forbearance. We explained how the Bank Board under Pratt had granted vastly more forbearance than the banking agencies and that continuing such extreme forbearance would increase losses.

Second, we pointed out a revealing flaw in the forbearance language. It applied only to the Bank Board. If it was good policy, why should it apply only to the Bank Board and not to the banking regulatory agencies? The answer could not be that the banking regulatory agencies had all along followed the policies that Congress was proposing to mandate now for the Bank Board; the banking regulatory agencies had been classifying assets for scores of years.

Third, we talked to House Banking Committee members and staff and Senator Gramm and his staff about the merits of the forbearance language. We defended our policies on the merits and explained how the so-called forbearance provisions would benefit control frauds and harm honest S&Ls. The control frauds increased interest expenses and decreased asset yields. The sooner the Bank Board closed them, the better for honest firms. We noted that Representative Barnard had praised the Bank Board's R41c appraisal standard and recommended that it serve as a model for other banking regulators. His subcommittee's hearings documented pervasive abuses by appraisers inflating values for control frauds. The appraisal industry had no uniform, national licensing standards or professional guidance. Virtually all appraisers supported R41c's requirement that they use market value.

We also explained in detail exactly how forbearance would inflate values, gut the agency's powers, make it far harder to take the necessary actions to get the criminals under control, and raise costs to the taxpayers. We made this our consistent message to reporters and began to generate a series of stories attacking the forbearance provisions.

The fourth way that we sought to counter the forbearance provisions was to draft substitutes that sounded similar to those proposed by the control frauds but with small differences that greatly reduced the damage they would do. We also worked up language for committee reports and colloquies that would allow courts to interpret the provisions in the least harmful fashion. A colloquy is a planned question-and-answer exchange done on the public record by two members of Congress for the purpose of providing the intent underlying a particular legislative provision.

Representative Leach and Senator Gramm greatly aided these endeavors. They, and their staff, worked with us to gain expertise in the subtle and arcane means by which the proposed forbearance language would emasculate the Bank Board's power to act against the control frauds. Senator Gramm always kept a foot in both camps. His speeches were consistently sympathetic to the plights of Texas banks and S&Ls. Behind the scenes, he believed that it was essential to close the control frauds. The proposed forbearance language offended him.

Representative Leach worked full throttle against the control frauds and the league. He took the lead in defeating the worst forbearance provisions. Overall, we were effective beyond our most optimistic expectations in limiting the damage caused by the forbearance proposals.

One of our best wins was the addition of a single clause to the provision stating that the Bank Board could not require the recognition of losses beyond those required under GAAP. We were able, by working with Leach and Gramm, to amend that provision by adding "except for supervisory purposes and to the extent consistent with the practices of banking regulatory agencies." We only acted "for supervisory purposes," so the "exception" covered everything we were concerned about. The

Bank Board's opponents could hardly object to the agency acting in a manner consistent with its sister agencies, because the premise of their (false) argument was that the Bank Board was acting like nazis.

Cranston and his staff, acting at Keating's behest, worked in the Senate to defeat our efforts to counter the original forbearance language. Overall, the Senate was no better than the House. It voted out a $7.5 billion recap bill with forbearance. Senators Cranston, Riegle, and Sanford (all Democrats) took the lead in killing the $15 billion proposal.[6] Garn was the strongest proponent of a $15 billion recap bill, but he could not carry the Senate Banking Committee, and neither he nor Danny Wall, his top aide who was about to become Bank Board chairman, was useful in fighting the forbearance proposals. This made Gramm's help critical.

Senator Proxmire was an obstacle, not an ally. Indeed, the league sent a letter to its members quoting him as saying:

> [In the next few weeks] we will see stories about how FSLIC is almost out of money, about how there may be one or two large thrift failures just around the corner that will supposedly bust the remaining funds. . . . I predict these stories will be deliberately leaked to stampede the Congress into acting. (Black 1993, 50)

In fact, soon after Proxmire spoke, the run at American Savings intensified and the Bank Board met urgently with Volcker, who was convinced that an overall S&L collapse could be imminent. Losses at other S&Ls were growing massively. The FSLIC was running on fumes: the total FSLIC fund was down to $500 million dollars. The industry had roughly a trillion dollars of deposits. Gray asked permission to brief closed sessions of the FSLIC's oversight committees to make them aware of how dire the situation was. Incredibly, St Germain refused permission. Proxmire assumed he was dealing with the usual bureaucratic game: exaggerate your problems and ask for a bigger budget. Officials know that there are more fictional than real crises in Washington, D.C., but that knowledge can delay the recognition of real crises.

Bringing the facts about the extent of the S&L crisis to the attention of Congress was the Bank Board's only possible counter to the league's stupendous lobbying power. This is why the league launched a preemptive attack on Gray using the Proxmire quotation. This league strategy caused the FSLIC to remain extremely conservative in its loss estimates.

St Germain blunders

St Germain remained under the Speaker's thumb even after the May 5 massacre. His staff requested routine testimony from the Bank Board on money laundering and other topics. However, one of the paragraphs in the invitation letter quoted a Justice Department official about the extensive role of fraud in the Southwest and asked the Bank Board to provide testimony on whether that problem affected or involved S&Ls. It was a heaven-sent opening. We wondered whether someone on his staff blundered or had intentionally given us the opportunity. Either way, it was too good an opportunity to pass up.

I recommended to Gray that we prepare testimony that addressed all the committee's questions but focused on the Texas control frauds and how forbearance would make it far more difficult to restrain them and bring them to justice. We could get invaluable exposure for our arguments by testifying about these issues. Rosemary Stewart argued against this strategy, counseling that it would upset St Germain. I agreed that it would upset St Germain, but thought that it was still our best strategy to defeat forbearance. Gray agreed.

My aides and I prepared a powerful presentation on the forbearance-related issues, and we incorporated the work of others dealing with the other topics on which St Germain has asked for our testimony. We filed the testimony with the committee the day before the hearing. Bill Robertson was to present it with me. He was still trying to get over our last joint foray, our disastrous February 10 peace meeting with the Speaker.

When we arrived in the hearing room and started to set up our materials, St Germain's legal counsel, Dick Still, called us forward. Dick informed us, seconds before we were to begin our testimony, that St Germain had "disinvited" us. We were not to testify; he returned our written testimony to us; and he told us to leave. He told us we were testifying about things the committee had not asked us about. I read the portion of St Germain's letter that had expressly asked for our views on S&L fraud in the Southwest and how to deal with it. He said we had misinterpreted the letter and that we were not to testify.

This was an unwise act on St Germain's part. There are few things better calculated to attract widespread press interest than a governmental attempt to prevent someone from testifying on a subject after inviting him to testify on that subject. The blunder thrilled me. I began seeking out reporters and explaining that the committee had disinvited us after reading our testimony that disclosed how severe the problem of fraud was among

Texas S&Ls and how seriously the forbearance provisions pushed by the Speaker, the Texas control frauds, and the league would harm our efforts to control that fraud. I gave them copies of our testimony complete with the charts and graphs that documented our position.

The press immediately put St Germain's staff on the defensive. We pointed out to the reporters the portion of St Germain's letter that explicitly asked for our testimony on the extent of the fraud and the steps needed to control it, and showed them that our testimony responded to every question in the letter. It was obvious to the reporters that St Germain or his staff might have screwed up in drafting the letter, but we had not done anything wrong in our response. That meant that St Germain was disinviting us to avoid any public exposure of the Texas control frauds and the resultant embarrassment to St Germain and the Speaker. That raised the obvious question of whether Wright had ordered St Germain to disinvite me, particularly given his personal attack on me at the February 10 meeting.

Warren Brookes, a columnist who wrote about economic issues, wrote a column in the *Washington Times* blasting St Germain and the Speaker for suppressing our testimony. Brookes claimed that the Speaker ordered St Germain to block our testimony.

Unfortunately, Gray cracked at this juncture, just as the crude suppression of our testimony was helping us generate a major story in the national media attacking the forbearance provisions as scandalous—drafted by thieves to benefit thieves. St Germain called Gray in a rage. Gray hurried to the Hill to meet him. St Germain excoriated him for our testimony. Gray, according to Gary Bowser, the committee aide who had helped investigate the FHLB-Dallas, blamed it on me. I had acted without authority. Gray ordered us to stop talking to reporters about the incident.

The problem was that Gray's term was about to end. He had no job, no realistic prospect of getting a good one, and large debts. One of the last things he had going for him was the goodwill of St Germain. I think that goodwill was genuine. St Germain was an atrocious legislator and human being in many ways, but he was capable of supporting others who were basically well motivated.

"HIGHEST PRIORITY—GET BLACK"

Brookes's July 9, 1987, column attacking Speaker Wright for killing my testimony about fraudulent Texas S&Ls, along with the earlier *Houston*

Chronicle article in which I criticized Speaker Wright's intervention on behalf of Gaubert and Dixon, found their way to Keating's desk. He wrote to Grogan, his political fixer. Grogan had helped get Henkel appointed and had arranged the Keating Five meeting. Both masterstrokes had not only failed (with Gray and the FHLBSF) but had turned into acute embarrassments. Keating offered Grogan a chance to redeem himself in a memorandum (reproduced as Appendix C) dated July 15, 1987, that enclosed both articles:

> HIGHEST PRIORITY—*GET BLACK*
> GOOD GRIEF—IF YOU CAN'T GET WRIGHT AND
> CONGRESS TO GET BLACK—KILL HIM DEAD—
> YOU OUGHT TO RETIRE[7]

GRAY'S VALEDICTORY WITH DINGELL

Dingell was an even more complicated person than St Germain. He and his wife were personal friends of the Speaker and his second wife Betty. Barry (1989, 730) describes Dingell as a "rock" of support for the Speaker throughout his ethics crises. Dingell began his investigations of Gray in a fashion that was brutal even by Dingell's standards. Recall that the infamous memorandum by Keating's lawyer (Mickey Gardner) told of their work behind the scenes with Dingell to try to destroy Gray's reputation. Dingell had followed up with successive investigations that kept the Bank Board reeling. In the face of my vigorous defense of the agency and Gray, Dingell (my hometown congressman!) had threatened me with jail (because of Gray's resistance to turning over documents about open institutions to him).

Now, in the last month of Gray's term, June 1987, Dingell conducted one last hearing about the Bank Board. The witnesses were White, Gray, and Black (I joked that we were the "Monochrome Coalition"). Gray had recovered his nerve and decided to go out standing tall. We made my testimony to St Germain an exhibit to our testimony to Dingell, and made sure the press was aware of St Germain's suppression of it. Dingell understood what we were trying to do by making the suppressed testimony an exhibit and knew that our testimony was intended to generate press stories calling for the defeat of the forbearance provisions. This meant that our testimony would be extremely embarrassing for St Germain and the Speaker. Dingell, the rock on which the Speaker built his ethics defense and Gray's most effective past critic, would seem to have two choices. He could suppress our testimony, or permit it and try to rebut it by flaying us alive.

Dingell, however, had come to understand who Gray was and what he was trying to do. He understood what Gray was up against better than almost anyone because he was canny and because he knew how Keating and the control frauds operated. Dingell appreciated Gray's willingness to take on the Reagan administration and push for reregulation. Dingell took a special interest in securities regulation and was a bitter foe of accounting abuses. He was particularly pleased with Gray's efforts to end Pratt's creative RAP. Dingell was a fierce opponent of powerful criminals, and he knew that the control frauds had drafted the forbearance language and enlisted the Speaker as their patron.

So Dingell found a third option: embracing Gray and Gray's positions. He called Gray forward to pose for pictures shaking his hand. He praised Gray's initiatives and courage. He let us lambaste forbearance and highlight our suppressed testimony. Then, with a twinkle in his eye, he said it was time to move on to the focus of the hearing. It was remarkable. Being somewhat paranoid myself by this time, I wondered initially whether he was praising us just to set us up for a fall. It was soon clear that he meant every kind word he said about Gray. Dingell could not possibly gain politically from what he was doing, and he risked a great deal. I am convinced that he did it because he thought it was the right and fair thing to do (and perhaps from a bit of guilt about how badly he had treated Gray). Dingell's response helped Gray a great deal psychologically. If a virulent critic like Dingell was now saying kind words about him, then there was reason to hope. It was proof that Gray had tried to do the right thing and that people were beginning to realize and acknowledge publicly that he had tried to do his duty even when doing so was dangerous and almost certain to fail.

THE FINAL FSLIC BILL

The final FSLIC recap bill was an embarrassment, but not a catastrophe. Once Wall replaced Gray, the control frauds' and the league's concerns about the amount of money given to the FSLIC declined greatly. Wall and the administration supported forbearance.

With Gray gone, President Reagan was willing to exert some effort on behalf of the bill. He issued a veto threat as the recap bill went to the conference committee. The veto threat related only to the inadequate amount of FSLIC funding in the bills, not the forbearance provisions.

The conference committee adopted a $10 billion recap bill, despite the House having voted for $5 billion and the Senate $7.5 billion.[8] The media labeled this a win for the administration because a conference committee normally compromises between the House and Senate versions, and $10 billion was bigger than either side had voted for.

Our congressional allies were even more successful on forbearance. My aides kept providing assistance even after Gray's term ended and I left to assume full-time duties as general counsel to the FHLBSF. Wall was trying to put his team in place and, fortunately, did not understand our role in counteracting forbearance or our ties to Senator Gramm and Representative Leach. Congress killed the scam of amortizing loan losses and adopted the "supervisory exception" that we drafted. The Bank Board could counter the damage the control frauds intended to inflict on the agency if it took full advantage of the exception.

THE IMPORTANCE OF THE BANK
BOARD'S CRITICISMS OF THE SPEAKER

The idea that Gray, hated by the administration, the industry, most of Congress, and much of the media, could successfully expose and fight the Speaker's ability to hold the FSLIC recap bill hostage was close to delusional. Barry (1989, 234), however, confirms that in his and Wright's view:

> the [February 10, 1987] meeting would ultimately have an impact far beyond the savings and loan industry; it would play a key role in Gingrich's effort to destroy Jim Wright.

Barry also quotes with approval Gingrich's conclusion that the S&L matters were decisive in removing Wright from power because they made him seem corrupt and because they were current (1989, 215–216).

8. M. DANNY WALL: "CHILD OF THE SENATE"

THE ADMINISTRATION'S AND WALL'S INITIAL SYMBOLIC STEPS

In the absence of a serious scandal, there is a ritual when the administration appoints a chairman to succeed its prior appointee. The outgoing chairman praises his successor at the ceremony where the new chairman takes the oath of office. The successor praises his predecessor's accomplishments and speaks of how they have made his own task much easier. The president lauds both of his appointees. But President Reagan did not invite Gray to the podium or praise him, and Wall did not mention him in the speech he made at the ceremony (Binstein and Bowden 1993, 298). The administration and Wall signaled a complete break with Gray's policies, not continuity. They also signaled the severity of their displeasure with Gray. The process inflicted a last bit of humiliation on him.

Wall sincerely believed that Gray's policies were disastrous for the Bank Board, the industry, and Gray. Mayer (1990, 242) sums it up: "For Danny Wall, Ed Gray was the enemy." Wall knew that Gray's status as the most unpopular regulator in the nation offered him an opportunity to gain by making clear his break from Gray's policies. Initially, Wall played this very well. He picked a symbolic change that was sure to receive favorable publicity. Gray had placed an unarmed guard at the door leading to the portion of the headquarters in which the Bank Board members' offices were located. Wall removed him and ensured that the act gained wide publicity, "spun" as a break with Gray's legacy of distrust and paranoia. It earned him prominent, glowing stories in the *Washington Post* and the trade press.

WALL'S PERSONNEL CHANGES

Wall believed that Gray had far too many officials reporting to him (over fifteen). He created a new layer of "executive directors," managers above the level of office director, to reduce the number of direct reports. Wall did not retain anyone involved in making policy during Gray's term as a direct report. The president also appointed Roger Martin to the Bank Board. He was a real estate developer, a Republican donor, and a friend of one of Keating's closest allies.

Wall appointed Darrell Dochow as executive director of the Office of Regulatory Policy, Oversight and Supervision (ORPOS). Dochow had spent most of his career at the Office of the Comptroller of the Currency (OCC) until being recruited to be the director of agency functions at the FHLB-Seattle. His specialty was electronic data processing. Despite the name "Policy" in the title, ORPOS did not take a lead role in setting regulatory policy under either Gray or Wall.

Wall recruited Jordan Luke to serve as his executive director for legal functions. Luke was a commercial lawyer. He promptly barred bringing any new suits against accounting firms. Wall and Luke were not close. Wall had a dim view of lawyers (a common view). Wall generally did not seek to manage the legal function. Luke saw his role primarily as that of a technician providing support to policy makers.

Wall understandably considered himself an expert in congressional relations. He brought Karl Hoyle, a PR specialist, to the agency as executive director for congressional relations and PR. Hoyle was close to Wall, but generally was not involved in policy.

Jim Boland, Wall's chief of staff, was his closest advisor at the agency. Boland was a congressional staffer and friend. The other individuals that influenced Wall's policies were his closest friend, Rick Hohlt, and to a lesser extent "Snake" Freeman. Both men were senior league lobbyists.

Roy Green, president of the FHLB-Dallas, retired soon after Wall became chairman. Wall chose George Barclay, a senior official on the banking side of the FHLB-Dallas, to replace him. Barclay had no experience as a supervisor. Barclay and Wall then forced Selby to resign (Mayer 1990, 211).

WALL'S POLICY INITIATIVES

Wall advanced two interrelated policy changes. He dramatically adopted forbearance, and he wanted the GAO to declare the FSLIC solvent. Both of Wall's top priorities focused on changing the behavior of government, not the industry. Like President Reagan, Wall believed that government was the problem. He believed that Gray and his key appointees, working together with the GAO, had created an unnecessary S&L crisis.

Wall believed in forbearance. He implicitly endorsed the industry's primary charge against Gray by pledging that he would usher in a new approach that would never "regulate to the lowest common denominator." He ended reregulation.

Recall his support for removing Scott Schultz and for preventing any suit against Craig Hall; recall also the statement he made to Speaker Wright soon after becoming chairman:

> We did have a clown in the Craig Hall thing. He would have brought down the daisy chain [of S&Ls in Texas]. (Barry 1989, 218)

His statement to Wright was in private, but Wall publicly stated, "By definition, we don't shut down Texas institutions" (Mayer 1990, 235). Takeovers of Texas S&Ls soon slowed to a trickle. Growth rates of high fliers in the Southwest, particularly in Texas, increased sharply as enforcement actions against those who broke the rules fell markedly and Jordan Luke stated publicly that he hoped that the Bank Board would continue to decrease the number of enforcement actions in 1988 (U.S. House Banking Committee 1989, 2:599; 5:307).

Wall embraced forbearance in several other ways. Gray had proposed a rule that would have ended the last vestiges of creative RAP. The Bank Board delayed that rule for over a year (U.S. House Banking Committee 1989, 2:321).

The FSLIC recap bill, as passed, required changes in the agency's net-worth requirements that would allow S&Ls to overstate their true net worth. The Bank Board adopted a rule with statutory forbearance provisions that went well beyond those required by the new law.

It appeared to me that this might have been unintentional or that the drafters had not understood the supervisory implications, so I asked Jim Barth, the new chief economist, to find out how many S&Ls would fail their net-worth requirement under the statute and under the proposed rule. Barth ran the numbers and found that a material number of S&Ls that would have failed their net-worth requirement under the statutory standard would meet it under the proposed rule. Barth understood the significance of the data. The Bank Board had far greater supervisory powers over S&Ls that failed their net-worth requirements. The proposed rule would reduce the agency's power to prevent abuses at the S&Ls that posed the greatest risk. He told his superiors at the Bank Board what he had found and, being an honorable scholar, gave me credit for sparking the research.

Wall was unhappy that Barth had performed this analysis. Richard Haas, the executive director whom Barth reported to, called him into his office and questioned Barth sharply about it. Then Haas questioned him about why I had wanted the analysis done. Barth responded that the data showed why I wanted the analysis: we were unnecessarily and sharply limiting our supervisory powers over S&Ls we badly needed to get under control. Haas made clear to him that he was never to do a study again at my suggestion, at least not without his bosses' express approval. Wall was deeply upset that this study had been done, even though it was never released to the public and remained a secret. Barth told me how he had been called on the carpet, warned me about how Wall viewed me, and explained why he could not be seen as being close to me.

The new statute also required the Bank Board to revise the classification-of-assets rule; it now had to comply with the forbearance provisions barring the agency from requiring loss recognition greater than that required under GAAP. This forbearance clause was the gravest threat to our supervisory powers, and the inclusion of the "except for supervisory purposes" phrase had been our top priority. The preceding chapter explained how Representative Leach and Senator Gramm led the successful effort to include our language. Wall decided not to take advantage of the supervisory exception in the revised rule. As a result, the rule resulted in much greater forbearance than that required by the statute.

Wall's highest priority was to change the FSLIC's internal accounting so that it could report its own solvency. Wall believed that the FSLIC's acknowledgment of its insolvency was responsible for the industry's difficulties (as opposed to the industry's problems having caused the FSLIC's insolvency). He believed that the FSLIC's insolvency caused every S&L to pay substantially higher interest rates in order to attract deposits. Wall thought that the public would believe the FSLIC if it declared itself solvent and if the GAO "blessed" that claim.

Wall was incredulous that Gray had acknowledged that the FSLIC was insolvent. He complained years later in an interview:

> Ed Gray sat at this table with Charles Bowsher [the comptroller general], and they had a bidding war about how big the losses were at the FSLIC. *And Gray's numbers were bigger than Bowsher's.* To the visitor, that made sense: Gray knew more about it than Bowsher. To Wall it was the essence of disloyalty. As late as the summer of 1987 he was insisting to Bowsher that "you only have a $2 billion problem here." (Mayer 1990, 244; emphasis in original)

The FSLIC's enormous contingent liabilities (insurance obligations to depositors of hopelessly insolvent S&Ls) caused the FSLIC and the GAO to recognize that the FSLIC was insolvent. Wall's problem was that there were even more insolvent S&Ls—and they were far more deeply insolvent—in fiscal year (FY) 1987 than there had been in FY 1986 when Gray recognized that the FSLIC was insolvent. The FSLIC's contingent liabilities were therefore larger, and the FSLIC was more insolvent, in FY 1987 than in FY 1986.

Wall could use forbearance, however, to reduce dramatically the FSLIC's contingent liabilities. He simply assumed that forbearance would work and that far fewer S&Ls would fail than Gray had predicted. The result was a sharp fall in the FSLIC's estimate of its contingent liabilities.

There were other ways the dramatic increase in forbearance could help Wall declare the FSLIC solvent. The money the FSLIC typically needed to resolve failed S&Ls was vastly greater than the amounts estimated by GAAP. GAAP underestimated losses particularly badly for control frauds and did worst of all for Texas control frauds. Every government takeover of a failed S&L directly increased the FSLIC's estimate of the cost of resolving that S&L. The FSLIC's predictions of the cost of resolution (prior to takeover) consistently underestimated actual losses, so it seemed as if the GAO should require the FSLIC to recognize dramatically greater contingent liabilities for future losses.

Wall had a five-part plan for getting the FSLIC declared solvent. I have explained the first three steps: designing accounting and regulatory changes that would make the industry report that it was healthier, stopping virtually all expensive takeovers, and revising the FSLIC's financial statements (to indicate that forbearance would substantially reduce the FSLIC's contingent liabilities). The fourth step was an ancillary benefit of stopping the takeovers. It allowed Wall to dramatically increase the amount of money in the FSLIC fund. He took the $2.3 billion in annual FSLIC insurance-premium income and the slightly larger annual funds received from FICO bond sales under the FSLIC recap and left them in the FSLIC fund. This allowed the fund to grow at an annual rate of roughly $5 billion. Wall told us that he was greatly increasing the FSLIC's cash reserves in order to convince the GAO that the FSLIC was solvent. Wall was running a negative arbitrage: the interest expense on the FICO bonds was far greater than the interest rate the treasury paid the FSLIC on its reserves. This waste, though enormous, was dwarfed by the opportunity cost of not using the fund to close the worst control frauds.

Wall's belief—that if the FSLIC fund had more cash in it, then it must be solvent—had no support under accounting theory, but he believed that politics, not accounting principles, would determine whether the GAO blessed the FSLIC's revised financial statements and reported that it was now solvent. Wall built up the liquidity of the FSLIC fund to provide the GAO with the political cover he believed it needed. His fifth step was to put political pressure on the GAO to provide that blessing. The effort failed. The GAO was livid that Wall would try to damage its professional reputation (Day 1993, 289).

THE IMPLICATIONS OF WALL'S AND MARTIN'S VIEW THAT GRAY WAS THE ENEMY

Wall was convinced that Gray had deliberately gamed the numbers to make the FSLIC appear insolvent to get the recap passed. He said this at a lunch in San Francisco where we shared a table. He sounded strikingly similar to Senator Proxmire (in the passage quoted in the last chapter) predicting that the FSLIC would create false publicity about an S&L crisis in order to induce Congress to pass an excessively large FSLIC recap bill. Proxmire, a prominent Democrat who had long chaired Senate Banking, was Wall's chief opponent on myriad issues for many years. The similarity of Proxmire's and Wall's views adds to the likelihood that when Wall became chairman he really believed that there was no S&L crisis and that forbearance was the key to preventing a crisis from developing. The industry and the administration had pushed this view since 1981, so it is understandable that Wall shared their beliefs. Congress had just voted overwhelmingly to mandate greater forbearance, and a majority in both parties had supported it. Gray was the outlier, not Wall. The administration, Congress, the industry, and Wall all agreed on three things. There was no real crisis, Gray was the problem, and forbearance was the solution.

The claim that Gray knowingly manufactured a false crisis to get the FSLIC recap passed required an explanation of why Gray made its passage his top priority. If he knew there was no crisis, he had little to gain from passage of the bill and a great deal to lose from Speaker Wright's extortion. Why would Gray have reintroduced the bill in 1987, a move likely to provoke further extortion from Wright? The control frauds offered the only logically coherent explanation: Gray was vindictive. He wanted the extra money to punish his political opponents. (In a classic example of "too many c(r)ooks spoil the soup," this logical coherence was destroyed because the control frauds offered two contradictory theories of Gray's vindictiveness. The California control frauds said that Gray was out to destroy Republican contributors; the Texas control frauds said that Gray was out to destroy Democratic contributors.) From Wall's perspective, however, the point was that everyone he talked to agreed that Gray was vindictive. Wall's view of Gray as a man who had undercut the administration's deregulatory policies, artificially created a crisis, and vindictively targeted S&Ls for closure was a common view in 1987. The control frauds and the league had spent lavishly to spread that message for years.

One testament to the success of this big-lie technique was the reaction of Larry White, the new Bank Board member, to the campaign. He began his term by soliciting complaints against Bank Board supervisors, and he insisted on hearings on whether to renew the direct-investment rule. Documents we discovered after Lincoln Savings was finally closed confirmed what I told White at the hearings: Keating had stacked the Bank Board hearing. He arranged to have a dozen prestigious (and purportedly independent) entities support his criticisms of the direct-investment rule and the agency. He secretly coordinated the testimony.

All the witnesses claimed that the Bank Board frequently acted abusively: the proof was that institutions were so afraid of reprisals that none of them would come forward to complain. I told White that this was absurd: we were guilty because no one would provide an example of our guilt. It was logically impossible to refute their claim, and an assertion that cannot be falsified is a statement of faith, not fact. I added that the truth was that Bank Board regulation still remained far weaker

than banking regulation. White told me, "Bill, they can't all be lying."
I lost credibility with him when I responded, "Yes, Larry, they can and
they are." He said that my response showed that I was acting like an
advocate.

White's view, and his conclusion that I lacked objectivity, was a natural human reaction. Consider the effect of 150 people saying the same
thing—that is how many people met with Wright at Ridglea to attack
Gray. The Bank Board member heard the same message from the administration, the league, S&L CEOs, and real estate developers. Surely
they couldn't all be lying? White knew that Gray was not a monster, but
their personalities and approaches to decision-making were so different
that they were never close. White was always wary of Gray. The charges
of abuse created smoke, and White feared that though he never saw it
himself, there might be fire. The control frauds advanced under cover
of the smoke screen they laid down.

The newest Bank Board Member, Roger Martin, adopted the views
of his fellow real estate developer, Charles Keating, even more completely than Wall did. As Mayer (1990, 242) notes, for Wall, Gray was
the enemy. Martin shared that view, but added fervor.

Just like Wright and the Keating Five, the Bank Board members
heard that Selby and Patriarca, the directors of agency function at the
FHLB-Dallas and the FHLBSF, were vindictive. Gray had personally
selected them, so their vindictiveness confirmed Gray's. The leader is
normally decisive in establishing group culture, so it followed that the
industry complaints that the FHLB-Dallas and the FHLBSF staffs were
vindictive and overly aggressive were credible. Forbearance requires
passivity, not aggressiveness. I also had a reputation for being aggressive and close to Gray.

Wall never had much success converting the field to his type of agency
culture. The central problem was that Gray put in place a normal financial regulatory culture: he personally recruited many of the best banking regulators and put them in charge of supervising the most troubled
field offices. They, in turn, raided their former agencies for many of the
best up-and-coming staff and hired new, professional staff that emu-
lated their bosses. Other FHLB presidents, at Gray's urging, recruited
banking regulators as their own top supervisors. These officials were
chosen because they were thought to exemplify the strengths of banking regulatory culture: good judgment and no-nonsense supervision.
The banking regulatory agencies were much more prestigious than the
Bank Board. The FHLB field officials thrived under the influence of the

banking regulatory culture. Danny Wall, a minor political figure with no experience in supervision, could not make them repudiate that culture.

A related problem was that the top people who joined the Bank Board from the OCC, Selby and Patriarca, were considerably more prestigious and accomplished than Wall. Selby had served in about every senior position at the OCC and had then run it. Patriarca was the *wunderkind* whose career was an improbably meteoric rise from the most junior of enforcement attorneys to the head of the most difficult and prestigious job: head of the multinational group supervising the largest, most complex banks in America. How was Wall supposed to convince other field supervisors, Selby's and Patriarca's former subordinates at the OCC, that they should ignore Selby's and Patriacrca's advice and follow his?

In a sane world, Wall would have welcomed the presence of Selby and Patriarca in the two most troubled regions, sought their advice, and learned from them. Unfortunately, in Wall's eyes Gray had tainted Selby and Patriarca by selecting them. By doing their jobs well, Selby and Patriarca had angered ultrapowerful politicians. Wall wanted to avoid confrontation.

Wall could fire FHLB officials only "for cause." This was a major limitation on his managerial sway because the field did all the direct examination and supervision. Wall potentially had leverage with the principal supervisory agents (PSA). Each FHLB CEO was also the PSA for his (they were all male) district. The Bank Board chairman, not the FHLB, determined the PSA designation. This meant that the chairman had substantial leverage over the choice of a successor when an FHLB CEO resigned. He could block any candidate by refusing to designate him as the PSA. Gray caused shock waves when he removed the PSA designation from Joe Settle (which effectively forced him to resign as FHLB-Dallas CEO). The FHLBs and their presidents formed powerful duchies that the Bank Board could interfere with only in egregious circumstances.

There were, however, important people on the Bank Board staff who supported the views that forbearance was desirable and that Gray, Selby, Patriarca, and I were too aggressive. The most important of these was Rosemary Stewart, OE's head. Stewart believed that all four of us were too aggressive, and she eventually came to believe that Gray and I had a "vendetta attitude" against Charles Keating (U.S. Senate Committee 1990–1991a, 4:153–156, 324; 5:19). Stewart's views lent great credibility to the complaints about the Bank Board under Gray. Gray, Selby, Partriarca, and I were upset with Stewart's performance; this further testified to her rightness when Wall accepted her view that we criticized her because she had blocked our misuse of the agency's enforcement powers to punish innocent S&L owners, principally Charles Keating. Stewart eventually came to believe that Gray wanted to punish Keating for opposing reregulation. She was the only Gray-appointed office director (in a nonadministrative capacity) that Wall left in charge of a department. Stewart played a vital role in confirming Wall's and Martin's conclusion that Gray, Selby, Patriarca, and I were the problem and that Keating was the solution.

Wall and Martin had, from their perspective, inherited control of a dangerously flawed agency. If their plan had been to regulate aggressively but fairly, then having two key field offices under the control of vindictive leaders would have been an almost insuperable problem, because the Bank Board could regulate aggressively only through the field. Because, however, Wall and Martin believed that the answer was to end aggressive regulation, they had a real chance of success. The Bank Board could block any aggressive action by its field offices. The only vital change needed at headquarters was to remove Robertson's control over ORPOS. Wall achieved that goal by appointing Dochow as ORPOS's executive director.

The field could not take any enforcement action or close any S&Ls without the Bank Board's approval. Green's resignation as president of the FHLB-Dallas allowed Wall to remove Selby and dramatically change the culture of the FSLIC's most important district. If Cirona were to resign as FHLBSF president, Wall could do the same at the FHLBSF, the FSLIC's second-most important district. Wall could make life sufficiently unpleasant for Cirona that he was likely to resign.

WALL'S STRATEGIC GAMBLE

If Wall were wrong about forbearance, he would increase the eventual bailout costs to the taxpayers by tens of billions of dollars. Wall and his team assumed that control frauds were rare. They also assumed that they could distinguish those rare frauds from honest but troubled S&Ls. If Wall's team were not able to distinguish the control frauds, and if the frauds were not rare, then the team would be extraordinarily vulnerable to being manipulated by the frauds. One reason that Reagan appointed Wall was that both believed government to be the problem. This predisposed Wall to believe industry complaints about aggressive regulators. Because Wall's team viewed Gray and his people as the enemy and as vindictive, they believed control frauds' claims about vindictive field regulators. The control frauds' only expertise was in manipulating people. Wall's team would be lambs to the slaughter if control frauds existed in huge numbers. Wall's efforts at deregulation and creative accounting, like Pratt's, improved the environment for control frauds and weakened the Bank Board's ability to fight them.

Wall's actions exposed the nation and his reputation to two other risks. He weakened supervision by removing the nation's top financial regulator (Selby) from the region that most needed tougher supervision and placing Barclay in charge. The loss of supervisory talent would have been enormous in any case, but Wall greatly compounded the loss by removing Selby in an attempt to placate Speaker Wright. The message to the supervisors was clear: do not upset the politically powerful. If Selby and Patriarca were right, if control frauds were important, and if they routinely developed political patrons, then this was the worst possible message Wall could have sent. If Wall succeeded in sending a similar message to the FHLBSF staff, the control frauds' victory would be complete. The losses to the taxpayers would mount tremendously.

Wall would suffer personally if he failed to change the culture of the FHLBSF and if he were wrong about the importance of frauds and the presumed vindictiveness of the FHLBSF. If the FHLBSF were fair and professional as well as correct about the nature of the control frauds, then Wall would have to block takeovers and enforcement actions supported by well-researched and well-reasoned memoranda and data. The FHLBSF led the nation in closing failed S&Ls, particularly control frauds. It had recommended thirty-five closures; the Bank Board had closed all thirty-five; and the Bank Board had never lost a case that challenged a closure recommended by the FHLBSF (U.S. House Banking Committee 1989, 5:159). All the recommendation memoranda passed my desk for review when I was the Bank Board's litigation director. The FHLBSF had, by far, the best-documented memoranda of any district.

It should also have been clear that the FHLBSF would continue to recommend closures even if Wall did not want to close failed S&Ls. Indeed, Cirona explicitly told Wall that when he visited San Francisco early in his term. Wall complained that we recommended actions even when we knew he would reject them: this, he said, could make him look bad. Cirona told him that our job was to give him our best advice; he would decide whether to take it. Wall glared back but said nothing.

Cirona and Patriarca shaped the FHLBSF's culture. The FHLBSF made possible Gray's reregulation by closing so many control frauds more quickly than the FHLB-Dallas district could. These closures provided the facts to support a strong rationale for reregulation. An FHLBSF senior supervisor, Chuck Deardorff, conducted a study of fraud and abuse that helped the Bank Board identify the pattern of control frauds. The FHLBSF recommended that conservators be appointed for control frauds before they had been proven insolvent. The law allowed this, and courts upheld the takeovers, but this required very well-supported recommendations. Cirona, Deardorff, and Dirk Adams provided the leadership for this policy of earlier—and it was still far too late—intervention, and Rod Peck and Bruce Ericson of Pillsbury, Madison and Sutro, the FHLBSF's outside counsel, were critical to the implementation of the strategy. Patriarca inherited this strong team and honed the regulatory culture into an even more effective strike force against the control frauds. The senior FHLBSF managers had the freedom that comes from knowing that we could double our salaries and reduce our workweek by going to the private sector if Wall found a way to force us out. No one was willing to endanger her reputation by being intimidated by Wall, and Wall had no leverage over Patriarca.

If the FHLBSF's recommendations were correct, the frauds would fail and cause far greater losses. Wall would have to explain why he had ignored the recommendations. In this scenario, the FHLBSF would be vindicated and Wall's reputation could be ruined. Wall seems to have been so convinced of Gray's (and his top lieutenants') perfidy that he never considered this possibility.

EUREKA! I'VE FOUND IT!

The first sign of the difficulties that the FHLBSF would have with Wall involved the town in which my family lives, San Carlos, California. San Carlos had a large S&L, Eureka Federal, that failed because of its investments in mob-related real estate in Las Vegas (Pizzo, Fricker, and Muolo 1991, 221–227). It was placed in the MCP program. The FHLBSF's goals for MCPs were to stop ongoing frauds, clean up the files and record keeping, stop all new risky investments, and shrink the S&Ls. The MCP teams came from S&Ls thought to be well managed. The MCP program reached these goals, particularly in California, where the FHLBSF exercised real oversight of the MCP managers. The

FHLBSF had only one serious problem: the MCP team leader guiding Eureka Federal. Despite warnings, he continued to violate directives to stop risky investments and growth. The FHLBSF removed him in mid-1987.

Within days, we received a letter from the Bank Board directing us to rescind our removal. We were stunned that senior Bank Board officials even knew this person existed. It turned out that he was a contributor to the Republican Party. When we fired him, he flew on his private plane to Washington, D.C., where he immediately got a personal meeting with Danny Wall. Wall heard his complaint without informing the FHLBSF of the meeting or arranging for the FHLBSF to join the meeting by telephone conference. Wall did not even ask the FHLBSF to respond to the complaint; he simply ordered the FHLBSF to rescind its decision.

At the time, Wall's action seemed inexplicable to the FHLBSF. No one in the industry or in academia thought that MCPs should grow and invest in risky assets. The only industry complaints were that the FHLBSF had not forced the MCPs to shrink even more quickly. It was (and remains) impossible to know what the S&L executive told Wall, because Wall never informed the FHLBSF of the complaint or of the reasons he was ordering that the man be rehired. The only logical possibility is that the executive convinced Wall that Eureka could eliminate its losses by "growing out of its problems."

The MCP manager was a Republican, a minor politico like Wall (who shared his love for talking politics), and an innovative "can do" type with a private plane. This was exactly the kind of manager Wall wanted in the industry and the kind of man he instinctively trusted. The FHLBSF was biased against high-risk investments. Wall supported deregulation and greater asset powers, especially for sophisticated managers like the man before him. Boland, Wall's chief of staff, had a favorite analogy for describing Wall's views of why deregulation was desirable. He said that if he were to drive 80 mph down a well-known (and dangerous) parkway in the Washington, D.C. area, doing so would be unsafe, but it would be safe for a professional race car driver to do it. It was critical to avoid "regulating to the lowest denominator" so that the Bank Board did not exclude the racing pros. Plainly, the FHLBSF's decision was the product of Gray's policies; Wall's policies required the reversal of the FHLBSF decision. No input was needed from the FHLBSF, because the issue was what policy to follow and Wall knew his policies.

Wall's actions violated normal management principles. But Wall knew that the FHLBSF shared Gray's views about reregulation and forbearance. That made the FHLBSF Wall's enemy. Wall had nothing to learn from the enemy, and if the incident humiliated the FHLBSF, that was a side benefit. It would show his displeasure, serve as a warning against future acts of regulatory zeal, and increase the chance that the senior staff would leave.

What Wall failed to understand was that these actions would upset not only the FHLBSF, but every other FHLB and a good part of the Bank Board's staff as well. Wall was the leader of the entire Bank Board system. The FHLBSF was part of that system. We were his agents. Wall went out of his way to signal the industry: I do not trust my field staff, and if they displease you, please meet secretly with me and I will reverse their actions. As President Reagan said, "The government is not the solution; the government is the problem."

The FHLBSF initially found Wall's actions incomprehensible. We did not know the depth of the distrust and animus Wall had for us when he became chairman. Cirona, Patriarca, and I had had professional and amicable dealings with Wall when he was on the Senate Banking staff. We were baffled at the change.

The FHLBSF tried to implement Wall's order to reinstate the MCP manager, but was overjoyed when his greed posed an obstacle. He demanded a long-term contract and a substantial raise! This was a golden opportunity to put our side of the matter before Wall. We explained the normal restraints on growth and risky investments by MCPs and why the rules were desirable. We explained the efforts we had made to get the manager to comply. We explained that he was already unusually well-compensated, that the raise he was demanding was excessive, and that a long-term contract made no sense since MCPs were supposed to be temporary. We were sure that Wall's order had been some snafu and that now that he knew the facts, he would use the manager's greed as a graceful way to climb down from his prior order. We were wrong. Wall ordered that we give the manager the raise and the long-term contract and that we let him expand the S&L by investing in risky investments. This sent a chill throughout the FHLBSF.[1]

Years later at a FHLBSF conference, the CEO of the S&L that acquired Eureka Federal told us what a bad job we had done during the MCP because we had permitted the S&L to grow and invest in risky assets that had had horrible default rates.[2]

GROWING OUT OF YOUR PROBLEMS—
AND INTO A CATASTROPHE

Eureka's MCP manager proposed a silver bullet to Wall. If Eureka Federal were allowed to "grow out of its problems," there would be no need for FSLIC assistance. Wall never saw a "silver bullet" he did not want for his bandolier. He adopted the same silver bullet, but with a magnum load, for the largest S&L, American Savings, at the start of his term (again, over the objections of the FHLBSF). That silver bullet missed, and the ricochet would have taken out Wall but for the most improbable stroke of luck.

Wall would later testify that when he became chairman he discovered that the largest S&L, American Savings, was "being run out of the Chairman's office" and that he promptly put an end to that. American Savings was run by its CEO, Bill Popejoy, under both Gray and Wall. Gray and Wall both failed, in part, because they ignored the FHLBSF's views and adopted Popejoy's plan to grow American Savings out of its problems.

What was run "out of the Chairman's office" by both Gray and Wall was the FHLBSF's efforts to supervise the S&L. Ann Fairbanks, Gray's chief of staff, intervened to quash the adverse findings of the FHLBSF examiners led by George Kodani. Fairbanks even threatened Kodani's job. After Gray acceded to Patriarca's pleas, which I had endorsed and forwarded to him in January 1987, to allow the FHLBSF to regulate American Savings, the examiners found additional losses. Gray decided that he had made a mistake in approving Popejoy's plan to grow American Savings out of its problems, and he put the S&L on a fast track for a FSLIC-assisted merger. That was the situation that Wall inherited.

American Savings' management now drafted a "doomsday" letter to its outside auditors suggesting that the S&L was no longer a "going concern." This is accounting jargon meaning that the firm has failed, and it triggers the most adverse accounting "basis" and results in substantial write-downs of asset values. The S&L management said that it would send such a letter to the auditors unless the Bank Board backed off and stated that American Savings would not be taken over. In substance, the S&L was holding a gun to its own head and threatening to shoot.[3]

Washington headquarters and the Corporate and Securities Division of the Office of General Counsel informed Mike and me of this shortly after Wall became chairman on July 1, 1987. I must confess that when we first heard this, we began to consider what sort of letters we could send to American Savings to prevent them from sending such a letter to their auditors. Fortunately, the securities attorney pulled us up short by asking why we would do anything of the kind. The attorney reminded us that the Bank Board was a securities-law regulator of S&Ls and that the S&L managers' underlying purpose was to avoid disclosing losses that they should, in fact, reveal. Mike and I, quite embarrassed, said that we were wrong and that the Bank Board should refuse to send any letter.[4] This appeared to be the consensus staff view.

The next day, Mike, his deputy Eric Shand, Shand's supervisory team, and I were on a telephone conference with Wall and his senior staff about American Savings' request. Mike and I explained why we opposed sending any letter. To our surprise, we were now alone in supporting that position. Wall was the most insistent on the need to send the letter in order to avert a run on American Savings that could take down the FSLIC and lead to a nationwide run. Everyone at the Bank Board feared a nationwide run, but we felt confident that we could put American Savings in the MCP program and promptly stop any run, even if Popejoy made good on his threat.

I tried to talk Wall out of sending the letter. I noted that Congress had been quite adversarial in its hearings on the Bank Board, that Dingell would claim jurisdiction over any securities-law matter, and that he opposed the Bank Board's securities-law jurisdiction. I cited the securities attorney's argument that the Bank Board's only reason for sending the requested letter would be to prevent appropriate disclosures, and that acting in this manner would undercut our moral, political, and legal authority. How could we take enforcement action against others for failing to disclose losses if we acted to prevent the disclosure of similar losses at American Savings?[5]

The securities attorney, to our confusion and consternation, compounded our difficulties by speaking up and saying that we had been prepared to countenance a Bank Board letter last night. That was quite true, but we had promptly reversed ourselves in response to his arguments. The staff consensus had evaporated; the FHLBSF was the only one opposing the letter. Wall ordered it sent.

An analogous dispute soon arose. The FHLBSF had found evidence of pension-law violations by American Savings while it was under Charles Knapp's leadership. Knapp was the most infamous of the high fliers who had caused American Savings' insolvency. In such a case, the field office would refer the matter to the Washington office, which would forward it to the Department of Labor. The problem was that Washington sat on the referral for months. We pointed this out to Wall, in writing, and urged action. To my knowledge, Washington never made the referral. I know of no other S&L which received such favorable treatment on a pension-law violation.

Wall continued to direct the supervision of American Savings from his office. He made a major change almost immediately. Gray had urgently directed the FSLIC to find an acquirer, and the FSLIC had selected Ford Motor Co., which already owned First Nationwide, a large S&L based in San Francisco. Wall now reversed course and endorsed Bill Popejoy's plan to grow rapidly by borrowing in the short run and investing in long-term assets.[6] This, of course, exposed an insolvent S&L to severe interest-rate risk, which is what started the debacle! The FHLBSF vehemently opposed this plan as being imprudent. (Actually, it was insane, but you have to be polite even when your boss seriously proposes jumping off a cliff.)

With Wall's blessing, American Savings increased its interest-rate-risk exposure in the summer of 1987—and interest rates shot up. Soon, the S&L had an unrealized loss of over $2 billion from this failed interest-rate gamble. It was already seriously insolvent from fraud losses, so every penny of the new losses would be borne by the taxpayers. American Savings funded its purchase of longterm securities with very short-term Reverse Repurchase Obligations (REPOs). REPO loans are collateralized by high-quality fixed-rate bonds. When interest rates increase, those bonds lose value and the REPO contract imposes a "margin call" that requires the borrower to immediately post enough new high-quality bonds to protect the lender against any loss. This means that American Savings faced a double whammy: the increase in interest rates both reduced the value of its huge bond portfolio by over $2 billion and produced repetitive margin calls that created a severe liquidity problem. This same dynamic later caused Orange County's bankruptcy.

Wall and his top advisors met one weekend that fall. American Savings would collapse on Monday when it could not meet its margin calls. That was inevitable. Wall's staff was in emergency meetings with the Federal Reserve to try to get large amounts of cash in order to fend off any runs that might be triggered by closing the nation's largest S&L in a liquidity-and-solvency crisis. The FHLBSF was suddenly (and temporarily) back in Wall's good graces. I was leading an emergency effort to prepare the legal and factual grounds for a takeover. Wall faced imminent disgrace.

Then Monday came—"Black Monday," October 19, 1987. The largest stock market loss in American history occurred that day. Frightened investors sold stocks and bought bonds, which caused interest rates to fall. American Savings did not have to meet any margin calls, and over half the losses on its interest-rate-risk gamble were made good. Black Monday brought gloom worldwide, except in a tiny pocket at the Bank Board's headquarters, which found renewed faith in God. It was the miracle on 1700 G Street. Proposed as a movie plot, the story would be rejected as too contrived.[7]

WRIGHT ATTEMPTS TO GET WALL TO FIRE ME

After the February 10, 1987, meeting, and after my criticisms of the Speaker began appearing in the press, he added me to his "to fire" list.

> On July 29, 1987, Wall paid a courtesy visit on Wright. While Wall was waiting in Wright's offices, some of Wright's staff asked whether William Black was still employed by the Bank Board. . . . Wall said he responded that Black was no longer on the staff of the Bank Board, but was on the staff of the FHLB-San Francisco, an independent entity. When Wall entered Wright's office, Wright asked the same question about Black and Wall gave the same answer.
>
> According to Wall, sometime after November 20, 1987, and perhaps as late as early 1988, Wright's aide Phil Duncan called [K]arl Hoyle, the Bank Board's director of Congressional and Public Affairs. According to Wall, Duncan told Hoyle that Wall's response that Black was now employed by the FHLB-San Francisco, and thus out of the Bank Board's responsibility, was not satisfactory. Duncan did not accept that. He wanted Black fired. (U.S. House Conduct Committee 1989, 274; transcript citations omitted)

Wall personally passed on to Cirona, the president of the FHLBSF, Wright's desires that I be fired. Cirona, however, supported me. He simply warned me that Wright was trying to get me fired and to avoid giving Wall any pretext of "cause" for firing me. Wall did the only thing he could: he ordered me not to talk to the press. Charles Babcock, a *Washington Post* reporter, was amused to hear Wright use obscenities in his attack on me during their interview (May 1, 1988, memorandum memorializing telephone call with Charles Babcock).

Wall also suggested that his general counsel, Jordan Luke, tell me that Wright wanted me fired. I asked Luke why Wall was so upset with me, particularly because we had never had any problem before he became chairman. Luke said Wall was upset that I had taken on Wright. Wall felt that Wright was so powerful and vindictive that I had endangered the entire agency by criticizing him. Wall also felt that I had acted in a manner so contrary to my own interests that he did not trust my judgment. If I criticized Wright, I would surely have no compunction in criticizing Wall if I felt he acted improperly. Both of Wall's reasons were logically coherent.

LINCOLN SAVINGS: ACCEPTING THE WEREWOLF'S ADVICE ABOUT SILVER BULLETS

Wall made serious mistakes after taking advice from people who believed in silver bullets, including Eureka's MCP manager and Bill Popejoy, but at least none of them were evil. Within weeks of becoming chairman, Wall began committing the mistakes that would force him to resign. Wall took Charles Keating's advice about how to solve the Bank Board's problems with Lincoln Savings and the FHLBSF. The same silver bullet would slay both problems. The Bank Board's problems with Lincoln Savings and Wall's problems with the FHLBSF were, as Wall perceived them, the same. The FHLBSF enraged Keating and his political allies in the White House and Congress. The "silver bullet" was to remove the FHLBSF's jurisdiction over Lincoln Savings.

The difficult thing, given that the reader knows the story will end badly, is to recreate how Keating could induce Wall to reach decisions that now seem suicidal. It appeared the opposite to Wall in 1987 and 1988. In 1987 and 1988, Wall considered Gray's actions suicidal. Keating was someone who top politicians strove to meet at parties. He had close ties to the White House, the House and the Senate, and top state officials in Arizona and California. He was a major subject of a *60 Minutes* segment about the "New Southwest" that focused on his novel way of doing business and suggested that Lincoln Savings must be enormously profitable. Top-tier audit firms gave his financials "clean opinions" and decried the FHLBSF's criticisms. Lincoln Savings reported at times that it was the most profitable S&L in the country. Again, Boland is the one who had the telling phrase to describe Wall's perspective. Keating was so powerful and so nasty that, in Boland's catchphrase, "he can get you in ways you'll never know you've been got." Keating was a political force of nature the likes of which none of us, including Wall, had ever seen.

Years later, William Seidman, the FDIC chairman, told us that he had met Wall shortly after his term began and inquired how he was going to deal with the problems at Lincoln Savings. Wall replied that there were no problems; he had taken care of the whole matter. Wall inherited an FHLBSF recommendation to appoint a conservator for the S&L when he took office on July 1, 1987. The Bank Board's power to appoint a conservator for a California-chartered S&L was restored on August 10, 1987, when President Reagan signed the FSLIC recap bill into law.

By late July 1987, it was clear that the FSLIC recap bill would soon become law. Bill Robertson, the director of ORPOS, wrote a memorandum to the Bank Board on July 23, 1987, in which he recommended that a conservator be appointed for Lincoln Savings. He was particularly disturbed by the evidence of efforts to deceive the examiners that Anne Sobol had gathered in her enforcement investigation. He asked for an opportunity to brief the entire Bank Board (U.S. House Banking Committee 1989, 5:598–615).

Robertson's staff made the routine scheduling calls to Wall's assistant to arrange a briefing on the FHLBSF's recommendation to appoint a conservator. Wall's assistant did not respond to their calls, so they e-mailed him. He did not respond to the e-mails (the Bank Board system allowed the sender to know whether the message was ever opened; the ORPOS e-mails were opened but never responded to [U.S. Senate Committee 1990–1991b, Special Counsel Exhibit 238]). This was unprecedented. (That is a phrase that is going to recur in this discussion of Lincoln Savings.) The FHLBSF's recommendation to appoint a conservator for Lincoln Savings was never heard by the Bank Board under Wall. The FHLBSF was never permitted to brief the Bank Board on Lincoln Savings. That was unprecedented.

While the Washington and FHLBSF supervisory staffs moved to try to put Lincoln Savings into conservatorship, Keating raced to cut off those attempts. On the same day, July 23, 1987, that Robertson sent a memorandum to Wall recommending that a conservator be appointed, Wall's closest aide, Jim Boland, accompanied by Dorothy Nichols, my former deputy and now my successor as litigation director, met with counsel for Lincoln Savings. Lincoln's lawyers withdrew their suit against the agency, expressing their confidence that Wall would stop the abuses they claimed Gray committed. This was clever: prosecuting the lawsuit would have led to an embarrassing loss. Dropping the suit cost Keating nothing and allowed him to appear reasonable.

Earlier, on July 1, 1987, Lincoln Savings had filed the most massive response to an examination report in history. Over 750 pages long, it had many boxes of exhibits in support. Keating boasted that Lincoln Savings had spent millions of dollars preparing the response. The cost was primarily for Kaye, Scholer's legal fees, since they authored the response. It was, superficially, quite good, but disingenuous.

Kaye, Scholer's response triggered a large number of questions at the FHLBSF. The firm represented, on Lincoln Savings' behalf, that a series of facts the examiners had found were not facts. For example, the examiners found that the loan files contained no credit checks or appraisals. Kaye, Scholer represented that the loan files contained both. In fact, both statements could be literally true. When the examiners reviewed a particular file, it had no credit check or appraisal; later, when Kaye, Scholer wrote its response, it represented that the file then had both documents. The FHLBSF's newly acquired knowledge that Lincoln Savings was stuffing the files with documents created after the loan had been made suggested a need to check for even more widespread deception. Had the FHLBSF known that Jones, Day's "regulatory audit" confirmed all the examiners' key findings about the total lack of appropriate underwriting, and that Lincoln Savings used the the Jones, Day write-ups of document deficiencies as a road map for creating new documents and engaging in additional file stuffing, its concerns would have been even deeper.

The FHLBSF staff, outside counsel, and accounting experts reviewed the response. They found other things that made no sense and suggested that the responses were structured to mislead the examiners. Dividing the review of the examination response among us, we analyzed its errors and made a list of the most serious concerns; these needed to be reviewed immediately during a two-week "field visit" (jargon for a short, focused examination rather than a "full scope" examination). The topics to be covered by the examiners in the field visit and the timing were provided to the S&L in writing on August 28, 1987 (U.S. House Banking Committee 1989, 5:508). The OE and ORPOS concurred in providing this notice—which was standard procedure—to Lincoln Savings.

Among the topics for the field visit was the "tax sharing" agreement between Lincoln Savings and its parent holding company, ACC (U.S. House Banking Committee 1989, 5:621). Another topic was a suspicious transaction involving a property with a large loss that was suddenly sold for an enormous gain. For reasons that were not known by either the Bank Board or the FHLBSF in fall 1987, Keating could not allow the agency to learn of the extraordinary abuses involving either the agreement or the real-estate transaction. It was imperative that he prevent the field visit if he were to avoid a Bank Board takeover. I explain why in the next chapter.

Thereafter, nothing was ever normal again about the supervision of Lincoln Savings. On July 31, 1987, Wall made Darrell Dochow, the lead supervisor of the FHLB-Seattle, the "executive director" of supervision, which effectively demoted Bill Robertson to an ill-defined deputy position (U.S. House Banking Committee 1989, 5:507).

On September 2, 1987, only five days after the FHLBSF sent its letter to Lincoln Savings about the field visit, Lincoln Savings' counsel met with Boland and Jordan Luke, Wall's new general counsel (ibid., 5:521). The purpose of the meeting was to hear Lincoln Savings threaten to sue the Bank Board if the field visit took place. No one from the FHLBSF was informed of this request for a meeting with the Bank Board; no one at the FHLBSF was informed that senior Bank Board managers would meet with Lincoln Savings; obviously, the FHLBSF did not participate in the meeting; and the Bank Board did not request the FHLBSF's views prior to making decisions in response to the threat to sue.

Jordan Luke was not a litigator, yet he did not alert the Litigation Division about the meeting, brought no litigator with him to the meeting, and did not ask his Litigation Division for its views prior to reaching a decision, even though the issue (ostensibly) threatened litigation. Boland and Luke did not consult Dochow prior to reaching their decision or alert him to the meeting. Dochow was Wall's newly minted executive director of ORPOS (i.e., their colleague whose office presumably should have had the lead on matters involving examinations). Then, adding insult to injury, they made Dochow call the FHLBSF the next day and halt the planned field visit. All of these actions were unprecedented (unless you count the end run by the MCP manager of Eureka as an analog). Boland and Luke recommended to Wall (and there is every reason to believe that they recommended what they knew Wall wanted) that he prevent the field visit. Wall ordered that the scheduled field examination not go forward. At this point, Dochow was informed of the decision, and he communicated it to the FHLBSF. No examination had ever been halted in American financial regulatory history because of a threat of suit.

The violations of good management practices are so obvious that they do not require discussion. The incident shows how quickly Wall was able to transform the headquarters culture. By creating another layer of management and recruiting non–Bank Board staff to fill it, he could be sure that those who reported directly to him were strong supporters of his policies and mode of operating and that they could keep in check any holdovers from Gray's regime.

The incident also shows the types of staffers Wall favored: technicians who defined their job as trying to implement smoothly their boss' policies. They were dedicated to getting the trains to run on time; where they ran and what they carried were not their department. They also shared Wall's obsession with secrecy.

Wall's success in creating a supportive headquarters culture so quickly was all the more remarkable because the actions he needed support for were so antithetical to every normal supervisory reflex. The normal response of an agency lawyer, when a regulatee's lawyer threatens suit if your client acts within its statutory mandate, is to make it unmistakably clear that the effort to intimidate will fail. Few things could be more clearly within the Bank Board's mandate than the examination of an S&L. If he had sued, Keating would have lost, which would have created a desirable precedent for the Bank Board. Indeed, his lawyers could have been sanctioned for bringing a frivolous suit. More to the point, Keating could not sue to halt the examination, because the suit would be public, and depositors, bondholders, and shareholders of Lincoln Savings and its parent holding company, ACC, would have asked what Keating was trying to hide from the examiners. The Bank Board would have answered that question, in court, with the findings of the FHLBSF examination that demonstrated how badly mismanaged and abused the S&L was. The "short" selling alone (jargon for investments made in the belief that the share price will soon fall sharply) would have tanked ACC's stock and Keating's wealth. The Bank Board knew exactly how specious Keating's claims were likely to be because he had recently filed his claim of purported bias by Gray, and that motion contained many pages of invective against Gray, but not a single act or statement of bias against Keating. Moreover, Gray had had no involvement in the FHLBSF's examination—and he was gone. Keating's legal claims, therefore, were frivolous.

General counsels normally respond to threats of litigation by energizing their staff to work tenaciously to ensure that the agency wins in court. New general counsels are normally eager to establish that no outside lawyer can push them around. Every natural instinct, honed by law school, should have driven Luke to respond to Keating's litigation threats with the Clint Eastwood line "Go ahead. Make my day!" Instead, Luke went along with Wall's decision to spike the field visit. Luke did not even make the most minimal effort to learn the facts before recommending capitulation. Again, this goes against every legal instinct and practice.

Dochow's actions were even more inexplicable. Luke was brand new and had never been a supervisor. It was conceivable that he did not understand how much damage he was doing to all Bank Board regulators, indeed all financial regulators. Dochow was personally chosen by Wall to serve as executive director of the Office of Regulatory Policy and Supervision (ORPOS), yet Wall had excluded him and his people (both in the field and at headquarters) from any role in an unprecedented decision that could do incalculable harm to all financial regulators. They did not even inform him of the meeting in advance. The normal instinct of any supervisor upon hearing that the regulatee is desperate to avoid being examined is to assume that there must be a very good reason for the desperation. The normal response is to put the examiners in the shop immediately, beef up the team, and tell them to look intensively to find what the S&L or bank is trying to hide. The obvious suspects were the topics the FHLBSF had informed Lincoln Savings would be the subject of the field visit. This was a dispute whose resolution was of transcendent importance for the continued survival of the Bank Board. In any normal world, Dochow would have taken the lead in the meeting and insisted that the field visit go forward.

Any normal top supervisor treated the way Wall treated Dochow on this secret meeting with Lincoln Savings would have made clear that he would resign if the decision were not reversed forthwith. Wall's deliberate exclusion of Dochow was a slap in the face. It was also a slap in the face of Dochow's largest single group of supervisors, the FHLBSF. Dochow could not keep any credibility with his troops in the field if he allowed this kind of end run and surrender. Dochow, however, appears to have taken the way he was treated as proof of his need to get into Wall's good graces. Wall obviously viewed the FHLBSF as the enemy. If Dochow stood with the FHLBSF, Wall would treat him like the enemy.

The substance of the September 2 agreement was that the field visit was postponed indefinitely. The Bank Board would rereview the examination report and Lincoln Savings' massive response to it, and would then independently determine whether a field visit would be appropriate. Such a rereview by headquarters was unprecedented. If the rereview concluded that the FHLBSF had acted properly, our normal supervisory powers would be restored. Again, this was unprecedented.

Lincoln Savings, at a minimum, had bought itself many months in which it could not be examined. It reacted, of course, by speeding up its growth and frauds. Keating, knowing that no examiners would be permitted into the S&L, used this period of immunity to commit his most intense looting, adding massively to Lincoln Savings' ultimate losses.

The FHLBSF was dumbfounded by the order not to examine Lincoln Savings. It was startling to see how quickly and totally the emerging agency culture of regulatory vigor and courage had been ended at headquarters. (It is a measure of Wall's ability to select true toadies that not one of them ever opposed his policies on Lincoln Savings.)

Dochow told the FHLBSF that he was looking for some "middle ground" in the dispute about the field visit. This may appear innocuous, but it reveals how Dochow saw his role and the relationship between the FHLBSF and the Bank Board. Another quotation from Dochow may help illustrate the point. This quotation is from much later, on November 21, 1989, at the House Banking Committee hearings on the Lincoln Savings fiasco. It is important to emphasize that this testimony came after Lincoln Savings' collapse was known to be the most expensive S&L failure in history and Keating was known to be a fraud. Dochow was answering a hostile question about why he had agreed to Keating's demand that I be excluded from any meetings with Lincoln Savings' representatives.

> In one last effort to try to come to resolution between the institution and the [FHLBSF], with me quite frankly trying to serve as the *referee*, I decided that it was appropriate to go ahead and see if we could get Mr. Keating in the room with Mr. Patriarca and with myself. (U.S. House Banking Committee 1989, 5:107–108; emphasis added)

"Middle ground" and "referee" make clear how Dochow saw his role and the Bank Board system. A referee is a neutral between two contesting parties. To Dochow, we were not part of the Bank Board, so he could be neutral in a dispute between the FHLBSF and Keating. To us, the FHLBSF was an integral part of the Bank Board. We were the Bank Board's field unit for California, Arizona, and Nevada. We were intensely loyal to the Bank Board's mission and to the Bank Board as an institution. The FHLBSF supervisors knew they were in a knife fight with Keating. They wanted a leader who would support his troops (or clean house if there was deadwood or abuses). Moreover, no one at the FHLBSF saw Dochow as a neutral referee. The FHLBSF thought that Dochow was in Keating's corner.

Wall, who spoke of his open-door policy, never permitted a briefing by the FHLBSF (or ORPOS) on the FHLBSF recommendation to appoint a conservator for Lincoln Savings. Wall, Martin, and headquarters senior staff, however, met dozens of times with Lincoln Savings to get its views. This, too, was unprecedented. Bank Board officials met with Lincoln Savings representatives on three more occasions in September and October 1987 (U.S. House Banking Committee 1989, 5:506–596). Wall met with Keating in September. The FHLBSF was not represented at any of these meetings and often was not even informed they were to occur.

WALL AND DOCHOW MEET PROFESSIONAL RESISTANCE FROM ORPOS STAFF

Although stopping the field examination was an enormous victory, Keating (and Wall) suffered a serious setback in fall 1987. Dochow had promised to review a 750-page document with many boxes of exhibits, the FHLBSF examination report and supervisory correspondence, the results of Anne Sobol's enforcement investigation, and the FHLBSF's response to Lincoln Savings' rebuttal. Many of the materials were complex, involving arcane accounting and finance issues. Others involved legal interpretations. Dochow could not possibly review this mass of materials by himself. But now the limitations of Wall's efforts to replace Gray's supervisory culture surfaced. Dochow called on his staffers who were liaisons with the FHLBSF, and who were already familiar with the examination report and the supervisory correspondence, to do the review. The official in charge was Al Smuzynski; his principal aide was Kevin O'Connell. Kevin had worked for an S&L and then the FHLB-Chicago before joining the Bank Board. He was a prodigious worker with good analytical skills and a phenomenal memory. He was also a son of the S&L League's executive director, William O'Connell. Al was an "old timer" with broad experience. He was steady and calm. Kevin was impassioned and had a wicked sense of humor. They made a good team. Dochow's problem was that he had no one at ORPOS who was loyal primarily to him (as opposed to the Bank Board's mission).

O'Connell was also a problem for Dochow and Wall because he was too candid. He told a Bank Board attorney handling a fairly minor application by Lincoln Savings that Wall had ordered Dochow to have the S&L rescind the application because Wall did not want to have to make any decisions concerning Lincoln Savings. O'Connell warned her that any matter involving Lincoln Savings was "politically dangerous" (U.S. House Banking Committee 1989, 5:674). She was so startled and upset that she wrote down what he said as soon as he left her office and then memorialized it in a memorandum to the file.

The more fundamental problem for Wall and his senior staff was that Lincoln Savings was always an easy call. Anyone with any experience knew it would be a catastrophic failure. It fit the pattern of control frauds, and they all ended the same way. This was why it had been a straightforward task for me to draft a memorandum in 1985 for Norm Raiden's and Bill Schilling's signature recommending that Lincoln Savings' application to exceed the direct-investment threshold be denied (U.S. House Banking Committee 1989, 2:370–386). Because Dochow did not yet have staff who would serve as unthinking yes-men and yes-women but did have a record establishing that Lincoln Savings was the last S&L that should be given regulatory concessions, he was digging his own professional grave (one big enough to hold Danny Wall also) when he assigned Smuzynski and O'Connell to independently review the examination and Lincoln Savings' response. Smuzynski was already well known for his (correct) position that the FHLBSF had erred in supervising Keating by taking too long to stop his abuses.

Keating had two primary arguments. First, bias. Gray had hated him because he opposed Gray's direct-investment rule. Gray's bias had infected the FHLBSF when he sent Patriarca as its chief supervisor and when I became its general counsel. The problem was that there was zero evidence of any personal bias against Keating on any of our parts (for the very good reason that there was no such bias). Smuzynski had dealt with Patriarca, Gray, and myself on hundreds of occasions and knew these claims were spurious. More to the point, Smuzynski and O'Connell knew that other control frauds routinely made similar claims of bias against whoever was supervising them.

Keating's second argument was on the substance of the examination. Yes, the examiners had found many technical violations and paperwork problems, but they had missed the bottom line: Lincoln Savings was highly profitable. That second argument was also certain to fail with O'Connell and Smuzynski. The underlying problem again was the already clear pattern of the control frauds: Lincoln Savings fit it to a

T. Vernon Savings had earlier claimed that it was the most profitable
S&L, then failed. All the high-flier Ponzis reported exceptionally
strong profits, and all of them were catastrophic failures. Moreover,
the FHLBSF had already found that the losses were growing and that
Lincoln Savings was covering them up. The FHLBSF write-ups were
extremely tightly reasoned, documented, and professional.

In addition to these weaknesses in his case, Keating had created an
additional insuperable problem for himself. Lincoln Savings had de-
ceived the agency. That was what the forging of documents and signatures and the file stuffing were all about, and Sobol had documented
both offenses. That was decisive in Robertson's recommendation to the
Bank Board that nothing short of a takeover would be adequate (U.S.
House Banking Committee 1989, 5:602). It was certain that Smuzynski
had been heavily involved in drafting Robertson's memorandum. The
FHLBSF had reacted the same as Robertson and Smuzynski: when you
lie to the regulator, you cannot be trusted and you are trying to hide
something very bad. Until Dochow, this was universally the reaction of
regulators to Lincoln Savings' deception.

The result of O'Connell and Smuzynski's review was devastating for
Keating's case. They found that the examination report was overwhelmingly correct, the claims of bias spurious; they emphasized the criminal
attempt to deceive the agency; they pointed out that Lincoln Savings
was following the classic high-flier pattern; and they predicted that, like
all the others, it would crash and burn. They thought it would probably
cost the FSLIC roughly $500 million to resolve the failure, and noted
that the cost would increase the longer Lincoln Savings remained open
(U.S. House Banking Committee 1989, 2:603–618).

FALSE HOPES ON THE ROAD TO MUNICH

O'Connell and Smuzynski reported their results to us and Dochow
at an October 7, 1987, meeting at the Bank Board. Rosemary Stewart,
Dorothy Nichols, and Carol Larson, a Bank Board accountant, also attended the meeting. Dochow was plainly the odd man out. He spoke up
to say that he was very concerned about the risks posed to the FSLIC
by the way Lincoln Savings was operating, but he was not sure Keating
was all that bad. The entire group (other than Stewart) hammered him
about the file stuffing and the backdating and forging of documents and
signatures. He admitted that he was wrong. He told us that a conserva-

torship was out of the question because it was politically unacceptable to the Bank Board. Indeed, he told us that some members of the Bank Board felt that our recommending a conservatorship showed that we were overly aggressive.

We began, collectively, to rough out a stringent cease-and-desist (C&D) order to stop Lincoln Savings' unsafe practices. I spoke of the need to have a "united front" when dealing with the S&L, and Smuzynski responded that he thought we had one. Rosemary Stewart expressed no opposition to seeking a C&D. Mike Patriarca, trying to mend fences, sent a memorandum to Dochow on October 8 applauding the united front and asking for permission to conduct the field visit.

Dochow then met with Lincoln Savings representatives on October 21 to give them the results of Smuzynski and O'Connell's findings. Again, the FHLBSF was excluded from the meeting, even though the review had vindicated us. Dochow sent a memorandum to Patriarca two days later with his summary of the meeting. Dochow said that Lincoln Savings understood that its examination and supervision should return to normal and that the examiners would return by the beginning of 1988. Keating's threats had bought at least a four-month halt to any examination. Dochow reported that the S&L's lawyers acknowledged that they needed to improve their operations:

> I don't think they want to continue the fight and appear willing to take the proper corrective actions if we (the FHLB of San Francisco and ORPOS) also remained reasonable. (U.S. House Banking Committee 1989, 5:667)

Dochow badly misread Keating and his lieutenants. First, the implication was that Lincoln Savings would be fine if only its managers took "the proper corrective actions." But what the FHLBSF and Anne Sobol had found, and ORPOS had confirmed, was that Lincoln Savings was run by dishonest people in the classic high-flier manner, which inevitably meant disaster. Dochow thought that if they just put some systems in place (that was Dochow's area of expertise and his mantra), all would be well.

Second, the belief that Keating did not "want to continue the fight" sent the Bank Board down the road to Munich, with Wall reprising the role of Neville Chamberlain. Keating loved to fight, and by threatening to bring an utterly baseless suit, he had killed the field visit. Keating was sure to reprise tactics that had proven so successful. Moreover, Keating could not allow the examiners to discover his massive frauds involving the tax-sharing agreement.

Third, Dochow implicitly stated that Keating's team was acting "reasonably" and would continue to do so if only the FHLBSF would also do so. What did "reasonable" mean in this context? Dochow made that clearer in the remainder of his memorandum. He asked Patriarca to consider taking no enforcement action and to put the corrective action in an unenforceable, voluntary agreement with Keating. The united-front meeting had unanimously and explicitly opposed any action below the level of a C&D. Now, Dochow suggested that it would be reasonable not to take any enforcement action and rely on Keating's promises. The united-front meeting, of course, had concluded that the Bank Board's most acute concern was that Keating had repeatedly lied to the agency and that Lincoln Savings' efforts to deceive the agency were criminal. It was clear at that meeting that Dochow was the weakest link, and this confirmed it.

Worse, Dochow ended the memorandum with a new, ominous threat to the integrity of the agency. He informed Patriarca that Lincoln Savings was "very anxious" to change its supervisors; he had told it that if it acquired an S&L in another FHLB district and headquartered there, it could be supervised by the other FHLB. This too was unprecedented. No S&L had ever been permitted to acquire another S&L for the purpose of escaping supervisors it found to be too vigilant.

In addition to the obvious impropriety of rewarding someone like Keating who behaved abusively and deceptively and was leading an S&L into a catastrophic failure, this "supervisor shopping" was inappropriate for several less-obvious reasons. The law required S&Ls to have a satisfactory Community Reinvestment Act (CRA) record. Lincoln Savings made zero investments in its community. It made virtually no home loans (eleven in roughly eighteen months, and those were special favors reciprocating favors done by others), and virtually all of its investments were in Arizona real estate projects. It was a California S&L with its branches in Southern California. Its CRA record was probably the worst in the nation.

S&Ls that are serious supervisory problems, and Dochow had just agreed at the meeting with us that Lincoln Savings was a severe supervisory problem, are not permitted to buy other S&Ls. Dochow had strongly agreed with the unanimous view at the united-front meeting that Lincoln Savings was critically undercapitalized relative to its extremely risky investments and that its growth must be stopped. Yet Dochow, only two weeks later, was now contemplating approving massive growth through acquisition.

At this point, Keating drew a new card and played it brilliantly. He announced that Bill Hinz would be the new CEO of Lincoln Savings. Hinz was a well-respected S&L executive of unquestioned integrity and someone Jim Cirona knew well. Hinz met with Cirona and assured him that Keating had given him carte blanche to transform Lincoln Savings into a well-run institution. It was, of course, too good to be true, but Cirona trusted Hinz and felt pressure from Dochow to act "reasonably," as he explained:

> I have known Hinz for years. He came to see me and told me that he had never seen "such a goddamn mess" as he encountered at Lincoln. He started saying all these wonderful things about how he was going to make Lincoln into a traditional savings and loan association. (U.S. House Banking Committee 1989, 2:826)

An FHLB-Seattle official added:

> Lincoln told us that Hinz is on his way out. He was hired to work things out with Cirona but is on his way out because he failed. (ibid.)

Hinz reported to Cirona weeks later that Keating had reneged on the initial agreement and was personally directing the investment areas the Bank Board was most concerned about. Hinz, to his discredit, stayed on as an extremely well-paid figurehead for many months. Keating had bought himself another several weeks and had gotten to the end of 1987 with no examination, no supervision (Lincoln Savings refused, in writing, to comply with FHLBSF directives after Wall became chairman), and no enforcement.

We felt bitterly disappointed as 1987 came to an end, but hopeful that the stringent C&D would soon be issued and the examination resumed. Patriarca kept pressing for the return of normal examination-and-supervision authority to the FHLBSF, for the issuance of the C&D, and for sending examiners into Lincoln Savings. Dochow avoided saying either yes or no to these requests. The FHLBSF was left twisting slowly in the wind.

THE REVOLT AGAINST APPEASING KEATING SPREADS
THROUGH THE FIELD OFFICES

Wall and Dochow were confident that another FHLB would agree to allow Lincoln Savings to purchase an S&L in its district and take on the task of supervising Keating. Dochow had been director of Agency Functions at the FHLB-Seattle. Jim Faulstich, the president of the Seattle Bank, had recommended Dochow to Wall. Dochow asked Faulstich to allow Lincoln Savings to buy a district S&L and transfer its supervision to Seattle. No FHLB president in his right mind would have wanted to supervise Keating, and Faulstich made clear that he had no interest in the proposal. Dochow and Wall continued to pressure Faulstich. He agreed to have his supervisory staff meet with Keating and hear his proposal.

The meeting was a failure for Keating, Wall, and Dochow. This was another instance of Keating's behavior producing immediate distrust in people who had just met him. The Seattle staff asked Keating why he was not an officer or director of Lincoln Savings: "He responded to the effect that he did not trust the regulators and did not want to go to jail" (U.S. House Banking Committee 1989, 3:7). The staff was also upset by his willingness to purchase any S&L in Seattle, sight unseen. He obviously had only one interest: escaping the FHLBSF's jurisdiction. If Seattle said yes, it would, implicitly, send the message that it believed in weaker supervision. Seattle also studied the FHLBSF examination, the recommendation to appoint a conservator, and the ORPOS work confirming San Francisco's findings. FHLB-Seattle representatives notified Dochow that they agreed with the FHLBSF findings and opposed Keating's proposal to purchase a Seattle S&L (ibid., 2:961). Dochow and Wall did not take "no" for an answer. They asked Seattle to reconsider—and were rejected.

The FHLBs engaged in periodic peer reviews. The FHLBSF underwent such a review of its operations in late 1987. The peer review team criticized the Bank Board's interference with the FHLBSF's examination-and-supervision powers over Lincoln Savings (U.S. House Banking Committee 1989, 5:514).

By early 1988, Wall was having significant trouble neutralizing the FHLBSF's effort to close Lincoln Savings. Dochow's key staff had confirmed that the FHLBSF's findings were correct, found that there was no evidence of improper actions by the FHLBSF, and predicted that if Lincoln Savings were not closed promptly, it would cause very large losses (U.S. House Banking Committee 1989, 2:603–618). The FHLB-Seattle had killed the elegant solution of transferring jurisdiction over Lincoln Savings, and had put its agreement with the FHLBSF and ORPOS staff in writing. The peer review had supported the FHLBSF. The California Department of Savings and Loans (CDSL) supported the takeover (ibid., 2:960). Dochow and Stewart had agreed that the minimum acceptable response to Lincoln Savings' violations was an extremely stringent C&D order (ibid., 2:452–463). Hiring Hinz had been exposed as another of Keating's endless line of stall tactics. Dochow had proved ineffectual in derailing the FHLBSF's efforts to close Lincoln Savings.

The staff knew that the C&D would lead to the recognition that Lincoln Savings was already insolvent. The C&D would require Lincoln Savings to sell $600 million in direct investments that it had made in violation of the rule. Stewart, Dochow, O'Connell, Smuzynski, and Robertson agreed with the FHLBSF that the S&L had severe losses that would be exposed by the sale. It had taken far too long, and Wall's order killing the field visit had led to horrific additional losses, but the professional staff had finally reached an agreement that would lead inevitably to closing Lincoln Savings. Unfortunately, Keating understood that too, and he had another political card to play.

KEATING ADDS SPEAKER WRIGHT TO THE KEATING FIVE AND WALL ORDERS APPEASEMENT

Keating used two of the Keating Five to checkmate Wall. First, Keating convinced Senator Glenn to invite Speaker Wright to meet Keating and Glenn on January 28, 1988, to discuss Lincoln Savings' complaints against the FHLBSF. Keating's chief political fixer, and former Glenn aide, Jim Grogan attended. The Senate Ethics Committee later gave Grogan immunity in order to induce him to testify. He remained a fervent supporter of Keating's, so his admissions against Keating's interests are particularly credible.[8] Grogan testified that Keating habitually dominated all conversations. Wright, however, was so demonstrative at the luncheon meeting that Keating could hardly get a word in. Wright spent the lunch denouncing Gray and me. After lunch, Wright invited Keating and Grogan to his offices to continue the discussion and to plan actions against Gray and me. Wright kept demanding plans to have me fired and to have Gray and me sued (U.S. Senate Committee 1990–1991a, Part 1 closed, 85–89; Part 2 open, 237).

Keating then left for a meeting with Wall. Senator Cranston, another member of the Keating Five, arranged this meeting. Keating began the meeting by emphasizing that he still had the Keating Five's support and had added the Speaker's support. Keating told Wall he had just come from personal meetings with Senator Glenn and the Speaker. Referring to the Speaker, he told Wall "that is one man in Congress you would get along with much, much better if you took care of the problem in San Francisco. There is a red-bearded lawyer that's a real problem. If you took care of that problem, you would get along much better with Speaker Wright" (U.S. Senate Committee 1990–1991a, December 13, 1990, transcript 31). Keating was referring to me. Plainly, he did not think that Wall would react badly to a naked invocation of political power designed to remove one of Wall's senior officials in the field. Keating renewed his threat to sue the Bank Board if he did not escape the FHLBSF's jurisdiction.

The incident also shows that Speaker Wright ended up helping the two most notorious S&L control frauds and that he was willing to intervene despite being threatened with ethics charges stemming from his analogous acts on behalf of the Texas control frauds. His willingness, indeed zest, to take such a politically imprudent act demonstrates the ferocity of the Speaker's animus and the complete frustration he felt at being unable to stop press criticism.

This series of January 28, 1988, meetings proved decisive. Wall told Keating at that meeting that he would direct Dochow to reach an "amicable solution" to the dispute (U.S. Senate Committee 1990–1991b, Special Counsel Exhibit 150, 2–3, 5). Dochow told his aides and Patriarca of Wall's direction. Kevin O'Connell told his FHLBSF counterparts working on the Lincoln case about Wall's orders. They memorialized the directive in a February 8, 1988, e-mail message (U.S. House Banking Committee 1989, 5:559). The meaning was obvious: "amicable" meant that there would be no litigation (ibid., 5:96). Anyone who had ever dealt with Keating knew that he would not agree to anything other than the Bank Board's surrender. Moreover, Wall had just demonstrated that political pressure and litigation threats could cause him to capitulate. It was certain that Keating would use the same tactics to override any resistance by Dochow's professional staff to the order to appease Keating.

UP AGAINST THE WALL

Wall needed political cover for the order to appease Keating. The newly created Enforcement Review Committee (ERC) was used to try to provide that cover. This was a logical tactic, but it backfired, and caused further humiliation for Wall and his lieutenants. First, Dochow tried a last, desperate measure to convince the FHLBSF to cave in to Keating's demands. This was hopeless, and it further embarrassed the agency in unexpected ways. The FHLBSF team met with Dochow on February 3, 1988. Dochow informed us that Keating was demanding that our jurisdiction over Lincoln Savings be removed, that Dochow believed he would recommend that the agency accede to that demand, and that the agency was already negotiating a memorandum of understanding with Keating's lawyers that would remove our jurisdiction.

In short, the ERC was a fig leaf giving the vaguest cover to an act of naked political power. In addition to Dochow, Barclay and Luke were the voting members of the ERC. The choice of Barclay for the committee revealed a great deal about the ERC. Wall chose him, the only principal supervisory agent (PSA) with no supervisory or enforcement experience. Barclay was the only PSA who owed his appointment to Wall and the only PSA that Wall had leverage over. Barclay's vote, therefore, was a foregone conclusion. Luke, who had no supervisory experience and had followed without protest Wall's mandate to accede to Keating's demand that the field visit be halted, would make the vote unanimous. The two nonvoting members of the ERC were Rosemary Stewart and Karl Hoyle (Wall's congressional relations man). They voted, however, on one enforcement case, Lincoln Savings, providing greater cover to Wall and Martin. (Allowing nonvoting members to vote in favor of nonenforcement had a certain baroque symmetry.) Stewart detested the FHLBSF and was Keating's greatest defender on the staff, so her vote was never at issue, and Karl Hoyle's job was to keep Wall from suffering Gray's fate, so a unanimous vote in favor of appeasing Keating was inevitable. In (mild) defense of the ERC members, they rarely tried to hide the fact that removal of the FHLBSF's jurisdiction was certain because Keating demanded it as a precondition.

Dochow inadvertently informed us at the February 3 meeting that Keating had provided Martin with a file that was supposed to have adverse information about Cirona and me. Naturally, we asked to see it so we could respond. Dochow said he could not show it to us without Martin's permission. We told him that was outrageous, and we insisted on seeing the file that day (U.S. House Banking Committee 1989, 2:877–896).

We then discussed the proposed meeting with Keating. (This was the meeting that Dochow was referring to in the testimony I quoted previously about how he saw his role as a "referee" between Keating and the FHLBSF.) Dochow told us that Keating insisted that I be excluded from the meeting and that he, Dochow, believed that if that was what Keating wanted, I should be excluded. Again, for obvious reasons, all of this was unprecedented. Cirona told Dochow that was unacceptable. I was his general counsel; he had confidence in my integrity. Keating wanted me excluded because of my abilities and knowledge. No regulator could function if the regulatees could exclude the regulators they found most effective. Further, Keating was threatening to sue the FHLBSF and the Bank Board, and Cirona said that I was the first person he would pick to accompany him to a meeting with Keating. Dochow said he would still recommend that I be excluded. Cirona said that if the Bank Board gave Keating a veto over FHLBSF participants, no one from the FHLBSF would meet with him. Dochow responded that he had hoped Cirona would not say that because his recommendation would be to meet with Keating without any FHLBSF representatives. Cirona requested the right to meet with the Bank Board Members about the file that Keating had given Martin and about Keating's demands to exclude me from the meeting.

We called over to headquarters and found that White was the only Board Member who would make himself available for a meeting. Martin's special assistant also attended the meeting. White told Dochow that he should provide us with what had become dubbed "the secret file" and said that permitting Keating to veto the agency's representatives at the meeting could set a bad precedent. The Bank Board members would have to meet to decide whether to acquiesce in Keating's demand. Given White's views, we told him we would return to San Francisco to await the Bank Board's decision on the meeting.

Martin's special assistant contacted him. Martin ordered her to retrieve Dochow's copy of the secret file to prevent us from seeing and responding to it. Martin alerted Wall to Cirona's position about the meeting and to our having flown home to await the agency's decision. Wall and Martin decided to go forward with the meeting without FHLBSF representatives.

KEATING: "I DIDN'T THINK ANYONE WOULD BELIEVE ME." / STEWART: "I BELIEVED HIM."

That meeting, and a subsequent ERC meeting, produced a further humiliation for Wall and his team. (I was also excluded from the ERC meeting at which Keating and his representatives made a five-hour presentation. The FHLBSF was permitted to have a representative present only as an observer. The ERC forbade our representative to ask any questions or respond to Keating's claims.) Keating renewed his claim that Gray and I had a vendetta against him. His evidence of this vendetta was the following story (which we learned the details about over a year later, when Keating's lawyers deposed Stewart and my lawyer deposed Keating). Keating said that he attended a league convention in Hawaii and had noticed at one point that Gray was looking at him. A man came up to Keating and said that he had overheard Gray speaking to other Bank Board officials at his table. The man reported that Gray pointed at Keating and said, "That's Charles Keating. I'm going to get that cocksucker." Stewart testified at her deposition that "I believed him" (she believed Keating when he told this anecdote). The anecdote is powerful. It offers direct support of Keating's claim that Gray had a vendetta against him. Indeed, Stewart found it so powerful and believed it so completely that it led her—after Lincoln Savings was finally taken over and proved beyond any doubt to be the nation's worst control fraud—to testify under oath that Gray had "a vendetta attitude" against Keating (U.S. House Banking Committee 1989, 5:19).

Stewart and Dochow led the Bank Board delegation that met with Keating. Neither of them asked Keating any questions about this anecdote. This is why Keating had to exclude me from the meeting. In 1989, Keating brought a *Bivens* lawsuit against me for $400 million. The key to such a lawsuit is that it allows you to sue the federal employee in his individual capacity. The only silver lining to this is that we were finally able to take Keating's testimony under oath. My attorney and I crafted a series of questions about the anecdote.[9] Here is my recollection of the substance of Keating's responses.

Q. Who told you that Gray made these statements?
A. I don't know.
Q. When did he tell you that Gray made these statements?
A. I don't know.

Q. Which year did he tell you?

A. I don't know.

Q. Where were you when he told you?

A. I don't know.

Q. Were you in Hawaii when he told you?

A. I don't know.

Q. Did you take any steps to check on the accuracy of what he told you?

A. Yes.

Q. What did you do?

A. I talked to former members of Gray's staff who sat with him at the table in Hawaii.

Q. What did they say?

A. They said that Gray did not make any such remark.

Q. Why didn't you include this alleged statement by Gray in the motion you filed to recuse Gray on the grounds of bias against you?

A. (Keating, looking very sheepish) Given what we've just gone through, I didn't think anyone would believe me.

I was not in Hawaii, but I can attest that Gray never made any statement like this about anyone in my presence or to my knowledge. He also did not use that kind of vulgar language.

Stewart was the director of enforcement. By training, experience, and personality one would think that she would be certain to ask exactly the questions that immediately popped into my head when I finally heard Keating's claims about Gray. But Stewart had logical reasons to detest Gray, Patriarca, and me. We believed that the Bank Board needed a new, more vigorous head of enforcement. Patriarca and I led the effort to get her pushed laterally into some newly created office with a fine title and no real responsibility so that Gray could appoint a new director. Stewart believed that Gray, Cirona, Patriarca, Selby, and I were too aggressive. Keating was criticizing people she was predisposed to believe the worst of, and she chose to believe him uncritically. Luke, of course, lacked this excuse. One would have expected the agency's general counsel to probe Keating's claim, but Luke did not.

Again, Dochow is harder to explain. Part of the problem, well known to criminologists who study fraud, is that we are not inclined to believe that respectable people will blatantly lie to us. Dochow is a fastidious man whose expertise was systems, not frauds. The FHLB-Seattle did not have a substantial problem with control frauds. Keating wore expensive clothes, and he looked like a former champion swimmer (which he was) and a highly respectable businessman (which he was not). Dochow explained to the ERC that he was comfortable with Keating because "he looked me straight in the eye" (U.S. House Banking Committee 1989, 2:974). Control frauds, of course, can lie fluently while looking one directly in the eye and swearing simultaneously on a holy text and their mother's honor. The more important reason for Dochow's behavior was that Wall had given Dochow his orders and Dochow followed orders. Wall did not tolerate dissent, and he could remove Dochow at will. Keating conned Dochow, but Dochow made the task simple by shutting down his critical reasoning abilities.

We followed up with formal demands for copies of the secret file and an opportunity to respond. Martin's initial response to that demand was that he could not give the file to us without *Keating's permission* (U.S. House Banking Committee 1989, 2:979–981). It turned out that Martin had obtained the secret file at his own request. Keating, in one of his many meetings with the Bank Board members (all of which we were excluded from), launched one of his many personal attacks on senior FHLBSF officials and Gray. He referred to a file while making the attacks. Martin asked him for a copy. Martin then circulated it to senior Bank Board officials without informing us of the file. When we persisted in demanding the file, Martin gathered up all copies of the files at the Bank Board and returned them to Keating. He did so for the express purpose of preventing us from responding to the charges.

Dochow, supported by other staff, and Martin told two inconsistent stories about the contents of the secret file. Dochow said it simply had old newspaper clippings of stories criticizing Keating and Lincoln Savings but no information about Cirona or me. Luke and Stewart said it had two documents: Lincoln Savings' motion to recuse Gray (which contained no evidence of bias of Gray and did not deal with me or Cirona) and Keating's general counsel's memorandum of "talking points" that the Bank Board officials said had "nothing new" (U.S. House Banking Committee 1989, 2:912–913).

Martin, however, approached Cirona at a party and told him that he thought that the Bank Board would have to give Keating what he wanted. Cirona asked why. Martin said that Keating was threatening to sue the agency. Cirona responded that threats of lawsuits, and actual lawsuits, were common in America. It did not mean that you stopped doing what was right. Martin said that this was different: he had seen a Lincoln Savings file, and it had enough embarrassing dirt to make settlement prudent.

I believe Dochow's version. Once the Bank Board finally took over Lincoln Savings, there were many lawsuits, hundreds of depositions, and tens of thousands of documents produced. If Keating had had any dirt, he would not have hesitated to use it, and no dirt ever emerged. It did not exist. Keating's claims of a vendetta were pure fiction. The secret file remains important for four reasons. First, pretending it contained embarrassing information about us was a reprehensible way for Wall, Martin, and Dochow to treat their staff. Second, it enraged us and made the dispute personal. Third, it was critical that we not be given the file because our response would have been devastating and on the written record. Fourth, and most important, Martin's seizing on a group of articles that had no negative information about Cirona and me and concluding that it proved that we were engaged in personal misconduct demonstrates the degree of personal animosity he felt.

We later received confirmation of the intensity and persistence of his hate. Years later, the Bank Board was able to see the work done by Lincoln Savings' outside counsel. One memorandum sets forth the basis for bringing a *Bivens* lawsuit against me.[10] It has a long passage discussing Martin. The context is that Michael Binstein, a reporter who worked for the syndicated columnist Jack Anderson, had written articles describing the February 10, 1987, Bank Board meeting with Speaker Wright and the April 9, 1987, meeting with the Keating Five. Both articles were critical of the politicians. The legal memorandum argues that I must have been the source for both articles because I was the only person present at both meetings. The conclusion was logically and factually fallacious; I was not Binstein's source for either article. But the memorandum continued:

> Perhaps the most significant evidence that Black is Binstein's source is an investigation conducted by Roger Martin. Martin has stated to Jim Grogan that he has no doubt that Black is the individual who has provided Lincoln's confidential information to Binstein and to other reporters. Martin's conclusion is based on an investigation he conducted of an anonymous letter received shortly after the initiation of settlement discussions between Lincoln and the FHLBB. The anonymous letter, in Martin's words, called him "on the carpet" for helping Keating. The letter stated that Keating was actually Martin's enemy. Martin has told Grogan he is certain that the anonymous letter came from Black. Martin said that after he received the letter he authorized an investigation to

determine if the postmark on the letter could be matched with the travel schedules of various Eleventh District personnel. Martin discovered that the letter was postmarked from the city in which Black and an assistant to Black had traveled to on government business on the day the letter was mailed. (Kaye 1988, 4–5)

Kaye, Scholer's description of Martin's role is priceless. Remember the context. Lincoln Savings was constantly threatening to sue the Bank Board for a vindictive campaign of leaks of confidential information. Martin, even more than Wall, believed that the threat of suit (plus the political pressure) required the Bank Board to capitulate to Keating. In these circumstances, Martin told Grogan (Keating's in-house lawyer and chief political fixer) that he was sure that a Bank Board official had violated the law and harmed Lincoln Savings. That would have made Martin the star witness for Keating in the lawsuit. Martin would have confessed that the agency was guilty.

If Martin really believed that he had proof that I was leaking documents to damage Keating, he had a clear duty. That would constitute cause to fire me, and I should have been fired immediately. Martin, of course, never tried to fire me, because there was no basis for the claim. It is also revealing that Martin spent his time investigating the Bank Board's field personnel and reporting the results to Keating instead of investigating Keating and sharing the findings with the field. Of course, his idea of an "investigation" or of "proof" was idiosyncratic. When the president defines the government as "the problem," and appoints leaders who treat their staff as "the problem" and the thieves as their confidants, the thieves have a field day.

Martin was so supportive of Keating that he served as a confidant even regarding information about Wall's private views. On May 6, 1988, Keating called Senator Cranston's top aide and complained that "Black . . . precipitated this whole thing" and that "Danny Wall is too weak to stand up against him." Keating said that "Rodger [*sic*] Martin . . . said as much to him"(U.S. Senate Committee 1990–1991b, Special Counsel Exhibit 150, 2–3).

Martin's belief in the FHLBSF's perfidy was so complete that, like Stewart, he retained his belief that the FHLBSF was worse than Keating, even after Keating had been shown to be the worst S&L control fraud. When Patriarca left government service and joined Wells Fargo Bank, a San Francisco newspaper wrote the traditional blurb announc-

ing the new hire and noting how he had warned the Bank Board that
Lincoln Savings should be closed. Martin wrote the reporter a letter on
February 24, 1992, attacking Patriarca. The first paragraph showed that
Martin's inferential skills and standards of proof remained unchanged:

> I read with interest your flattering article of [*sic*] Michael Patriarca. Per-
> haps you wrote this because he leaked information to you.[11]

The ERC process continued to produce new problems for the Bank
Board. Barclay had Selby accompany him to all ERC meetings until
Selby agreed with the FHLBSF when it argued against removing Lincoln Savings from its jurisdiction. After that, Selby later testified, Barclay "disinvited" him to all future ERC meetings (U.S. House Banking
Committee 1989, 2:1048). The SEC then informed the Bank Board that
its investigation corroborated the FHLBSF's criticisms of Lincoln Savings, and the Justice Department began a criminal investigation of Lincoln Savings' massive file stuffing and document and signature forgeries
(ibid., 5:676–677).

The ERC seized on a new leak about Lincoln Savings as a justifi-
cation for removing Lincoln Savings from the FHLBSF's jurisdiction.
Unfortunately for their purposes, the source of the leak proved to be a
relatively recently created document that the FHLBSF (and Gray) had
never had access to. The Bank Board could have been the source of the
leak, but the far more likely explanation is that it came from Congress
(which the Bank Board had supplied with the document). Despite the
logical difficulties of using this as a basis for removing the FHLBSF's
jurisdiction, the ERC implied that it was a valid basis.

Meanwhile, the Munich negotiations continued, and produced further problems for the Bank Board. The documents that were emerging
would, purportedly, "freeze" the S&L's risk. The actual documents,
however, did not freeze any aspect of the S&L's risks. Lincoln Savings
was permitted to grow rapidly using high-risk assets, including direct investments (despite its massive violation of the rule) and junk bonds (because the Bank Board did not understand the authority of California-
chartered S&Ls). The Bank Board's ignorance was understandable
because it deliberately excluded the FHLBSF and the CDSL from the
negotiations. The only persons knowledgeable about the S&L's investment powers were Lincoln Savings' counsel. They did not find it prudent to point out that the Bank Board had left a gaping loophole through

which the S&L would soon drive an enormous increase in junk bonds, just as the junk bond market tanked.

It misses the primary point, however, to focus on the Bank Board negotiators' failures. Dochow and Stewart were in an impossible position. The central problem was that Wall's order (fully supported by Martin) to negotiate an agreement that Keating would approve required the Bank Board to surrender unconditionally. Keating was not aiming for a toothless enforcement agreement; he insisted on a nonenforcement agreement with serrated teeth that would slice through the Bank Board's enforcement powers. Any enforcement agreement that Keating agreed to sign would, from the Bank Board's standpoint, literally be worse than no agreement at all. Here Dochow was at a critical disadvantage, for he did not understand the Bank Board's enforcement powers and was not gifted at interpreting complex legalese. He had to rely on Stewart, and she was the staffer most supportive of Keating. This would eventually lead to a breakdown of their relationship as Dochow came to believe that Stewart had misled him about how seriously the agreements restricted the Bank Board's normal supervisory and enforcement powers.

Stewart compounded her eventual problems by personally signing a "side letter" to Lincoln Savings saying that the Bank Board had "no present intention" of filing criminal- or securities-law referrals against Lincoln Savings (U.S. House Banking Committee 1989, 2:1004). The Bank Board did have substantial new evidence of additional criminal acts by Lincoln Savings officials at the time she signed the letter, so the agency should have updated the criminal referrals. Stewart negotiated the side letter at Keating's request, but the Bank Board authorized her to sign it. Nevertheless, the personal signature was sure to make her the focus of investigators' wrath if Keating proved to be a fraud. Both the Justice Department and the SEC were likely to be furious with her (not just with Wall and Martin). The existence of the side letter was kept secret from the field.[12]

Keating's primary outside law firms for dealing with the Bank Board, Kaye, Scholer and Sidley & Austin, competed to see which could pummel the helpless Bank Board negotiators harder. They knew that Keating graded law firms on results and aggressiveness (U.S. Senate Committee 1990–1991a, 6:323–324). Margery Waxman, Sidley's lead partner on the matter (and Henkel's ethically challenged ethics counsel) wrote a January 22, 1988, memorandum to Keating discussing the February 5 meeting.

If we bring a lawsuit against San Francisco before the meeting, Bill Black
. . . will advise them not to meet with us. This will give Black and everyone else in San Francisco who is out to get us the leverage to pull the
case out of Washington. "They" have been saying we are incapable of
sitting down and rationally discussing the exam. Dochow knows that
isn't true but he won't have a choice after we sue. *Even Jordan Luke* will
advise him against talking to us after the lawsuit is filed. . . .[13]

If you can't reach a settlement with Dochow . . . then launch your
nuclear offensive . . . they will deserve everything they get. (Waxman
1988a, emphasis added)

Keating forced Dochow to agree to exclude me from meetings. Keating then convinced Dochow to exclude the agency's outside accounting
firm, Kenneth Leventhal—which the FHLBSF had hired at the recommendation of ORPOS because of the firm's real-estate expertise and
reputation for honesty—from visiting Keating's hotel, the Phoenecian
(which ultimately suffered a $100 million loss). In another of those small
things that show so much, Dochow kept referring to the FHLBSF as
having an "aggressive" edge in examining Lincoln Savings. When we
pressed, the example he came up with to support this claim was that
the FHLBSF had hired Kenneth Leventhal—which, we pointed out,
we had done at ORPOS's recommendation. Dochow had no response
at this meeting, but we later learned that he continued to criticize us
as "aggressive" when we were not present. Dochow believed that an
aggressive supervisor was so self-evidently a bad thing that he never explained why the label should not be considered a compliment.

When the FHLBSF commissioned an independent appraisal that
showed a large loss on the hotel, Keating swung into high gear. Lincoln
Savings paid a bank over $20 million in "fees" to arrange for the Kuwaiti
Investment Office (KIO) to purchase a major interest in the hotel at a
price suggesting that the hotel's market value was well in excess of the
value found by the appraiser. Simultaneously, Lincoln Savings had an
outside law firm research the Foreign Corrupt Practices Act, which pro-
hibits U.S. companies from bribing foreign officials. I joked that we now
had good evidence of the market price of bribing a Kuwaiti prince (the
royal family runs the KIO), not the market value of the hotel.

In response to the FHLBSF's warning that excluding me from meetings would set a terrible precedent, Dochow said that he saw no precedent. Keating reached the opposite conclusion. Encouraged by its
success in excluding first me and then the agency's accountants, Kaye,

Scholer induced Dochow to exclude O'Connell from any subsequent examination of Lincoln Savings and further stipulated that the Bank Board

> will give us names of everyone on the examination team for FHLB before hand and Dochow said he would listen to any objections that we might have as to suggested people. (U.S. Senate Committee 1990–1991a, 4:258)

Dochow went even further on January 3, 1989. He formally removed O'Connell from all matters involving Lincoln Savings (U.S. House Banking Committee 1989, 5:856). With the FHLBSF removed, O'Connell had emerged as the most vigorous and effective critic of Lincoln Savings. Keating, logically, targeted the officials who he most feared would stop his crimes. By 1989, however, Dochow knew that Keating was a control fraud and that he had looted Lincoln Savings so severely that it was certain to fail. Dochow also knew that the FHLBSF and the CDSL would be harshly critical of his supervision of the S&L. Dochow could not afford to have O'Connell turn on him. O'Connell understood his leverage and had a firm moral compass. He told Dochow he would resign if he were removed from the case. Dochow quickly rescinded his earlier order but tried to keep O'Connell away from taking any visible role on the case.

The FHLBSF compounded Wall's problems in the run-up to Munich. Patriarca told Dochow that the precedents the Bank Board was setting would irreparably damage the agency. He also noted a central logical flaw. If the FHLBSF was engaged in a vendetta against Keating, its leadership had to be removed. It could not be left in charge of the largest district (with over 30 percent of the industry's total assets). Patriarca and Cirona asked Dochow to fire us if he believed Lincoln's claims. (We were not offering to resign, and we would have used the effort to fire us to expose Wall's capitulation to Keating and the damage it would inflict.) Patriarca appeared, accurately, as the essence of professionalism, whereas the reputations of Wall's lieutenants' fell.

The FHLBSF also kept its cool. We were dragged back to headquarters on minimal notice, taking "red eye" flights in and flights back that same night. We were then attacked personally by our colleagues and treated as the enemy while we were exhausted. But we never lost our cool or responded with personal attacks against the ERC members, Wall, or Martin while there was still a chance we could convince them that they erred. Instead, we documented why the path they were advising would produce a disaster. The FHLBSF knew far more about Lincoln Savings, about control frauds, and about Keating than any of the ERC members. Our advantage was in logical analysis, and we maximized that advantage by concentrating all our efforts there. This meant that the record before the ERC would be acutely embarrassing to the Bank Board when Lincoln Savings failed.

9. Final Surrender: Wall Takes Up Neville Chamberlain's Umbrella

The ERC gave Wall all the cover it could, unanimously recommending the removal of the FHLBSF's jurisdiction over Lincoln Savings. The ERC members knew that they had Wall and Martin's votes. The issue was not whether their recommendation for removing the FHLBSF's jurisdiction would be adopted, but whether they could avoid embarrassment.

White was the only Bank Board member willing to be briefed by the FHLBSF. At the end of our briefing he explained that he would vote against removing the FHLBSF's jurisdiction, but would not make the matter a *cause célèbre*, because he "had bigger fish to fry." He explained that Wall and Martin's inept sales of failed S&Ls could cost the taxpayers many billions of dollars. If he went to the mat with Wall on Lincoln Savings, Wall would thereafter freeze him out, and he would be unable to stop worse scandals in the sales. White never understood the human dimension of regulation and leadership. Removing the FHLBSF's jurisdiction at Keating's behest was of transcendent importance to the Bank Board, and it was important to every regulatory agency (Seidman 1993, 188). There were billions of dollars directly at stake in Lincoln Savings (more than White could have saved on any other FSLIC deal), but the indirect cost of capitulating to Keating was far greater.

Dochow and Stewart realized that their greatest risk of embarrassment came from the FHLBSF. Their solution was straightforward: they recommended that the FHLBSF not be permitted to address the Bank Board on the most critical matter the Bank Board and the FHLBSF had ever dealt with. Bank Board meetings to consider enforcement actions always included the FHLB with jurisdiction over the S&L in question. Nevertheless, the FHLBSF was not invited to participate in the May 5, 1988, meeting. Indeed, the Bank Board kept the date of the meeting secret from the FHLBSF. Similarly, Dorothy Nichols, the litigation director, and Anne Sobol, who led the OE investigation of Lincoln Savings and recommended that the agency make a criminal referral, were not invited to attend the meeting. The CDSL and the SEC were not invited to or informed of the meeting.

But fate was unkind to the ERC members. Luke, the ERC chairman, had sent Cirona a copy of the ERC's recommendation to remove the FHLBSF's jurisdiction over Lincoln, and Cirona called Luke on May 4. Luke did not see the message slip until the morning of May 5. Luke told the Bank Board meeting that Cirona had called, but he had not responded. Luke was concerned that Cirona would attack them for secretly rushing through the ERC's recommendation at a hastily called Bank Board meeting kept secret from Cirona (U.S. House Banking Committee 1989, 6:407–408). Wall responded to Luke's concerns an hour later (9:20 a.m. in Washington, D.C.). The meeting transcript captures his characteristically convoluted style of speech.

> Let me just make the announcement that we are trying to locate Jim (Cirona) as long as was reasonable, given the difference in time, to see if he can get on the bridge [conference call]. I think it's appropriate to give them an opportunity; on the other hand, the observation has been made that the other side, the Lincoln side, is—would not be a participant. I think we have certainly heard, I think, a fair, and what appears to be even-handed presentation and it's appropriate, I think, for us to give consideration, specifically, to part of the System, in this particular case, the—our regulatory arm. So we'll see if we can get him involved (U.S. House Banking Committee 1989, 6:437–438; subsequent citations for this meeting come from this source).

It may be obvious, but here is what was going on. The Bank Board began its meeting at what was 5:20 a.m. in California. An hour later, after the ERC presentation, it woke up Cirona at his home in San Francisco (at 6:20 a.m.). (Cirona's home phone number was on a card carried by Wall's senior staff, and since it took under ten seconds to add someone to the conference line, the delay was intentional.) Cirona did not hear any of the presentation; he had no materials at home; he was half-asleep; and he was not the FHLBSF expert on Lincoln Savings—

we, his senior staff, were. Despite the palpable cynicism underlying the call, Cirona, ever the gentleman, simply declined to take part in those circumstances.

Dochow first noted that he doubted the Bank Board members had read the FHLBSF memorandum to the ERC. He said that although he knew it was "unfair" to do it this way, he would read the captions from the memorandum to explain the FHLBSF's position (435).

Freed of any knowledgeable opposition, Dochow, Stewart, Hershkowitz, Hoyle, Barclay, and Wall produced such revealing quotations that they ultimately sealed their own fates. It worked out better that we were excluded from the meeting.

The transcript is replete with tragicomic vignettes, but it can be boiled down to three areas. First, there are odes to Keating. Dochow's recommendation was premised on the belief that Keating had not been sufficiently involved in running Lincoln Savings and that the solution was to have Keating take full control of the S&L. The theme of "Keating as paragon" spread. Dochow said that any deficiencies at Lincoln Savings, e.g., its misrepresentations to the agency, had occurred when Keating was not "focused" on the matter (414). Anything Keating focused on was apparently a success. Dochow told the Bank Board:

> It's my personal belief that Mr. Keating is probably a very fine real estate developer, and so many things come to mind that, in my opinion, would indicate that (416).

Indeed, the key was to let Keating do *more*, to cut back supervisory restrictions, and, in Dochow's phrase, to let him "have a little bit of room" (418). Dochow paraphrased Keating's plea as "Trust me."

Hoyle predicted that Keating would prove "a good regulatory citizen" because he owned substantial stock in ACC (434–435). Hoyle did not have any expertise in regulation, so he may not have known that the worst S&L control frauds invariably owned substantial stock in the S&Ls they looted.

Wall spoke of his personal regard for Keating's business acumen.

> It seems to me that Mr. Keating, in my own knowledge, has been a very active, and a very entrepreneurial businessman for at least the last 13 years, that I've known him only known him basically and very much at a distance, but he is clearly not a flash in the pan and he's not a Don Dixon [who looted Vernon Savings] (450).

The second major embarrassment involved apologies for Keating's misconduct. I discussed one major example, the claim that the agency had been repeatedly lied to only because Keating had not focused on the matter. But the OE, through Stewart and her deputy Hershkowitz, mounted grander defenses of Keating. Stewart began by claiming that there was no evidence of "abnormal risk" at Lincoln Savings (422). In fact, there had never been a more sophisticated and ample documentation of "abnormal risk" by any Bank Board entity in the history of the agency than that presented by the FHLBSF and its outside experts. Dochow had just finished explaining how Lincoln Savings was replete with abnormal risk. No one pointed out the contradiction or asked how enforcement attorneys had become experts on risk.

Stewart hit her stride with her description of Sobol's findings.

A lot of depositions were taken, and people do disagree about the conclusions. I find them not particularly startling, not particularly indicative of criminal activity except by some fairly low level folks at Lincoln. (423)

The depositions proved that Lincoln Savings had engaged in massive file stuffing to deceive the examiners about its lack of meaningful underwriting of loans and investments. They also proved that hundreds of forged documents and signatures were intended to deceive the agency into believing that hundreds of millions of dollars of direct investments had been made much earlier and then "grandfathered." Everyone at the agency other than Stewart and Hershkowitz found this both startling and indicative of criminal activity. Stewart even claimed that Keating's lawyers had a "plausible" explanation for why it was permissible to *forge* documents and signatures.

The files were stuffed and the documents and signatures forged by "fairly low level folks at Lincoln" (and Arthur Andersen). But no one believed that these secretaries and paralegals decided on their own to engage in these enormous fraudulent exercises. Top lawyers ran both forms of criminality out of the Lincoln Savings and ACC legal departments. Stewart, Dochow, Wall, and Martin continued to meet with those lawyers in order to negotiate the Bank Board's surrender to Keating even though the Bank Board had filed a criminal referral against them. Indeed, Stewart had concurred in the appropriateness of that referral. Nobody at the agency thought that the lawyers were engaged in some frolic of their own not ordered by Keating. Powerful lawyers who force "low level folks" to commit forgeries are culpable and contemptible.[1]

Stewart's most novel support for Lincoln Savings, however, came when she brought up the subject of leaks.

> Finally, I believe very strongly that Lincoln has been victimized by deliberate leaks of information. My own recommendation is, in large part, based upon that belief. How the Bank Board deals with that kind of situation, when we do not have a person that we can prove is responsible for those leaks, becomes difficult. . . .
>
> So, in an indirect way, [the ERC's recommendations] address those illegal leaks of information and the harm to Lincoln. Much like Affirmative Action addresses discrimination, it's not directly in response, and yet it seems to be a fair way to deal with what we have on the table. (423–424)

This may be the single most muddleheaded analogy in regulatory history. It was not spontaneous: Stewart had been trying it out on others for months. The irony of Stewart calling for "Affirmative Action" for Keating, one of the most privileged human beings on the planet, was rich. She was probably not aware that he was a racist and sexist bigot of truly epic proportions and that he despised affirmative action (Binstein and Bowden 1993, 236, 248, 380).

Regardless of Stewart's analogy, there was no evidence that anyone at the FHLBSF had leaked anything or that the most recent leaks could possibly have come from the FHLBSF. How could removing the FHLBSF's jurisdiction over Lincoln Savings be the appropriate remedy? But no one told the Bank Board that the leak could not have come from the FHLBSF, even when Wall intimated that the FHLBSF was the most likely source of the leaks (U.S. House Banking Committee 1989, 6:808). In any event, Keating, not the press, victimized Lincoln Savings.

Hershkowitz's defense of Keating was even more robust. Stewart had said, in essence, maybe he's not crooked; maybe it's just his secretaries. Hershkowitz went much further: he seemed to be saying that the Bank Board should take no action regarding Keating, except perhaps to praise him.

> The documents that we've been talking about are all traditional enforcement documents. But this is not a traditional regulatory case. The

institution is not doing anything illegal; in fact it is engaging in those types of transactions that have been contemplated by Congress and contemplated by this Board as the general direction that the industry might go in order to increase its profits outside traditional business. . . . [M]anagement [has] a personal stake in the transactions and have been successful in turning real profits, not paper profits, in these kinds of transactions. (432)

This was an extraordinary defense of Keating. Even Stewart conceded that Lincoln Savings had committed illegal acts. How did an enforcement attorney know that Keating was producing real profits when Dochow's staff found it was producing real losses? Congress prohibited federally chartered S&Ls from engaging in almost all direct investments. But Hershkowitz was presumably reflecting accurately what was "contemplated by this [Bank] Board." Wall and Martin thought that direct investment was sure to "increase . . . profits." The argument that Keating posed no risk to the FSLIC because he had "a personal stake in the transactions" ignored the fact that officers and directors are not supposed to have "personal stakes" in S&L transactions. Such a personal stake creates a conflict of interest that violated Bank Board rules. Keating did, in fact, have such conflicts in several transactions, and they produced large real (not paper) losses. The FHLBSF examination had documented, and ORPOS had confirmed, that virtually all of Lincoln Savings' claimed "profits" were paper, not real.

The third area of embarrassment was the adoption of a bizarre, mirror-image sort of logic. Lincoln Savings was certain to fail, and fail catastrophically, if it was supervised conventionally. But using the Bank Board's logic, what appeared to be Keating's greatest weaknesses flipped, and became strengths. Keating's abusive, confrontational style and his disdain for regulation meant that Lincoln Savings' survival depended on a hands-off style of regulation. Hershkowitz explained it this way:

Based on what I've seen, and I think I've talked to Kevin [O'Connell] about this, we agree that if the institution remains in its current supervisory situation, it will, inevitably, fail. An institution that engages in high-risk transactions requires extra supervisory surveillance, and it needs a regulator that will permit management to make management decisions. San Francisco has demonstrated in the past with this institution that it believes that its current assets and risk profile is such that it will not permit them to do that. (433)

Keating's use of political power against the Bank Board should have been a major problem for him, but it became his greatest strength. The great hope became that Keating would use his political power to get favors from local and state governments, and that this would cause the value of Lincoln Savings' real estate investments to surge. Under this logic, the worse off Lincoln Savings became, the more essential it was to keep Keating in charge and free of regulatory restrictions. (Of course, they ignored the fact that Lincoln Savings was steadily getting worse precisely because Keating controlled it.) Each of these points is exemplified by Barclay's comments to the Bank Board.

> I believe also that Keating probably is the only one who can preserve a significant amount of value for Lincoln. I believe that he is a—and he proved to us, he is a very strong sales oriented individual and I believe, although he says he has no political connections, that only he can get some of the zoning changes that are necessary to enhance the value of the properties [that] otherwise would be substantial losses for the institution. (419)

Barclay went even further about fifteen minutes later, expressing concern should the Bank Board win an enforcement action against Lincoln Savings.

> And the chances of . . . if we are successful in court, would be to have the people who are most qualified to enhance and preserve value gone and the cost [to the] FSLIC would be excessively greater. (429)

Barclay voiced the *reductio ad absurdum:* when the S&L fails, the Bank Board will have to rely on Keating's political power to reduce losses. No one asked *why* Lincoln Savings was failing if Keating was such a superb real estate developer and was supported by politicians who provided him with optimal zoning and easy permit approval.

Wall and Martin voted to remove the FHLBSF's jurisdiction over Lincoln Savings. White dissented. Ever nonvigilant, the Wall Bank Board was later shocked when Keating wanted an even more abject surrender, and threatened the Bank Board politically and with litigation until it surrendered unconditionally.

WAXMAN: "YOU HAVE THE [BANK] BOARD RIGHT WHERE YOU WANT THEM"

The Bank Board's May 5 vote gave Keating everything he demanded. Characteristically, he responded to appeasement by increasing his demands. He and his lobbyists contacted members of the Keating Five to have them pressure the Bank Board into giving in to Keating's newest demands.

Once the FHLBSF had been excluded, Waxman was confident of complete success. As she gloated in her May 10, 1988, memorandum:

> You have the Board right where you want them and you should be able to reach an agreement tomorrow which will completely satisfy you.
>
> As you know, I have put pressure on Wall to work toward meeting your demands and he has so instructed his staff. They all know the Wednesday meeting is crucial to their future. If they mess up this time, it is all over. The points that you should come out with tomorrow are: San Francisco is finished. [N]othing can be done to follow up their exam. (U.S. Senate Committee 1990–1991a, Vol. 2, pp. 180–181)

The remainder of the memorandum (accurately) predicted the details of the Bank Board's surrender, which was formalized ten days later.

Grogan was so excited by the victory that he told a CDSL supervisor that Keating and Lincoln Savings "got everything they wanted from the Bank Board" (MDL #OTS-D11-0553847). The CDSL learned of the Bank Board's May 5 meeting and decisions through Grogan, not the Bank Board. This, predictably, added to Commissioner Crawford's rage against Wall.

OTHER HUMILIATIONS

The Bank Board's capitulation to Lincoln Savings was delayed both by Keating's desire to place even more restrictions on the agency and by O'Connell's tenacious rearguard action. By the time the Bank Board signed the instruments of surrender on May 20, 1988, the facts had developed so as to ensure that Wall's peers would view his action as indefensible. Wall's central problem was that Lincoln Savings was following the classic control-fraud pattern, which would inevitably lead to failure. As 1987 and 1988 rolled on, dozens more of the high-fliers were proven to be, despite forbearance, failed control frauds. The growth rule was killing the Ponzis, though forbearance and the slowdown in enforcement had extended their lives and deepened their damage.

The track record was even more dismal for S&Ls that had invested primarily in direct investments. Every S&L that had invested more than 10 percent of its total assets in direct investments in 1983 (the ones Benston had praised) had failed by 1988. Wall was betting that Lincoln Savings would be the only survivor.

Before the Bank Board could reach an agreement with Keating, it was embarrassed by an incoming tide of developments involving Lincoln Savings. The agency dealt with those embarrassments instructively. Shortly after Robertson recommended that Lincoln Savings be taken over, Wall removed his authority over it. After Selby supported the FHLBSF, Barclay barred him from attending any future ERC meetings. After the Seattle bank supported the FHLBSF, it was excluded from the May 5 meeting even though the deal contemplated eventually moving Lincoln Savings to their district.

The SEC found that the FHLBSF was correct about numerous acts of securities fraud by ACC that arose from Lincoln Savings overstating the value of its assets. The SEC also found that ACC/Lincoln Savings and their new outside auditor, Arthur Young, were so uncooperative that it was forced to institute a formal investigation. (Contemporaneously, Dochow assured the Bank Board that Keating had turned over a new leaf and was now a good regulatory citizen.) So, naturally, the SEC was not informed of the Bank Board's meeting or the planned agreements with Keating, even though they obviously undercut the SEC's case against ACC for securities fraud. The CDSL supported the FHLBSF's actions. It was, contrary to uniform Bank Board practice, excluded from the May 5 meeting. The ERC at least told the Bank Board that the CDSL opposed the proposed agreements, but it said that the CDSL's views were not entitled to any weight because it had been influenced by the FHLBSF. (Yes, the CDSL listened to our arguments, and to Dochow and Stewart's arguments, and it agreed with us. That was not a reason to disparage its views unless Dochow viewed the FHLBSF as an infectious agent.)

The ERC did not inform the Bank Board that the peer review of the FHLBSF had opposed the Bank Board's removal of its jurisdiction. Then, between May 5 and May 20, the Justice Department, which had (because of resource constraints) originally indicated that it would not investigate the FHLBSF's criminal referrals, informed the Bank Board that it had begun the investigation. O'Connell made a last ditch, impassioned effort to convince Dochow not to sign the agreements, but the only effect of his plea was to convince Dochow that he should greatly limit O'Connell's role in the examination.

Wall and Martin's gamble became desperate. If Keating turned out to be a crook, everyone would have the evidence and the incentive to say that they had warned the Bank Board not to capitulate. Dochow had a similar problem. After rejecting O'Connell's pleas, he made his own plea to Keating (through Keating's lawyers). Their notes show that he recognized there were enormous loopholes in the agreements that would allow Keating to greatly increase Lincoln Savings' size and risk. Dochow told Keating's lawyers that he was staking his reputation on the belief that Keating would not exploit the loopholes. To throw oneself on Keating's mercy was a remarkable act. Unfortunately, Dochow was entrusting the public purse along with his personal reputation to Keating's mercy. Again, it has to be stressed that the people who directed him to appease Keating (and the administration that appointed them) are most responsible for this scandal.

THE INSTRUMENTS OF SURRENDER

The agreements signed were, of course, unprecedented. They represent the only time in history that a financial regulatory agency consented to what was, in substance, a cease-and-desist order *against the agency* and permitted an institution that it had found to be in massive violation of its rules to increase those violations. The Bank Board got no meaningful restrictions on Lincoln Savings; instead it surrendered unconditionally and provided reparations ("affirmative action," in Stewart's parlance). There were three documents signed on May 20, 1988. The Bank Board eventually gave copies of two of them to the CDSL, which gave us copies. The third document was not disclosed outside a small group at headquarters (and Lincoln Savings). The Bank Board got two things in the agreement: ACC agreed to contribute $10 million to Lincoln Savings to increase its capital, and Lincoln Savings agreed to recognize a relatively small number of accounting adjustments that would have the effect of reducing its capital. The bad news, which was not in the agreement, was that ACC and the Keating family had taken roughly $120 million out of Lincoln Savings and ACC during the time the Bank Board had forbidden the FHLBSF to examine or supervise Lincoln Savings. Returning $10 million left Keating over $100 million to the good. The agreement allowed Lincoln Savings to "un"-adjust its accounts to "un"-

recognize the loss of capital if its accountants agreed, and the Bank Board knew that Arthur Young agreed with Keating that the adjustments should not be made. The provision, therefore, proved illusory.

Sadly, the Bank Board claimed a third advantage to the agreement, the right to examine Lincoln Savings. The Bank Board had an absolute right to examine any S&L, and as I explained, Lincoln Savings could not get a court to block its examination. The agreement had a number of other illusory provisions in which Lincoln Savings agreed not to do things it could not lawfully do.

The memorandum of understanding (MOU) was the first agreement a regulator ever made in which it effectively consented to a cease-and-desist order against its own supervisory powers. Recall that ORPOS and the SEC had confirmed the accuracy of the FHLBSF examination. The Bank Board nevertheless agreed that it could not use that examination to support any action against Lincoln Savings or ACC or any of their officers. Worse, in a very broadly drafted section, the Bank Board agreed that it could not bring an enforcement action against these entities even if it independently verified violations that arose from matters criticized by the FHLBSF examiners. The Bank Board agreed to remove the FHLBSF's jurisdiction over Lincoln Savings and bar its personnel from any examination. The Bank Board also agreed to limit its power to bring even enforcement actions that were unrelated to the FHLBSF findings. The MOU even allowed Lincoln Savings to expand its direct investments in ways that otherwise would have been unlawful.

Keating achieved more with the MOU than he had attempted to obtain through Henkel's subterfuge or the Keating Five's political pressure. Henkel and the Keating Five would have obtained immunity only for Lincoln Savings' existing violations of the rule. The MOU not only provided the long-sought immunity, but also allowed Lincoln Savings to make even greater direct investments with impunity. The Bank Board never brought an enforcement action against Lincoln Savings for violating the direct-investment rule, despite ORPOS's confirmation that the FHLBSF examiners were correct and Sobol's findings of widespread fraud designed to make such investments appear lawful. The political pressure finally paid off on May 20, 1988. Substantively, the MOU was the disastrous document.

The third agreement incurred the most intense wrath because it best captured the nature of the agency's surrender. It was the document kept secret from the CDSL. Stewart, at the direction of the Bank Board and the demand of Keating's lawyers, signed a side letter saying that the Bank

Board had "no present intention" of making any referrals to the Department of Justice and the SEC. Again, although Stewart recommended providing the letter and drafted it, the blame has to be placed on Wall and Martin. Even if the Bank Board had not signed the side letter, it would have been extremely loath to make additional referrals against Keating, so the letter probably had little substantive effect. The letter became a flash point in the 1989 House Banking Committee investigation of Lincoln Savings' failure.

KEATING'S VICTORY PARTY

I have quoted the memoranda showing that Keating got everything he desired from the Bank Board, but the best evidence of how happy Keating was with the deal was the party he threw when the Bank Board signed the deal on May 20, 1988. Keating, the antiporn activist, celebrated Wall's surrender with a wild party at which he taped together men and women facing each other and poured Dom Perignon down women's blouses. The revelers threw a computer out the window for good measure (Binstein and Bowden 1993, 71–72). The Bank Board's humiliation seemed complete, but it would yet deepen.

THE WHITEWASH FAILS: THE 1988 BANK BOARD EXAMINATION OF LINCOLN SAVINGS

Keating's celebration was so intense because his victory over the Bank Board was so complete. The agreements made the task of the examiners more difficult because they impaired the Bank Board's normal powers of examination, supervision, and enforcement. They also made the promptness and the effectiveness of the examination more critical because they authorized Lincoln Savings to make additional high-risk investments that would have been unlawful but for the deal. Lincoln Savings continued to grow rapidly and to place virtually all of its investments in ultra-high-risk assets. Worse, the investments were made in fraudulent transactions.

The Bank Board faced the problem of doing something it had never done: run an examination. It had to draw on the FHLBs to do that, and that posed many problems for Dochow. No FHLBSF examiners were permitted. None came from the FHLB-Dallas because its staff remained overwhelmed by local control frauds. That left ten districts, and Dochow created a team drawn from nine of them. It was, of course, difficult to assemble such a team, and the time passed. By the time the examination finally began in mid-1988, no full examination team from the Bank Board had been on-site for over a year and a half. Lincoln Savings, of course, had used that time to defraud.

Control frauds that relied on direct investments and ADC loans were clustered in the states that had deregulated the most. That meant that FHLBSF and FHLB-Dallas examiners and supervisors had by far the most experience evaluating such frauds. The FHLBSF had far more experience with control frauds that relied on direct investments because only California permitted its S&Ls to invest 100 percent of their assets in direct investments. The result was that new entrants intending to use direct investments as their primary fraud mechanism overwhelmingly sought California charters. By excluding staff from Dallas and San Francisco, Dochow had eliminated most of his expertise. Lincoln Savings was known to be the most complex S&L in the nation, so expertise was vital.

Dochow's selections of senior examination staff exacerbated the expertise problem. Dochow could not solve the expertise deficit by drawing on former colleagues at the Office of the Comptroller of the Currency because national banks are forbidden to make direct investments. Dochow selected Steven Scott from the Seattle bank to run the examination team even though he had never conducted an Office of Thrift Supervision (OTS) examination and lacked experience with the types of assets Lincoln Savings invested in. Also selected were an examiner from the Pittsburgh bank to review Lincoln Savings' real estate (which made up about 80 percent of its total assets), and an examiner from the Indianapolis bank to review the $1 billion junk-bond portfolio. The Pittsburgh and Indianapolis examiners were junior enough that I will not use their names. They had no experience with complex ADC loans, direct investments, junk bonds, or frauds. The blame for their mistakes belongs with Dochow (or Wall and Martin).

Scott was an unfortunate choice. He, like Dochow and Keating, was a fastidious dresser who believed himself to be financially sophisticated. This is the easiest personality type for a financial fraud to con. One incident captured this point for me. After Keating's massive frauds were fully exposed (no thanks to Scott), Scott met with Patriarca and me to brief us on the current condition of Lincoln Savings: the Bank Board was about to restore the FHLBSF's jurisdiction over Lincoln Savings. Scott gave us a dispassionate description of one fraud after another. At lunch, he switched subjects and went on, at great length and with real passion, about how superb Keating's private jet was. It had one of the best sound systems he had ever heard, the wood paneling was rich and tasteful, and the seats were luxurious and comfortable. Keating had superb taste. Scott was so intent on this narrative that he did not notice that Mike and I were staring at him in horror. Scott had still not lost his intense admiration for Keating.

Scott was so open in his admiration for Keating during the 1988 exam that he caused a revolt among the other examiners, state and federal. David Riley, an FHLB-Atlanta examiner, testified about how Scott instructed new examiners when they arrived in Phoenix (Lincoln Savings was a California S&L, but all its senior management and its records were in Phoenix, where Keating ran ACC):

> Scott . . . informed the examiners that the examination of Lincoln would start from a clean slate. He said that we would not be provided a copy of the previous examination report. He explained that we would not be allowed general access to ACC/Lincoln offices or employees, nor would we generally be allowed access to original documents. Instead, all questions or requests were to be directed to Tim Kruckeberg of ACC/Lincoln. . . . Scott expressly prohibited our access to ACC's main headquarters building where the offices of Mr. Charles Keating, ACC Chairman of the Board, and the other top officers were located. Steve further said that any examiner who harbored any prejudicial attitudes toward Lincoln should go home. (U.S. House Banking Committee 1989, 3:513–514)

Riley went on to testify that each of these restrictions was unprecedented and each imperiled the exam's accuracy (ibid., 514). The staff revolt, and CDSL protests, eventually caused Dochow to reduce—but not remove—these limits. In addition to these overall restrictions, Scott imposed additional unprecedented, harmful restrictions on Riley in the course of his particular assignment. Riley concluded that those restrictions were designed to blunt criticism of Lincoln Savings' asset quality and its management abuses. He and several examiners from other FHLBs complained to Scott without avail. They then complained to senior officials at their home FHLBs and were told to start documenting the problems (ibid., 514–517). The revolt became so widespread that Dochow had to visit Phoenix and assure the exam teams that he did not desire a whitewash.

The FHLBSF heard from several FHLBs and the CDSL that the

1988 examination was a whitewash. We were told that Scott had explained to new examiners that the Lincoln Savings/ACC managers were so brilliant that they were out of the Bank Board's league. Scott's most disturbing statements, however, were that everything would be fine because Keating and his lieutenants were so smart that they could prevent losses even when they made bad investments (U.S. House Banking Committee 1989, 3:64). This was obviously a troubling statement for those fearing a whitewash, but it was also a strange statement. Lincoln Savings and ACC managers were obviously inferior. For the most part they were inexperienced graduates of second- and third-tier schools (with large chips on their shoulders about status). Keating deliberately hired callow yes-men (Black 2001; Binstein and Bowden 1993, 163).

Hiring people for their weak moral fiber exposed Keating to the risk that they would steal from Lincoln Savings. Keating's audacity came to the fore when Mark Sauter, Lincoln Savings' director of regulatory compliance, was the lieutenant placed in charge of the file stuffing and forgeries. Sauter had also embezzled from Lincoln Savings. Keating eventually discovered this. Keating had a serious problem: he had to remove Sauter, but if he fired him, Sauter would make a deal with the prosecutors investigating the file stuffing and forgeries. He would plead guilty to the crimes and reveal that they his superiors had ordered the fraud. That disclosure would endanger Keating directly, but it would also embarrass the Bank Board and vindicate the FHLBSF. The press and Congress would place enormous pressure on the Bank Board to remove Keating and clean the stables.

Keating's answer to the problem of phony documents was to craft two more false documents. He reprised the strategy he had used with his Arthur Andersen resignation letter by writing a letter to Dochow and enclosing a letter from Sauter to Keating. The Sauter letter announced that he was resigning. Sauter's letter recounted how he had been eager to work with the regulators to show that an entrepreneurial S&L could be both innovative and a superb regulatory citizen. The letter then praised Keating's brilliance, ethics, etc. Sauter then explained that he was resigning because he had become convinced that the FHLBSF and Gray had a vendetta against Keating and were out to destroy him. Keating's letter to Dochow opined that it was a travesty when abusive government officials drove such a fine young man to despair and to lose faith in his own government. Dochow and Stewart did not investigate to find out why Sauter really resigned. Instead, they accepted Keating's letter as further proof of the FHLBSF's abuses. Keating's audacity conquered the credulous once more. Sauter would eventually plead guilty to the felonies outlined in the FHLBSF's criminal referrals for file stuffing and forgery, but Lincoln Savings was long dead by then.

Combining inexperienced examiners and a supervisor who supported Keating produced an examination that found only minor losses at Lincoln Savings. The S&L was insolvent by roughly $3 billion by late summer 1988, but the federal examiners had identified less than $10 million (and perhaps as little as $5 million) in real-estate losses by what they intended to be their last week on-site (U.S. House Banking Committee 1989, 3:16).

Please consider what would have happened if the examination had truly found only small losses at Lincoln Savings. The Bank Board would, implicitly, have confirmed that Lincoln Savings was profitable and exceeded its capital requirements. Keating would have been permitted to grow and to change FHLB districts by acquiring another S&L. Lincoln Savings' growth rate would have increased, and all of its new investments would have been in high-risk assets. (Virtually all of the new investments would also have been fraudulent.) It would have grown by roughly $1.25 billion in the first year, and by more than that each year it remained open. It would have lost more than this amount each year because the new real estate it financed would have deepened the glut, causing larger losses to its existing real estate. All other Arizona real estate owners would also have suffered increased losses. Lincoln Savings, and the politicians who intervened on its behalf, would have been vindicated and emboldened. Keating would have found it far easier to garner support if future examinations found problems. The FHLBSF would have been completely discredited, and other control frauds would have successfully emulated Keating's tactics to escape its jurisdiction. Control frauds in other FHLB districts would have followed the same strategy. Keating would have corrupted the entire FHLB system. The results would have been catastrophic.

"GO FOR THE THROAT"

As with the fortuitous defeat of the administration's effort to give Keating control of the Bank Board by appointing Henkel and Benston, the nation got lucky. Once more, effective public servants were essential to our good fortune. Keating was within days of his greatest triumph — a Bank Board examination that "proved" he ran a superior S&L — when he was brought down by the CDSL (Crawford, his deputy and successor Bill

Davis, Gene Stelzer, and Dick Newsom), O'Connell, Smuzynski, and two examiners from the FHLB-Chicago, John Meek and Alex Barabolak. Others deserve substantial credit for fighting bravely against Scott's efforts, but they were not in a position to deliver a decisive blow.

Crawford was the essential man. The FHLBSF had recommended that the Bank Board examine Lincoln Savings, its holding company, the tax-sharing agreement, and suspicious transactions that transmuted losses found by the FHLBSF into purported highly profitable "sales" of real estate. The Bank Board did not follow up on any of these recommendations. (If we had been cleverer, we would have begged the Bank Board *not* to investigate these subjects.) Crawford later told Dochow that the tax agreement smelled, and needed to be examined. The revolt (which Crawford supported) against the whitewash led Dochow to see the advantage of appearing responsive to such a recommendation.

In August 1988, ORPOS accountants looked at the impact of the tax-sharing agreement on Lincoln Savings (which is what the September 1987 field examination would have done). They found that Lincoln Savings had sent $94 million in cash to ACC (the parent holding company) under the purported authority of a tax-sharing agreement between ACC and Lincoln Savings.[2]

The tax-sharing fraud relied on a "cash for trash" scheme to transmute real losses into phony profits. The "profits" were so large that the tax-sharing agreement required Lincoln Savings to pay the $94 million to ACC. ACC, however, did not owe any taxes, so it was illegal for Lincoln Savings to make what was, in essence, an unsecured $94 million loan to its parent. That would have been true regardless of the financial condition of the parent, but it was a disaster given ACC's financial condition.

It was a personal disaster for Dochow. Keating had personally assured him that he did not take a dime out of Lincoln Savings. Because of that assurance, Dochow had always dismissed criticisms of Keating's (and his kin's) outrageously large salaries and his rampant nepotism. ACC had long been deeply insolvent on a stand-alone basis (i.e., without Lincoln Savings) and sharply unprofitable. That meant that ACC could not repay Lincoln Savings. It was also clear that Keating would not voluntarily repay Lincoln Savings even if he could. ACC, of course, had failed to recognize the $94 million debt to Lincoln Savings as a liability, so the Bank Board had yet another reason to know that ACC was committing securities fraud by selling worthless junk bonds to widows and stock to the general public.

Indeed, now that Dochow knew that ACC was looting Lincoln Savings through tax-sharing payments, he had to order an immediate halt to any further payments to ACC. He did so on September 6, 1988 (the best birthday present I received that year). ACC had only two positive sources of cash flow—tax-sharing payments and the junk bond sales to widows. ACC lost money on operations at a prodigious rate, mainly because of the grossly excessive salaries paid to Keating and kin. The Bank Board knew that by stopping the tax-sharing payments it was ensuring that ACC would have to increase greatly the rate at which it defrauded the widows.

The Bank Board also knew that ACC would inevitably default and cause many thousands of widows to lose hundreds of millions of dollars. This would transform the arcane S&L crisis into a political scandal. For the first time, identifiable human victims would exist. We empathize with individuals, not statistics. These victims would have faces—grandmothers' faces. There were tens of thousands of elderly victims, and there were "deep pockets" like the multitude of law firms, and three of the Big 8 audit firms, that helped Keating loot Lincoln Savings. That meant there would be private plaintiffs' counsel and congressional hearings. The lawyers and congressional aides would search for victims who were personable and articulate and had heart-wrenching stories. As a longtime congressional aide, Wall knew what was coming. He could not know specifics such as the elderly man who committed suicide when he learned that he had lost his life's savings. Or the mother who told Keating's bond seller that she was investing her savings to earn enough interest to make a down payment on a wheelchair-accessible van—for her daughter who had suffered "catastrophic brain stem damage" (U.S. House Banking Committee 1989, 4:142).

The young man (so polite, so clean cut) explained to her why she should put *all* her savings in ACC's junk bonds. The young bond seller earned a very nice bonus, and a "bond for glory" T-shirt. Maybe he had enough decency to refrain from mocking his victims at the ACC Christmas skits that made fun of the elderly who bought what one expert had publicly implied was "the worst" investment in America (U.S. House Banking Committee 1989, 2:471). In fairness to them, the bond sellers were so young and unqualified that some of them bought ACC bonds. The central point, however, is that it was Keating who devised the scheme and pressured his aides to maximize the take from the widows. He bears the moral culpability. The efforts of his defenders to excuse him on the grounds that he did not sell the securities himself, but caused callow youths to carry out the actual fraudulent sales, miss the point (Fischel 1995; Black 2001). He is more culpable, not less, and certainly more craven, because he twisted these young people (in ways that must have damaged them) into weapons against the widows.

The tax-sharing deal also meant that Lincoln Savings had made an unlawful $94 million loan that clearly could not and would not be repaid, so it needed to recognize a $94 million loss, which would cause it to fail its net-worth requirement. Killing the field visit had allowed Keating to evade the FHLBSF's order barring Lincoln Savings from paying dividends to ACC. ACC had looted Lincoln Savings of $94 million, most of it after Wall's ability to close Lincoln Savings was restored by passage of the Competitive Equality Banking Act (CEBA) in August 1987.

Dochow knew that this was only the beginning of the bad news. It was more than suspicious that Lincoln Savings claimed to have sold real estate for massive gains in a glutted real estate market. Since the FHLBSF had shown that the real estate came with large losses, the odds were good that the purported profits were phony and that the deals were "cash for trash" scams. If they were scams, then $94 million did not begin to suggest the depth of the losses. To produce $94 million in tax payments, Lincoln Savings had to have produced roughly $300 million in profits. If the profits were fictitious, then Lincoln Savings would have to reverse the recognition of over $200 million in income, and that would mean that Lincoln Savings was hopelessly insolvent. Even the $200 million loss figure did not capture Lincoln Savings' full loss exposure. In a cash-for-trash deal, the amount of cash the S&L loaned was several times larger than the fictitious profits. Lincoln Savings, therefore, could well have losses approaching $500 million from about ten loans likely to be cash-for-trash scams. Each of the borrowers defaulted.

Dochow also had to keep in mind our constant warning: CEOs that lie to the agency about one area are likely to lie about many areas. Kenneth Leventhal, the real estate specialists, eventually issued a report saying that every Lincoln Savings deal that they had reviewed was fraudulent, explaining that "Lincoln was manufacturing profits by giving its money away" (U.S. House Banking Committee 1989, 2:298).

Dochow faced a crisis in his examination. His examiners had not found a loss in any of the likely cash-for-trash deals. Indeed, the 1988 examination did not recognize that the deals, on their face, had every indicia of being cash-for-trash scams. They had missed the link between the deals and the tax-sharing agreement. The examination was criticized as a whitewash, and Dochow had personally chosen all the key individuals conducting the examination.

Dochow decided that he needed to heed the FHLBSF's and the CDSL's advice to examine ACC. Indeed, the CDSL, despite its very limited resources, informed Dochow that it would examine ACC. O'Connell was put in charge of recruiting the exam team. He came from the Chicago-FHLB and knew a holding company exam specialist, Alex Barabolak. Barabolak brought (the inaptly named) John Meek as his deputy. Together, they led an examination team that uncovered and documented new abuses, many of them criminal, everywhere they looked. Barabolak reported directly to O'Connell, not Scott. Barabolak and Meek knew that they were dealing with a control fraud. They were calm, professional, and insistent. Keating and his troops, who had been praising Scott and Dochow, soon raged at Barabolak and Meek.

The arrival of the Chicago examiners freed the CDSL to examine Lincoln Savings. Crawford's instructions to his team were to "go for the throat" (U.S. House Banking Committee 1989, 3:56). Gene Stelzer and Richard Newsom were unleashed on Keating. They, within ten days, had found three times as many losses as Scott's examination (ibid., 3:16, 269). Moreover, their conclusions were well documented, and the S&L's initial responses often dug Keating's grave deeper. Newsom was a real-life Detective Columbo. It was a special horror for the ever-elegant Keating to be taken down by such a slovenly character who also turned out to be whip smart, tenacious, fearless, and extremely competent. Within a month, Newsom had identified over $50 million in losses — over five times more than Scott's team (ibid., 3:271).

In a speech in Berlin in 1963, President Kennedy noted that "Dante once said that the hottest places in hell are reserved for those who in a period of moral crisis maintain their neutrality."[3] The Bank Board should have considered that, just as it should have known that Lincoln Savings was a control fraud before it surrendered so abjectly to Keating in May 1988. But by early September 1988 there was no doubt that the Bank Board knew that Lincoln Savings and ACC were deeply insolvent, that Keating was running an enormous control fraud, and that ACC was targeting widows and using fraud to sell them worthless junk bonds. The Bank Board had clear authority to stop the sales. The CDSL, Barabolak and Meek, and many others in the field recommended that the Bank Board stop the sales immediately and beseeched senior Bank Board officials to act (U.S. House Banking Committee 1989, 3:57).

The Bank Board, however, took no action to halt or even slow the sales or to warn the widows. The CDSL did what it could, ordering Lincoln Savings not to sell ACC's junk bonds and desperately seeking a change in state law that would authorize it to place in conservatorship a state-chartered S&L engaged in serious violations of law or safety, even if it had not yet been proven insolvent. The CDSL informed Wall that it would close Lincoln immediately if the law passed.

Wall and Martin faced disgrace if they stopped ACC's junk bond sales. The junk bond sales to the widows were a Ponzi scheme. ACC was insolvent and losing money. If the Bank Board stopped the sales, ACC would fail within weeks because it could not pay its debts. It would default on the junk bonds and over ten thousand widows would lose much of their life savings. ACC would file for bankruptcy protection. The widows would line up outside Lincoln Savings branches holding signs protesting the fraud. By bowing to pressure from the Keating Five and Speaker Wright, preventing the FHLBSF examination, and removing its jurisdiction over Lincoln, Wall and Martin had ensured weeks of national news coverage of the scandal. At a minimum, they would lose their jobs. It was more likely, however, that they would also be pilloried in public. The administration would be furious. Awkward questions would be asked about who had led the push to deregulate S&Ls (answer: Vice President Bush). Lincoln Savings was the biggest proponent of deregulation and the worst exemplar of it. The administration's effort to give Keating control of the Bank Board would also be acutely embarrassing in an election year. Wall and Martin, loyal Republicans, would not close Lincoln Savings before the election.[4]

No one leaked the findings to the press to warn the widows. The examiners knew that if they blew the whistle, the Bank Board would fire them on the spot, make a criminal referral against them, and try to suppress publication of the story. Keating's law firms, he had roughly 100 of them on retainer, would sue the examiner in his individual capacity for hundreds of millions of dollars. The release of the information would (appear to) damage ACC; in fact, it would precipitate its failure. Keating would blame the failure on the Bank Board, and faced with a lawsuit that finally had some (apparent) validity, Wall and Martin would cave in to the threat of litigation. By blowing the whistle, the examiner would have been committing professional and financial suicide and aiding Keating instead of the widows.[5]

Only White was in a position to effectively demand action, but he still declined to make Keating's, Wall's, and Martin's actions a *cause célè-*

bre, ACC was able to defraud thousands of new victims, mostly widows, of tens of millions of dollars. Although Edmund Burke did not write the words so often attributed to him, the words remain apt: "All that is necessary for evil to triumph is for good men to do nothing."

Wall's bigger problem was that St Germain was the rare committee chairman defeated for reelection in 1988. Gonzalez became chairman of the House Banking Committee. Gonzalez believed that it was his duty to remove Wall from office. As one of his first acts as chairman, he held field hearings in San Francisco in January 1989 and invited FHLBSF witnesses as well as Dochow and O'Connell. The FHLBSF had briefed the committee's investigators on the Bank Board's appeasement of Keating while St Germain chaired the committee. Gary Bowser, Jim Deveney, and their staff leader, Jake Lewis, were up to speed on the facts, convinced that the Bank Board had acted badly, and eager to remove the blot that St Germain had placed on the committee's reputation when he rejected their recommendation to hold hearings and told them to end their investigation.

The Bank Board was in an impossible situation. Its examination had shown that the FHLBSF was correct about the true state of Lincoln Savings and of Keating's character. Dochow was already negotiating with Cirona about how to return Lincoln Savings to the FHLBSF's jurisdiction. Dochow could not attack the FHLBSF, and Wall would not permit him to acknowledge that the Bank Board had made a mistake. The FHLBSF witnesses would criticize the Bank Board's actions if they were permitted to testify about Lincoln Savings. O'Connell might join in that criticism. Dochow deliberately made O'Connell unavailable for the hearing, but he could not keep the FHLBSF witnesses away. Wall used his only real option: he ordered us not to testify about Lincoln Savings and refused to allow the committee to see any of the examination findings about Lincoln Savings and ACC (U.S. House Banking Committee 1989, 5:927). Gonzalez ordered us to testify, and Wall backed down. Our testimony made it clear that we were intensely critical of the Bank Board's surrender and its failure to stop Keating's ongoing abuses. The Bank Board finally ended the bond sales shortly after Gonzalez indicated that he would conduct a series of full committee hearings on the Bank Board's handling of Lincoln Savings. ACC stopped selling bonds on Valentine's Day 1989, over five months after ORPOS figured out the tax-sharing fraud (ibid., 4:268). Gonzalez had shown that exposing the Bank Board's actions to public scrutiny worked.

"PULL A RABBIT OUT OF THE HAT": M. DANNY WALL

The Bank Board had to act, but it could not act. ACC had unlawfully taken $94 million from Lincoln Savings. The Bank Board could not permit that. Dochow directed Lincoln Savings to demand the money back from ACC; Lincoln Savings refused. Dochow went to Stewart to get her to bring a temporary cease-and-desist order against ACC ordering it to repay Lincoln Savings. A temporary C&D is effective immediately; ACC would have been required to repay Lincoln Savings at once. Stewart knew that ACC could not repay Lincoln Savings, so a temporary C&D would force ACC to file for bankruptcy, which would expose the scandal. She refused to bring the C&D order, arguing that the MOU she and Keating's lawyers had drafted forbade bringing such an order without prior negotiation with the S&L. This incident created a serious rift between Dochow and Stewart. She had personally assured him that nothing in the MOU restricted the Bank Board's normal enforcement powers. That assurance was now shown to be false. The larger point, however, is that Stewart refused to bring any enforcement action against ACC and Lincoln Savings; indeed, she declined even to *investigate*, Stewart knew that any enforcement action would have the same effect as ordering a halt to the junk bond sales to the widows: it would expose the failure of ACC and Lincoln Savings as well as her leadership role in the Bank Board's acquiescence in Keating's demands.

Stewart had championed affirmative action for Keating on the grounds that newspaper articles had (accurately) exposed his misdeeds. She now decided that the Bank Board should take no meaningful affirmative action on behalf of the widows or the taxpayers. Dochow, shorn of any enforcement support, issued an unenforceable "directive" to Lincoln Savings to stop a significant number of acts, but he had issued no directive to ACC to stop the bond sales in 1988. Keating, of course, violated the directive with impunity. The Bank Board took no enforcement action in response to the violations. Stewart did not even investigate the violations.

The Bank Board indisputably needed to close Lincoln Savings immediately. Keating began to tell Scott that if the Bank Board took over the S&L it would cost the FSLIC $2 billion. That was tantamount to admitting that it was insolvent by $2 billion. Keating also began to line up the traditional scam acquirer groups that would purportedly solve the problem by buying the S&L without any FSLIC assistance.[6] The

Bank Board had a great deal of experience with such scams, and normally did not let them stall enforcement action.

The details are too complex for a book of this length, but it is easy to summarize the three problems all such deals shared. First, they were based on accounting scams. The novel aspect in this case was that the accounting fraud was disclosed.[7] The CDSL forcefully made it clear that it would not approve any scam deal and that any deal to buy an S&L that was insolvent by over $2 billion without FSLIC assistance was a scam. That was the second thing wrong with every one of the proposed deals. The third problem was that each deal was designed to keep Keating in total control of Lincoln Savings, ruling through straw parties. The saddest variant brought former Bank Board member Hovde in (he offered his services to Keating, he was not recruited) as a straw for Keating.

Despite these facts, Wall and Martin pushed Dochow to try to negotiate a deal with each new shill. Keating bombarded Cranston and DeConcini with pleas to pressure the Bank Board. His messages—often in writing—were crude. He warned that Lincoln Savings would soon fail and that the failure would harm the senators' careers. He asked for a "politically powerful person" to call Wall and Martin and pressure them (U.S. Senate Committee 1990–1991b, April 8, 1988, Special Counsel Exhibit 178).

Even when the Bank Board finally decided on April 5, 1989, to reject the latest scam deal and ready itself to appoint a conservator for what it now knew was likely to be the most expensive S&L or bank failure in U.S. history, Wall said the following about Keating:

> [W]e are dealing with someone who has . . . been very successful in financial transactions of one kind or another, it seems to me that we could see the ultimate proffer of an offer to buy this institution on a totally arms length basis. And frankly, I will not be surprised if that happens. I have no knowledge of anything other than my understanding and perspective as to this man's success over the years. And it is clear to me he may well pull a rabbit out of the hat. . . . So I submit we may not necessarily [*sic*] going only to a conservativeship [*sic*]. We may be looking at another kind of an acquisition put forward very quickly. (U.S. House Banking Committee 1989, 5:904–905)

Wall's "understanding and perspective as to this man's success over the years" was so erroneous and so unshakeable that even when he had been shown that the "success" was really failure hiding behind a fraudulent façade, he retained his faith in Keating's myth. Alternatively, perhaps Wall believed that Keating was so accomplished a fraud that he could con an independent party into purchasing the most insolvent S&L in history without any FSLIC assistance. No rabbit popped out of the hat, and the Bank Board took over Lincoln Savings two years after the FHLBSF recommended it do so.[8]

Keating responded with a barrage of lawsuits challenging the appointment of the conservator and suing many officials in their individual capacities through *Bivens* actions. (He sued me for $400 million.) Keating then uttered the words that so injured the Keating Five. He called a press conference. Keating gave a presentation to the press: written questions to him and written answers to those questions, which he read aloud. He did not permit the press to ask any questions. (That enraged the press.) The important point is that Keating's remarks were not a spontaneous miscue.

> One question . . . had to do with whether my financial support in any way influenced several political figures to take up my cause. I want to say in the most forceful way I can: I certainly hope so. (U.S. Senate Committee 1990–1991a, 1:1116)

WHEN YOU GO TO KILL THE KING . . . YOU BETTER SUCCEED

Vice President Bush won the 1988 presidential election. Wright ruined the S&L debacle as a Democratic Party campaign issue. One of the new president's first acts was to order Wall to stop all "Southwest Plan" deals and to appoint the FDIC, not the FSLIC, conservator or receiver. Bush also made it clear that the FSLIC and the Bank Board would be eliminated: the insurance function would be transferred to the FDIC and to a new regulatory bureau, which became known as the Office of Thrift Supervision (OTS).[9] This was an obvious slap in the face to the Wall. William Seidman, the FDIC chairman, writes that Wall launched into a fierce personal attack on him when the new Bush administration briefed them both on the plan (Seidman 1993, 196).

President Bush, however, was personally loyal to Wall. He introduced legislation in early 1989 to deal with the S&L crisis. It provided that Wall be made director of OTS, without the "advice and consent" of the Senate and the normal confirmation hearings. Scholars warned the administration that this might well be unconstitutional, which it was later found to be.[10]

Riegle, Cranston, and Garn were on the Senate conference committee that would negotiate a compromise bill with its House counterpart, chaired by Gonzalez. Gonzalez maximized his negotiating leverage by making his top priority blocking Wall's appointment. He was able to win concessions in many other areas by finally agreeing not to insist on confirmation hearings. He did not give up on his belief that the government must remove Wall from office.

Gonzalez attacked Wall publicly by holding a series of hearings on the failure of Lincoln Savings. This took considerable courage on his part, because it was certain that the hearings would embarrass the Keating Five, and four of the senators were fellow Democrats. The party pressured Gonzalez to stop the hearings, but Gonzalez was relentless.

The FHLBSF was determined to tell the full truth about Wall. We believed that he had degraded the reputation of the agency and that he would cause new scandals if he were subjected to similar pressure. But the event that had enraged us was the Bank Board's decision to let Keating defraud the widows in the hopes that this would delay ACC's failure and allow him "to pull a rabbit out of the hat."[11] Wall compounded his mistake by ordering Patriarca and me to headquarters to coordinate our testimony with his staff's testimony (U.S. House Banking Committee 1989, 2:89–90). We were told that if we agreed to place the blame on our staff (for purportedly failing to document Keating's abuses adequately), Wall's staff would praise our efforts to bring Keating to justice. We were offended that they thought there was any chance we would agree to such a proposal. We resolved to go full bore. The meeting had one advantage: it led inadvertently to my discovery of Stewart's side letter.[12]

Wall, Dochow, and Stewart were hurt badly by the Gonzalez hearings. The first witness was FDIC chairman Seidman. He damaged the Bank Board's strategy of blaming everything on the FHLBSF. He testified that FDIC officials had reviewed the FHLBSF findings and concluded that they would have responded to such evidence by promptly imposing a stringent cease-and-desist order or placing the S&L in conservatorship (U.S. House Banking Committee 1989, 1:21). He presented the Resolution Trust Corporation's (RTC) lawsuit against Keating, which described his claims of FHLBSF bias as "baseless" and noted that Keating had been able to remove our jurisdiction through "political pressure" (ibid., 1:168). Seidman did not say a single supportive thing about Wall and his lieutenants.[13]

Patriarca and I testified at the next hearing. Wall launched a preemptive attack, providing the committee and the media with a chronology

that was written to support his position. We were able to make that strategy backfire because the chronology was too selective in its omissions.
We highlighted two: it did not contain ORPOS's written recommendation to Wall on July 23, 1987, endorsing the FHLBSF's recommendation
that the Bank Board appoint a conservator for Lincoln Savings; it also
failed to note that Bill Robertson, the ORPOS director who made the
recommendation, was demoted days after he wrote the memorandum
and that the Bank Board never allowed either the FHLBSF or ORPOS
to brief it on the recommendation. We explained that this was unprecedented (U.S. House Banking Committee 1989, 2:17–18, 23).

Wall's chronology also described the MOU and the agreement but
did not reveal Rosemary Stewart's side letter. I read the side letter to
the committee, explained why it was such a harmful (and revealing)
symbolic act, and noted that we referred to it as "Rosemary's Baby"
after the movie in which the husband makes a deal with the devil (U.S.
House Banking Committee 1989, 2:25–26). The committee took up the
phrase with relish. We also filed highly detailed and documented analytical testimony that explained the substance of what Wall and Martin
had done wrong and rebutted the attack on our staff. The testimony
generated very adverse publicity for Wall, provided a roadmap for critics, and made public many documents revealing the extent, nature, and
consequences of the appeasement. We put the responsibility squarely
on Wall.

Selby and the CDSL's leaders (Crawford and Davis) testified with
us on the same panel. Selby testified about the ERC members' being
driven by fear of litigation and "political retaliation," explained that
he was "disinvited" from ERC meetings immediately after he wrote a
memorandum supporting the FHLBSF's position, and emphasized
that the OE's poor performance at Lincoln Savings reflected their general failings, which he attributed to the "overriding fear by OE of losing a case" (U.S. House Banking Committee 1989, 2:32, 1048–1049;
5:1005–1006).

Davis revealed that Lincoln Savings had bugged the examiners'
phones (ibid., 2:35, 1149–1155). Crawford explained Keating's efforts
to get his bosses to fire him (ibid., 2:38). Davis bemoaned Wall and
Martin's lack of "courage" (ibid., 2:100).

Federal and state examiners who participated in the 1988 examinations of Lincoln Savings and ACC, along with the FHLB-Seattle supervisors who met with Keating, testified next as a panel. Their testimony
emphasized three themes. First, Scott was a strong supporter of Keat-

ing's operations, and this resulted in minimal "loss" findings until New-som, Barabolak, and Meek exposed the attempted whitewash. Second, Lincoln Savings and ACC were pervasively corrupt. Third, Keating's approach to the FHLB-Seattle was so outrageous that it alerted them, and should have alerted any competent regulator, that Keating was a crook (U.S. House Banking Committee 1989, 3:54–55, 75–79).

The FHLB-Seattle witnesses emphasized headquarters' pervasive fear of litigation (ibid., 3:13). They noted their amazement that Keating had boasted about getting Henkel appointed to the Bank Board, and had said that it proved that he could accomplish anything with his political power (ibid., 3:54, 71). The FHLB-Seattle knew that Henkel had resigned in disgrace after being caught trying to immunize Lincoln Savings' $600 million violation of the direct-investment rule, so it was appalled by Keating's boasts. Representative Leach asked a question that showed that he understood the FHLB-Seattle's professional staff better than Dochow, their former leader:

> Mr. Leach: You knew that you were being asked to be dupes for the San Francisco office, to replace them as weaker regulators, which I think you should have found very offensive.
>
> Mr. Clarke: We did. That thought did occur to us. (ibid., 3:55)

Clarke then gave the best four word summation of the Bank Board's removal of the FHLBSF's jurisdiction: "very strange, unprecedented, wrong" (U.S. House Banking Committee 1989, 3:56).

The single most damaging moment came when Representative Schumer asked the entire panel: "[W]ould any of you disagree . . . that Washington knew . . . the subordinated debt was virtually worthless, and still allowed the sale to proceed?" (U.S. House Banking Committee 1989, 3:74). No one disagreed.

Both FHLB-Seattle witnesses then responded to Schumer's question whether there was any "plausible explanation" for Dochow's conduct.

> Mr. Clarke: There is no plausible explanation that was ever given to us, and I cannot think of one, frankly. . . .
>
> Ms. McJoynt: No. (U.S. House Banking Committee 1989, 3:77)

SEC chairman Richard Breedon's testimony delivered the next heavy blow to Wall. He said that the MOU had destroyed the SEC's ability to bring a timely enforcement action against ACC for securities fraud; that the Bank Board had entered into the MOU without consulting or notifying the SEC; that the Bank Board had caved in on taking action against the accounting fraud at Lincoln Savings; and that both Arthur Young and ACC/Lincoln had obstructed the SEC's investigation while Dochow was telling the Bank Board that Keating was committed to being a good corporate citizen (U.S. House Banking Committee 1989, 4:47, 52, 54, 76, 154–156).

Wall, Dochow, and Stewart testified on November 21, 1989. Their first strategic mistake was not to admit that they had made a mistake. Their second was to direct the vast bulk of their testimony, and all of their fervor, at attacking their critics instead of Keating. Their third was using Stewart to lead the attack.

Stewart concentrated her attack on Gray, Patriarca, me, and the FHLBSF as a whole. She had suffered the most personal attack ("Rosemary's baby"), and the committee members believed that her side letter was indefensible. She also had the greatest antipathy for Gray, Patriarca, and me. This put her in an inherently poor position as Wall's primary defender.[14] The central problem, however, was that Stewart's rage at us caused her still to believe that Keating was the victim and we were the villains. She testified, under oath, that Keating's theory of the case (he was innocent victim of vendetta because he opposed reregulation) was correct. I, for example, was a "perjur[er]" because I had read the text of her side letter and criticized it (U.S. House Banking Committee 1989, 5:22). One does not have to be a lawyer to know that this could not constitute perjury.

Stewart's testimony, of course, was so over the top and so unsupported that it was disastrous for Wall and Dochow as well. She told Representative Kanjorski that he was engaged in "an absolute falsehood" (U.S. House Banking Committee 1989, 5:181). Wall ("child of the Senate" and veteran of hundreds of hearings) cringed and began whispering furiously in her ear, but the damage was irretrievable. The hearing closed on a bipartisan note that sealed Wall's fate:

Chairman Gonzalez: The Chair is compelled at this point, in view of that outburst . . . [to note,] Ms. Stewart, your attack on your current and former agency colleagues—and now added Mr. Kanjorski, not to mention former Chairman Gray—is scathing and unrelentless.

On behalf of the taxpayers of America who will pick up the bill for the savings and loan nightmare, I offer the following thought: How much money could have been saved if you had pursued these high-flying S&L operators . . . with the same intensity? Your performance in that regard is well documented . . . and no amount of attacking others will absolve you of that regard.

Mr. Leach: . . . Ms. Stewart did not have authority to make these decisions on her own. [T]he Bank board is to be accountable. (ibid., 5:181)

Stewart's testimony was a godsend to Keating. He had pending litigation challenging the appointment of the receiver and his *Bivens* actions against Gray, others, and me. Stewart, a senior agency official, had just testified that Keating's lawsuits were correct. Gray, Patriarca, and I had a "hidden agenda" to "punish" Lincoln Savings because it opposed the direct-investment rule; we exhibited a "vendetta attitude" against Keating; and a campaign of leaks had damaged Lincoln Savings (U.S. House Banking Committee 1989, 5:19). She intimated that we were probably the source of the leaks. She also told the press that Lincoln's losses were caused by a bad economy, not by any fraud on Keating's part. Further, her testimony was under oath, so it would be admissible in court.

Keating's lawyers understandably rushed to take her deposition in order to find additional support for her charges. The great irony is that her deposition, combined with my attorney's deposition of Keating, destroyed the value of her committee testimony for Keating. The further irony is that the competence of Keating's lawyer rendered her testimony useless. One can only imagine his dawning horror as his persistent questioning drew out that Stewart's sole basis for her charge of abuses was what Keating had told her. She had no personal knowledge of any misconduct by any Bank Board official—*none*, the only personal animus she witnessed was by Keating (U.S. Senate Committee 1990–1991a, 4:337).

I quoted earlier her deposition testimony that "she believed" Keating when he told her (in early 1988) that Gray had called him a vulgar name and vowed to destroy him. I also explained how asking the most obvious questions would have exposed the lie. The remarkable fact is that Stewart continued to believe Keating's fables in 1990, after the 1988 federal and CDSL examinations, Kenneth Leventhal, the RTC, the SEC, and the Justice Department had all established that the FHLBSF was correct in warning that Keating routinely misrepresented the facts. Moreover, she testified that she had never taken any steps to check whether Keating's claims of bias were correct (U.S. Senate Committee 1990–1991a, 4:338).

Stewart's House Banking Committee testimony and her deposition ended any chance that Wall had of remaining in office. President Bush soon indicated his lack of confidence and Wall resigned, with a personal attack on Gonzalez. The testimony also doomed Keating's suit against Gray and me. My attorney sent a Rule 11 letter notifying Keating's counsel that continuing the suit, which Stewart and Keating's deposition testimony had proven to be baseless, would lead us to seek sanctions against the attorney. Keating dismissed the suit.

THE NEW BROOM

Bush appointed Tim Ryan to replace Wall as OTS director. Ryan brought in Harris Weinstein as chief counsel. Ryan and Weinstein made their mandate explicit: they had been appointed to make it clear that the administration favored aggressive enforcement, supervision, and regulation. That meant pursuing the most infamous control frauds, their law firms, and their accounting firms. Weinstein delegated enforcement powers to the field and placed senior field attorneys with litigation experience (like me) in charge of regional enforcement groups. Stewart left the agency to work with the Jones, Day law firm. Dochow returned to the FHLB-Seattle as its lead supervisor. Weinstein ended Luke's prohibition on suing audit firms. The agency began to litigate cases and set favorable precedents. The number of cases more than doubled, and the significance of the cases and the remedies sought increased dramatically. The OTS and the RTC combined to recover well over $1 billion from law and audit firms. Other than an unsuccessful White House effort to remove the OTS's jurisdiction to bring an enforcement action against the president's son, Neil Bush, for his contribution to the expensive failure of Silverado Savings (Seidman 1993), political intervention with the OTS halted.

Milken's guilty plea removed him as the de facto head of Drexel. Without his ability to manipulate the "captives," the true default risk of junk bonds was revealed, and their value fell sharply. All of the S&L captives failed; their other frauds would have sunk them even without the junk bond collapse.

Keating's forces went out with a last blast at San Francisco. Lawyers for one of his principal lieutenants were deposing one of our midlevel supervisors. They began asking her which of our employees were homosexual. The OTS lawyer representing her objected, so there was a telephonic hearing with the judge. Keating's lawyer represented to the court that he had concrete facts that established a good-faith basis for believing that there was a conspiracy among homosexual regulators in San Francisco to destroy Keating. Based on these representations, Chief Judge Bilby directed her to answer the questions. The lawyer's next question was whether she had heard any "rumors" that employees were homosexuals. The young OTS lawyer from headquarters, unfortunately, did not object immediately. Fortunately, the lunch break occurred shortly after this series of questions. Our supervisor returned to the office in tears, humiliated and outraged at having to testify about rumors regarding who might be a homosexual. I told the OTS attorney to inform opposing counsel that the deposition was over and that we would file an emergency motion with the judge asking him to overturn his order.

According to the opposing lawyer's conspiracy theory, (1) Keating was intensely homophobic; (2) Keating was a strong opponent of pornography; (3) the FHLBSF employed homosexuals; and (4) therefore (?), homosexual regulators conspired to destroy Keating.[15] The lawyer's explanation for having no evidence to support the last point was that homosexuals are hidden and can conspire secretly. Judge Bilby realized that he had been misled into authorizing an outrageous witch hunt. Furious, he started the hearing. The opposing lawyer immediately dug his grave deeper by demanding that I be excluded from the courtroom. That had worked with Wall, but federal judges do not take kindly to such tactics. The judge proceeded to tear into the opposing lawyer for his misrepresentations and tactics. He ordered a halt to any such questions and the destruction of all records of the questions and responses.

This incident revealed to Judge Bilby the nature of our opponents. He later discovered that Arthur Young had put the disgraced Jack Atchison back on its payroll as a consultant. Judge Bilby was hearing the RTC and ACC bondholders' case against Young when he learned of this deeply inappropriate arrangement. He announced that his dad, a judge, had told him that a judge always has the power to order a "skunk" out of his courtroom. Young decided to settle the case for a very large sum.

THE END OF THE S&L CONTROL FRAUDS

The important control frauds all failed before Ryan became chairman. The failures occurred despite Wall's vulnerability to political and legal pressure and his support for forbearance. They failed because of Gray's reregulation (principally the growth restrictions), because of the vigorous field regulators who Gray recruited, and because the 1986 Tax Reform Act and the failure of other control frauds led to the collapse of regional real estate bubbles.

The OTS's vigor under Ryan and Weinstein was, of course, far too little, far too late. But it showed what could have been done if the administration and the Bank Board had engaged in vigorous enforcement in the 1980s.

10. It's the Things You Do Know, but Aren't So, That Cause Disasters

Keating's control fraud could have taught us the lessons we needed to learn to avoid the ongoing wave of control fraud. Consider Greenspan's, Benston's, and Fischel's evaluations of Lincoln Savings. Greenspan said it "posed no foreseeable risk" to the FSLIC (Mayer 1990, appendix C; U.S. House Banking Committee 1989, 3:603–606).[1] Benston said Lincoln Savings should serve as the model for the industry. Fischel proved it was the best S&L in the nation. Three of the nation's top financial experts took the worst corporation in the nation (perhaps the worst in the world) and pronounced it superb. That is the measure of how successful control frauds are in deceiving experts who do not understand fraud mechanisms and assume that CEOs cannot be crooks.

Our failure to learn the lessons of the S&L debacle led to the new wave of control fraud.

THE LESSONS WE SHOULD HAVE LEARNED FROM THE S&L DEBACLE

1. FRAUD MATTERS, AND CONTROL FRAUDS POSE UNIQUE RISKS.

Control fraud was one of the largest causes of losses during the debacle, and other frauds were material. Control fraud caused the current wave of financial scandals.

Unfortunately, the conventional economic wisdom failed to learn this lesson. As stated in Easterbrook and Fischel (1991, 285), that wisdom asserts:

[A] rule against fraud is not an essential or even necessarily an important ingredient of securities markets.

2. IT IS IMPORTANT TO UNDERSTAND FRAUD MECHANISMS.

Many of the financial experts' most embarrassing predictive and analytical failures arose because they did not understand how control frauds operate. For example, Bert Ely, a financial consultant, thought fraud was trivial because there were few cases of CEOs taking money out of the till (Ely 1990). Control frauds were consistently able to fool top economists because they did not understand how CEOs turn accountants and accounting principles from a restraint into a weapon of fraud and a shield against the regulators.

Economists receive no training about fraud risk, incidence, or mechanisms (beyond the conventional wisdom that it was trivial, a distraction during the debacle). Lawyers receive no fraud training. Joe Wells's Association for Certified Fraud Examiners (ACFE) offers free materials to any business school that will teach a course in fraud examination. Only a small number of business schools took up the offer prior to the Enron scandal. The number even now remains scandalously low. The average new accountant receives no meaningful training about fraud and no training at all about control fraud.

3. CONTROL FRAUD CAN OCCUR IN WAVES.

Control fraud is not random. Criminologists know that some environments produce increased crime. The S&L industry in the first half of the 1980s was a nearly optimal environment for control fraud. The incentive to engage in both reactive and opportunistic control fraud increased sharply. Entry was easy. Opportunistic control frauds flocked to the industry.

The ongoing wave of control fraud, by contrast, arose from the growth and collapse of an enormous financial bubble and the evisceration of regulatory and ethical restraints on fraud. We can identify the environments that produce waves of control fraud and avoid or greatly reduce the problem if we change our approach to regulation and corporate compensation.

Similar waves of control fraud have occurred in many countries (La Porta, Lopez-de-Silanes, and Zamarripa 2003; Johnson, La Porta, Lopez-de-Silanes, and Shleifer 2000). Conventional economists' efforts to guide the transition of Russia to capitalism were disastrous because they failed to understand both governmental (kleptocratic) and corporate control fraud (Stiglitz 2003, 21).

4. WAVES OF CONTROL FRAUD CAUSE IMMENSE DAMAGE.

Individual cases of control fraud cause severe losses, but waves of control fraud cause systemic injury. The direct financial damage is staggering: many tens of billions of dollars during the debacle and hundreds of billions in the ongoing scandals.

The indirect financial damage is far greater. During the debacle, the indirect financial injury was primarily the inflating of regional real estate bubbles. This deepened the real estate glut and ultimately worsened the severe drop of values that harmed even honest real estate participants. Bubbles waste societal resources through misallocation both when they inflate and when they collapse. Fraud sends inaccurate price signals that move markets ever farther away from efficiency. The S&L control frauds kept real estate prices artificially high by increasing the levels of ADC lending and direct real-estate investments in markets that had vacancy rates seen only in the severest recessions. The fraudulent investments contributed to regional recessions in Texas, Louisiana, and Arizona. Other indirect financial injuries were inflicted on S&L employees, who lost their jobs and pensions when control frauds destroyed the S&L; innocent stockholders; and the victims of ACC's worthless junk bond sales. The S&L industry was not a major purchaser of junk bonds, but it provided Milken's most important group of "captives." They were critical to the overstating of junk bond values, which misallocates and wastes societal resources.

The indirect financial damage during the ongoing scandals has been far greater. They have again created wasteful gluts, particularly in broadband. However, the ongoing scandals' most harmful indirect economic effect has been to reduce trust. Frauds operate by creating—and abusing—trust. As a result, fraud is the most powerful acid extant for eating away trust. We are now beginning to understand how important trust is to an economy. Economists of all ideological stripes agree that trust is one of the most important resources (Stiglitz 2003, 274; Fukuyama 1995). One way to conceptualize Akerlof's classic 1970 article on lemons markets is that it shows how widespread control fraud eviscerates trust.[2] A broad range of scholars and market participants have concluded that the erosion of trust caused by the ongoing wave of control fraud significantly influenced millions of investors to withdraw from the stock market, which caused a staggering loss of market capitalization (Stiglitz 2003, 274). That loss was $9 trillion, so if the consensus is correct that the erosion of trust contributed materially to that loss at its peak, the indirect losses from control fraud were crushing.[3]

Current scandals have generated many other indirect economic costs; lost jobs and pensions again predominate. Enron and its fellow conspirators (virtually every major energy trader in America and several electrical generators) caused blackouts in California, raised the price of electrical power dramatically, and bankrupted California's electrical utilities. (These control frauds were aimed at customers, not creditors.) Similarly, corporate tax fraud surged as some of the nation's top audit and law firms pushed fraudulent tax shelters and schemes for using tax havens to avoid taxation. Enron was so active in these frauds that it marketed its services as a consultant for eliminating corporate taxes.

The indirect, nonfinancial impacts of the S&L control frauds cannot be quantified. One of these impacts is political scandal. The control frauds' manipulation of Speaker Wright became widely known. The disclosure weakened Wright while he was in office and contributed to his decision to resign. Keating's enlistment of the Keating Five greatly damaged Senator McCain's ambition to become president. He was the Republican Party's rising star in early 1987 but a political liability by September 1987. He now campaigns for political reform. Is he, and is the nation, better or worse off because Keating convinced him to add his leverage against the Bank Board? The most I can say is that the S&L control frauds powerfully affected our political system. My personal view is that they damaged it.

The social and political effects of waves of control fraud are clear, and in Russia and some of the other former Soviet bloc nations, they are tragic. Life expectancy has fallen dramatically, violence has increased, respect for Western institutions has plummeted, and poverty and disease rates have surged. These social and political effects have made many Russians hostile to the United States, and the effects feed back into economic policies that can cause further damage (Stiglitz 2003).

Effective markets are neither natural nor inevitable. Markets are institutions shaped by law, culture, and morals. They are vulnerable to control frauds. Such frauds cannot be defeated for all time; eternal vigilance is essential. Effective regulation is essential if modern markets are to remain honest and efficient.

5. CONTROL FRAUDS CONVERT CONVENTIONAL
RESTRAINTS ON ABUSE INTO AIDS TO FRAUD.

Control frauds do not simply defeat internal and external controls such as outside auditors. They pervert intended controls into allies. We need to listen to Keating. Grogan, his political fixer, warned Keating that hiring Atchison away from Arthur Young just after he gave Lincoln Savings a clean audit opinion (and quadrupling his salary) would discredit Atchison.[4] Atchison was critical to ACC/Lincoln Savings' getting clean audit opinions, recruiting the Keating Five, and making presentations to the Bank Board, so Grogan apparently did not want to repeat Keating's mistake with Henkel, i.e., ruining such a valuable asset. Grogan describes Keating's response:

> [He] was white hot. He said that spineless lawyers would ruin this company, that he had to have talented accounting people. That lawyers never made a nickel for the company. . . . And that the accountants and business people made the money for the company. (U.S. Senate Committee 1990–1991a, December 14, 1990, a.m. session, transcript 49)

He meant it literally: the accountants "made the money" (albeit fictitiously). All the S&L control frauds were accounting frauds. All of them were able to get clean audit opinions from top-tier audit firms, typically for many years. No audit firm exposed an S&L control fraud.

Even after two top-tier audit firms resigned from their audit engagement with Lincoln Savings, and after Keating was widely known as a control fraud, Peat, Marwick aggressively "pitched" Keating for the account. It then issued opinions supporting both a scam sale designed to create a massive fictitious profit and a scam reciprocal transaction designed to create a scam sale of Lincoln Savings. Both scams were designed to fend off a regulatory takeover.

Keating showed that control frauds use outside auditors to do far more than bless fraudulent deals and accounting. He used Arthur Andersen to stuff the junk-bond underwriting files in order to deceive the examiners. He used Andersen's shameful, dishonest resignation letter as well as Atchison's equally disgraceful letter attacking the FHLBSF examination to help recruit the Keating Five.[5] The senators stressed that Andersen's and Young's reputations as top-tier audit firms led them to believe Keating's representations (U.S. House Banking Committee

1989, 3:669–671); Stewart and Dochow were similarly duped. ACC could not have defrauded the widows without Arthur Young's clean opinion.

Control frauds routinely enlisted top lawyers and academics to aid their frauds. Lawyers drafted the reciprocal deals that covered up the initial frauds. Shopping for appraisers was even easier than shopping for auditors and attorneys. Appraisers' grossly inflated valuations underlay all the S&L control frauds. The inflated values allowed the auditors to "rely" on the appraisers. This provided the outside auditor and the control fraud important protection against a civil suit.

As Mayer (1991, 285) explained, "Disreputable clients, after all, pay better." Control frauds pay best: money is no object; they control how much will be spent; and the experts and professionals they hire to defend the firm will actually spend their time defending the CEO while he loots the firm. Zealous advocacy on behalf of the client is perverted into slavish, but lucrative, aid to the CEO looting the firm. The regulators they fought were the ones zealously advocating the interests of the client.

Unfortunately, conventional economic wisdom learned none of these lessons. The legal profession and the accountants, in response to an embarrassing record of the top firms in their fields aiding control frauds, agreed on the primary strategic response: reduced professional liability. Leaders of the bar and the accounting industry testified before the National Commission on Financial Institution Reform, Recovery and Enforcement in 1993. They angrily denounced the OTS and RTC suits that had led, collectively, to over a billion dollars in settlements. They did not offer any apologies, accept any responsibility, or suggest any reforms of their practices.

My original profession, law, was the least professional. It made no reforms until the current wave of control fraud hit, a decade after the S&L debacle. The top law firms in the nation have, again, zealously aided the control frauds in destroying the client. (Shades of "it became necessary to destroy the village in order to save it.") Even then, they resisted all change, and had to be forced into finally reforming their (unethical) ethics rules barring lawyers from revealing ongoing financial crimes.

The record of the accounting profession has been more mixed. It tried to clean up a number of accounting standards that were abused during the debacle. Overall, though, it thought the debacle had nothing to teach it about auditing. A contemporaneous document compellingly shows this. From an interview with Dan Guy, the head of auditing for the American Institute of Certified Public Accountants (AICPA) in January 1994:

> Q. To what extent do you think deficiencies in the audit process contributed to the alleged audit failures in the savings and loan industry? [R]egulators . . . point out two major deficiencies in audits they have seen: a lack of professional skepticism and a willingness to accept the client's position.
> A. I can't think of any problem with standards that was identified by regulators looking at the S&L mess. (Craig 1994)

This same complacency existed even among accountants who specialized in fraud detection. A major work, *Accountant's Guide to Fraud Detection and Control* (2nd ed.), had the misfortune to be published in March 2000 (before Enron filed for bankruptcy) with a publisher's press release stating that "[Securities] fraud is being adequately detected by independent auditors (CPAs) in their annual audits."

Later, however, the profession tried, over great rank-and-file resistance, to get auditors to consider fraud risk when planning audits. The Financial Accounting Standards Board (FASB), to its great credit, tried to require that stock options be expensed. SEC chairman Arthur Levitt strongly supported this initiative. I explain below why this could be important for reducing control fraud. For now, it is enough that the FASB and Levitt knew that the proposal, while clearly correct, would expose them to attack.

The high-tech industries, the top-tier audit firms (under the leadership of Harvey Pitt), Clinton's Treasury Department, and a bipartisan coalition of legislators led by Senator Lieberman used intense, crude political power to intimidate the FASB and the SEC. Although many were guilty, none paid any political price. Clinton did not back Levitt; Levitt asked the FASB to cave in to the political pressure. He says it was his biggest mistake (Levitt 2002, 10–11, 12).

Accountants led the move to reduce the ability of victims of security fraud to recover their losses. This movement was, cleverly, labeled tort reform. (Everything Congress proposes is a "reform," no matter how pernicious its effect.)[6]

Fifteen years ago, when the financial world was rocked by the savings and loan scandal, the accounting industry faced a crisis not unlike the one it faces today. Lawsuits were mounting, millions of dollars were paid out in settlements, and the image of accountants was plummeting. . . .

Jack Henry, a retired managing partner in Andersen's Phoenix office, said that at the time of the S&L crisis there was a major change in the industry, caused by mounting litigation. "We were tired of getting the crap kicked out of us. . . ."

The nation's largest accounting firms, including Chicago-based Andersen decided to fight back. They formed a lobbying coalition. They poured millions of dollars into political campaigns. . . .

[T]he top accounting firms successfully lobbied for a federal law that makes it more difficult for investors to sue them. The 1995 law was a major victory for the profession and was achieved only after Congress voted to override a veto by President Bill Clinton—his first ever. (*Chicago Tribune*, February 13, 2002)

Easterbrook and Fischel (1991, 282) wrote, after Fischel knew from personal experience representing S&L control frauds that the claim was untenable,[7] that:

High quality firms must take additional steps to convince investors of their quality. One traditional step is [outside audits]. [The auditor] has a reputational interest—and thus a possible loss—much larger than the gains to be made from slipshod or false certification of a particular firm. . . . The larger the auditor . . . relative to the size of an issuer, the more effective these methods of verification are.

The Keating Five made the same argument to us.

DeConcini: Why would AY say these things, they have to guard their credibility too. They put the firm's neck out with this letter.
Patriarca: They have a client . . .
DeConcini: You believe they'd prostitute themselves for a client?
Patriarca: Absolutely, it happens all the time.[8] (U.S. Senate Committee 1990–1991a, 1:1059)

6. CONFLICTS OF INTEREST MATTER.

The S&L debacle proved that human nature had not changed; conflicts of interest still cause damage. Keating's actions demonstrate that he believed that maximizing conflicts of interest made it easier for him to suborn auditors and attorneys. He engineered Andersen's and Arthur

Young's involvement in nonaudit work while they were the auditors. Keating placed the accountants in an advocacy role requiring them to attack the FHLBSF examination and examiners in order to help Keating retain control of Lincoln Savings. Andersen's resignation letter and Atchison's letter to the Keating Five were blatant, false advocacy pieces. Auditors are supposed to be independent and objective; they must never become advocates for the client. Here, they became advocates for the individual destroying the client because he was the person who hired and fired them (and in Atchison's case, quadrupled his salary).

Keating bragged to the FHLB-Seattle that he spent $50 million hiring outside professionals to fight the 1986 FHLBSF examination (U.S. House Banking Committee 1989, 3:776). Some of that was for consultants such as Fischel and Benston, but it went overwhelmingly to Arthur Young and to Keating's top outside law firms: Kaye, Scholer and Jones, Day. Young's consulting fees and litigation-assistance fees dwarfed its audit fees. Atchison became Keating's most effective advocate.

Henkel, serving as Keating's tax lawyer, business partner, borrower, and Bank Board mole, exemplified the dangers of conflicts of interest, as did his ethics counsel Waxman, was also counsel to Lincoln Savings. A Kaye, Scholer partner received a sweetheart loan from Lincoln Savings. Taggart, the CDSL commissioner who was Keating's fiercest state regulatory ally, received benefits from Keating shortly before he left office (U.S. House Banking Committee 1989, 2:328-330). Keating, of course, believed that political contributions were essential for recruiting the Keating Five (and many other federal and state politicians). Since Keating backed his beliefs with substantial expenditures and had great expertise and success in manipulating professionals and politicians, there is every reason to conclude from his conduct that conflicts of interest do matter.[9]

Unfortunately, the conventional economic wisdom taught the opposite. Conflicts became "synergies." Stiglitz (2003, 10, 133-139) explains how this mindset helped spur scandals. Former SEC chairman Levitt makes the same point in *Take on the Street* (2002, 114-119).

7. DEPOSIT INSURANCE WAS NOT ESSENTIAL TO S&L CONTROL FRAUDS.

S&L control frauds generally relied on deposit insurance to fund their Ponzi growth. Federal deposit insurance was a key attraction to opportunistic control frauds and the primary reason they clustered in the S&L industry. But that does not mean it was essential. S&L control frauds were consistently able to defraud uninsured private market actors. ACC/Lincoln Savings was able to sell over $250 million in worthless junk bonds — the worst security in America — primarily from three branches in one state. It is true that Keating targeted widows because they generally lacked financial sophistication, but Keating also sold ACC stock to sophisticated investors. He beat the "shorts," and (worthless) ACC stock sold at a substantial share price after five years of continuous fraud. Milken sold $125 million of (worthless) ACC junk bonds to (purportedly ultrasophisticated) investors in 1984.

S&L control frauds frequently sold subordinated debt because it could count as regulatory "capital." Subordinated debt is uninsured and inherently risky because the buyer receives nothing until all other creditors are paid. S&L sub debt issued by traditional, healthy S&Ls was far riskier than the norm because S&Ls had minimal capital. The risk from sub debt issued by the high fliers was off the charts. Such S&Ls always defaulted.

ACC is the only exception I recall, and it proves the rule. Milken sold, as I noted, $125 million in ACC sub debt at a high interest rate to the usual subjects: if Milken sold one's junk bonds, it was understood that one bought junk bonds issued by other Milken clients. The key to Milken's scheme was to reduce the apparent default rate, so it would not do to let ACC default on its Drexel-issued junk bonds. The situation was as elegant as it was cynical: ACC would sell junk bonds to widows (at a ludicrously low rate of interest) and use the proceeds to retire the Drexel-issued junk bonds sold (at a very high rate of interest) to Milken's minions.[10]

This scam simultaneously (1) avoided a default on Drexel-issued junk bonds, (2) considerably reduced ACC's interest expense, and (3) allowed ACC to book a gain from refinancing its debt at a lower interest rate.

We also should have learned from the debacle that junk bonds actually had fewer debt covenants than less risky debt (which contradicts the theory of private market discipline by creditors). In no case did sub debt holders exercise effective discipline over an S&L. Indeed, I do not recall any case in which they even attempted to impose discipline. All of these facts refute the theory that private creditors exercise effective discipline through debt covenants or similar means.

The other form of private market discipline that failed during the debacle was private deposit insurance. Control frauds caused the failure of private insurance systems for thrifts (state-chartered S&Ls that were not insured by the FSLIC) in Ohio, Maryland, and Utah. In no case did private insurers adopt regulations that conventional economists would consider rational, but that is hardly a defense of the concept of private deposit insurance, for the theory relies on the assumption that they will act rationally. There is no known case where a private thrift insurer successfully stopped a control fraud in time to avoid the collapse of the fund. All the private thrift-insurance funds that did not collapse saw their members convert to FSLIC- or FDIC-insured status because depositors lost confidence in them.

We should have learned from the S&L debacle that private market discipline does not stop control frauds effectively, that sub debt is not equivalent to capital for banks, and that private insurance does not effectively prevent, detect, or limit control fraud. Unfortunately, the conventional economic wisdom learned none of these points. Easterbrook and Fischel (1991, 282), for example, assert that if a firm issues debt, it "(a) forces the managers to pay out the profits, and (b) if there are no profits forces the firm into bankruptcy." But control frauds follow a third way. They create very large fictitious profits blessed by a top-tier audit firm. They then borrow more money or sell more stock and use part of the proceeds to pay interest on the prior debt.

Because the waves of S&L control frauds and the ongoing wave consistently fooled entities that had the incentive to exercise private market discipline, the efficient-market hypothesis has often been proven false. Control frauds can continue for many years, thereby moving prices further away from their "true" value. The efficient-market hypothesis is the bedrock of modern finance, so the ineffectiveness of markets against waves of control fraud is of major importance.

8. "SYSTEMS CAPACITY" PROBLEMS ARE ENDEMIC AND EXPOSE US TO HUGE DANGER.

Henry Pontell's systems-capacity theory can help us limit or even prevent future waves of control fraud. Systems capacity refers to the inability of the prosecutorial or regulatory system to cope with crime or misconduct adequately because of resource limitations, deficient authority, or lack of political will. Almost everyone agrees that the Bank Board exemplified each of these severe capacity problems and that the Justice Department was also badly understaffed and wholly unprepared to deal with the wave of control fraud. The Reagan administration bears the primary blame for these capacity limitations.

It is a self-fulfilling prophecy that government will be ineffective if one designs it to be ineffective. The systems-capacity problems of the SEC and the Bank Board are parallel. Both were forbidden to pay salaries competitive with those offered by the banking regulatory agencies (much less private firms). Both experienced rapid turnover and had to staff key operations with inexperienced personnel. Both faced vastly increased supervisory needs in quantity and complexity. The deluges overwhelmed both staffs. The frequency of examinations (or reviews) fell sharply. Government (the OMB during the Reagan administration, the House of Representatives in the case of the SEC) greatly exacerbated the capacity limitations by seeking to reduce the number of staff at a time both agencies were critically understaffed. Neither staff recognized the wave of control fraud until it was too late. If we had learned the lessons of the S&L debacle, we would have supercharged the SEC in the early 1990s, greatly reducing the control frauds.

The combination of our political, ideological, and budgetary mechanisms increase systems-capacity problems. No one in the OMB gets promoted for figuring out that vastly more money should be spent to increase the number of regulators. Again, we did not learn the appropriate lessons from the debacle. The "reinventing government" movement, for example, required every agency to develop formal mission statements and strategic plans, and led the GAO to designate high-risk activities. The SEC's recent annual reports stress that it is a civil "law enforcement agency." Nevertheless, the SEC annual reports, prior to Enron's failure, never identified waves of control frauds as a risk imperiling the success of its mission, and the GAO never designated the SEC's antifraud activities (or any other SEC activity) as high-risk. (As I write, it has still not done so.) The GAO standards for high-risk activities emphasize fraud risk, but only fraud risk in which the government is directly defrauded. In designating high-risk activities, the GAO should consider the harm that will befall the public if regulators fail to achieve their missions.

One of the great advantages of control frauds is their ability to cause the firm to make political contributions. Audacious control frauds use this ability to help shape their regulatory environment. They seek to undercut effective regulation. There is no "Brotherhood of Burglars" that has apparent respectability and regularly lobbies for restrictions on the quality of door locks or the number of police assigned to neighborhood patrols. The GAO needs to develop a team tasked with looking for critically underregulated areas that put the nation at risk.

9. REGULATORY AND PRESIDENTIAL
LEADERSHIP IS VITALLY IMPORTANT.

The S&L debacle should have made both of these points clear. Pratt, Gray, and Wall were more different than similar. Bank Board policies changed radically and quickly when the chairman changed, even though the same president appointed them. These changes, however, did not appear to reflect any change in the Reagan administration's regulatory policies.

Ryan was very different from Wall, even though President Bush appointed both of them OTS directors. Ryan's appointment signaled a sharp change in presidential policy concerning regulation, and Ryan changed OTS policy abruptly.

In general then, the debacle was not a case where entrenched bureaucrats drove policies irrespective of presidential or agency leadership. Indeed, the closest example of entrenched bureaucrats making contrary policy was the FHLBSF's vigorous resistance to Wall's regulation of Lincoln Savings and American Savings (and Gray's regulation of American Savings). If Wall had been able to fire the FHLBSF personnel who led this resistance (as he could have done after the creation of the OTS in August 1989), he might have been able to crush that resistance by removing its leaders.

The debacle demonstrated that "the vision thing" is central to regulatory success in a crisis. Pratt was brilliant, charismatic, and had a distinct vision. He also was the regulator who, according to Martin Mayer (1990, 61), would win the prize for most to blame for the debacle. His vision was disastrously wrong, and his brilliance and creativity made the problem worse: he exemplified the phrase "too clever by half." He believed that some clever fudge (almost always an accounting gimmick) would get him through the latest crisis. He had an uncanny ability to optimize the regulatory environment for control fraud.

Gray got the vision thing right, which is why his critics will never forgive him. Mayer told me that as soon as it became known that he was writing a book about the debacle, many individuals wrote or called him to try to make sure that he attacked Gray. They still believe the control frauds' very expensive propaganda that tried to paint an intelligent man as stupid.

Gray had many weaknesses, but he had six great strengths that proved decisive in preventing the debacle from becoming a catastrophe. First, he understood, as early as anyone at the agency, that all the high fliers were following the same basic pattern and that their claims of high income and low losses were produced by accounting fraud. Second, he understood that limiting their growth was essential. Third, he understood that the agency was critically understaffed and that he would have to change the structure radically and to openly defy the OMB and the administration. Fourth, he was a very good judge of supervisory talent. He personally recruited Patriarca and Selby to deal with the two districts leading the fight against the control frauds. Fifth, he had a sense of duty that led him to sacrifice his career and defy an astonishing array of powerful opponents in order to defeat the wave of control frauds (which we then called "high fliers"). It also led him to overturn his ideological opposition to reregulation and to be willing to act contrary to the wishes of the president he loved. Sixth, he did not want yes-men or yes-women, and he was comfortable working with people like Selby and Patriarca who had supervisory expertise that far exceeded his own.

Wall remains the enigma with regard to the S&L control frauds. He was such an obsessively secretive man that only a few relevant contemporaneous comments exist on the record. Even a few days before he voted to appoint a conservator for Lincoln Savings, he did not accept the fact that Keating was a fraud. Instead, he continued to praise Keating's purported business skills. His fellow Bank Board member, Roger Martin, was even more loyal to Keating. Neither of them ever pushed the agency to take action against the high fliers. The nation is fortunate that the growth rule caused each of the remaining high fliers to collapse while Wall was Bank Board chairman. Forbearance delayed these collapses and materially increased the ultimate cost to the taxpayers, but it could not save these Ponzi schemes. In short, Wall and Martin did considerable damage, but they would have done vast damage had they preceded Gray instead of following him.

Both Pratt and Wall demonstrated a recurrent problem with modern regulation. Placing an individual who does not believe in regulation in charge of a regulatory agency can cause great damage, especially if that agency has to deal with control frauds. Deregulatory economists argue that private market mechanisms deal adequately with control fraud. People who believe that claim (and those who have taken one course in law and economics are often its most fervent adherents) believe that financial statements are truthful and that auditors will not aid control frauds. They are taught that public-choice theory has shown that it is naïve to believe that government workers act in the public interest (instead of simply maximizing their personal self-interest). Agencies are routinely captured by the regulatees, according to the economic theory of regulation. Government officials who argue that control fraud is material exemplify an agency problem: they are trying to distract attention from their own failures. Externalities such as pollution are not a valid rationale for regulation; they just represent a failure to adequately assign property rights pursuant to the Coase theorem. Antitrust laws need not, and should not, be enforced, because markets quickly sweep away the rare problems that arise, and antitrust laws are used primarily by unsuccessful competitors to bludgeon rivals they could not outcompete.

The book I use to teach intermediate microeconomics makes most of these points. It is intensely antiregulatory, which means that it presents the conventional neoclassical view. Anyone who believes all (or even most) of the propositions in the above paragraph is going to be personally unprepared to identify or deal with a wave of control frauds. Indeed, such a wave is impossible under their beliefs. Further, if fraud is immaterial, then there is no reason to learn about fraud mechanisms or the means to reduce fraud. If the person who believes such theories is a senior regulatory leader, the agency will be unprepared to deal with a wave of control frauds. Indeed, such a leader would be strongly inclined to believe that any employee who vigorously argued that a corporation reporting strong profits (blessed by a top-tier audit firm) should be closed must have taken leave of his senses or be engaged in a vendetta.

Pratt did not close any control frauds. Therefore, his potential vulnerability to their pleas was untested. Wall appears to be an example of this root vulnerability, which Keating then exploited by demonizing Gray and his lieutenants, threatening personal suits, and bringing political pressure to bear.

None of the four top federal S&L leaders that dealt with the debacle was captured by the industry. The S&L league developed such bad relations with Pratt that they barred him from their meetings. The industry fought against each of Gray's major regulatory initiatives and the FSLIC recap. After a honeymoon period, the league warred with Wall. Indeed, all three chairmen shared utter contempt for the league. Ryan had no use for it, and it was in any event reduced to a weak group by the time he became OTS director.

Public-choice theory fails to explain the actions of Pratt, Gray, and Wall. Gray is the most obvious case. He acted directly contrary to his self-interest. Wall shows a subtler problem with the theory. Assume for the sake of discussion that Wall chose to appease Keating out of pure self-interest. How could he know that appeasement would best aid his

self-interest? His surrender to political pressure and threats of litigation eventually cost him his job and reputation. Perhaps public-sector
employees, to maximize their self-interest, act in the public's interest,
because doing so improves their chances of retention and promotion
and helps them develop a favorable (and valuable) reputation.

The new wave of control fraud shows that we have again failed to
learn the necessary lessons from the S&L debacle. First, Levitt blinked
during his ultimate confrontation and gave up on expensing options.
His surrender is now his greatest regret. He could have learned from
Gray that he would be far happier if he had tried to do the right thing
and lost. Note that Levitt (whom I think highly of) is wealthy and that
the SEC is considerably more prestigious than the Bank Board. Gray
was in a far worse position but persevered. I write this not to disparage
Levitt, but to point out that Gray's courage was unusual.

President George W. Bush appointed Levitt's successor, Harvey Pitt.
Pitt exemplified the danger of appointing regulatory leaders who do not
believe that conflicts of interest matter and do not believe that waves of
control fraud can occur. Bush made Pitt the SEC chairman because he
was the nation's leading opponent of accounting and audit reform. During a speech Pitt promptly gave to an audience of accountants, he reminded me of Wall and Henkel. He began by expressing his regret that
the SEC was not always a "kinder and gentler place" for accountants.
He blamed the strained relations between accountants and the SEC on
the SEC staff (and implicitly blamed their conduct on Levitt). He eventually resigned after his continued efforts to block the appointment of
real reformers (which he did at the request of the White House and Representative Oxley) proved clumsy and embarrassed the administration.

One of the lessons of the S&L debacle is that our nation was very
lucky. (I know that a $150 billion debacle does not sound "lucky," but
without Gray's reregulation and the war against the control frauds, the
debacle would have cost over a trillion dollars.) We were thrice lucky
in having Gray. First, Reagan appointed him to deregulate. He could
not have been appointed if he had supported reregulation. He then underwent a fortunate transformation and became the nation's leading reregulator. "Reregulator" was the greatest possible insult in the Reagan
administration, and normally would have led to his removal. Gray survived solely because he was a personal friend of the Reagans.

Second, he got it largely right when he reregulated. He got brokered
deposits wrong, but he sealed the fate of the control frauds when he adopted the growth rule. Third, he was willing to take on opponents that

dwarfed even those that attacked Levitt. We were also lucky because the administration's effort to give Keating control of the Bank Board failed and because Keating used Henkel so crudely that he could be removed from office before he could destroy reregulation. Henkel would have caused enormous damage if he had remained Keating's mole.

We cannot afford to rely on luck. We have to take the selection of senior regulators more seriously. That requires us to discuss the role of the president in regulation. President Reagan failed in this role. His administration (and it is important to remember that Vice President Bush was in charge of financial deregulation) took the following actions:

- Insisted on deregulating at a time of mass insolvency
- Insisted on covering up the scope of the crisis
- Barred Pratt from briefing the cabinet finance committee
- Argued in favor of running insolvent S&Ls like Ponzi schemes
- Repeatedly cut the number of examiners
- Fought the agency's use of the FHLB system to double the number of examiners and supervisors at no cost to the Treasury
- Opposed Gray's efforts to reregulate
- Refused to allow the FSLIC to obtain any money from Treasury
- Tried to give Keating majority control of the Bank Board
- Appointed Keating's mole, Henkel, to the Bank Board
- Accepted (through Bush) a $100,000 contribution from Keating even after Senator Riegle had returned his contributions in light of the Keating Five scandal
- Reappointed Henkel to the Bank Board after he tried to immunize Lincoln Savings' violations
- Tried (through Don Regan) to embarrass Gray into resigning
- Threatened to prosecute Pratt and Gray for closing insolvent S&Ls
- Threatened to prosecute FDIC chairman Seidman for closing banks
- Reached a deal with Speaker Wright to support forbearance and not reappoint Gray
- Conducted a criminal investigation of the FHLBSF at Keating's request
- Provided no White House support for the FSLIC recap until Gray left office
- Regan testified that while Gray warned of the coming crisis, he, Regan, ignored the warnings
- Not only did President Reagan never request a briefing from Gray about the debacle, but they never discussed it personally after Reagan appointed Gray

- President Bush insisted on appointing Wall as director of the OTS without the advice and consent of the Senate, which was ruled unconstitutional
- Bush appointed Wall OTS director even after he had appeased Keating

10. ETHICS AND SOCIAL FORCES ARE
CRITICAL RESTRAINTS ON FRAUD AND ABUSE.

Only a small percentage of traditional S&Ls that did not change owner-ship in 1981–1984 engaged in control fraud. A CEO who spends her professional career at an S&L working her way to the top generally has substantial loyalty to the institution, staff, and customers. The combi-nation of personal ethics and social ties makes control fraud far more unlikely. Conversely, as I explained earlier, conflicts of interest matter. Real estate developers who bought S&Ls during 1981–1984 were the CEOs most likely to become control frauds. They had serious conflicts of interest and few institutional or personal loyalties.

Whistle-blowers were rare at S&L control frauds. One of the lessons we should have learned from the debacle is that control frauds' ability to hire and fire personnel makes whistle-blowing an extremely risky act. True whistle-blowers—those who inform the public or the authorities of control fraud—have been rare during the current wave of financial scandals. We cannot rely on whistle-blowers to do the work regulators and the criminal justice system should do against control fraud.

11. DEREGULATION MATTERS AND ASSETS MATTER.

Deregulation can aid control fraud in four ways. It can radically change the environment because we are poor at predicting untested dynamic events. For example, in the S&L debacle, even though an economic theory predicted "competition in laxity," Pratt did not anticipate Cali-fornia's reaction to the Garn–St Germain Act of 1982. He did not antici-pate how his dozens of regulatory changes interacted to create a perfect environment for control fraud. (I call it "faith-based" deregulation.) Sec-ond, deregulation may increase system-capacity problems. ADC loans were often over 100 times more time-consuming to review than single-family home loans. Third, deregulation may allow investment in assets that lack a readily ascertainable market value. One of the keys to ac-counting fraud is to find such assets, like the large commercial ADC projects in Dallas. They may create guaranteed (though fictitious) in-come and hide true losses. Fourth, deregulation may provide the au-thority to enter into reciprocal (fraudulent) transactions used to transmute bad investments into good ones. It may also provide the authority to create an entity that will be used as a straw party.

12. WHY DOESN'T THE SEC HAVE A CHIEF CRIMINOLOGIST?

Virtually every federal agency in America has a chief economist. Most have several chief economists at various subunits. As far as I can tell, no federal agency has a chief criminologist. The federal government does not have a job classification labeled criminologist. All financial regulatory agencies are civil law-enforcement agencies that must concern themselves with control fraud (and many other crimes). They are commonly staffed, however, with people who have received no professional training about fraud. Lawyers, accountants, and finance and economics majors dominate the SEC. None of these disciplines, traditionally, have studied fraud. (A few accounting students now take a class in fraud auditing.)

I do not suggest that the chief criminologist must have a degree in criminology. The goal is to have someone who thinks like a criminologist and is familiar with fraud techniques and indicia of fraud.

We know enough to do much better against control fraud. We can tell what environments are most likely to produce waves of control fraud. We can figure out the fraud schemes that are most prevalent and the best ways to identify such schemes.

There is a basic paradox about trust in the regulatory context, one that the Bank Board under Wall got wrong in their fateful decision to accept Keating's plea of "trust me." Trust is vital for efficient commerce, social harmony, and intimacy. But some of us must remain intensely skeptical so that others can continue to trust. The regulators need to be skeptical (accountants and most lawyers also have to rediscover skepticism). That does not mean automatically assuming the worst, but it does mean that one checks hard and skillfully. It also means that if the party being examined interferes with the review, lies, or attempts to intimidate the reviewer, the reviewer's skepticism should spike and the superiors should support the reviewer.

We can do far better investigations. The S&L debacle is again instructive. Mario Renda was a control fraud who helped loot dozens of S&Ls and banks. A Bank Board enforcement attorney, Hershkowitz, investigated him. Unfortunately, the OE had no experience in complex investigations, and he missed the fraud when he took Renda's deposition (Binstein and Bowden 1993, 196). Fortunately, Michael

Manning of Morrison & Hecker, outside counsel for the FDIC, discovered it (ibid., 214). Manning contacted me, and we (the FSLIC and the FDIC) shared the expense of his investigation that uncovered the widespread fraud. The lesson is that even fairly small numbers of highly experienced, tenacious investigators can greatly increase performance. Too many regulatory agencies refuse to use outside counsel to aid their investigations.

Daisy chains make it harder for examiners looking at one entity to spot reciprocal transactions. But daisy chains are also a weakness if one investigates properly, for they can lead the investigator to identify a large portion of the most dangerous control frauds.

The criminal justice system can do a far better job of investigating waves of control fraud. Daisy chains are highly susceptible to sting operations, as are S&L and bank control frauds. Undercover employees could easily be placed in corrupt financial institutions. FBI and IRS agents often have the necessary expertise. Electronic surveillance could provide direct evidence of conspiracy in reciprocal transactions. None of these techniques was used in any material manner during the S&L debacle. The Dallas Task Force was very effective without these means, but it would have been considerably more effective if it had used them. In our experience, detailing our examiners and supervisors to assist criminal investigations made all the difference. The SEC, of course, is so short of experienced staff that it cannot afford to detail the type of staff that would most aid the criminal investigation.

The SEC also needs to litigate more cases and sign far fewer consent agreements. The SEC negotiates consents disproportionately with failed smaller firms. The commission often gets no meaningful relief in such consents. The greater the system-capacity problems, the greater the tendency to accept a consent agreement rather than litigate. The agency, however, suffers when it relies almost entirely on consents. It does not establish precedents; its enforcement attorneys lack experience and may fear litigation; and the relief granted against serious wrongs will often be inadequate.

Tougher prison sentences in real prisons remain the best hope for deterrence. Keating caused Andersen to stuff the junk bond files in order to deceive the examiners. If the Justice Department had brought a criminal action against Andersen in 1987 for this crime, the accounting profession would have had a powerful incentive to clean up its act. This could have reduced the ongoing wave of accounting scandals.

13. CONTROL FRAUDS DEFEAT CORPORATE GOVERNANCE PROTECTIONS AND REFORMS.

The S&L debacle should have taught us that control frauds were able to defeat a broad range of corporate governance principles. Control frauds control the election of the board of directors. They pick outside directors who are the equivalent of inside directors. Efforts to improve corporate governance may be desirable for other reasons (though we must not lose sight of the cost), but they are unlikely to be effective against control fraud, and we certainly should not rely on their effectiveness. The new Sarbanes-Oxley reform legislation primarily relies on improving corporate governance. Since control frauds have caused the ongoing financial scandals, that is discouraging.

The one hope that the S&L debacle offers in this regard is that S&L control frauds preferred the 100 percent ownership model. They viewed even outside directors picked entirely from business associates as a hindrance. There are virtually no cases in which an S&L board of directors caused any known difficulty for a control fraud. This, however, is still another area in which we have failed to learn the lessons of the debacle. According to Easterbrook and Fischel (1991, 10, 70–75, 133, 282), the ideal form of ownership is the sole owner and CEO because it eliminates agency problems. That may be a disadvantage in the context of control fraud. An agency problem is likely to be either an officer like Mark Sauter, who embezzled from Lincoln Savings, or a whistle-blower who exposes the fraud. Single-ownership will not stop the embezzler, but it may stop the whistle-blower and allow the fraud to grow.

14. STOCK OPTIONS INCREASE LOOTING BY CONTROL FRAUDS.

Control frauds decide how stock options will be structured. They design options to permit easier looting. Typically, this means tying stock options to short-term economic performance, which is easier for the control fraud to distort. Control frauds delight in using seemingly legitimate corporate mechanisms to transfer firm assets to their personal use. According to Easterbrook and Fischel (1991, 282), however, "[With] stock options ... If the firm does poorly, the managers lose with the other investors." By now, this needs no refutation. It should not have needed refutation when written, because S&L control frauds had demonstrated that the CEO could do very well regardless of the fate of the shareholders.

**15. WE NEED TO REINVENT THE "REINVENTING GOVERNMENT"
MOVEMENT TO DEAL EFFECTIVELY WITH CONTROL FRAUD.**

The Clinton-Gore effort to reinvent government did not leave us any
better prepared for the current wave of control fraud. Three changes
would be helpful. First, the existing strategic plans of few regulatory
agencies meaningfully analyze the primary risks threatening the agency's
ability to meet its mission. In plain English, a goal of the SEC should be
to prevent waves of control fraud. Second, the GAO should change its
definition of high risk to include risks to the public should the agency
fail in its mission. It is embarrassing that the GAO, as I write, still does
not consider the SEC's antifraud activities a high-risk function. Third,
both the OMB and the GAO should establish divisions to locate units
suffering system-capacity problems and to recommend steps to fix the
problem. Someone needs to be rewarded and promoted for recommending more regulation and more spending when that is necessary.

Appendix A: Keating's Plan of Attack on Gray and Reregulation

AKIN, GUMP, STRAUSS, HAUER & FELD

[illegible]

WASHINGTON, D.C. 20036

[illegible]

August 28, 1985

<u>CLIENT CONFIDENTIAL</u>

Mr. Charles H. Keating, Jr.
Chairman of the Board
and President
American Continental Corporation
2735 East Camelback Road
Suite 150
Phoenix, AZ 85016

Dear Charlie:

Since our recent conversation about keeping the heat on the White House regarding Hovde's replacement and Gray's dismissal, I have talked to my expert colleagues in-house as well as some good friends in the Administration. Regrettably, the consensus is a bit gloomier in some repects than our earlier prognosis -- in large part because the President's illness has made it clear that the White House will have a very short list of priorities for action in the Fall. As significant as Gray's adverse impact is on Lincoln in particular and on the S&L industry as a whole, it is clear that Regan and Company are unlikely to focus on the Gray problem without a subtle and effective program to force their attention on the issue.

However, there is also some good news. Namely, there appears to be a reasonably good and current appreciation at the Don Regan level, in the Vice President's office and in certain important offices on the Hill, that Ed Gray is causing a major problem for the already shaky S&L industry.

The question then is how to reconcile the conflict between the intense pressure at the White House to focus <u>only</u> on the budget and tax bills, and the Gorbachov meeting, versus our goal of getting some near-term relief for Lincoln.

Instead of trying to sack Gray, who is unquestionably a disaster but still "a nice guy" to the Reagan-inner circle, our efforts should focus primarily on getting the White House to take a less controversial (and therefore highly desirable) remedial course of action: identifying and

EXHIBIT 2 MRG

nominating a Hovde replacement who would be acceptable to
you and other enlightened industry leaders. This more
conservative course of action is appropriate for a number of
reasons:

1) It is non-confrontational and therefore far more
feasible than ousting Gray, who enjoys the loyalties of
Reagan's people and who, like so many before him in this
Administration, would have to be criminally liable or worse
before they would be removed.

2) It would informally serve notice on Gray and his
staff in a discrete way that he is out of favor with the
White House. This is key since most Reagan-appointed Chairmen of regulatory commissions enjoy great influence over the
selection of their fellow commissioners. By robbing Gray of
this important perogative, you could hurt him both psychologically and practically, thereby making his early resignation
more likely.

3) Chairmen who lose their influence over Board appointments often find that the loyalties of their own staffs
become shallow at best. This could temper the action of key
FHLBB staff, both in Washington and in the regional offices,
such as San Francisco.

4) Once confirmed, the Hovde replacement immediately
could start to issue strong dissents that could provide your
litigators with some good material for appeals to the Federal
Courts.

5) With an enlightened Hovde replacement on the
horizon, the now-cowed female Member of the Board may take a
more independent approach, including occasionally dissenting
from the Chairman. The obvious displeasure of Texans,
including the Vice President, with the Gray Chairmanship
could further enhance this Member's independence from Gray
if she sensed she wasn't alone.

6) Congressional leaders would have a greatly improved
opportunity to show in public hearings the folly of the
Gray-approach since all three Board Members would be testifying
with the Hovde replacement presenting an opposing viewpoint
to Gray's. Nothing could better educate Members of Congress
and the Administration as to FHLBB problems and opportunities
than an enlightened Board Member who could publically disagree
with Gray.

7) Finally, the PR value of the Hovde replacement
would be unlimited. You would no longer have to rely exclu-

MBG

Mr. Charles E. Keating, Jr.
August 26, 1988
Page Three

Since your new Board Member could articulate an intelligent
approach, and do so with the mantel of authority that goes
along with membership (actual or designated) on the FHLBB.

At this point you are probably saying: "OK - wise guy,
how do we go after your modest goal and get around a very
reluctant White House?" You are probably also frustrated
because I'm saying Gray is likely to be around for awhile
unless we can make life so miserable that he resigns early.

To successfully replace Novde and to simultaneously
make life unbearable for Gray, I think we need to pursue a
number of actions in tandem as soon as the Labor Day Recess
is over.

1) Gershon Kekst and Company should mount a major
public relations program in responsible print media (i.e.
The American Banker piece) to highlight the deficiencies of
the Gray Board. Using a respected economist like Professor
Benston is an ideal way to magnify such flaws as: The
Board's failure to police situations in a timely fashion;
its efforts at "reregulation" in a manner inconsistent with
the Reagan Administration's open marketplace approach; the
troublesome conflict of interest questions; and the Chairman's
excessive travel schedule which has resulted in a lack of
attention to the Board's operations - these are all points
that can be developed in newspapers like The Wall Street Journal
and then offered as "objective" information pieces for
officials of the Executive Branch, Congressional members,
and even important Kitchen Cabinet Members.

In making this recommendation for an increased PR
effort, I continue to stop short of urging a personal attack
on Gray. While it may be a narrow line to walk, I think we
should be cautious about stirring a personal attack since
the old Reaganites have a lot of scar tissue and they circle
the wagons very quickly around one of their own when they
feel there has been a vindictive attack as opposed to substantive criticism.

2) Our Congressional program should have a three-part
goal:

a) We should use every possible hearing (oversight
or routine) as a means of assaulting Gray through planted,
informed questions. The recent Dingell Oversight Hearing
illustrated the aggressive approach that we should be taking
behind the scenes to make Gray, his staff, and other Board
Members feel extremely uncomfortable about current FHLBB

MRG

Mr. Charles H. Keating, Jr.
August 28, 1985
Page Four

operations. If done properly, the Board Members should not
necessarily know what segment of the industry is generating
the heat, only that the heat is there and will be increasing.
Following each of these hearings, letters asking for additional
information should inundate Gray's office from appropriate
Congressional sources. Together, these efforts should make
Gray feel very much under attack by responsible members of
Congress.

b) Congressional pressure also should be kept on
Don Regan and Bob Tuttle to insure that the White House
feels the <u>real</u> anxiety of key members of the Senate and
House about the Hovde replacement. This pressure should
start immediately after the Labor Day Recess and continue
throughout September and October when the White House will
probably be very much in need of Congressional votes on the
budget and tax bills. Achieving significant changes in the
make-up of the FHLBB by the Christmas recess must become the
quid pro quo for some key Members whose votes on these
crucial bills will be vital to the White House.

c) Surrogates like Professor Benston should be
used to call on key members and staff, and to testify in
open Congressional hearings about the counter-productive,
re-regulatory approach that the Gray Board is pursuing. If
we don't provide articulate surrogates for Lincoln, the
robust point of view that you need to have expressed simply
won't occur.

3) We need to brief a number of important members of
the Executive Branch and to rebrief those with whom you have
already talked. The Comptroller of the Currency designee
Bob Clark, the soon-to-be confirmed O.M.B. Chief Jim Miller,
Ken Cribb and others at Justice -- these are just a few of
the people who need to understand better the adverse impact
that a "well-intended Gray" is causing the S&L industry. Of
course, our PR efforts as outlined above could have a substantial positive impact on this effort if it is handled
properly.

The recommendations outlined above presume that your
Wall Street lawyers are protecting vital options with regard
to future litigation. Pursuit of these judicial options or,
as appropriate, a hold on them should be compatible with the
three-pronged recommendations outlined above.

As part of this approach, I urge you to consider putting
together an informal group of three or four of the most
distinguished industry leaders you know who could join you
occasionally in Washington for Executive Branch appearances.

MRG

Mr. Charles H. Keating, Jr.
August 28, 1985
Page Five

Congressional testimony and/or press interviews. I think
that a group concept is helpful if you select men of stature
such as Gordon Luce to join you in presenting the magnitude
of the problem for the industry. By identifying some articulate
allies, you may also limit the FHLBB staff from acting
punitively against Lincoln. While total avoidance of
punitive actions may be impossible, a group approach may
ameliorate some of the risk to Lincoln.

A final point that I discussed at length with Gershon
yesterday is timing. In my opinion (humble or not), it is
essential that your efforts be put into high gear in early
September. If you wait until October you will have lost
essential time for making even the modest gains that designation of a Hovde replacement can mean for Lincoln. In view
of the acute nature of your problems with the Gray Board and
the realities of this Administration's immediate priorities,
you simply cannot let one-third of the next three months go
unused. At present, we are barely a bleep on the far
right-hand corner of the White House's radar screen - if
we're idle for the next crucial 30 days, we might be forever
lost at sea.

Let me know your thoughts on the above. I am sorry I
cannot join you in New York on the 18th, but I am available
to join you there on the 19th or, alternatively, to see you
on the 19th or 20th in D.C.

Sincerely,

Michael R. Gardner

MRG/lpm
cc: Bob Hubbard

Appendix B: Hamstringing the Regulator

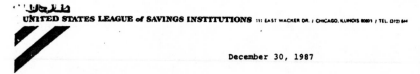

UNITED STATES LEAGUE of SAVINGS INSTITUTIONS 111 EAST WACKER DR. / CHICAGO, ILLINOIS 60601 / TEL. (312) 644

December 30, 1987

MEMORANDUM TO: Bill O'Connell

FROM: Norman Strunk   <u>PERSONAL</u>

I read the interview with Theo Pitt in the December issue of <u>Sav-ings Institutions</u> and had a problem with his comment about the crooks, responsible people in the business having pointed out who the crooks were, etc.-- left hand column on page 64.

As one who has done a lot of research on the causes of the fail-ures, I thought I might suggest some caution as you work through your new FSLIC Committee and get into this general area. In the first place, according to the material Rosemary Stewart recently put together for the Board to submit to the Barnard Committee, only 20% of the failures in the past three years (and 23% in the previous three-year period) were attributable to "fraud" and "in-sider abuses." The percentage of dollar losses, in contrast to number of institutions, might well be higher.

You know from your own observations and my manuscript that there were many reasons for the major losses suffered by the FSLIC in ad-dition to "dishonesty" and the "crooks." We have to recognize, of course, that a lot of loose talk contributed to the impression many have had that our business was ruined by the "crooks." You may re-member my quoting Paul Volcker to this effect.

I know that many in the business complained about some of the oper-ations that later resulted in failures and losses -- the "whistle blowers" -- but even if the bad operations were identified as in-volving substantial elements of fraud, the supervisors would have been unable to respond to such finger pointing, or at least res-pond very quickly.

The supervisory law passed in 1966 following substantial compromise negotiations between the Board under Chairman John Horne, the League, the Congress, the ABA and banks, etc., gave the Board power to re-move officers and directors, but surrounded this authority with a lot of "due process" protections. Specifically, in the case of dis-honesty the Board was given authority to remove an individual charged with a crime, dishonesty, etc., but, of course, only after an indi-vidual has actually been charged.

The supervisors have to be able to prove dishonesty to a court and such documentation can involve a lot of examiner time. The Board's Office of Enforcement has no authority to bring action with respect to criminal activity. All the Board can do is refer its suspicions and findings to the Department of Justice. The Department of Just-ice has white collar crime cases substantially backed up so even if the Board knew or had strong evidence to prove that there was dis-honesty, it would have been difficult for it to do anything about

THE AMERICAN HOME THE SAFEGUARD OF AMERICAN LIBERTIES

MEMORANDUM TO: Bill O'Connell   December 30, 1987
                Page 2

it in the way of removal action. The Board certainly can't
throw anyone out on suspicion of crime -- or accusation by a
competitor -- and we wouldn't want it to. Other grounds for
removal are equally surrounded by protective "due process"
provisions.

As my paper shows, the Board, along with the FDIC, has not
been able to use the temporary cease and desist order to stop
wrongdoing. When we participated in the writing of the supervisory law, hindsight shows that we probably gave the business
too much protection against unwarranted supervisory action,
thus protecting the crooks as well as the good guys and imped-
ing effective supervisory action against reckless management.
But, as you well know, the business doesn't take too kindly to
the idea of removing these protective features of the law. Ed
Gray did not get the changes in the supervisory law that he
sought in 1984. Thus the business itself is somewhat to blame
for the "failure" of the Board to use a "fast whistle!"

In making a case that "the government" was basically responsible
for the tragedy that befell the FSLIC, I think we have to be
careful that we do not put all the blame on the Home Loan Bank
Board, particularly the Board under Ed Gray. Goodness knows,
he called to everybody's attention the problems that were developing in the business -- to a point that the business got
tired of hearing about it -- and, as we have discussed, there
was widespread opposition to his regulatory initiatives.

The brokers and their association customers killed the proposed
reforms with respect to broker money. There was widespread opposition to his initiatives with respect to the net worth regulation. There was vehement opposition by many with respect to his
proposal for direct investments. He inherited an inadequate supervisory and examination staff for which substantial blame must
be placed on OMB. After considerable jawboning, he did get more
effective supervisory action from the regional banks.

I am writing this memo to suggest that as the League develops
its program with respect to the FSLIC that you do not get into
a finger pointing contest with Ed and some of his people. We
would not want him to sit at his typewriter again to make the
record, as he sees it, on this subject. The blame lies with
the Pratt Board, OMB, the Reagan Administration's philosophy of
deregulation, preferring decision making by the marketplace,
lack of congressional authorization earlier of the ARM, etc.

You can share this memo with Theo, if you like. It would not
be appropriate for me to write directly to him on this or any
other question.

                        N.S.

NS:ep

Appendix C: Get Black ...Kill Him Dead

**AMERICAN
CONTINENTAL
CORPORATION**

2725 East Camelback Road / Phoenix, Arizona 85016 / (602) 957-7170

TO: JIM GROGAN   DATE: 7/15/87

FROM: CHARLES H KEATING, JR.

SUBJECT:

HIGHEST PRIORITY - <u>GET BLACK</u>

<u>GOOD GRIEF</u> - IF YOU CAN'T GET WRIGHT AND
CONGRESS TO GET BLACK - KILL HIM DEAD -
YOU OUGHT TO RETIRE.

102629DM3

SB010 1301

NOTES

PREFACE

1. My regulatory career is profiled in Chapter 2 of Riccucci's study (1995).

CHAPTER 1

1. I use the term "CEO" because it is short and because CEOs typically control companies. I use "he" as the pronoun for CEO for similar reasons.

2. I do not assume that individuals are perfectly rational in evaluating risk. Individuals frequently misapprehend risks. It is enough for my purposes that they try to avoid situations in which detection and punishment of fraud is most likely.

3. A straw is someone who fronts for the real person at interest. An S&L generally cannot loan money to its CEO. The CEO finds an acquaintance who will sign the loan documents but give the proceeds to the CEO.

4. The same dynamic caused the current glut of broadband capacity.

5. The rule banning ARMs was not a product of S&L domination of the Bank Board. To the contrary, the industry, the agency, several presidents, and most of Congress wanted to overturn the ban on ARMs in order to reduce the industry's systemic exposure to interest-rate risk. The ban remained, however, because the powerful National Association of Home Builders and the National Association of Realtors (normally allies of the S&L trade association) feared that ARMs would reduce home purchases. The NAHB and NAR lobbied "proconsumer" congressional chairmen to block Bank Board approval of ARMs.

6. In addition to being awful economics and accounting, loan loss deferral was poor policy. It encouraged S&Ls to sell their home mortgages at enormous losses that locked in their real insolvency. The owners knew that the S&L was hopelessly

insolvent and that its reported profits were fictitious. "Profits" occurred solely because the deferred recognition of loan losses led to real losses being dramatically underreported. The owners also knew that the fictitious profits would disappear in about five years. Deferral, therefore, prompted two disastrous responses. First, S&Ls sold mortgages at what was likely to be the worst possible time (which magnified the eventual losses of the FSLIC). Second, there was a powerful incentive to engage in reactive control fraud.

7. An arbitrage is a risk-free exchange, so an RCA is a self-contradiction. There were no arbitrages available to S&Ls. Stripped of the veneer of financial mumbo jumbo that the task force tacked on to the proposal, an RCA was an instrument that grew rapidly and took moderate interest-rate risk. Loan loss deferral and RCAs are, however, contradictory proposals, a fact that escaped the task force's analysis. An RCA would prove profitable if interest rates fell; it would greatly increase losses if they rose. But if the agency was relying on a near-term fall in interest rates, then the last thing it should have done was to adopt loss deferral, which encouraged S&Ls to sell their traditional mortgages at large, real losses. If S&Ls held the mortgages and rates fell sharply, they would make enormous gains. This policy incoherence was characteristic of Pratt's tenure. His motif was to do everything possible for the industry even if the components were logically inconsistent.

8. Ed Kane (1985), however, predicted very early that the industry was headed for disaster, but he did not tie that accurate prediction to opposition to deregulation.

9. This political risk extended to Vice President Bush, for he was Reagan's head of financial deregulation.

10. For example, our analysts knew that the Soviet Union was deploying nuclear missiles in Cuba because our U-2s spotted the characteristic pattern of antiaircraft defenses the Soviets always used for nuclear missiles.

11. The same thing happened to the SEC in the 1990s. It became so short-staffed that it never knew a wave of control frauds had hit. It never identified patterns of conduct indicating that fraud was likely.

12. This provided a wonderful sight gag in *Jurassic Park* (Spielberg, 1993). The camera shows a view in a passenger-side mirror of the still-distant *Tyrannosaurus rex* pursuing the jeep and then cuts to a direct view of the action in which the *T. rex* is terrifyingly close.

13. Humbert Wolfe (1886–1940), "Over the Fire," from *The Uncelestial City* (New York: Alfred A. Knopf, 1930).

CHAPTER 2

1. Market value means just that. You assign current market prices to your assets and liabilities. A long-term fixed-rate debt loses much of its market value if interest rates increase sharply. Interest rates did that in 1979–1982, so S&Ls, with their 30-year fixed-rate mortgages, became massively insolvent.

2. Supply-siders argue that reduced taxes lead to economic and tax-revenue growth that will eliminate deficits. Bush aptly termed this "voodoo economics" when he was running against Reagan for the 1980 presidential nomination. The 1981 tax cuts led to record deficits.

3. GAAP changed subsequently to require recognition of these market-value losses. During the debacle, however, GAAP used the original or book-value basis for assets as long as they were held for investment (as opposed to sale or trading). S&Ls always claimed that they were holding for investment.

4. S&L mergers used "purchase" (often called "push down") accounting (rather than "pooling").

5. S&L liabilities were so short-term that they reflected market value and were unaffected by the "mark."

6. How often does the IRS provide a lagniappe? Is this a great country or what?

7. Discount was a "contra asset." It reflected the fact that even though the mortgages had a new (lower) GAAP basis after the mark-to-market, they could still pay off in full at their initial book value. Assume that in 1977 one bought a home with a $200,000 mortgage at an 8 percent interest rate, and then sold it in 1983 when the comparable mortgage interest rate was 14 percent and the market value of the mortgage was $160,000. One pays the S&L the contractual amount ($200,000 less down payment and amortized interest), not the reduced market value. (This assumes that the buyer does not assume the mortgage.) "Discount" provided the accounting mechanism to recognize the value of mortgage prepayments.

8. S&Ls amortized goodwill on a straight-line basis over forty years. Pratt ended the Bank Board rule that had limited amortization to a maximum of fifteen years, and he used creative RAP to continue the forty-year period even after the accounting profession revised GAAP to require a faster write-off of goodwill.

9. Discount was "accreted" to income over a much shorter time than forty years.

10. Accountants refer to this as a "timing difference." That is quite a euphemism in this context, for few acquirers were likely to survive long enough to have the curves "cross over."

11. To estimate the fictional accounting gain from discount, however, one also has to remember that the acquirer in my hypothetical was acquiring a net liability. Acquiring a net liability depresses real operating results. Taking this into consideration, the more insolvent the S&L acquired, the greater the fictional net income and the worse the cash position.

12. One got a bonus at the Bank Board by being "creative" or working exceptionally hard. Creative often meant finding a new way to abuse accounting. Working hard usually meant spending nights and weekends getting new goodwill mergers and new conversions from mutual to stock ownership approved. In the field, it meant finding someone willing to be a goodwill acquirer. The Bank Board under Pratt constantly reinforced the message that traditional S&Ls were the problem,

that new entrants were "entrepreneurs" and the solution, that abusing accounting was "clever" or "innovative" instead of immoral, and that the Bank Board's policies had brilliantly resolved the crisis. The Bank Board staff loved Pratt. He was quick, generous with praise, quick to make fun of himself, demanding, and hardworking. Pratt didn't intimidate staff members into agreeing with him; he swept them off their feet and turned them into disciples eager to spread his message and methods. This made the Bank Board staff certain not to see the new entrants as criminals. I asked an agency old-timer in 1985 how many "changes of control" the Bank Board had denied in her institutional memory; the answer was one.

13. For example, in 1988 the FHLB in San Francisco recommended Mera-Bank as an acceptable acquirer for three failed Texas S&Ls. The senior supervisor, Eric Shand, however, felt that something was wrong and asked me to look at the matter. It turned out that not only was MeraBank insolvent except for its (fictitious) goodwill, but that it was also operating at a loss, once the (fictitious) income from the accretion of discount was removed. Our line supervisors had not understood goodwill accounting. We changed our recommendation and notified the Bank Board that MeraBank would fail. Wall was furious at us and approved the acquisitions. MeraBank soon failed. In 1992, an experienced agency accountant with from the Dallas region joined our West Region. She was unaware that goodwill accounting produced fictitious income. It was lost knowledge after Pratt left.

14. Here's an example: year-end total liabilities at an S&L over the last five years were $10 million, $20 million, $30 million, $40 million, and $1 billion. If we measured the 3 percent capital requirement against current liabilities it would be $30 million. With five-year averaging, however, the capital requirement is 3 percent of $1.1 billion (the sum of the total liabilities over the five years) divided by five. The average total liability was $220 million, so the capital requirement is 3 percent of that, $6.6 million, which is slightly more than *one-half of one percent* of the actual total liabilities of $1 billion. If the S&L had grown more rapidly, the percentage requirement would have been even lower.

15. California legislators stood to lose substantial campaign contributions from S&Ls; a state legislator can neither hurt nor help a federally chartered S&L. The "supremacy clause" of the U.S. Constitution prevents states from restricting federally chartered S&Ls. California S&Ls had just gotten the governor of their dreams, George Deukmejian, elected. They would soon have the California Department of Savings and Loans (CDSL) commissioner of their dreams: Larry Taggart, son of the governor's largest campaign contributor. They could dominate the CDSL, but if they had to convert to federal charters they would lose influence. The CDSL was funded by assessments on state-chartered S&Ls. The conversion to federal charters devastated the CDSL. It fired three-quarters of its professional staff. The CDSL's survival depended on the Nolan Act, which had no opponents: all the risk lay with FSLIC, not California.

16. His defense was that he was impotent at the time. It is unlikely that this unique variant of "no harm, no foul" pleased his wife!

CHAPTER 3

1. Deposit brokers existed because of limits on deposit insurance and because S&Ls and banks paid a slightly higher interest rate for jumbo deposits of $100,000 or more. They "sliced and diced" the funds of corporations and very rich customers into fully insured $100,000 deposits at a number of banks or S&Ls. Deposit brokers also consolidated funds from many small depositors into fully insured jumbo accounts.

2. Losing the case was my first major act as the new litigation director. I joined the agency on our eldest child's second birthday, April 2, 1984.

3. This question was of particular importance to me when I joined the agency as his litigation director. I told him to go ahead. The worst that could happen would be an order to approve FSLIC insurance for the new charters.

4. A direct investment involves an express or implicit ownership interest in the investment, as opposed to being a creditor for the investor. Buying land or shares is a direct investment. Lending money makes one a creditor. There is a critical exception to this last statement that I will explain later.

5. GAAP did not permit this much fee income to be recognized as immediate income, but control frauds routinely did it anyway and got clean opinions. The Bank Board shares in this blame. S&Ls could report additional fee income under RAP.

6. Many current control frauds use an additional mechanism: huge corporate loans made directly to the CEO. The corporation may then forgive the loan or the CEO may fail to repay the loan. S&Ls did not use this device because it was generally unlawful for an S&L to loan money to its CEO.

7. The control frauds had an elegant means of finding bad real estate developers. They maximized "adverse selection." Economists first identified adverse selection in the insurance context. A company offering insurance against lung cancer faces the risk that the people most likely to buy coverage are the ones most likely to develop lung cancer. Insurance theory and practice have developed means of reducing adverse selection. Control frauds took the opposite steps. The best way to reduce adverse selection in lending is to ensure that the borrower will suffer financially should the loan default and to conduct superior underwriting of the borrower and the real estate project pledged as security for the loan. Control frauds structured ADC loans that required neither a down payment nor a personal guarantee in order to ensure that the borrower would not suffer any direct financial loss. They chose borrowers with poor reputations who would not suffer any indirect financial loss from a loan default, and avoided making loans to high-quality developers.

8. Worse, the United States Court of Appeals for the Fifth Circuit ruled that Arthur Young was not liable to Western Savings' honest shareholders because Western Savings was a control fraud! The auditors were immune from suit because they helped a control fraud cause a billion dollars in losses to the taxpayers. By protecting top-tier audit firms from liability for aiding control frauds, the courts (and later Congress) helped cause the current wave of scandals.

9. The property could also be real estate owned by the S&L as a result of foreclosing on a defaulted ADC loan.

10. Because a CEO did need not to expressly ask the employee or officer to engage in fraud, everyone enjoyed deniability—and almost no one wants to think of himself or herself as a criminal. People in these situations use all kinds of what criminologists call "neutralization" techniques to keep from looking at themselves as criminals. Control frauds reinforce these techniques. One of the most effective means, which Keating used to good effect, was to tell employees that they were geniuses and that the regulators were dumb, vicious perverts. He paid people well above competitive salaries. His outside professionals were generally top quality, but his in-house people overwhelmingly were graduates of second-tier schools. Telling them that they were geniuses and paying them far more than graduates of top schools at rival banks and S&Ls made for intense loyalty. The other inducement was negative. It is why I say that control frauds are control freaks (Black 2000). Asking questions was the one sure way to get fired by a control fraud. One could make loans with a 96 percent default rate (as happened at Vernon Savings) and get a huge bonus, but ask a question and one was gone. The control frauds hired yes-men and yes-women and got rid of inquiring minds.

Nevertheless, the officers and employees knew that they were helping a fraudulent scheme. People who were unwilling to do so left, and the ones hired to replace them were likely to be less ethical. S&L control frauds deliberately gutted internal controls designed to stop bad loans. It was easy to defraud S&L control frauds.

11. My favorite example of construction fraud victimized Guaranty Savings, an Arkansas control fraud. It disbursed all the loan proceeds—over $30 million—to build an underground health club in Dallas. Even without construction fraud this would have caused a huge loss, but with the fraud, the FSLIC became the owner of a block-long, five-story-deep hole in downtown Dallas. The hole was worse than worthless. If one removes that much dirt, the ground nearby begins to subside, and may collapse into the hole. Such a collapse would rupture water and sewer lines and natural gas pipes. Dumping the dirt back in the hole would not recreate its former condition. Dallas wanted us to spend over $5 million to turn the hole into the world's biggest concrete post! We, barely, convinced them there was a much cheaper way to compact the dirt safely.

12. Economists are like the guy in the old joke who loses his car keys one night on the north side of the parking lot but searches for them on the south side because the light is better there—they only study where they have data.

13. The context was that I had just lost the case defending the deposit broker rule (on the grounds that we had no statutory authority to adopt the rule).

14. I had useful skills to bring to the reregulatory task. I was a lawyer, so I understood the rules, the legalese, and our litigation opponents' strategy for overturning the rule. I was an economics major with over 60 semester hours of economics, and the University of Michigan accepted me into its PhD program in economics. (I went to its law school instead.) This did not make me an economist, though I teach

microeconomics, but it meant that I was sufficiently fluent in economics to serve as a translator between the lawyers and OPER.

I was also "chief coroner" for the agency. My role as litigation director required me to autopsy every S&L failure in preparation for defending our closure of the S&L against legal challenges and determining whether we should sue the officers, directors, and outside professionals. To do my job, I had to become familiar with how the agency examined and supervised, and I had to learn how S&L accounting and appraisals worked. I found this, having experts explain their fields to me, great fun.

This education process also meant that I developed a broad network of friends who respected me. People are flattered when you take a sincere interest in their field. They are impressed when you link their insights to an aspect of another field with an unforeseen connection and show that the combination produces an elegant Ponzi scheme.

Because I saw every failure, I was among the first to see the emerging failure pattern. The central fact about the high fliers is that virtually all of them were minor variants on the ADC Ponzi theme. Tom Segal, one of my litigation attorneys, also suggested that we establish an "early warning" system. All too often we would learn of a planned closure days before it happened, even though it had been in the works for months. Segal's suggestion was excellent, and it paid dividends during reregulation because we discovered that our supervisory staff regularly briefed Bank Board members on "significant supervisory cases." The briefing book was enormous. It had synopses on hundreds of S&Ls, and the worst ones, which I had generally never heard of, also fit the pattern of high-flier failures.

15. Gray did not know me. I had lost the first major case I had handled for him. When I lost the case, he lost his top priority. I was now advising him to defer, for months, his remaining top priorities. He knew, far better than I, that his political opponents would use that delay to savage him. I was the messenger of terrible news. Gray did not kill or abuse the messenger. Two things helped. I had the confidence of the Norm Raiden, who recruited me to the agency, and Norm had Ed's confidence. I had also advised, as did my predecessor, that we were likely to lose the deposit broker lawsuit.

16. The problem with economic studies of ADC Ponzis was just what I explained: they were certain to report record income. Moreover, few of them had collapsed even by fall 1984, when we reproposed the rules. We had to look at the relatively small group of failures, which is always a problem for statistical analysis, and even for those failures we could not rely on reported income figures, because they were fraudulent. My solution was to study the likelihood and the cost of failure and to show that the S&Ls that grew fastest had the same characteristics as the catastrophic failures.

This required a very difficult dance. I started out with a great deal of credibility with our economists, but they generally had no respect for Gray and reregulation. They knew that their profession would consider them prostitutes if they favored reregulation because regulation was so discredited among economists, and they feared that Keating's expert economists would end up as peer reviewers of their future academic articles and would trash them. They feared that I was the pimp out to prostitute them. I had to establish why economic theory predicted that control fraud was a rational response and to explain how an ADC Ponzi worked. I also had to make sure that they reviewed every sentence in the preambles discussing the economic arguments. It took time, but it added to my credibility and made them comfortable going forward.

In the process, I got an unusual boost to my credibility by saving two of the OPER studies. In 1984 our economist reported that the study supporting the capital rule, which focused on the problems of excessive growth, did not find the expected relationship. This could have killed the entire rule. I was sure, given my knowledge of the limited number of failures, that the study should show that excessive growth was associated with a host of problems characteristic of our worst failures. I asked to see the data entries. It turned out that OPER had entered data for a number of failures twice. The double-counted ones had shown the expected relationship only very weakly. When those entries were removed, the study offered strong support for the rule.

The second example occurred in 1987 when the Bank Board considered extending and strengthening the direct investment rule. The key OPER study tested whether S&Ls with greater direct investments cost the FSLIC more to resolve when they failed. I had suggested this study design. The OPER econometrician (an economist who specializes in statistics) told me the study found that greater direct investments led to *reduced* FSLIC expenses. He told me that a number of "outliers" (extreme values) drove this result. He was spending his time working on corrections for the serious heteroskedasticity that arose in large part from these outliers. I asked to see the data plot (which shows graphically each datum). It showed five failures with enormous amounts of direct investment — the largest ones in the entire sample — and the FSLIC had resolved each of them at zero cost! You can see why this would lead to a negative statistical relationship between direct investments and the cost of resolution. Unfortunately, the econometrician had not thought to check, nor had anyone in OPER checked, whether this result could be true. Had he known anything about the S&Ls that the Bank Board was closing, he would have known there was a mistake. To him, however, the closures were simply data, which was why he accepted the nonsensical results and continued calculating.

I asked him to tell me which failures the outliers represented. He looked up the identifier number for the first one and told me "American Diversified Savings Bank." I smiled. This control fraud had cost the FSLIC almost $1 billion to resolve. (It grew more than 1,000 percent.) The other outliers were all control frauds, and their "zero resolution cost" figures were, of course, wrong. Each of them was a catastrophic failure. The mistake occurred, once more, in data entry. The Bank Board had a new "Management Consignment Program" (MCP) that split the failed S&L's portfolio into good and bad assets and transferred only the good assets to a newly chartered S&L. The newly chartered S&L got an FSLIC financial guarantee that the good assets really were good. That meant that the newly chartered S&L had a zero (additional) cost of resolution to the FSLIC. The econometrician had entered that zero resolution cost for the five MCPs. The Bank Board generally used the MCP program for the worst failures with substantial direct investments, so these mistaken data entries created a severe bias in the statistical analysis. The econometrician corrected the data entries and the expected result emerged: the greater the amount of direct investment, the greater the cost to the FSLIC to resolve the failure.

CHAPTER 4

1. Gray's reregulation tightened the standards in 1985.

2. Milken recruited Keating (and other notorious control frauds such as David Paul and Ivan Boesky) to buy state-chartered S&Ls because they could grow massively, buy large amounts of Drexel junk bonds, and serve as Milken's "captives" (Akerlof and Romer 1993; Black 1993c). The Bank Board, in a rare victory, blocked Boesky's acquisition of a California-chartered S&L. Keating and Paul, however, became captives. They learned at the end of each day which junk bonds they now owned; they had no involvement in deciding what to buy or sell. Milken got, and exploited, three obvious advantages from his captives. They bought huge amounts of Drexel junk bonds. He churned the accounts (engaged in rapid, repeated trades). These tactics maximized Drexel's fee income. Milken was able to dump his junkiest junk on his captives. It did not matter that this made Lincoln Savings and CenTrust Savings more insolvent; their failures were certain. It helped Milken dump his biggest losers on his captives (Black 1993c).

The more subtle advantage was that Milken's control of the captives ensured that public offerings of junk bonds would succeed and that junk bonds issued by Drexel that were about to default would instead be restructured. Milken could cause the captives to purchase whatever junk bonds the market had refused to buy or restructure (Akerlof and Romer 1993). Reducing the reported default rate of a security makes it appear less risky; a bond that appears less risky rises in value. This is not a claim that Drexel ran a Ponzi scheme or that junk bonds were worthless. They were, however, materially overvalued. That made Milken a rich man, even after he was released from prison.

This explains why Milken made substantial efforts to induce control frauds like Keating, Paul, and Boesky to enter the S&L industry. We know from Boesky and Keating how Milken pitched the idea. He told them that a deregulated, state-chartered S&L would make them the equivalent of "a merchant prince" (NCFIRRE 1993, 15). Milken understood his fellow felons.

The Bank Board, however, did not understand Milken until it was too late. Gray's instincts again caused him to lean the right way. He was deeply suspicious of Milken and wanted to pass rules restricting junk bonds. OPER, however, said they could not support the rule. In this era, even the GAO's economists opined that junk bonds were an excellent investment (Stein 1992, 134–135). According to OPER, Milken was right: a diversified pool of junk bonds made a superior investment portfolio. Fortunately, S&Ls never held more than 10 percent of outstanding junk bonds (and usually far less), and 90 percent of all those junk bonds were held by a dozen S&Ls, all of which failed (Black 1993c; NCFIRRE 1993, 4). Many at the agency saw Lincoln's billion-dollar portfolio of junk bonds as a warning sign, but OPER did not. There were rumors that Drexel had captives, but that fact had not yet been proven.

3. The White House director of personnel told the Senate Ethics Committee investigating the Keating Five that he learned this when he inquired about Keating's reputation in Arizona (U.S. Senate Committee 1991, 3:705–707).

4. Greenmail is a form of extortion. The "corporate raider" buys a large stock position in the target firm and threatens a hostile takeover. The target firm's executives, who fear losing their high-status, high-pay positions if the takeover succeeds, cause the firm to buy back the raider's shares at a premium. Lincoln Savings bought a great deal of Gulf Broadcasting stock at above the market price. This investment could have easily rendered Lincoln Savings insolvent if the shares had fallen even slightly in price. It was a grossly imprudent investment for an S&L that had little or no capital. Gulf Broadcasting eventually bought Lincoln Savings' stock position at a premium, so the greenmail succeeded.

5. The tone of the letter is surreal: Gardner implies that Reagan should have been concentrating on assisting Keating instead of "the budget and tax bills, and the Gorbach[e]v meeting."

6. John Dingell is a Democratic congressman representing my hometown, Dearborn, Michigan (our neighbor directly across the street hosted a neighborhood meeting with him when I was a teenager).

7. By standing up to Dingell and launching a somewhat impassioned defense of the agency, Gray and I gained considerable stature within the agency. We had all been feeling down because Dingell had been able to embarrass the agency at the first hearing, and now we were fighting back and getting some respect for it from Dingell. Gray liked it, of course, because it was a defense of him and his agency. He circulated my remarks to the FHLB presidents. I had already been playing a wider and more prominent role at the agency because of my work on the critical reregulation rules, but after the second Dingell hearing I took on a prominent role at most of the key congressional hearings during Gray's term. He also frequently used me to head his highest-priority projects, even if they had no litigation component.

8. In 1984, Keating began recruiting the senators who would become known as the "Keating Five." Keating was an Arizona real estate developer, famous for making large political contributions. Senator DeConcini represented Arizona, and Keating contributed substantially to his campaigns. DeConcini became Keating's earliest and most loyal Senate patron, even though Keating was a Republican and DeConcini was a Democrat.

9. When I learned about this incident in 1990, it immediately reminded me of the devastating insult in *A Man for all Seasons*, Richard Rich perjures himself to provide the evidence that condemns Sir Thomas More. Rich passes by More as he leaves the witness box and More notices that he is wearing a new chain of office. He asks what it is and is told that Rich has just been appointed "Attorney-General for Wales." More responds, "Why, Richard, it profits a man nothing to give his soul for the whole world. [pause] But for Wales!" (Bolt 1990, 92). But for Manion!

10. I participated in the economic and econometric discussion at the Bank Board meeting when we adopted the tougher equity-risk investment rule to replace the direct investment rule. After the meeting, Larry White asked me, "You're ABD (all but dissertation) in economics, right? Where did you study?" I had to explain that I was "ABE" (all but everything!).

11. His other studies fared no better. The results of one strongly supported our position on the risks posed by such investments. His comments concluded that the finding was meaningless because it was not statistically significant. I looked at the values he reported and told our economists that my "quick and dirty" review (without the necessary tables) showed that the study was statistically significant very near the 90 percent confidence interval. They checked and it was. Shocked, they lost confidence in his work.

12. Recall that the fraud that led to Andersen's well-deserved demise involved destroying records after Enron's failure was made public. The document destruction was unlawful, but it did not harm investors. At Lincoln Savings, Andersen did something far worse: it helped keep a control fraud in operation, a control fraud that cost the taxpayers $3 billion.

13. A true, contemporaneous underwriting document could not have such information.

CHAPTER 5

1. I am biased, but I think that the contrast between the following excerpts from Barry's book (1989) reveal his central bias. The first description is of Marshall Lynam, Wright's number two aide, the second is of me (a Wright critic):

Tall, lean, white-bearded, only a few years younger than Wright, he handled Wright's personal business and constituent services. (72)

He was a full-bearded man in a city where beards were a badge of nonconformity, a leftover from the sixties. (236)

If you support Wright, a beard is . . . a beard. If you criticize Wright, a beard is fraught with peril.

2. The GAO had done a series of studies demonstrating that fraud and insider abuse was pervasive at the worst failures and that the control frauds were able

to get clean opinions from Big 8 audit firms. The GAO was, rightly, critical of how weak Bank Board regulation, supervision, and enforcement had typically been. The GAO had a generally strong reputation with Congress.

3. Until very recently, any Senator could do this secretly to any bill. There are ways to discharge the freeze, but it is a major obstacle. Such freezes were not common because they invited ruinous retaliation by other senators. Cranston's freezing a bill of national importance indicates how important Keating viewed the defeat of the FSLIC recap and Proxmire's measure to be, as well as how beholden Cranston was to Keating. Because the freeze was secret, the Bank Board did not even become aware of it until it was far too late.

Cranston was not the only senator willing to block the FSLIC recap. Senator David Pryor of Arkansas placed his own hold on the bill. Pryor wrote Gray on October 3, 1986:

> S&L officials in my state have called to my attention what appears to be a deliberate system of harassment. . . . Before the Bank Board receives any recapitalization authority from the Congress, you need to assure us that your supervisory resources are being used effectively and fairly. . . . I have put a "hold" on the Senate recapitalization bill and am anxious to receive assurances from you that you will correct the abuses which have been taking place in Arkansas and other states. I was pleased to learn that you have been discussing this problem with the House Majority Leader [James Wright]. (Mayer 1990, 232)

Pryor's letter was characteristic of the attitudes of the politicians who intervened with the Bank Board on behalf of the control frauds (which were endemic in Arkansas): it does not ask questions; it pronounces guilt and issues the sentence. But Pryor's letter is special because, in one of the grand jokes that fate plays, Pryor ended up on the Senate Ethics Committee investigating the Keating Five's analogous intervention on behalf of Charles Keating. The five senators couldn't complain of not having a jury of their peers!

4. This is a common practice in which lenders agree to reduce the interest rate and to delay payments. The GAAP accounting rules at that time (FAS 15) were extraordinarily easy to abuse. A lender who approved a "troubled debt restructuring" (TDR) did not have to recognize the loss currently. (When a lender accepts a lower interest rate and delayed payments, it suffers a real, immediate economic loss.) This GAAP treatment was, of course, very attractive to S&Ls that would have had to acknowledge their insolvency if they foreclosed on the defaulting borrower. If they entered into a TDR instead, they could delay recognition of their losses and claim that they were still solvent.

The Bank Board had taken over only one S&L that had lent to Hall, Westwood Savings, but it was the "lead lender" to Hall and had sold "loan participations" to twenty-nine other S&Ls. These S&Ls were eager to agree to the TDR and desperate to prevent any suit against Hall. Wright believed that since the other loan participants favored the TDR, Westwood Savings' objection to the TDR had to be irrational.

5. Barry offers insight into both Hall's central argument about the virtues of forbearance and Wright's (and Barry's) acceptance and adoption of those arguments. Barry (1989, 217) includes the following as if it were a factual statement:

> [Hall's] bankruptcy would flood the already-depressed Texas real estate market with tens of thousands of condominiums. That would drive real estate values down further and could spark a true depression in Texas.

Hall was bankrupt. That was a fact regardless of whether the parties called him bankrupt. He could not pay his debts when they came due, and his liabilities greatly exceeded his assets. The TDR would reduce his liquidity problems and delay his bankruptcy filing, but he would (and did) end up filing for bankruptcy. The condos would not flood the market when he declared bankruptcy; they were already in the Texas real estate market. Approving the TDR increased the glut by permitting Hall to complete the construction of new units, and caused property values to fall even more than they would have if Westwood had forced him into bankruptcy in 1986.

Wright believed Hall's experts' claim that his bankruptcy would "destroy twenty-nine S&Ls" (Barry 1989, 218). In fact, those S&Ls had already failed, and the TDRs locked in that failure. The TDRs, along with Wright's actions blocking the FSLIC recap, delayed the takeover of the twenty-nine failed S&Ls and greatly increased losses to the taxpayers and the harm to Texas's economy.

The glut of Texas real estate became much worse in 1987–1988 precisely because Wright delayed closure of so many control frauds (including many of the twenty-nine S&Ls behind Hall). The appointment of federal receivers for those twenty-nine S&Ls in 1986 would have led to similar lawsuits against defaulting borrowers and would have forced dozens of other Texas control frauds to report that they were insolvent. This would have helped bring down the control-fraud daisy chain that added to the glut of real estate in the Southwest and caused tens of billions of dollars in additional losses to the taxpayers every year it stayed in operation.

To defend Wright's putting a hold on the FSLIC recap, Barry (1989, 218) musters a quotation that is actually a devastating indictment of Wright and Danny Wall.

> M. Danny Wall, the Republican staff director of the Senate Banking Committee who succeeded Ed Gray, later told Wright, "We did have a clown in the Craig Hall thing. He would have brought down the daisy chain [of S&Ls in Texas]."

Wall made this statement as Bank Board chairman. The Bank Board's principal mission was to bring down the daisy chain. Wall and Wright believed that keeping the daisy chain of control frauds open was good for the FSLIC, Texas, and America; this explains why Wall and Wright combined to create one of the worst financial-policy fiascoes in history.

Wall's disparagement of Schultz as a "clown" is also revealing. Wall, Wright, and Barry have never met Schultz and know nothing of him. They relied on Hall's view of Schultz. Westwood's MCP managers decided to sue Hall. Schultz made sure that they considered Hall's arguments and thoroughly analyzed the options. Schultz then defended the managers' decision from extortion by powerful politicians (Wright and Wall, who was acting on behalf of Senator Garn) and pressure by Gray and Fairbanks. I cannot understand how any of this could possibly make him a clown.

Schultz went on to spot many of the problems with Lincoln Savings. Keating, like Hall, personally attacked Schultz. Wall never talked to Schultz; he relied on Hall's and Keating's criticisms to form his view of Schultz as a clown. I worked with Scott Schultz in both the Hall and the Keating disputes. I found him competent, principled, and brave. World Savings, the best-run S&L in the country, apparently agreed; it hired him away from us.

To Wall (and, it appears, to Wright and Barry), people like Schultz who stick to their guns when it is clear that their bosses and powerful politicians want a contrary result are objects of derision, naïve waifs. The anecdote also displays a weakness inherent in Wall's management style. A Bank Board employee trying to bring a politically well-connected control fraud to justice would feel no confidence going into the fight if Wall were the one watching her back.

6. Barry does not ponder why Raupe would not pass on such a message, which was clearly a warning to Wright from a highly reputable individual who was no friend of Gray's. Raupe was Wright's best friend and, according to Barry, the only aide who had the guts to disagree with Wright. Barry asked Raupe about this conversation with Smith several years later, at a point when it would have been intensely embarrassing for the Speaker to ignore such a warning.

7. The national recession of the early 1990s and the cut in defense spending made possible by the fall of the Soviet Union caused California real estate values to drop. One of the important reasons that the California real estate recession was far less severe than that in Texas is that the California control frauds were closed or brought under control well before the recession hit. As Chapter 4 explains, control frauds followed the same practices in California and Texas and failed for the same reasons, even when they were lending to a vibrant real estate market.

CHAPTER 6

1. Barry is very sympathetic to Mack. He quotes favorably a reporter who chastised the *Washington Post* for running a story that exposed Mack's background because the paper was making itself a party to an act of "vengeance" on the part of the *victim* of Mack's attempted rape and murder (Barry 1989, 734). If exposing

Mack's crime to the public is the limit of her "vengeance," then Mack can count himself the most fortunate of felons.

2. The House ethics investigation of St Germain focused on benefits he received from the league and individual S&Ls. He, and female guests, dined routinely with a league lobbyist, who picked up the tab, and an S&L gave him an ownership interest in an investment (Day 1993, 257–258, 298–299).

After St Germain delivered a committee vote on April 1, 1987, in favor of a $5 billion FSLIC recap bill with forbearance, the House Ethics Committee voted on April 9 to issue a report that reads like an indictment of his ethics but ends with a free pass (Barry 1989, 213–214). The ethics committee arranged a further favor by holding the report's release until the Easter recess to minimize publicity. The Speaker blocked Gingrich's efforts to reopen the St Germain ethics inquiry (ibid., 542–543). The actions of the House Ethics Committee regarding St Germain were viewed as a whitewash even by Congress. Wright protected St Germain from censure.

3. Wright had met Dixon. Indeed, Wright had sent Dixon an autographed picture of the two of them together on Dixon's yacht.

4. The league's executive director, William O'Connell, explained:

Ironically, Treasury Under-secretary George Gould would say on January 21, 1987, that "given its organizational restraints," that all the FSLIC could "efficiently use to resolve problem cases," over three years was $15 billion, or $5 billion a year. Gould's statement would be influential in the congressional debate (O'Connell 1992, 80n17).

CHAPTER 7

1. Stan Parris (a Virginia Republican) should get at least an honorable mention. He fought to get the public to realize the depth of the S&L crisis.

2. Although Gonzalez was from a very politically safe district, opening himself up to the charge of betraying Texas was one of the few ways he could have lost an election. Moreover, he did not need to lose an election to be hurt. The Speaker had boundless ways to make Gonzalez's life unpleasant.

3. *Henry Gonzalez:* Representative Gonzalez was the first Hispanic Texan elected to Congress. He was not a moderate, but he was so iconoclastic that he could appear moderate because his positions did not track a consistent partisan or ideological path. He was a big man with a huge craggy face dominated by a magnificent nose.

Gonzalez and Wright had similar backgrounds. Both were boxers who prized being tough. Both were populist Texas Democrats. They were from the same generation. They were quick to anger. Gonzalez, well into his 60s, tried to fight a man who called him a communist. They both loved to talk, and they were old-time populist orators who mixed an odd combination of folksy anecdotes, obscure references to Roman and Greek political philosophers, and ornate language into a political version of a religious revival meeting. By the mid-1980s, both men's orations had begun to grate on many of their colleagues. "Henry B," as he was called, was a lawyer and former math teacher (Day 1993, 317).

Gonzalez was seventy years old and had tremendous seniority. He was consistent about many things, especially championing civil rights and populist causes. Many of his colleagues thought he was a bit loopy. Those who liked him saw him as a modern Don Quixote de la Mancha, tilting at windmills and trying to save the oppressed. The ones who did not like him just thought he had a screw loose.

Gonzalez was patient and persistent. He made a good ally and a painful opponent. He figures prominently in later chapters that discuss events after he became chairman of the House Banking Committee. He died recently, and his son now represents his district.

Thomas Carper: Thomas Carper was nothing like Wright or Gonzalez in style or temperament. He was a pilot who volunteered to serve three tours flying surveillance aircraft off the coast of Vietnam during the war. He received an MBA from the University of Delaware. Trim and incredibly calm, he comes across as reserved, thoughtful, and highly professional. He later became governor of Delaware, and in 2001 he was elected junior U.S. senator from that state.

Jim Leach: He was a champion wrestler in a state (Iowa) obsessed by wrestling. His undergraduate degree is from Princeton, his MA (Russian studies) is from Johns Hopkins, and he then did further graduate study at the (very liberal) London School of Economics in economics and Soviet studies. He was chairman of the (liberal Republican) Ripon Society for many years.

A smart-as-a-whip Midwesterner, Leach is a very nice, fair-minded guy with high moral principles. He despises those who abuse power and was a passionate opponent of the control frauds. He was by far the most helpful member when we were trying to deal with the forbearance provisions. He is the only one of the four still in the House.

Buddy Roemer: Charles "Buddy" Roemer was a bit like Carper. His MBA was from Harvard and he dressed like a refined banker. He later became governor of Louisiana. He was the latest in a long line of reform governors who lasted one term. (Folks from Louisiana can stand good government only in very small doses.) He had changed parties and run for reelection as a Republican. You can glean most of what you need to know about Louisiana politics from Roemer's having finished a distant third against the neo-Nazi Klan leader David Duke and the crook Edwin Edwards. The race between Edwards and Duke produced the classic bumper sticker: "Vote for the Crook; It's Important."

4. I took extremely detailed notes of the April 9, 1987, meeting with the Keating Five that eventually led to the Senate ethics investigation. The complete text of my final notes can be found in the appendix to *Inside Job* by Pizzo, Fricker, and Muolo (1992, 2nd. ed.) and in U.S. House Banking Committee 1989, 2:745–773. Each of

the nine participants at the meeting testified to the accuracy of the notes. The most sincere compliment came from Senator Glenn. He testified (U.S. Senate Committee 1991, 5 : 198) that he knew my notes were extraordinarily accurate because

> even some of the phrasing I use and the way I say things were captured exactly — commas in the right places and the whole thing, exactly the way I would let it roll out at a meeting like that.
> It may be busted syntax, it is mine and I recognize it when it occurs. [laughter]

Two senators were convinced that they must have been tape-recorded (U.S. Senate Committee 1991, 3 : 302).

5. FAS 5 required recognition of "contingent liabilities" only when they were "estimable and probable." The control frauds abused this loose standard to avoid loss recognition. FAS 15 allowed firms to avoid recognizing currently their losses on TDRs. Even if an S&L foreclosed on the real estate pledged as collateral on a bad loan, it did not have to recognize the full market-value loss. Instead, GAAP permitted S&Ls to use "net realizable value" (NRV) to calculate the loss. This always caused losses to be underreported, but the distortion was particularly severe for federally insured depositories.

One estimates the market value of income-producing real estate by discounting back to present value the net cash flows over a lengthy time period (e.g., thirty years). The discount rate should reflect the risk of the particular investment being valued. The typical ADC loan by a control fraud would have borne an enormous market discount rate because the borrowers' creditworthiness was so poor, the business plans so pathetic, and the real estate markets so glutted that default and huge losses were almost certain. An NRV, however, used a discount rate that had no relationship to the risk of the investment being valued. The discount rate used in an NRV for an S&L was the interest rate the S&L paid on federally insured deposits (e.g., 5 percent). The lower the discount rate, the higher the "value" of the asset. Using NRVs, therefore, seriously overstated the value of the real estate securing defaulting ADC loans and understated the FSLIC's losses.

6. Sanford later served as cochairman of the Senate Ethics Committee investigation.

7. Grogan testified about the memorandum in the Senate ethics investigation of the Keating Five. The committee's independent counsel, Mr. Bennett, is the questioner (U.S. Senate Committee 1991, 87–88).

> [I]t was attached to an article where Black was publicly attacking Wright. It was a remarkable article that a federal bureaucrat would publicly, using his name, go on the record and attack the Speaker of the House. And what Keating's point was that, good grief, if this guy has got the gumption to . . . (laughter) . . . to take on the Speaker of the House, you ought to have an ally in the Speaker of

the House. And if you know anything about Capitol Hill, you ought to be able to go get some allies and take care of it.

Mr. Bennett: That was a great recovery, Mr. Grogan.

Witness: Thanks.

(Laughter.)

Mr. Bennett: You can strike that from the record also.

(Laughter.)

The bouts of laughter make sense if you understand that Grogan's "great recovery" was substituting "gumption" for a male anatomical reference at the last moment. Grogan was one of Senator Glenn's aides before he served Keating, and the Senate Ethics Committee treated him like he was a member of the club even when he was describing a vicious abuse of power. The committee thought it all quite humorous, which reveals a great deal about the committee.

8. The bill was nominally $10.8 billion, but $800 million of it was a bookkeeping scam to increase the reported net worth of the S&L industry by restoring the "secondary reserve" as an asset on their books. (The details are arcane, inane, and unnecessary.)

CHAPTER 8

1. Two postscripts. The manager's risky investments caused large new losses at Eurekea Federal. Wall decided Eureka needed to be sold with FSLIC assistance. The potential acquirer did not want to be bound by the MCP manager's long-term contract, did not want his services, and did not want to pay his exorbitant salary. The FSLIC fired the MCP manager! But Wall had insisted that we put him on a long-term contract, so the manager successfully sued for breach of that contract. The FSLIC had to reimburse the S&L's legal fees and pay a very large damage award to the MCP manager. I ended up being the soccer coach of a kid whose father was the MCP manager's lawyer. The lawyer could not understand why the Bank Board had acted so stupidly at every turn throughout the matter, but he was happy because the legal fees had paid for a very nice BMW. The taxpayers, of course, bought it for him, courtesy of Wall.

2. I was wearing my "Just Say No to Washington" button and came over to explain what had happened. At the end of my tale he asked me if I had a copy of the button he could wear.

3. We called it the *Blazing Saddles* ploy after the scene where the black sheriff pretends to hold himself hostage to stop the credulous, racist white town-folks from attacking him. Mel Brooks would be astounded to know that this ploy worked in real life.

4. I do not remember this attorney's name; Mike and I remain thankful that he turned us around.

5. In the course of this, I said that a congressman could ask Wall, "Jesus Christ!

What purpose could this letter have other than preventing disclosure?" Wall shot back, "There is no reason to invoke the deity in this discussion!" There followed about ten seconds of shocked silence while we looked around the conference table in San Francisco with dawning horror. Wall had obviously heard much worse than "Jesus Christ" at least hourly in the Senate. It was clear that either he had seized the opportunity to slam me personally, or he hated me so much that he could not contain himself. Either way, if how he handled this matter was indicative of his policies, I was in trouble, the FHLBSF was in trouble, and the Bank Board might be in trouble. Wall and his staff attempted no substantive defense of his position. As noted in Binstein and Bowden (1993, 299), "Thereafter, whenever Black is on the phone during a conference call with the staff in San Francisco, Wall will turn to his aides and mumble, 'Why did they put this asshole on?'"

6. American Savings borrowed money through Reverse Repurchase Obligations (REPOs), which though structured as "sales," are actually short-term loans invested in mortgage-backed securities, which are long-term, fixed-rate assets.

7. The Bank Board took two useful lessons from all this. It unwound American Savings' interest-rate gamble, and it renewed efforts to sell the S&L. The Bank Board excluded the FHLBSF from the effort to sell the S&L and chose Bob Bass as the acquirer. Bass is one of the famous "Bass brothers" who have made fortunes investing in corporations and in Texas real estate. This set up a future long-running controversy with the FHLBSF, which (when it was finally permitted to see the deal) pointed out severe problems with the agreement that exposed the FSLIC to enormous losses. The American Savings fiasco did not cure Wall's belief in silver bullets, and the miracle meant that there was no longer any reason to be nice to the FHLBSF. (A postscript: In late 1994 Orange County, California, became bankrupt. It had invested its funds in long-term bonds. Its investment fund grew rapidly by borrowing through short-term REPOs. Interest rates increased, producing a liquidity crisis. Orange County was not saved by a miracle. It lost $1.7 billion from interest-rate risk. Robert Citron, the disgraced treasurer, resigned, and the county replaced him with — Popejoy! [Jorion, 1995: 159 – 160])

8. Grogan had received Keating's order to "Get Black . . . kill him dead."

9. It would take too long to explain the series of obstacles the Bank Board put in the way of my retaining counsel, which led to my having to represent myself for a time. I am grateful, as always, to Cirona and the FHLBSF for displaying loyalty and preventing a travesty.

10. A September 26, 1986, Sidley & Austin memorandum suggests a plan to have many S&Ls bring dozens of *Bivens* lawsuits as "an offensive weapon" in order to paralyze the Bank Board. A Pierson, Ball & Dowd memorandum dated October 19, 1987, notes that they have hired a private investigative firm to investigate a carefully unidentified "subject," which Grogan testified was me. Keating spent tens of millions of dollars each year on lawyers and deliberately set them in competition with one another to find which firm was willing to be the most aggressive. Kaye, Scholer won this competition.

11. The rest of the letter is equally amusing. Martin led Wall's effort to understate greatly the cost of resolving the S&L debacle. The Bank Board mandated that the field offices use a methodology that would seriously understate losses. (Jim Barth provided them with five possible ways to estimate the losses; Wall chose the one that produced the lowest estimate.) The FHLBSF provided the number using the mandated methodology, but explained that it would seriously understate actual losses. The Bank Board criticized us heavily for that aspect of our response. Martin now cited our absurdly low estimate of losses—which he and Wall had mandated—as evidence of Patriarca's ineptness.

12. When we finally learned of the letter, we assumed it was unprecedented. We learned subsequently that Stewart had provided a least one similar letter over the FHLB-Chicago's opposition to an S&L it considered to be the victim of insider fraud. If Wall and Martin wanted the side letter issued, they should have shouldered the responsibility, not placed it on Stewart.

13. Luke's cautious nature became clearer when the ERC finally voted to approve a subpoena for Saratoga Savings. I told him that the Bank Board had taken six months to approve a routine matter that used to be handled in a week and that Saratoga's losses had grown steadily during the delay. He said, "But Bill, they threatened to sue us!"

CHAPTER 9

1. On a personal note, I appreciated the irony of these same Lincoln Savings lawyers successfully demanding that the Bank Board exclude me from meetings that they would attend.

2. Tax-sharing agreements are normally a routine means of reducing the cost of tax compliance. The parent company and its subsidiaries file a consolidated tax return for the overall entity, and the companies agree to pay their respective shares of the total taxes. Lincoln Savings and ACC, of course, routinely turned the routine into another opportunity for fraud, and the tax-sharing agreement was no exception. In this case, they defrauded the FHLBSF (and through it, the public). For obvious reasons, an S&L or a bank is not allowed to make loans to its parent holding company. In the tax-sharing context, this means that the S&L cannot send cash to the parent for taxes that are not currently payable to the IRS. Lincoln Savings had large net-operating-loss carryforwards, so it was able to offset current income and greatly reduce its taxes. ACC/Lincoln Savings submitted a draft tax-sharing agreement that would have required Lincoln Savings, whenever it earned profits, to upstream cash to the parent company in order to pay taxes that were not currently payable (and might never be payable). The FHLBSF analysts reviewed it and informed ACC/Lincoln Savings that the provision was unacceptable for these reasons. ACC/Lincoln Savings replied that the agreement had been redrafted, and this provision removed, in response to the FHLBSF's concerns. In fact, ACC/Lincoln Savings had substituted tax jargon that permitted the very payments the

transmittal letter assured the FHLBSF had been prohibited by the revisions. ACC's deception succeeded: the FHLBSF analysts did not understand that the tax jargon would have the opposite effect of the one purported. (The language was not run by the legal department, so my predecessor did not review it.) The Resolution Trust Corporation (RTC), the FSLIC's successor agency, later filed suit against ACC on the grounds that these false representations constituted fraud.

3. Kennedy's speechwriters apparently invented the quotation. Dante's *Divine Comedy* does place neutral angels in Hell, perpetually harried by insects and chasing banners of authority.

4. Similarly, the Bank Board waited until after the election to close Silverado Savings, in which the vice president's son Neil had played such a disreputable role (Wilmsen 1991, 182–183). Bank Board economists also informed a group of us at the FHLBSF that the newest projections on the need for, and cost of, a federal bailout of the FSLIC were complete but would not be released until after the election.

5. The Bank Board's acquiescence in Keating's tactic of branding as criminals those who blew the whistle on his misconduct turned the world upside down. Bank Board leaders tolerated the defrauding of widows in order to avoid embarrassing themselves and the Republican Party. That was morally acceptable to Wall, a man who carried a Bible next to his heart every workday. Exposing the fraud, and thereby protecting the widows, was the great evil.

6. Dixon pulled the same stall at Vernon Savings.

7. Arthur Young resigned as ACC's auditor when Keating ordered Janet Vincent (Jack Atchison's replacement as Lincoln Savings' audit partner) to do something explicitly prohibited by the accounting rules. She refused, and Keating demanded that Young fire her. By this time, Young knew that both Lincoln Savings and ACC were hopelessly insolvent and that Atchison had exposed the firm to enormous liability. It wanted out, and seized the opportunity to resign. Peat, Marwick promptly and eagerly sought to replace Young. Peat, Marwick, however, also knew that it might be stepping into a minefield. The new auditor decided to disclose publicly ACC's aggressive accounting practices and to seek the SEC's prior blessing for the particular accounting treatment that had led Young to resign. (The SEC's chief accountant listened to the new auditor's lengthy pitch for recognizing income from a particular transaction. His decision: "No recognition." End of meeting, end of Keating's control over Lincoln Savings.)

Similarly, Peat, Marwick explained the accounting scam underlying the proposed acquisition of Lincoln Savings. The buyer (the Trump Group—*not* related to Donald Trump) and Lincoln Savings would both overpay (by over $40 million) to purchase a subsidiary from each other. Lincoln Savings would pay cash; the Trump Group would give a note (an IOU). In short, Lincoln Savings was financing the entire "purchase." Peat, Marwick then issued the most unusual accounting opinion any of us had ever seen. In its opinion, these mirror purchases should be treated as independent, but if the Bank Board disagreed, the accounting opinion was automatically withdrawn.

8. It would require a far longer book to explain all the harm that befell the nation from September 1988 to late April 1989 when the Bank Board indisputably knew it was dealing with a massive fraud but took no effective action against it. In addition to the losses to those who bought ACC's worthless junk bonds and the enormous new losses to the taxpayers from the new fraudulent investments, the Bank Board gave Keating's lieutenants time to destroy documents and transfer surviving documents out of Lincoln Savings' offices. Similarly, virtually all of Lincoln Savings' (few) valuable assets were transferred to subsidiaries or pledged as collateral. ACC and Lincoln's subsidiaries then filed for bankruptcy just before the California law changed and the CDSL would have taken over Lincoln Savings. The Bank Board, despite protests from Barabolak and warnings from the FHLBSF, took no action to prevent these subterfuges or to prepare to deal with the voluntary bankruptcy strategy. By filing voluntary Chapter 11 bankruptcy petitions, Keating hoped to stay in control of ACC, Lincoln's subsidiaries, and Lincoln's assets. (The law imposes an automatic stay that bars creditors like the FSLIC from retrieving looted assets without special permission of the bankruptcy court.) The FHLBSF, fortunately, had hired private counsel in Phoenix.

The Bank Board finally placed Lincoln Savings in conservatorship the day after the bankruptcy filings. The conservator discovered that virtually all of Lincoln's valuable assets had been transferred to subsidiaries or sold. Lincoln Savings had no cash to stem the run. The Federal Reserve had to make unsecured loans to Lincoln Savings (U.S. House Banking Committee 1989, 1:15–16). Wall's lieutenants got to explain to the vice chairman of the Federal Reserve how the Bank Board, knowing that it was dealing with the worst S&L fraud of all time, had allowed Keating to loot Lincoln Savings and put the Fed in this position. The vice chairman excoriated them. I was one of the FHLBSF personnel who heard the tirade on the conference line.

9. Which led to one of the great typos of all time. We received in our San Francisco office a trade journal with the following address label: "Office of Theft Supervision." Too true.

10. The Keating Five and Senator Garn, however, would have found confirmation hearings for Wall acutely embarrassing. Riegle chaired Senate Banking, which would have had to conduct the hearings; Cranston was the most senior majority member of the committee; and Garn was the ranking minority member.

11. This was our *Henry V* moment. The French, losing the battle of Agincourt, violate the rules of war by slaughtering the English boys in the baggage trains. Henry announces that he has not been angry since entering France, but this barbarity enrages him (act 4, scene 7).

12. I had complained to O'Connell about a provision of the MOU; he said that I must not have the final MOU because he had had the same concern and had insisted the provision be changed. I went over to the Litigation Division, which was producing documents that Gonzalez had subpoenaed, and requested a copy of the final agreements. The MOU turned out to be identical to the copy we had;

O'Connell's memory was in error (a rare event). But the package also had the side letter. The side letter convinced us that we were dealing with a corrupt system that needed to be rooted out.

13. Jim Murphy, a partner at Squire, Sanders & Dempsey (the firm I had come from), met with Seidman shortly before this testimony to pitch him for some business. Murphy mentioned that I had been with the firm. Seidman responded, "I've never met him, but I know of him. He's the kind of guy they should put in charge of OTS. [pause] Of course, it will never happen."

14. It was ironic, after all of the odes sung by the ERC, Wall, and Martin on the necessity of remaining objective and nonaggressive to witnesses, that they responded to criticism so intemperately.

15. All of the FHLBSF's senior leadership that dealt with Keating happened to be openly heterosexual.

CHAPTER 10

1. For his book *Maestro* (2000), Bob Woodward interviewed Greenspan about the February 13, 1985, letter that contained this assertion.

Greenspan believed he would do it the same way again, given the information he had in 1985. When he reviewed Keating's balance sheets, he found them both quite impressive and fiscally sound. Keating had not done anything wrong at that point, or if he had it wasn't detectable. (66)

He wrote in support of Keating's application to make four times as many direct investments as other S&Ls were permitted. The memorandum that I wrote recommending denial (U.S. House Banking Committee 1989, 2:370–386) used information that Greenspan could have obtained from public sources or his client. A comparison of his letter and my memorandum demonstrates four things: Lincoln had done many things wrong at the time Greenspan wrote his letter; if he had investigated the financial statements, he could have detected a great deal; Keating's balance sheets were facially unsound and unimpressive; his other conclusions about the high quality of Lincoln Savings' managers were untenable.

2. All of the examples Akerlof uses in his article are control frauds in which the object is to defraud the customer instead of creditors and shareholders. The S&L control frauds and the ongoing wave of control frauds generally targeted creditors and shareholders. However, modern control frauds often target customers, e.g., Enron and its coconspirators created and exploited the California power "crisis"; mutual funds widely abused customers; Tenet Healthcare allegedly practiced unnecessary surgery at one hospital, leading to the death of several patients, and fraudulently overbilled government health insurance programs; and, earlier, Koch Industries committed fraud against small oil producers.

3. Loss of financial trust was not a major problem during the S&L debacle

because of deposit insurance. S&L creditors were almost entirely made up of insured depositors. They trusted the FSLIC, not the S&L. The FSLIC never lost that trust because the public was convinced that no president or Congress would permit the FSLIC to default (no political entity that did so could have survived). All the private funds that insured Ohio, Maryland, and Utah thrifts, by contrast, collapsed when depositors lost their trust.

4. Good advice, when talking about normal regulators. O'Connell reacted that way; Dochow, Stewart, Wall, and Martin, did not.

5. Andersen's resignation should have been a red flag about Keating. Instead he threatened to sue the firm, which then changed its resignation letter into an attack on the FHBLSF. Keating used the Andersen letter to help recruit the Keating Five.

6. I may have some culpability for helping prompt this movement, for as the Bank Board's litigation director I began suing the Big 8 accounting firms.

7. Black (2003, 22–40). Judges, especially appellate judges, have the unique advantage of being able to declare in court opinions that their theories are correct. Judge Easterbrook used this advantage to rule that a plaintiff would not be permitted to attempt to prove that an auditor was liable because it would be "irrational" for an auditor to do anything that would make him liable. Of course, a theory that cannot be falsified is not a theory, but dogma. Auditors, in fact, commonly give clean opinions to control frauds that are massively insolvent. Auditors, in fact, help control frauds create fictional income and hide real losses. Auditors do this primarily for rational reasons: because control frauds pay them enormous nonaudit fees and because of agency problems (the interests of the audit partner who is under severe pressure to bring in lucrative clients or be fired frequently diverge from the interests of the firm). But auditors also act in ways that Judge Easterbrook may consider "irrational." An article by my colleague Robert Prentice (2000) skewers the claim that auditors would never aid a control fraud.

8. DeConcini, a former prosecutor, was barking at Patriarca, trying to intimidate him. He used the most inflammatory language he could ("prostitute themselves") as a shutdown line, trying to force Patriarca to back down. Instead, Patriarca hit him square between the eyes: "Absolutely, it happens all the time." DeConcini was visibly stunned. I do not think he had ever met a bureaucrat like Patriarca.

9. Conflicts of interest mattered on the federal regulatory side. The FHLBs clearly had potential conflicts of interest because they were owned by the S&Ls in their districts, and the president of each bank was also the principal supervisory agent. Cirona insisted on hiring senior officers with strong backbones and great integrity precisely because of this potential conflict. If an S&L CEO who was also on the board of directors of the FHLBSF indicated to our examiners that they best not push too hard, Cirona wanted to be sure that the response would be instant. The next morning, an expanded crew of our best and toughest examiners would enter the S&L like avenging angels, and Patriarca would personally call the CEO and read him the riot act. This was not, however, the case in all district banks at

all times. The 1989 legislation removing the examination and supervision roles from the FHLBs was desirable. Similarly, the FHLBSF had stringent conflict-of-interest rules. We could not even get a home mortgage on demonstrably normal market terms from an S&L.

10. One-year ACC sub debt was issued at 9.50 percent interest on March 29, 1988, when the prime rate that banks charged healthy companies was 8.50 percent (U.S. House Banking Committee 1989, 4:255).

Names and Terms

1981 TAX ACT. Officially, the Economic Recovery Tax Act of 1981; law that reduced marginal income tax rates and boosted tax shelters.

1986 TAX REFORM ACT. Law that ended many abusive tax shelters.

AKERLOF, GEORGE. Nobel prize–winning economist.

AMBERG, RUTH. Bank Board counsel and my aide on FSLIC recap.

AMERICAN SAVINGS. Largest S&L, victimized by fraud.

ANDERSON, JACK. Syndicated columnist.

ANDREWS, MIKE (D-TX). Congressman allied with Jim Wright.

ANGOTTI, OTTAVIO. Senior officer at Consolidated Savings Bank.

ANNUNZIO, FRANK (D-IL). Member of the House Banking Committee.

ATCHISON, JACK. AY audit partner for Lincoln Savings.

BAKER, JAMES. Secretary of the Treasury under Ronald Reagan.

BANK BOARD. Federal regulator of Savings and Loans.

BARABOLAK, ALEX. Lead FHLB-Chicago examiner of ACC.

BARCLAY, GEORGE. CEO of FHLB-Dallas.

BARNARD, DRUIE DOUGLAS, JR. (D-GA). Member of the House Banking Committee.

BARRY, JOHN. Author of a book about Jim Wright.

BARTH, JIM. Bank Board chief economist.

BARTLETT, HARRY STEPHEN "STEVE" (R-TX). Member of the House Banking Committee.

BASS, ROBERT. Texas billionaire who acquired American Savings.

BEEBE, HERMANN K. Head of a daisy chain of control frauds.

BENNETT, ROBERT. Investigated the Keating Five for the Senate.

BENSTON, GEORGE. Economist for Lincoln Savings.

BEVERLY HILLS SAVINGS. Failed California S&L.

BIG 8. Top-tier accounting firms in the 1980s.

BILBY, RICHARD M. Judge who presided over Lincoln Savings cases.

BINSTEIN, MICHAEL. Reporter who exposed Charles Keating's crimes.

BIVENS SUIT. Suit against a government employee in his personal capacity, alleging violation of a constitutional right.

BREEDON, RICHARD. SEC chairman under George H. W. Bush.

BOESKY, IVAN. Insider-trading felon.

BOLAND, JAMES. Danny Wall's chief of staff.

BOWMAN, LIN. Texas S&L commissioner.

BOWSER, GARY. House Banking Committee aide.

BROOKES, WARREN. Columnist who criticized Jim Wright.

BROOKS, JACK. Texas congressman allied with Jim Wright.

BUSH, GEORGE H. W. Vice president under Ronald Reagan, put in charge of financial deregulation.

BUSH, NEIL. Silverado Savings director.

CARPER, THOMAS (D-DE). Member of the House Banking Committee.

CASH FOR TRASH. Fraud scheme in which S&Ls used "straw" purchasers to buy problem assets at inflated prices.

CHAPMAN, JAMES (D-TX). Won special election to the House with aid of Texas S&Ls.

CHENEY, RICHARD "DICK" (R-WY). Congressman, 1979–1990.

CIRONA, JAMES. President of the FHLBSF.

CITRON, ROBERT. Treasurer who caused the bankruptcy of Orange County.

CLARKE, RICHARD. FHLB-Seattle staff member who met with Charles Keating.

COELHO, ANTHONY "TONY" (D-CA). Chairman of the DCCC and House whip.

COMMODORE SAVINGS. Texas S&L that aided Gaubert's lobbying.

COMPETITION IN LAXITY. Environment in which state and federal regulatory agencies compete for regulatees by weakening regulation; also known as a "race to the bottom."

CONNALLY, JOHN. Former governor of Texas; defaulted on loans to Lincoln Savings.

CONSENT TO MERGER. Resolution by the board of a failing or failed S&L that allowed the FSLIC to try to arrange a merger partner.

CONTROL FRAUDS. Frauds by those who control a firm or country.

CRANSTON, ALAN (D-CA). Senator, member of the Keating Five.

CRAWFORD, WILLIAM. Commissioner of the CDSL.

CRIMINOGENIC. Describing an environment that encourages crime.

CURLEE, DURWARD. Organized Texas opposition to reregulation.

DAISY CHAIN. Informal group of control frauds that engaged in transactions with one another in order to hide their frauds from regulators.

DAVIS, WILLIAM. Deputy commissioner of the CDSL.

DAY, KATHLEEN. Business reporter for the *Washington Post.*

DeConcini, Dennis (D-AZ).   Senator, member of the Keating Five.

De novos.   Newly created and chartered S&Ls.

Desupervision.   Reduction of supervisory personnel or powers.

Deveney, James.   House Banking Committee aide.

Dingell, John (D-MI).   Chairman of the House Energy and Commerce Committee.

Dixon, Donald.   CEO of Vernon Savings.

Dochow, Darrel.   Head of Bank Board supervision.

Dornan, Robert (R-CA).   Congressman, 1977–1996.

Duncan, Phil.   Aide to Jim Wright.

Eckhardt, Robert (D-TX).   Congressman, ally of Jim Wright.

Ely, Bert.   Financial economist.

Empire Savings.   First major Texas control fraud failure.

Fairbanks, Ann.   Edwin Gray's chief of staff.

Faulk, Walter.   Senior FHLB-Dallas supervisor.

Faulstich, James.   President of the FHLB-Seattle.

Fed or **Federal Reserve.**   Board of governors of the Federal Reserve System.

Ferrante, Robert.   CEO of Consolidated Savings.

Field visit.   Short, focused audit rather than a "full scope" examination.

Fishbein, Peter.   Lincoln Savings' top outside counsel

Forbearance.   In financial regulation, the policy of not taking enforcement action against certain rule violations.

"Full scope" examination.   Audit that covers all safety and soundness issues and all business operations.

Gardner, Michael "Mickey."   Outside counsel for Charles Keating.

Garn–St Germain Act of 1982.   Principal federal deregulation legislation.

Garn, Edwin Jacob "Jake" (R-UT).   Senate Banking Committee chairman; also ranking minority member of the committee.

Gaubert, Thomas.   CEO of Independent American.

Gershon Kekst and Company.   Charles Keating's PR firm.

Glenn, John (D-OH).   Senator, member of the Keating Five.

Gingrich, Newton "Newt" (R-GA).   Congressman, later Speaker of the House.

Gonzalez, Henry B. (D-TX).   Chairman of the House Banking Committee (1989–1994).

Goodwill.   Accounting term for market value in excess of net tangible-asset value.

Gramm, Philip "Phil" (R-TX).   Member and later chairman of the Senate Banking Committee.

Gray, Edwin.   Bank Board chairman.

Green, Roy.   President of the FHLB-Dallas.

GREENMAIL.   Form of extortion in which a buyer threatens a hostile takeover in order to induce management to purchase the buyer's shares at a premium.

GREENSPAN, ALAN.   Chairman of the Fed.

GRIGSBY, MARY.   Bank Board member.

GROGAN, JAMES.   Charles Keating's principal lobbyist.

GUY, DAN.   AICPA's head of auditing in January 1994.

HAAS, RICHARD.   Executive director of the Bank Board under Danny Wall.

HALL, CRAIG.   Texas real estate developer, aided by Jim Wright.

HARWELL, AUBREY.   Outside counsel who investigated the Bank Board for Jim Wright.

HEMEL, ERIC.   Top economist on the Bank Board.

HENKEL, LEE.   Charles Keating's mole on the Bank Board.

HERSHKOWITZ, STEVE.   Deputy enforcement director for the Bank Board.

HETEROSKEDASTICITY.   Statistical term that indicates that the nature of the relationship between two variables is not constant.

"HIGH FLIERS."   Industry term for S&L control frauds.

HINZ, WILLIAM.   President of Lincoln Savings.

HOVDE, DONALD.   Bank Board member.

HOYLE, KARL.   Bank Board director of Congressional and Public Affairs.

INDEPENDENT AMERICAN.   Control fraud run by Thomas Gaubert.

JONES, DAY.   Law firm that conducted a "regulatory audit" for Lincoln Savings.

JUNOT, PHILIPPE.   Former husband of Princess Caroline of Monaco.

KAYE, SCHOLER.   Primary counsel for Lincoln Savings.

KEATING, CHARLES.   Controlled Lincoln Savings.

KEATING FIVE.   Group of five U.S. senators (Alan Cranston, Dennis DeConcini, John Glenn, John McCain, and Donald Riegle) who pressured the Bank Board at Charles Keating's behest.

KING, THOMAS.   Executive director of the Texas League.

KITCHEN CABINET.   Informal advisers to a president.

KLEPTOCRACY.   Government run by those seeking personal gain rather than the common good.

KNAPP, CHARLES.   CEO of American Savings.

KRUCKEBERG, TIMOTHY.   Inside lawyer for Charles Keating.

LAND FLIP.   Fraud scheme in which "straw" purchasers are used to sell the same property repeatedly in order to inflate its value.

LARSON, CAROL.   Bank Board accountant.

LEACH, JAMES (R-IA).   Member of the House Banking Committee.

LEAGUE, THE.   Principal S&L trade association.

LEMONS MARKET.   Market in which sellers can judge quality but buyers cannot.

LEVITT, ARTHUR.   SEC Chairman under Bill Clinton.

LEWIS, JAKE.   Senior aide to the House Banking Committee.

LINCOLN SAVINGS. California control fraud led by Charles Keating.

LINDNER, CARL. Charles Keating's mentor.

LUKE, JORDAN. Danny Wall's general counsel.

MACK, JOHN. Jim Wright's chief of staff.

MAHER, BISHOP LEO. Arranged Don Dixon's meeting with the pope.

MALLICK, GEORGE. Friend, employer, and partner of Jim Wright and his wife.

MANION, DANIEL A. Judge appointed by Reagan with the aid of Charles Keating.

MANNING, MICHAEL. Lawyer with Morrison & Hecker, outside counsel for the FDIC.

MARTIN, ROGER. Bank Board member.

MATTOX, JAMES. Attorney general of Texas.

MCALLISTER, WALTER "BO," III. President of the Texas League.

MCBIRNEY, EDWARD. CEO of Sunbelt Savings.

MCCAIN, JOHN (R-AZ). Senator, member of the Keating Five.

MCJOYNT, PATRICIA. FHLB-Seattle staff member who met with Charles Keating.

MEEK, JOHN J., II. FHLB-Chicago examiner of ACC.

MEESE, EDWIN. Attorney general under Ronald Reagan.

MEHLE, ROGER. Assistant Secretary of the Treasury.

MERRILL LYNCH. Investment banking firm and the largest deposit broker.

MILKEN, MICHAEL. Felon and leading junk bond manipulator.

MORAL HAZARD. Condition in which risks and benefits are asymmetrical, thereby encouraging excessive risk taking or fraud.

MORRISON & HECKER. Government's outside counsel in actions against Charles Keating.

MURPHY, JAMES. Partner at Squire, Sanders & Dempsey.

NEIBEL, JOHN. Dean of the University of Houston Law Center.

NELSON, PAUL. Senior aide to the House Banking Committee.

NEWSOM, RICHARD. CDSL examiner of Lincoln Savings.

NICHOLS, DOROTHY. Bank Board litigation director.

NOLAN, PAT. California state senator who authored S&L deregulation.

NOLAN ACT. 1983 law deregulating California-chartered S&Ls.

NORTH AMERICA SAVINGS. California control fraud.

O'CONNELL, KEVIN. Senior supervisor at the Bank Board.

O'CONNELL, WILLIAM. Head of the S&L trade association.

O'NEILL, THOMAS "TIP," JR. (D-MA). Speaker of the House, 1977–1987.

PARRIS, STANFORD "STAN" (R-VA). Member of the House Banking Committee.

PASHAYAN, CHARLES (R-CA). Congressman, ally of Charles Keating.

PATRIARCA, MIKE. Lead supervisor at the FHLBSF.

PAUL, DAVID. CEO of Centrust Savings.

PETERSON, RICHARD.   Douglas Barnard's top aide.

PITT, HARVEY.   SEC chairman under George H. W. Bush.

PONTELL, HENRY.   Criminologist who studied S&L fraud.

PONZI.   Fraudulent scheme in which new money is used to pay prior victims; named for Charles Ponzi, an American swindler.

POPEJOY, WILLIAM.   Charles Knapp's successor as CEO of American Savings.

PRATT, RICHARD.   Bank Board chairman.

PRINS, CURTIS.   Ottavio Annunzio's aide.

PROXMIRE, WILLIAM (D-WI).   Chairman of the Senate Banking Committee.

PRYOR, DAVID (D-AR).   Member of the Senate Ethics Committee; Bank Board critic.

"RACE TO THE BOTTOM."   *See* "Competition in laxity."

RAIDEN, NORM.   General counsel to the Bank Board.

RAUPE, CRAIG.   Close friend of Jim Wright.

REGAN, DONALD.   Ronald Reagan's first treasury secretary (1981–1985), later his chief of staff (1985–1987).

REGULATION Q.   Rule that restricted the interest rates that banks could pay depositors.

RENDA, MARIO.   Defrauded dozens of banks and S&Ls.

REREGULATOR.   The worst insult possible in the Reagan administration.

RIDGLEA MEETING.   Meeting between Jim Wright and opponents of the FSLIC recap.

RIEGLE, DONALD (D-MI).   Senator, member of the Keating Five.

RILEY, DAVID.   FHLB-Atlanta examiner of Lincoln Savings.

ROBERTSON, BILL.   Director of ORPOS.

ROEMER, CHARLES ELSON "BUDDY" (D-LA).   Member of the House Banking Committee.

"RULE 11" LETTER.   Threatens to seek sanctions against counsel.

RYAN, TIMOTHY.   Director of the OTS.

SAHADI, ROBERT.   Chief economist at the Bank Board.

SANFORD, JAMES TERRY (D-NC).   Member of the Senate Ethics Committee.

SARATOGA SAVINGS.   California control fraud.

SARBANES-OXLEY ACT.   Reform legislation addressing financial scandals.

SAUTER, MARK.   Director of regulatory compliance for Lincoln Savings.

SCHILLING, WILLIAM.   Head of Bank Board supervision.

SCHOTT, PAUL ALLEN.   Assistant general counsel for the Treasury Department.

SCHULTZ, SCOTT.   FHLBSF supervisor who angered Jim Wright.

SCOTT, STEVEN.   Bank Board examiner of Lincoln Savings in 1988.

SECONDARY RESERVE. Accounting term and concept that allowed the FSLIC insurance fund to count noncash reserves as if they were real.

SEIDMAN, WILLIAM. FDIC chairman.

SELBY, JOSEPH. Lead supervisor at the FHLB-Dallas.

SEGAL, TOM. Bank Board litigation attorney.

SHAND, ERIC. Senior supervisor at the FHLBSF.

SMUZYNSKI, AL. Senior supervisor at the Bank Board.

SOBOL, ANNE. Bank Board litigator who investigated Charles Keating.

SOLOMON, MIKE. Bank Board counsel and my aide on the FSLIC recap.

"SOUTHWEST PLAN." Controversial 1988 plan by Bank Board chairman Danny Wall to sell failed S&Ls in the southwestern United States.

SQUIRE, SANDERS & DEMPSEY. Counsel to the FHLBB.

STELZER, GENE. CDSL examiner of Lincoln Savings.

STEWART, ROSEMARY. Head of OE at the Bank Board.

ST GERMAIN, FERNAND (D-RI). House Banking Committee chairman.

STILL, RICHARD. House Banking Committee counsel.

STRAUSS, ROBERT "BOB." Democratic Party leader.

"STRAW." Someone purporting to act independently but secretly acting on another's behalf.

SUNBELT SAVINGS. One of the most notorious of the Texas control frauds.

SYSTEMS CAPACITY. Inability or unwillingness of an agency to take effective action against crime because of resource constraints.

TAGGART, LAWRENCE. California S&L commissioner.

"TAX SHARING" AGREEMENT. Agreement among affiliated companies to file a consolidated tax return and to allocate the tax liability among the affiliates.

TAYLOR, MARY ELLEN. Edwin Gray's principal aide for congressional relations.

TRUMP GROUP, THE. Proposed acquirer of Lincoln Savings (not affiliated with Donald Trump).

TUTTLE, ROBERT. White House personnel director under Ronald Reagan.

VERMIN. Term regulators used for Vernon Savings.

VERNON SAVINGS. Texas control fraud run by Don Dixon.

VINCENT, JANET. AY auditor who replaced Jack Atchison at Lincoln.

VOLCKER, PAUL. Chairman of the Fed.

WALL, M. DANNY. Bank Board chairman.

WAXMAN, MARGERY. Lawyer with Sidley & Austin; counsel to Charles Keating and Lee Henkel.

WEBSTER, (JUDGE) WILLIAM. FBI director.

WEINSTEIN, HARRIS. Chief counsel for the OTS.

WELLS, JOSEPH. Head of the ACFE.

WESTERN SAVINGS. Thrift that acquired failed Texas S&Ls before it itself failed.

REFERENCES

Adams, Jim Ring. 1990. *The Big Fix: Inside the S&L Scandal,* New York: John Wiley & Sons.

Akerlof, George. 1970. "The Market for 'Lemons': Quality, Uncertainty, and the Market Mechanism." *Quarterly Journal of Economics* 84 (3):488–500.

Akerlof, George, and Paul M. Romer. 1993. "Looting: The Economic Underworld of Bankruptcy for Profit." *Brookings Papers on Economic Activity* 2:1–73.

American Banker, 1987. Article dated February 10.

Barry, John M. 1989. *The Ambition and the Power: The Fall of Jim Wright; A True Story of Washington,* New York: Viking Penguin.

Binstein, Michael, and Charles Bowden. 1993. *Trust Me: Charles Keating and the Missing Billions,* New York: Random House.

Black, William K. 1985. Undated draft Bank Board memorandum for the signature of Norman Raiden and William Schilling to Chairman Gray recommending the denial of Lincoln Saving's application to exceed the direct investment rule. On file with the author.

———. 1993a. "Substantive Positions of S&L Trade Associations, 1979–1989." Staff Report No. 1 to the National Commission on Financial Institution Reform, Recovery and Enforcement.

———. 1993b. "ADC Lending." Staff Report No. 2 to the National Commission on Financial Institution Reform, Recovery and Enforcement.

———. 1993c. "Junk Bonds." Staff Report No. 7 to the National Commission on Financial Institution Reform, Recovery and Enforcement.

———. 1993d. "The Incidence and Cost of Fraud and Insider Abuse." Staff Report No. 13 to the National Commission on Financial Institution Reform, Recovery and Enforcement.

———. 1993e. "Thrift Accounting Principles and Practices." Staff Report No. 20

to the National Commission on Financial Institution Reform, Recovery and Enforcement.

——. 1998. "The Best Way to Rob a Bank Is to Own One: Control Fraud and the Savings and Loan Debacle." Unpublished dissertation. University of California, Irvine.

——. 2000. "Control Fraud and Control Freaks." In *Contemporary Issues in Crime and Criminal Justice: Essays in Honor of Gilbert Geis,* ed. Henry N. Pontell and David Shichor, 67–80. Upper Saddle River, N.J.: Prentice Hall.

——. 2001. "Control Fraud and Control Freaks." In *Contemporary Issues in Crime and Criminal Justice,* Henry N. Pontell and David Shichor, eds. Upper Saddle River, N.J.: Prentice Hall.

——. 2003. "Reexamining the Law-and-Economics Theory of Corporate Governance." *Challenge* 46 (2):22–40.

Black, William K., Kitty Calavita, and Henry N. Pontell. 1995. "The Savings and Loan Debacle of the 1980's: White-Collar Crime or Risky Business?" *Law and Policy* 17:23–55.

Bolt, Robert. 1990. *A Man for All Seasons.* New York: Vintage.

Brookes, Warren. 1987. "Knee-deep in S&Leaze?" *Washington Times.* July 9: D1.

Calavita, Kitty, Henry N. Pontell, and Robert H. Tillman. 1997. *Big Money: Fraud and Politics in the Savings and Loan Crisis,* Berkeley and Los Angeles: Univ. of California Press.

Chicago Tribune. 2002. "Accounting Industry Puts Profit Above Integrity, Critics Say." February 13. *http://finance.pro2net.com/x32941.xml.*

Craig, James L., Jr. 1994. "Serving the Profession's Assurance Function." *The CPA Journal Online* (January). *http://www.nysscpa.org/cpajournal/old/14979915 .htm.* Accessed January 22, 2004.

Day, Kathleen. 1993. *S&L Hell: The People and the Politics behind the $1 Trillion Savings and Loan Scandal,* New York: W. W. Norton.

Easterbrook, Frank H., and Daniel R. Fischel. 1991. *The Economic Structure of Corporate Law,* Cambridge, Mass.: Harvard Univ. Press.

Ely, Bert. 1990. "FSLIC's Losses—When and How They Accumulated." Unpublished paper. On file with the author.

Financial Accounting Standards Board (FASB) Statement 72. *http://www.fasb .org/.* Accessed July 18, 2004.

Fischel, Daniel R. 1995. *Payback: The Conspiracy to Destroy Michael Milken and His Financial Revolution,* New York: HarperBusiness.

Fukuyama, Francis. 1995. *Trust: The Social Virtues and the Creation of Prosperity,* New York: Free Press.

General Accounting Office (GAO) *Thrift Failures.* 1989.

Jackson, Brooks. 1988. *Honest Graft: Big Money and the American Political Process.* New York: Knopf.

Johnson, Simon, Rafael La Porta, Florencio Lopez-de-Silanes, and Andrei

Shleifer. 2000. "Tunnelling." *American Economic Association Papers and Precedings* 90 (2):22–26.

Jorion, Phillipe. 1995. *Big Bets Gone Bad,* San Diego: Academic Press.

Kammer, Jerry. 1987. *Arizona Republic,* July 1.

Kane, Edward J. 1985. *The Gathering Crisis in Federal Deposit Insurance,* Cambridge, Mass.: MIT Press.

———. 1989. *The S&L Insurance Mess: How Did it Happen?* Washington, D.C.: Urban Institute Press.

Kaye, Scholer. 1998. Undated internal legal memorandum. On file with the author.

La Porta, Rafael, Florencio Lopez-de-Silanes, and Guillermo Zamarripa. 2003. "Related Lending." *Quarterly Journal of Economics* 118 (1):231–267.

Levitt, Arthur. 2002. *Take on the Street: What Wall Street and Corporate America Don't Want You To Know; What You Can Do to Fight Back,* With Paula Dwyer. New York: Pantheon.

Lowy, Martin. 1991. *High Rollers: Inside the Savings and Loan Debacle.* New York: Praeger.

Mayer, Martin. 1990. *The Greatest-Ever Bank Robbery: The Collapse of the Savings and Loan Industry,* New York: Macmillan.

MDL (multi-district litigation). Documents connected with federal litigation relating to suits against Keating, Lincoln Savings, and outside professionals. On file with the author.

National Comission on Financial Institution Reform, Recovery and Enforcement (NCFIRRE). 1993a. *Origins and Causes of the S&L Debacle: A Blueprint for Reform,* A Report to the President and Congress of the United States. Washington, D.C.: Government Printing Office.

National Comission on Financial Institution Reform, Recovery and Enforcement (NCFIRRE). 1993b. Staff interview with Paul Allen Schott. On file with the author.

National Comission on Financial Institution Reform, Recovery and Enforcement (NCFIRRE). 1993c. Testimony of William O'Connell. On file with the author.

National Comission on Financial Institution Reform, Recovery and Enforcement (NCFIRRE). 1993d. Testimony of Richard Pratt. On file with the author.

National Comission on Financial Institution Reform, Recovery and Enforcement (NCFIRRE). 1993e. Testimony of Jim Wright. On file with the author.

National Thrift News, 1986. May 26.

O'Shea, James. 1991. *The Daisy Chain: How Borrowed Billions Sank a Texas S&L,* New York: Pocket Books.

Patriarca, Michael. 1987. November 2. Unpublished memorandum. On file with the author.

Pierce, James. 1993. Unpublished address at the annual meeting of the American Economics Association. On file with the author.

Pizzo, Stephen, Mary Fricker, and Paul Muolo. 1991. *Inside Job: The Looting of America's Savings and Loans.* New York: HarperCollins.

Prentice, Robert. 2000. "The Case of the Irrational Accountant: A Behavioral Insight into Securities Fraud Litigation." *Northwestern University Law Review* 95 (1):133–220.

"Report on the Texas Thrift and Real Estate Crises." 1987. October 30. Unpublished U.S. League of Savings Institutions report. On file with the author.

Riccucci, Norma. 1995. *Unsung Heroes: Federal Execucrats Making a Difference.* Washington, D.C.: Georgetown Univ. Press.

Rom, Mark. 1996. *Public Spirit in the Thrift Tragedy.* Pittsburgh: University of Pittsburgh Press.

Securities and Exchange Commission (SEC) Annual Report. 2002. *http://www .sec.gov/pdf/annrep02/ar02fm.pdf,* p. 1. Accessed June 18, 2004.

Seidman, William L. 1993. *Full Faith and Credit: The Great S&L Debacle and Other Washington Sagas.* New York: Random House.

Shefrin, Hersh. 1999. *Beyond Greed and Fear: Understanding Behavioral Finance and the Psychology of Investing.* Cambridge, Mass.: Harvard Business School Press.

Stein, Benjamin. 1992. *License to Steal: The Untold Story of Michael Milken and the Conspiracy to Bilk the Nation.* New York: Simon & Schuster.

Stewart, Amy. 1988. Memo to Lorna Thompson dated March 1, 1988. On file with the author.

Stiglitz, Joseph E. 2003. *The Roaring Nineties: A New History of the World's Most Prosperous Decade.* New York: W. W. Norton.

Strunk, Norman, and Fred Case. 1988. *Where Deregulation Went Wrong.* Washington, D.C.: United States League of Savings Institutions.

Tillman, Robert H., and Henry N. Pontell. 1995. "Organizations and Fraud in the Savings and Loan Industry." *Social Forces* 73 (4):1439–1463.

Tuohey, Mark H., III. 1987. Memo to David Evans dated October 19, 1987. On file with the author.

U.S. Congress. House. Committee on Government Operations. 1988. 100th Cong., 2d sess.

U.S. Congress. Senate. Open Session Hearings before the Select Committee on Ethics. 1990–1991a. *Preliminary Inquiry into Allegations Regarding Senators Cranston, DeConcini, Glenn, McCain, and Riegle, and Lincoln Savings and Loan.* 101st Cong., 2d sess. November 11, 1990–January 16, 1991. Pts. 1–5.

U.S. Congress. Senate. Open Session Hearings before the Select Committee on Ethics. 1990–1991b. Special Counsel Exhibits. On file with the author.

———. Hearings before the Committee on Banking, Finance and Urban Affairs. 1989. *Investigation of Lincoln Savings & Loan Association.* 101st Cong., 1st sess. October 12 and 17. Pts. 1–6.

———. Committee on Standards of Official Conduct. 1989. *Report of the Special Outside Counsel in the Matter of Speaker James C. Wright, Jr.* Report to the

Committee by Special Outside Counsel, Richard J. Phelan. 101st Cong., 1st sess. February 21.

U.S. League of Savings Institutions. Unpublished documents discussing deregulation, reregulation, and FSLIC recap. On file with the author.

Washington Post. 1988. Article on Thomas Gaubert. May 5.

Waxman, Margery. 1988a. Memo to Charles Keating and Robert Kielty dated January 22. (MDL Doc. #WH000339). On file with the author.

Wheeler, Stanton, and Mitchell Lewis Rothman. 1982. "The Organization as Weapon in White Collar Crime." *Michigan Law Review* 80 (7):1403–1426.

White, Lawrence. 1991. *The S&L Debacle: Public Policy Lessons for Bank and Thrift Regulation.* New York: Oxford Univ. Press.

Williamson, George. 1990. *San Francisco Chronicle.* October 18: A1.

———. 1991. "Keating Allegedly Claimed Clout in Senate." *San Francisco Chronicle.* January 11.

Wilmsen, Steven K. 1991. *Silverado: Neil Bush and the Savings and Loan Scandal.* Washington D.C.: National Press Books.

Woodward, Bob. 2000. *Maestro: Greenspan's Fed and the American Boom.* New York: Simon and Schuster.

INDEX

LaVergne, TN USA
16 September 2009
157947LV00003B/4/P